Mozart's Piano Concertos

D0087310

In memory of my father, Alan Arthur Irving (1915–98).
He loved Mozart's piano concertos.

Mozart's Piano Concertos

John Irving

University of Bristol

ASHGATE

© John Irving, 2003

All rights reserved. No part of this publication may be reproduced, stored in a retrieval system, or transmitted in any form or by any means, electronic, mechanical, photocopying, recording, or otherwise without the prior permission of the publisher.

The author has asserted his moral right under the Copyright, Designs and Patents Act, 1988, to be identified as author of this work.

Published by
Ashgate Publishing Limited
Gower House
Croft Road
Aldershot
Hants GU11 3HR
England

Ashgate Publishing Company
Suite 420
101 Cherry Street
Burlington VT 05401–4405 USA

Ashgate website: http://www.ashgate.com

British Library Cataloguing in Publication Data

Irving, John, 1959–
    Mozart's Piano Concertos
    1. Mozart, Wolfgang Amadeus, 1756–1791. Concertos, piano
    2. Concerto
    I. Title
    786.2'186

Library of Congress Cataloging-in-Publication Data

Irving, John, 1959–
    Mozart's Piano Concertos / John Irving.
        p.   cm.
    1. Mozart, Wolfgang Amadeus, 1756–1791. Concertos, piano, orchestra.
    2. Concertos (Piano)–History and criticism. I. Title.
    ML410.M91738 2003

    784.2'62'092–dc21
    2002023246

ISBN 0 7546 0707 0

Typeset by Q3 Bookwork, Loughborough, Leicestershire
Printed in Great Britain by MPG Books Ltd, Bodmin, Cornwall

Contents

List of Music Examples

List of Tables

List of Figures

Abbreviations and Conventions

Bibliographic

K⁶	Köchel, Ludwig von, *Chronologisch-thematisches Verzeichnis sämtliche Tonwerke Wolfgang Amadé Mozarts, nebst Angabe der verlorengegangenen, angefangenen, von fremder Hand bearbeiteten, zweifelhaften und unterschobenen Kompositionen*, ed. Franz Giegling, Alexander Weinmann and Gerd Sievers, 6th edn, Wiesbaden: Brietkopf & Härtel (1964).
NMA	*Wolfgang Amadeus Mozart: Neue Ausgabe Sämtliche Werke [Neue Mozart-Ausgabe (NMA)]*, Kassel: Bärenreiter/Salzburg: Internationale Stiftung Mozarteum (1955–98).
deest	work not included in the Köchel catalogue
K.Anh.	Appendix to the Köchel catalogue

Library sigla

A-M	Benediktiner-Stift Melk an der Donau (Musik-Archiv)
A-Sm	Salzburg, Internationale Stiftung Mozarteum
A-Ssp	Salzburg, Musikalien-Archiv der Benediktiner-Erzabtei St. Peter
A-Wgm	Wien, Gesellschaft der Musikfreunde
A-Wn	Wien, Österreichische National-Bibliothek
CZ-Bm	Brno, Ústav Dějin Hudbi Moravského Musea hudebněhistoriké odděleni
CZ-CH	Státní okresni archiv v Chebu
CZ-K	Český Krumlov, pracoviště Státního Archivu Třeboň – pobočka Jindrichuv Hradec
CZ-KRa	Kroměříž, Státní Zámek a Zahrady, Historiko-Umělecké Fondy, Hudební-Arhiv
CZ-Pu	Prague, University Libruary (Clementinum)
D-B	Staatsbibliothek zu Berlin (Musikabteilung)
D-WRz	Herzogin Anna Amalie Bibliothek (Thüringische Landesbibliothek), Weimar
F-Pn	Paris, Bibliothèque Nationale (Département de la Musique)
GB-Lbl	London, British Library

GB-Lcm	London, Royal College of Music
I-Mc	Milan, Conservatorio di Musica Giuseppi Verdi, Fonds Noseda
PL-Kj	Kraków, Jagiellonian University Library
RO-Ba	Bucuresti, Natinal Academy of Sciences
Rus-Mem	Moscow, M. I. Glinka Museum (Gosuderstvennïy Tsentral'nïy Muzey Muzïkal'noy Kul'turïimeni M. I. Gliniki)
US-NYp	New York Public Library, Lincoln Center
US-NYpm	New York, Pierpoint Morgan Library
US-Wc	Library of Congress, Washington, D.C.
US-STu	Stanford, University Memorial Library

Music notation

Upper-case roman numerals denote major keys; lower-case, minor keys; V^7 means dominant seventh; V/ denotes the dominant of a key (thus, V/G means the dominant of G major); numbers of the form '6/4' refer to chords; numbers of the form '$\frac{6}{8}$' are time signatures.

Preface

Mozart's piano concertos are deservedly famous and familiar, standing alongside his operas and symphonies as his most frequently performed and best loved music. They are as popular today as they have been at any time since their composition; seldom absent from radio schedules for more than a day or two; prominent on any CD collector's shelf (and available in literally dozens of different recordings); a staple of music history courses, biographies, and pianists' repertoires. For many, these works represent the epitome of the concerto genre. They have attracted the attention of generations of musicologists who have explored their manifold meanings from a variety of viewpoints, including not only analytic or style-critical approaches to the notes themselves, but also aspects such as performance practice (taking into account, for instance, surviving performance materials from Mozart's own time and iconographical evidence of various sorts) and compositional genesis, based on detailed investigation of the composer's handwriting, the inks and papers he used, sketches, drafts and so on. Recent scholarship, within which the editorial work of the Neue Mozart-Ausgabe (NMA) is fundamental, has provided fascinating insights into this repertoire.

A new book on Mozart's piano concertos therefore requires some justification. Partly that justification lies in the sheer availability of information. Some staple texts are general and unashamedly subjective in their treatment, written in an age when descriptive narrative was all that was required, such as Girdlestone, 1958 or Hutchings, 1948; 1998. Others are excellent but necessarily (and frustratingly) cursory, such as Radcliffe, 1978. Yet others, including Zaslaw, 1996b, present extremely specialised accounts by a variety of present-day scholars expert in particular areas, that speak on a high professional level to other specialists in the field (historians of style, analysts, performance practitioners, palaeographers, and so on), rather than, say, graduate students or musically literate and sophisticated non-specialists seeking a reliable and current guide to this popular repertory and its critical environments. Yet others treat one or two key works in great detail, such as Tovey, 1936 and Grayson, 1999. No mention has yet been made of the extraordinarily broad range of treatment found in specialised music periodicals. Articles on just about every conceivable aspect of Mozart's piano concertos are to be found in *Acta Mozartiana*, *Current Musicology*, *Die Musikforschung*, *Early Music*, *Journal of the American Musicological Society*, *The Journal of Musicology*, *Journal of the Royal Musical Association*, *Mozart-Jahrbuch*, *Music and Letters*, *The Musical Quarterly*, *Studi Musicali*, *Zeitschrift für Musikwissenschaft* and many more. Not every music-lover (nor, indeed, every undergraduate) will have such literature – or at least a representative sampling of it – at the fingertips. Nor, in the normal course of events, will the German musicological literature on the concertos (such as Küster, 1991 and the *Kritische Berichte* to piano concerto volumes of the NMA, Serie V/15) be readily available to many. Another crucial and exciting dimension of recent Mozart scholarship that touches directly on the piano concertos is represented by Alan Tyson's work on the watermarks in Mozart's autograph manuscripts. This has provided valuable insights into Mozart's compositional process, occasionally leading to significant redatings of some works. So far as the piano concertos are concerned, Tyson's findings argue strongly for a revision in our understanding of the genesis of some of the most popular concertos, suggesting plausible redatings not accounted for in the older literature.

Forming anything approaching a comprehensive picture of Mozart's piano concertos is thus dependent upon an ability to juggle a huge quantity of material of different sorts in the memory (analytical, archival, editorial, palaeographical, stylistic, historical – including definitions of the genre itself, patterns of influence within it and Mozart's own development of it). It is the aim of this study of Mozart's piano concertos to attempt a conflation of the various strands of musical scholarship, and thereby to go some way towards fulfilling the need among university students, CD collectors, concert goers and pianists for an accessible, up-to-date handbook to this familiar repertoire.

Within the present study Mozart's piano concertos are approached from two contrasting perspectives. In Part One the focus is on broad thematic issues, including eighteenth-century theoretical frameworks for the understanding of movement forms, concentrating especially upon the extensive writings on this subject by Heinrich Christoph Koch; the origin of Mozart's concertos in earlier traditions of eighteenth-century concerto writing; subsequent historical shifts in the perception of the concerto's form; listening strategies, including those derived from rhetoric and topics; aesthetic and philosophical frameworks of understanding; and performance practices.

In contrast to the contextual progress of Part One, Part Two focuses on individual concertos. It presents a 'documentary register', proceeding chronologically through all 23 original works and drawing together information on the source materials: Mozart's autograph scores, sketches and cadenzas; authentic copies made by the Mozart family or their close associates in Salzburg, including existing performance materials; other early copies (cadenzas, scores and playing parts) that may have a close connection to the composer;[1] first editions; and relevant textual matters. Accounts of the concertos' compositional genesis, early performance history and reception are also included here, drawing extensively on the Mozart family correspondence and other contemporary reports. While each entry is designed to provide a summary of information relevant to the particular work, cross-references are given, where appropriate, to other entries. The entry for each concerto is intended to serve as an accessible introduction to that work. Part Two is not intended to be a comprehensive source listing. That is one function of a critical commentary, and for information on sources at one or more generations' remove from Mozart (for example, the manuscript scores and parts from the Doppler, Fuchs, Hatwig and Horak collections) the reader is referred to the relevant *Kritische Berichte* volumes of the NMA, Serie V/15. Typically these 'second generation' manuscript scores or parts were compiled from early printed editions in the first two or three decades of the nineteenth century.[2] Originating in the main in the 1830s and 1840s, these copies comprise part of the nineteenth-century project to 'invent' Mozart: a project that also includes the provision of 'critical' editions, and their philosophical and methodological premises; the increasing extent to which his music is included in the theoretical writings of Czerny and others; its place within emergent public concert life; the reception of Mozart's music – that is, both in print and in concert – in newspaper criticism and in academic journals; his institutionalisation, whether in scholarly foundations, in academic curricula, or as the subject of biographies. Consideration of the 'secondary' layer of source materials for the concertos properly belongs within a different and wider study of the construction and reception of Mozart that probably lies beyond the grasp of a single author.

Historically, Mozart's piano concertos have assumed a variety of roles. For the late eighteenth-century theorist, Heinrich Christoph Koch, they were ideal examples of the concerto genre. In his *Musikalisches Lexicon* (Koch, 1802) he described them as 'displaying all the characteristics of a good concerto'. Valorisation of practice in theory is a significant occurrence. Music theory had a long and distinguished history within the eighteenth century, and, situated within the Enlightenment project of testable, reliable, authoritative and, above all, public discourse (of which the *Encyclopédie* is only the best-known illustration), music theoretical pronouncements of the later eighteenth century acquired a doctrinal status. Koch had previously devoted considerable attention to theoretical discussions of the concerto, synthesising earlier and current understandings of the genre and its formal characteristics. Coming little more than a decade after Mozart's death, Koch's sanctioning of his concertos within the 'official' embrace of theory represents one important stage on the road to their (and his) canonicity.

The dissemination of the concertos in print is another route by which this was achieved. At approximately the same time as Koch was preparing the *Lexicon*, Mozart's widow was engaged in protracted (and possibly duplicitous) negotiations with publishers for the rights to print authoritative editions of her late husband's works, based upon the autograph manuscripts still in her possession; she ultimately concluded an agreement with the music dealer and publisher Johann Anton André of Offenbach-am-Main in November 1799. In fact, André had already begun to issue prints of some of Mozart's piano concertos during the 1790s, basing them on versions of varying quality that were already circulating in manuscript, or else, perhaps, pirated from Parisian editions. Armed with the autographs, however, he could begin on a more authoritative project of editions 'faite[s] d'après la partition en manuscrit' – an appellation that he proudly displayed on his title-pages. In 1800, André issued *Six grands Concertos dédiés au Prince Louis Ferdinand de Prusse, Op.82* (Mozart, 1800e), comprising Mozart's K.467, K.482, K.488, K.491, K.503 and K.595. He also published a volume of cadenzas to 'Op.82' (Hoffmann, 1801–3), composed by the Mainz virtuoso, Philipp Karl Hoffmann (1769–1842). Little more than a decade after Mozart's death, all of his piano concertos had appeared in print, a factor that was to ease their assimilation into the repertoire of pianists active within the emergent institution of the public concert during the early decades of the nineteenth century.

A related agenda was the provision of arrangements of the concertos during the 1820s and 1830s by Johann Baptist Cramer (Cramer, 1825–37) and Johann Nepomuk Hummel (Hummel, 1828–42).[3] Both Cramer's and Hummel's arrangements of Mozart's concertos included substantial embellishments of the original piano parts. It seems clear that this enterprise was at least partly undertaken to ensure the preservation of Mozart's concertos by adapting them to the emergent ethos of virtuosity in contemporary concert pianism. Both men were selective in their refurbishments of Mozart's concertos: Cramer offered K.459, K.450, K.467, K.482, K.466 and K.491; Hummel offered K.466, K.503, K.365 (originally for two pianos, arranged for piano solo), K.491, K.537, K.482 and K.456. Considered alongside Mozart, 1800e, Cramer's and Hummel's arrangements may be seen to establish K.466, K.467, K.482, K.491 and K.503 as particular favourites, a trend reinforced by surviving newspaper reviews of Mozart concerto performances in major European cities during the first three decades of the nineteenth century. These point to the early popularity of K.466 in D minor and K.491 in C minor (both were in the repertoire of Mendelssohn during the 1830s and 1840s, for instance).[4] To judge from these reviews, the appeal of these minor-key works evidently lay in their perceived emotional turbulence, speaking of a world that lay beyond ordinary experience, mysteriously encoding within the notes that Hegelian 'striving-to-become' so central to the aesthetic of the early romantic movement. Undoubtedly, Mozart's piano concertos played a part in the early nineteenth century's reinvention of his *persona* and, more generally, the invention of the 'Viennese Classical Style' against which the modern romantic productions of Chopin, Schumann, Mendelssohn et al. might be measured (and, consequently, validated).

Each of these particular cases touches upon socially produced meanings that Mozart's piano concertos have enjoyed in their history. Others include their usefulness to writers of *Formenlehre* textbooks from Czerny to Riemann; their positioning within a pedagogic hierarchy in nineteenth- and twentieth-century conservatoires (in which they are felt to be valuable as 'preparatory' studies laying a technical foundation for the performance of more 'advanced' virtuoso concertos by Liszt, Brahms and Tchaikowsky); their epitomising once again of eighteenth-century values of elegance and proportion as part of the twentieth century's neo-classical reaction to romantic excess (their imagined, idealised sound-world lies behind Ravel's G major Piano Concerto (1930–1), for instance); their usefulness as vehicles for the propagation of analytical creeds of various sorts;[5] their appropriation by performers of 'period' instruments, whose performances and recordings claim a territory in which academic scholarship is married to practical realisation (implicitly in contrast to previous approaches); and more recently (and horribly) their representation as 'soft focus' stereotypes to be tapped at will by marketing consultants. Lying beneath each of these approaches is a particular constituency of listener or practitioner who interprets Mozart's piano concertos according to a (consciously or unconsciously) defined set of criteria, 'interpretive communities', as Stanley Fish has defined them (Fish, 1980).

Central to these interpretations, in turn, is the status of the Text, and whether it is to be regarded as synonymous with the Work it represents. For some earlier commentators on these works, such a question would have had little import. Both Girdlestone and Hutchings, for instance, assume an identity of Text and Work, allowing each of Mozart's piano concertos to be treated to a chapter in turn. More recent philosophical standpoints have, in contrast, rejected that comfortable identity, refocusing attention on the reader's significance in apportioning meaning:

> a text is made of multiple writings, drawn from many cultures and entering into mutual relations of dialogue, parody, conversation, but there is one place where this multiplicity is focused and that place is the reader ... a text's unity lies not in its origin but in its destination ... the reader ... is simply that *someone* who holds together in a single field all the traces by which the written text is constituted (Barthes, 1977, p. 148).

Barthes's thesis is certainly persuasive, and points up the contrast between the philosophical certitude of the musicology of Girdlestone and Hutchings and the anxiety over shifting meanings that characterises our own. For Girdlestone and Hutchings, a Mozart piano concerto was an object (that is, a Text, encoding a Work) whose musical meaning could be revealed with certitude by penetrating analysis. Nowadays, we are unsure even what a 'text' of a Mozart piano concerto is. Mozart, like all other authors, could not legislate for the unknown cultural contributions of future generations (which may be both positive and negative in their impact). For example, the D minor concerto K.466 will always speak differently to different generations, even to members of the same generation, whose responses will always be contingent upon experiences that the composer cannot predict. In a performance of K.466, an audience of

300 will all hear the same piece, and yet all will, in a sense, hear what they want to hear, unconsciously (perhaps) bringing to this particular presentation the totality of their musical experience of K.466, of Mozart's other concertos, of his operas, of later concertos in the virtuoso tradition by Brahms, Tchaikowsky, Rachmaninov and others. In each case, the response that K.466 provokes will be different. For some, it will be a delight in a surfeit of beautiful melody; for others, perhaps, it will be irritation at what is heard as 'super-fluous' melody; others will derive pleasure – consciously or unconsciously – from the formal proportions of a movement; yet others will be listening for traces of particular performance practices; some will approach the piece through their own experience of playing Mozart's sonatas; some will hear K.466 as a rather slender forerunner of such romantic warhorses as Brahms's 1st or Rachmaninov's 3rd concertos; some, on the other hand, will try to listen as a contemporary of Mozart's might have done, attempting to remove (or at least forget) the nineteenth-century obstacles, cultural and theoretical, to such a position.

A guide such as this inevitably rests upon a broad range of existing research. Especially in Chapter Seven, on performance practice, the account offered presents a summary of the most relevant issues which are argued in more extended detail in specialist articles, for which specific citations are given in footnotes. The information about the individual concertos in Part Two draws substantially on the correspondence of Mozart, on surviving contemporary reports and documentary materials, and on existing archival studies. While autograph and other contemporary sources have been independently exam-ined, the conclusions presented here do not significantly depart from those expressed in many scattered locations across the published Mozart literature (or, at least, not often). Translations of passages from Mozart's correspond-ence are generally from Anderson, 1983, unless otherwise specified. Transla-tions of extracts from letters not in Anderson but in Bauer, Deutsch and Eibl, 1962–75 are my own. The pioneering documentary work of Otto Erich Deutsch (Deutsch, 1961; Deutsch, 1965) has provided an invaluable starting-point for many studies of Mozart's music, and this one is no exception. (Deutsch's work has more recently been supplemented by that of Cliff Eisen (Eisen, 1991a), to which reference is also made here.) Archival and biblio-graphical studies on Mozart are never-ending and reveal important information surrounding the genesis and transmission of Mozart's compositions, including, of course, the piano concertos. While the 6th edition of *Köchel* provides a useful assembly of information on the survival and location of autographs, first editions, early copies and other relevant materials to do with the concertos, it reflects a state of research hampered by the disappearance of many autographs from the former Berlin Staatsbibliothek, Preußischer Kulturbesitz at the end of World War II. In fact, the autographs listed in *Köchel* as lost were indirectly transferred to the Jagiellonian University Library in Kraków (Poland) during the 1940s, and resurfaced gradually only in the late 1970s and 1980s, thereafter becoming more readily available to researchers. The discussions of each concerto in Part Two of this study take account of these rediscovered scores as well as of more recent archival work – for instance that of Gertraut Haberkamp and Dexter Edge – on related source materials.

It will be obvious that there are very few musical examples in this book. Access to a good edition, preferably the NMA (in which important and interesting facsimile reproductions sometimes referred to in Part Two are also to be found), is assumed throughout. Eulenburg miniature scores will prove sufficient in most cases; two-piano reductions – with rehearsal letters, rather than bar-numbers – less so.

It is my pleasant duty to record my grateful thanks to the staffs of the various libraries in which I have worked for their patience and kindness in retrieving from their collections a variety of materials that have proved invaluable in the writing of this book. Several themes pursued in Part One and some of the material on individual concertos in Part Two were first trawled in postgraduate seminars in the Music Department at the University of Bristol, and in an undergraduate seminar course on Mozart's Piano Concertos. I am grateful to my colleagues and students for enduring these assaults so patiently, and to Sarah Dodds, who set the musical examples. During the course of the research for this study I was awarded a semester of sabbatical leave by the University of Bristol, and a travel bursary by the Bristol University Alumni Foundation. My thanks are also due to Professor Konrad Küster for permission to reproduce in a modified form part of an article that first appeared in the *Mozart-Jahrbuch* (Irving, 1998). For advice in matters of production I am much indebted to Rachel Lynch of Ashgate Press and her excellent team of in-house editors and, for her scrutiny of the typescript at the copy-editing stage, to Virginia Catmur. Although my mother has been a welcome source of encouragement in the rather slow progress of this book, it was my late father, Alan Irving, who initially badgered me into writing about Mozart's piano concertos. Among all classical composers, Mozart was his favourite, and he held the piano concertos in particular affection. He had not the slightest technical knowledge of music, though that was never an impediment to his grasp of these wonderful pieces. I wish I knew how he did it.

The University of Bristol
September 2001

Notes

1. Listing and discussion of manuscript copies in Part Two is, in the main, restricted to those produced by Mozart's father and sister, or by the Mozarts' preferred copyists, Joseph Richard Estlinger and Felix Hofstätter, and now in the library of St Peter's Abbey, Salzburg. Copies at the Státní Zámek a Zahrady, Historiko-Umělecké Fondy, Hudební-Archiv in Kroměříž (Czech Republic) are also included, as there is a demonstrable connection in at least one case (K.365) to these two copyists, suggesting that other sources of Mozart's concertos at the Kroměříž castle archive may emanate directly or indirectly from the composer's circle. In addition, the Kroměříž parts contain an autograph cadenza for the finale of K.365. Other sets of parts in this archive (for instance, K.456, K.466 and K.491) appear to be Viennese copies made during Mozart's lifetime. Kroměříž was the seat of the Prince-Bishops of Olomouc; from the seventeenth century, musical life there was especially rich. For information on the extensive Kroměříž collection of classical orchestral repertory, see Senhal, 1971 and Senhal, 1978. On the authentic copies of Mozart's works, see Senn, 1962; Schmid, 1970; Hintermaier, 1972; Eisen, 1991b; Eisen, 1996; and Edge, 1996c.
2. For instance, the score of K.488 now in the University Library (Clementinum), Prague, Sig. M II/13, no.2, was compiled from the parts issued by Breitkopf and Härtel, c.1800, as part of the 'Oeuvres Complettes de Mozart' (Mozart, 1800f).
3. For a detailed assessment of these arrangements, see Grayson, 1996.
4. See the entries for these works in Part Two below. Further evidence of the early popularity of K.466 is the production in 1809 by Johann Anton André of a version arranged for two pianos: 'Pour faciliter l'acquisition de ce Concerto aux amateurs qui possèdent déjà l'oeuvre 54 [that is, André's first edition of K.466 (1796)], ayant en soin de conserver l'accompagnement de l'orchestre l'on vend séparément les parties des deux Pianos à fl.2 [2 florins]'; see the entry for K.466 in Haberkamp, 1986.
5. For example, organicism; see Keller, 1956a.

PART ONE
Contexts: Form, Reception and Performance

CHAPTER ONE

Heinrich Koch and the Classical Concerto

The concerto genre was discussed at considerable length by the foremost late eighteenth-century music theorist, Heinrich Christoph Koch (1749–1816). While best known for his theoretical writings, Koch had a background as a practical musician, serving for much of his career in the Hofkapelle at Rudolstadt (his birthplace), being appointed Kapellmeister there in 1792. He was also a composer of cantatas, sacred vocal music and some instrumental works (all lost). His most famous and extensive theoretical text is the *Versuch einer Anleitung zur Composition* (Koch, 1782–93), a comprehensive account of musical theory and aesthetics published in three volumes (1782, 1787, 1793). It draws on the repertoire of its own day, and builds on earlier theory such as that of Riepel (Riepel 1752; Riepel, 1755), particularly in the importance accorded to melody in volumes ii and iii. Koch termed these sections 'The Mechanical Rules of Melody', and in them its constructive principles are treated in well-nigh exhaustive depth (see Baker, 1976). Koch's melodic theories pay particular attention to periodicity, taking as a starting-point the notion of the four-bar phrase, and treating its conjunction to other phrases in exact symmetrical relation as axiomatic in composition. Symmetry, to Koch, was naturally pleasing, even suggestive of an ideal 'order'. Phrases were most effectively grouped in larger paragraphs and, in turn, in balancing sections: most famously, this type of step-by-step extension is illustrated by an eight-bar minuet, expanded to 32 bars by such techniques as repetition, repetition in sequence, phrase insertion, interruption and the multiplication of phrase-endings and of cadences, either half- or full (see Sisman, 1982). The systematic extension of this fundamental principle leads to a discussion of the main outline divisions within a movement in which tonal – rather than thematic – factors play a major role in the conception. Neither melody nor harmony was of absolute primary significance in music, according to Koch (although each could temporarily take primacy within a phrase). Rather, key, or mode, is its primary substance (Koch calls it 'Urstoff ' – see Baker, 1988). The *Versuch* contains a great many musical examples by Koch himself, but is notable for its reference to recent or contemporary compositions including excerpts from Haydn symphonies, and keyboard sonatas and concertos by C. P. E. Bach. He also lavished praise on Mozart's 'Haydn' Quartets (published in 1785). Koch's other major contribution to music theory was the *Musikalisches Lexicon* (Koch, 1802) organised, as its name suggests, more as an inventory of terms rather than as a discursive discussion. Koch's aesthetics is indebted to the work of Batteux (Batteux, 1746) and Sulzer (Sulzer, 1771; Baker and Christensen, 1996), namely that the purpose of music (indeed, of the fine arts generally) was to awaken feelings in the listeners so as to inspire them to noble deeds.[1] Both the *Versuch* and the *Lexicon* influenced early-nineteenth-century theorists such as Gottfried Weber, though as the century progressed, the work of Reicha, Czerny and Marx tended to accord a greater role to theme in the representation of structure than had characterised Koch's work.[2]

Koch approached the concerto twice in his widely influential published writings. The more extended treatment appears in the third and final volume (1793) of the *Versuch* (Koch, 1782–83, iii, §120; Baker, 1983, pp.210–12; Baker and Christensen, 1996, pp.132–3, 153–4; 175–6). A briefer account, drawn essentially from the description originally printed in the *Versuch*, occurs in the *Lexicon* (Koch, 1802, columns 349–55). Probably Koch knew none of Mozart's piano concertos in the 1780s and early 1790s when he was compiling and publishing the *Versuch*; indeed, to begin with, his structural ideal in the concerto genre was represented by the work of C. P. E. Bach.[3] But by 1802, when the *Lexicon* was published, Mozart's work had come to represent for Koch the epitome of what was achievable within the concerto genre, and he generously concluded his description of the concerto by describing Mozart's examples as masterpieces representative of all of the characteristics of a good concerto.[4] A review of Koch's survey of the solo concerto therefore seems appropriate in a study of Mozart's piano concertos.

Koch and the concerto genre

Koch tells us that a concerto is a three-movement structure, consisting of two Allegros and a central Adagio, which 'can assume every mood which music is capable of expressing. It is that piece with which the virtuosos usually may be heard on their instrument' (Baker, 1983, p.208). He goes on to affirm that it is only possible to write an effective concerto for an instrument which one plays oneself. In these general areas Koch is in agreement with Daniel Gottlob Türk's description of the concerto in his *Clavierschule* (Türk, 1789; Haggh, 1982, iv, §27).[5] Whereas Koch deals with the first movement at considerable length, the slow movement and finale are dismissed in two and one paragraphs, respectively (Baker and Christensen, 1996, pp.212–13). He differs in his assessment of the concerto from his mentor, Johann Georg Sulzer, author of the important *Allgemeine Theorie der schönen Künste* (Leipzig, 1771–4; Baker and Christensen, 1996), whose views on music (and the arts more generally) he usually takes over *verbatim* both here in the *Versuch* and in the later *Musikalisches Lexicon*. Sulzer's opinion of the concerto was not high: 'basically nothing but an exercise for composer and player and an entirely indeterminate pleasure for the ear, aiming at nothing more' (Sulzer, 1771, i, p.229). Koch believed that this view was unfair:

> But consider a well-worked-out concerto [movement] in which, during the solo, the accompanying voices are not merely there to sound this or that missing interval of the chords between the soprano and bass. There is a passionate dialogue between the concerto player and the accompanying orchestra. He expresses his feelings to the orchestra, and it signals him through short interspersed phrases sometimes approval, sometimes acceptance of his noble feelings ... now it commiserates, now it comforts him in the adagio. In short, by a concerto I imagine something similar to a tragedy of the ancients, where the actor expresses his feelings not towards the pit [meaning the audience], but to the chorus [which, in a Greek tragedy, stood between the actor and the audience in a section of the theatre known as the 'orchestra']. The chorus was involved most closely with the action and was at the same time justified in participating in the expression of feelings. Then the listener, without losing anything, is just the third person who can take part in the passionate performance of the concerto player and the accompanying orchestra (Koch, 1782–93, iii, §119; Baker, 1983, p.209).

Subsequently Koch draws the same analogy between concerto and tragedy in the *Lexicon*. Central to Koch's model is the implication that the chorus in the ancient Greek tragedies of, for example, Aeschylus, Sophocles and Euripides was analogous to the tutti in the classical concerto, and functioned as a 'mediator' between actor (soloist) and audience. Evidently Koch felt that the interaction of a soloist and orchestra in the concerto paralleled to some degree that of actor and a chorus in the tragedy (Keefe, 1998; Keefe, 2001; Schulenberg, 1984, pp.28, 133). Probably he intended his analogy only in general terms and not as a direct parallel to the actual structure of classical Greek tragedy. For instance, a scene within a tragedy unfolds diachronically, reaching forwards in time from one defined situation to another. In the tragedy as a whole, the end-point in this diachronic progression involves the resolution of the intertwined threads of the plot. Obviously, the unfolding of a concerto movement (or even an entire three-movement work) does not literally parallel the narrative unfolding of a scene within a tragedy. For example, there are frequent reprises of some themes, acting as articulating moments in the musical form;[6] the tutti and soloist frequently share the same material (not commonly a feature of tragedy); and the tutti's role within the concerto is not restricted to self-contained segments, for instance, but invades solo episodes too, sometimes engaging in dialogue with the soloist.

Central to late-eighteenth-century understanding of the tragedy was Aristotle's portrayal of the genre in the *Poetics* (*Ars Poetica*), a treatise central to the developing tradition of art criticism since the renaissance. Despite a growing contemporary awareness of the doctrines of Plato (specifically the *Republic*, but also *Ion* and *Phaedrus*) and an increasing interest in the notion of the Sublime, gained largely through Boileau's 1674 translation of the classical treatise, *On the Sublime*,[7] Aristotle's description of the tragic genre remained the classic textbook account of the manner in which an individual and a group interact in the presentation of dramatic ideas.[8] Within the Greek tragedy, the function of the chorus is often to comment on the progress of the drama, and the manner in which the distinction is drawn depends largely on the opposition of different metres: iambic trimeters in which the actor usually speaks (advancing the drama) and lyric metres for the chorus, mapped out in broad strophes and antistrophes, tending towards stasis (reflecting on the situation).[9] Contrasting metres (iambic and lyric) thus encode different dramatic attributes: the episodes for the actor sustain the plot's forward momentum, while the chorus provides punctuating *stasima*. The strict opposition between *epeisodia* (scenes for one or more actors) and *stasima* diminished somewhat during the evolution of the tragic genre, especially in the work of Euripides, who introduced a greater variety of metres, breaking down the stylistic distinction between chorus and actor. While tragedy and concerto each unfold in an episodic manner, alternating 'tuttis' and 'solos', there is an important distinction to be made, for within the Mozart piano concerto, textural opposition and similarity coexist, involving actual sharing of material between solo and tutti on the one hand (as found, for instance, throughout much of the first movement of K.491), and extreme contrast on the other (for instance in the frequent virtuosic episodes within the first movements of K.450 in B flat and K.451 in D). Insofar as there is a generic correspondence between tragedy and concerto, Mozart's concertos, with their closer mingling of tutti and chorus, come closer to the tragedies of Euripides than those of Aeschylus, which separate the roles of chorus and actor rather rigidly in their contrast of metres – a stylistic trait keenly observed in Aristophanes's comedy, *The Frogs*.[10] An example of Euripides's metrical flexibility within a solo speech is to be found in the monody of the Phrygian in *Orestes*, a long speech, mixing during its course a variety of metres (anapests, cretics, bacchics, iambic dimeters and dochmiacs), punctuated on several occasions by the chorus which, however, retains its iambic trimeters throughout. Euripides applies his command of metre in order to delineate clearly the respective roles of the Phrygian and the chorus, whose identities derive from a deliberate contrast of 'dynamic' and 'static' metres – an especially satisfying case of technique applied in the service of genre.[11] A similar approach to the relation of solo and tutti is found in some movements of Mozart's piano concertos. As in the case of Euripedes's *Orestes* just discussed, the specific identities are defined by the appropriate application of a technique, in this case by contrasting a pronounced flexibility of phraseology within solo episodes against a somewhat 'squarer' profile in the surrounding tuttis. As an illustration of this practice, we may take the Siciliana from the Adagio of the A major concerto, K.488. It begins by setting out the solo and tutti paragraphs in opposition: an unsupported solo phrase is answered by the tutti, which, in turn, gives way once again to the solo (the two are not heard in combination until bar 25). Within such a structure the individual characteristics of solo and tutti emerge clearly and whereas the solo's opening ten-bar phrase unfolds as a theme and accompaniment, whose scansion moves exclusively from 'strong' (first beat) to 'weak' (second beat) in a clear periodic balance, the tutti's answer is contrasting in both respects. It features shorter, fragmentary phrase-units which overlap in counterpoint, so that, while its statement is actually eight bars long, it is seamlessly woven, mixing together different scansions, rather than being cadentially 'rhymed'. In its next episode the solo's phrasing becomes more sophisticated. Its opening turn figure gives it an 'upbeat' scansion, in contrast to the 'downbeat' scansion of the previous material. In particular, the shape of the melodic line gives prominence to the repeated treble A on the second beat, which progressively acquires an accentual stress greater than the first beat. The scansion throughout this phrase is thus weak–strong. It begins with periodic balance (bars 20–2 feature a four-beat unit, symmetrically answered in bars 22–4). Bars 24–6 (highlighted by the *piano* entry of the tutti) sound like a predictable continuation of this even-numbered scheme, but during the ensuing phrase there is a subtle gear-change. By the beginning of bar 28 the first beat of the bar has regained its natural stress (partly for harmonic reasons), reinforced by the entry of the horns in octaves. From this point there is a contrasting periodic balance, strong–weak, up to the next tutti entry in bar 35. This merging of different scansions within the episode is to some degree an adaptation of the solo's 'character' to that of the tutti. It retains the function of a 'dynamic' solo episode, though, in that it is here that the decisive modulation (to the relative major, A) is achieved.

Idiosyncratic phraseology is likewise a defining characteristic of the solo episode beginning at bar 49 of the Larghetto of K.595 in B flat. In contrast to regular four- and eight-bar periodicity earlier in the movement, it features a shift to five-bar phrases at bars 49–58 (the second phrase is a decorated reprise of the first), and further irregularities follow. Bars 60^3–62^2 begin as a decorated repeat of 58^3–60^2, but are extended into a six-bar pattern, clinching a modulation into G flat (and subsequently V/E flat, preparing the later reprise at bar 82). This episode is quite consistent in itself; all the phrase irregularities are achieved by 'internal' repetition of a melodic element (the phrase beginning at bar 49, for instance, is extended by sequential repetition of the falling scale steps of bar 50^1 in bar 51). The result, however, is a contrasting 'dynamic' as opposed to 'static' effect, which marks out the episode from its surroundings.

It should be reiterated, finally, that the purpose of this section is purely to investigate one way in which late-eighteenth-century criticism attempted to deal with observable differences (perhaps encoded in contrasting phraseologies) between the kind of discourse pursued by the soloist and that of the tutti. It is not proposed that the first movement form operates as a 'tragedy' in the sense that it unfolds a specific narrative. If there is a narrative here, then that narrative is typological only: the particular turns of phrase announced by the solo do not equate to a crucial event, such as the revelation of a character's true identity, or similar moment of *anagnorisis*, so central to tragic narrative. The analogy is more general than generic. The roles of solo and tutti are, on the whole, distinct in the sense that their mode of delivery, as opposed to material content (which they frequently share), is representative of perspectives emanating from different sources – sometimes opposing, sometimes conspiring – which are played out in a public forum of presentation, communicating a particular material content within a scheme that was believed by Koch to bear analogy with the 'tragedy of the ancients'. Perhaps Koch imagined the tragedy to be an idealised artistic medium for the representation of the individual and the social within ancient Greece; in which case, he may have seen the concerto, by analogy, as a similarly ideal artistic encapsulation of the Enlightenment.

Koch and concerto first-movement form

Fundamental to Koch's appreciation of concerto first-movement form is an ordered succession of tuttis and solos following ritornello procedures developed earlier in the eighteenth century. His model in the *Versuch* (Koch, 1782–93, iii, pp.338–9; Baker, 1983, pp.210–12) consists of four tuttis enclosing three solos which may be diagrammatically expressed as in Figure 1.1. It

T1	S1	T2	S2	T3	S3	T4
I	I–V	V	modulation (often to vi at furthest point)	retransition to V–I	I	I

Figure 1.1   Model of Koch's first-movement form

differs from the structure that was later to be typical of Mozart's normal practice principally in the organisation of T3 and S3. In Koch, the retransition (T3) was left to the tutti, modulating either sequentially, or else by means of a circle of fifths back from whatever remote key had been clinched at the end of S2 towards a dominant preparation for the reprise of the tonic key. The reprise itself was co-ordinated with the reprise of the opening (tutti) theme, but was entrusted to the soloist (S3). By contrast, Mozart's retransition normally involves the soloist right until the arrival of the tonic, at which point the tonal and thematic reprise is entrusted to the tutti.[12]

Concerning possibilities for the design of the opening tutti ritornello, Koch notes that it had formerly remained within the tonic but that more modern examples include digressions to the dominant. These are of two kinds. The first is seemingly derived from binary form in that, following the statement of the main theme in the tonic, there is a modulation towards the dominant, concluded by a half-close on the dominant, after which a secondary, cantabile theme is introduced, terminated by a cadence confirming the dominant; following this is further thematic material heading eventually back to the tonic key and co-ordinated with the reappearance of one of the themes from the opening section (usually, in fact, the main theme), closing in the tonic before the entry of the soloist. This specific pattern is not found in Mozart's concertos, but relates quite closely to those of C. P. E. Bach, which, as noted previously, had served Koch as a model in the preparation of his *Versuch* during the 1780s and early 1790s before he had encountered Mozart's works.[13] The second includes a real modulation into the dominant region, followed by one or more themes (which Koch terms 'ein melodisches Haupttheil') in that key (as in the first movement of K.449 in E flat, for instance, arriving at V/B flat in bar 31, and continuing with the secondary theme in the new key at bar 37). By contrast with the 'binary form' model, there is no articulating central cadence, but a smooth transition between the different stages in the unfolding sequence of keys. Whatever the detailed procedure from this point on, the opening tutti ritornello always reverts to the tonic at its end, concluding with a formal cadence before the first appearance of the soloist (Baker, 1983, p.120).[14]

Koch notes that the first solo entry typically arrives after a full cadence in the tutti (that is, without any overlap, as is found in the first movements of K.450 and K.503), but that later solo entries tend to overlap with tutti cadences: 'the melody of the main [solo] part is sometimes interrupted by the orchestra with short passages, which consist either of repeated segments of the principal melody or of phrases which occurred only in the ritornello' (Baker, 1983, p.211). This is Mozart's procedure in the first movement of K.453, for instance, which frequently includes dialogues and dovetailed overlaps between the solo piano and the woodwind. Regarding the end of the first solo, Koch comments that the orchestral tutti following the soloist's prominent right-hand trill and decisive cadence on the dominant

> begins again with the main phrase. It repeats a few melodic sections which were already contained in the first ritornello and closes likewise with a formal cadence in the key of the fifth [dominant] ... the second solo usually starts with a melodic section which was not contained in the first period ... This period is treated like the second main period of the first allegro of the symphony ... In its form, the third solo part in the concerto again resembles the third main period of the first allegro of the symphony. [Following the cadenza, the closing ritornello] generally consists of the last melodic sections of the initial ritornello, with which the entire first allegro concludes (Baker, 1983, p.211).

The description of the second and third solos in relation to 'the first allegro of the symphony' is highly significant, for although presented primarily in terms of a succession of tutti and solo sections, clearly demarcated by thematic, tonal and textural characteristics, Koch's outline of the concerto first-movement form, and especially its solo sections, was profoundly influenced by contemporary understandings of sonata form. So far as he was concerned, the three solos equated in thematic and tonal function to the three principal sections of a sonata movement. Koch's description of sonata form (which he terms 'the first allegro of the symphony') is as follows:

> the first allegro of the symphony ... has two sections which may be performed with or without repetition. The first of these consists only of a single main period [the 'exposition'], and contains the plan of the symphony; that is, the main melodic phrases are presented in their original order and afterwards a few of them are fragmented ... The second section consists of two main periods, of which the first [what was later recognised as the 'development section'] tends to have greatly diverse structures ... The last period of our first allegro [the 'recapitulation'], which is devoted above all to the main key, most frequently begins with the [opening] theme in this key, but occasionally may also start with another main melodic idea ... Finally, the second half of the first period which followed the V-phrase in the fifth [=dominant key], is repeated in the main key and with this the allegro ends (Baker, 1983, pp.199–200).[15]

According to Koch, the first Allegro of the symphony and the first movement of a concerto were fundamentally similar in tonal terms, the differences between the two residing principally in the character of themes and their continuation:

> The structure [of the exposition in a symphony first movement] differs from that of the sonata and the concerto not through modulations to other keys, nor through a specific succession or alternation of I- or V-phrases. Rather it differs in that (1) its melodic successions tend to be more extended already with their first presentation than in other compositions, and especially (2) these melodic sections usually are more attached to each other and flow more forcefully than in the periods of other pieces, that is, they are linked so that their phrase-endings are less perceptible (Baker, 1983, p.211).

On the 'structural' level of tonal succession, then, the course of events in a concerto first movement and in a sonata form are well-nigh indistinguishable. There is a modulation to the dominant region in each case; there is an important central section characterised by modulation; and there is a return to the opening tonality within which some previous events are reprised before the movement's close.

In relation to the concerto, it is just the solo sections that Koch treats as analogous to sonata structure, as the following suggests: 'Nothing remains to be noted in connection with the three main periods of the solo part, for they have the same external arrangement and the same course of modulation as the three main periods of the first allegro of the symphony [that is, sonata form]' (Baker, 1983, p.211). In the *Versuch*, he notes that 'the first allegro of the concerto contains three main periods performed by the soloist, which are enclosed by four subsidiary periods performed by the orchestra as ritornellos' (Baker, 1983, p.213).[16] Apparently, then, the tuttis have merely introductory or punctuating functions within this scheme;[17] the main burden of the structure is carried by the solo sections. In the *Lexicon* (Koch, 1802) the role of the opening tutti is more directly stated: 'The first entry of the solo part is preceded by an *introductory ritornello* [emphasis added], in which the listeners are made familiar with the [forthcoming] content of the solo, and in which the principal themes of the entire movements are announced.'[18] Furthermore, whereas in the *Versuch* Koch had justified the third tutti as a brief connective link between the second and third solos, typically ending with a dominant pedal and confirming the return to the tonic, in the *Lexicon* it is excluded altogether, the structure being explained as two solos surrounded by three tuttis. In this plan, the 'second solo' is in two halves, the first conforming to the expected modulatory pattern, while the second, following on without any explicit punctuation from the tutti, marks the return of the main theme and the home key.[19] It would seem that the status of tutti elements is progressively diminished in Koch's sonata-derived theory of the concerto form. The 'dynamic' qualities of the classical sonata form (for instance, its capacity to advance the 'argument' through hierarchies of tonal tension and resolution) are imputed to the solo sections; the tuttis are relatively 'static'.[20]

Especially important in this regard is the relationship of solo and tutti advocated by Koch. He considered the content of the first *solo* section, and not the opening tutti, to comprise the *Anlage* ('plan') of the concerto, in which the movement's key ideas are already interconnected, appearing to the composer as a complete whole, including all the main themes and figurations and their accompanying parts (Koch, 1782–93, ii, p.54; Baker and Christensen, 1996, p.161). Such a comment implies that not only were the solos 'primary' and the tuttis 'secondary' in structural significance (as in Vogler's description), but that the opening ritornello was actually composed 'retrospectively' in relation to an *already-existing* first solo (tonally adjusted, of course) and incorporating some, but not necessarily all of its themes:

> The difference between the form of an initial ritornello and the following main period of the composition [that is, the first solo] is principally that it closes in the main key and not in the most closely related key as does the [solo] period ... *Although* [the first ritornello] *includes sections of the main period, it does not (particularly in the concerto) contain each and every phrase of it* (Baker, 1983, pp.244–5; emphasis added).

This regimented approach is doubtless more akin to the instructional setting of a formal treatise than 'live' musical composition as practised by experienced masters and is not borne out by detailed analysis of Mozart's concertos. Mozart's first solos are frequently recompositions of the opening tuttis, typically introducing material not previously stated by the tutti (especially 'new' themes and transitional extensions associated with the defining modulatory function of the solo section)[21] and understandable only in relation to the opening paragraphs of the movement. For example, it is obvious that the piano's sequential continuation at bar 30 foll. in the first movement of K.413 is an adaptation of the pattern established at bars 24–41 in the preceding tutti, in which a dominant statement (bar 24) of the secondary theme is balanced by a tonic counterstatement (bar 32). According to Koch's concept of the *Anlage*, the opposite would be true. An admittedly extreme case is the first solo of K.482's first movement which is virtually unconnected materially with the preceding tutti; by no stretch of the imagination can bars 1–76 be said to derive from bars 77–198. In only a very few cases is the relationship of first solo to first tutti anything like as close as is suggested by Koch's prescription (the first movement of K.488 being one example).

Neither does the surviving manuscript evidence support Koch's implication that the solos were composed first of all. For Mozart, the autograph scores were generally also the composing scores, not 'fair copies', and of course they all start at the beginning of the movement with the first tutti, continuing directly into the ensuing solo after a few folios. In no case is there any physical indication that the solo sections were pre-composed.[22] A second type of source is the sketchleaf. Of the seven separate sketch leaves that survive for the piano concertos, six relate to the solo part, of which three belong to movements in ritornello form: (i) a continuity draft relating to bars 86–91 and 118–26 in the first movement of K.414; (ii) a revision of an already drafted section in the first movement of K.449 (bars 183–203); and (iii) preliminary versions of the opening solo phrase in the first movement of K.503 (bars 96–112).[23] In all three cases the sketches demonstrably arose during the process of writing out the autograph ('side-sketches', as László Somfai has termed them: Somfai, 1996) and not prior to that process. In the case of K.503 the sketchleaf contains progressive refinements of a passage already written into f.5v of the autograph score (proceeding directly from the closing bars of the first tutti). Once Mozart had decided upon a final version of the opening solo he cancelled the earlier version on f.5v of the autograph and copied the new one into the (blank) trumpet and timpani staves in his score.

A third way in which Koch's template does not adequately reflect Mozart's practice concerns the linkage of the first tutti and first solo sections. Mozart sometimes plays with the conventional expectations of tutti punctuation between the first two main periods, blurring the divisions between 'tutti' and 'solo' expositions. In nine cases, the first entry of the soloist coincides not with the restatement of the main theme but with the introduction of new material postponing the expected arrival of the main theme by some 10–20 bars. Moreover, when the theme eventually arrives, the piano does not play its opening, but completes in some way a restatement begun in the tutti.

Several approaches are encountered, the simplest of which is overlapping of the first solo entry with the end of the tutti. In K.271, the piano enters with an extended trill at bar 56, that is, during the tutti's codetta figure, continuing with a new introductory theme and closing into a *forte* restatement of the Allegro's main theme shared antiphonally by tutti and solo (bars 63–9). K.413 presents a rather different situation. Here, the precise location of the tutti's final cadence is quite ambiguous. A full close on F occurs at bar 53, but this is followed by an 'appendix', consisting of a further five bars of contrapuntal entries in the strings over a dominant pedal, whose eventual resolution over-laps with the piano's first appearance in bar 58. The continuation, a lyrical passage for the piano alone, incorporates a digression to the supertonic G minor and prepares for the tonic restatement of the main theme by the tutti at bar 68. In K.450, too, the piano's first entry overlaps with subsidiary cadential progressions in the strings following the apparent final cadence in bar 59, but launches instead into virtuosic display, entirely unthematic in character, built around scalic and arpeggiaic passages (bars 59–70), and ending with a fermata, possibly indicating that a brief cadenza is to be improvised before the long-postponed main theme, whose eventual arrival after an extended tonic pedal is all the more effective. In the first movement of K.467, following an emphatic tutti cadence in the tonic C major at bar 68, the soloist enters (this time after a brief woodwind link) with semiquaver passagework at bar 74, all founded on the dominant and evolving into extended virtuoso display, culmi-nating once more in a fermata (to be elaborated with an improvised cadenza?); this is succeeded by a trill (bar 80) sounded against the restatement of the main march theme begun by the strings and completed antiphonally by the piano (bar 84 foll.). The effect of each of these passages is to announce the soloist's individuality by means of a dramatic interruption of the flow, a denial of the temporary finality occasioned, for instance, by the tutti's decisive cadential arrival on the tonic. By entering with some provocative display of virtuosity, particularly one which strongly emphasizes the dominant chord by insistent and extended repetition, the soloist both reserves to itself a special sonorous space (in contrast to the tutti) and exploits an aesthetic precondition of classical tonality, namely that the protracted suspension of a regular 'tread' of harmonic progressions is a sure sign that some moment of dramatic resolution, some 'turning-point', is about to be reached. That moment is inevitably the restate-ment of the main theme that previously had opened the movement, and it does not diminish the special character of the soloist's entry if the ensuing thematic statement is *forte* or *piano*. The point is to arrest the attention of the listener by means of an unmistakable breach in the prevailing idiom of continuity.

A related strategy for spotlighting the soloist is the incorporation of a brief 'insert' between the tutti and solo expositions, found in K.415, K.466, K.482, K.491 and K.503. Following a full tonic cadence at the end of the tutti exposi-tion, the soloist enters (usually alone) with entirely new thematic material which is extended in a 'developmental' way throughout several related phrases, frequently outlining their own cadential environment, moving momentarily away from the 'home' tonic to explore closely related implied keys. The degree of thematic concentration in these 'inserts' is quite remarkable, especially in K.466 and K.491, in both of which the material leading to the eventual tutti restatement of the main theme evolves from the piano's first two or three bars; in both cases, thematic material from this 'insert' serves as the foundation for the central development section later in the movement.

While Koch's treatment of the concerto first-movement form is the most detailed of its time and holds generally true for classical concertos, especially those of C. P. E and J. C. Bach, one wonders if it would have been radically different had he been aware of Mozart's Viennese concertos before the appearance of the final volume of his *Versuch* in 1793. As it stands, his description, hovering between an appreciation of the element of texture-contrast and the tonal logic of the sonata, only imperfectly represents Mozart's sophisticated concerto structures. For instance, there is nothing in his account of either tutti or solo organisation that reflects the crucial element of dialogue between strings and wind in the opening ritornellos of, for instance, K.450, K.453 or K.482; or between the piano and the wind that is so essential a characteristic in the narrative continuity of these works. Neither is the structural interrelationship of tutti and solo sections sufficiently refined in Koch's scheme to handle the magical reformulation of a tutti at bars 143–9 in the first movement of K.488 as a solo at bar 261 foll. Ultimately, Koch's account of concerto first-movement form as practised in the late eighteenth century is an efficient summary of procedures, couched in a form that would be of practical benefit to a beginning composer. In relation to Mozart's finished examples it serves to highlight their radical departures from such conventional theoretical templates. Reflecting on Koch's detailed assessment of the concerto, one is struck by the gulf between his theory and Mozart's practice.

There are compensations, however. If Koch's 'structural' account of the concerto form proves insufficient in relation to Mozart's practice, then his rigorous account of *Melodielehre* in the *Versuch* offers a useful model for understanding the melodic, harmonic and tonal elements that lend coherence to Mozart's broader structures. Koch demonstrates how the shape of a tonal movement, considered hierarchically on the levels of phrase, section and whole, depends crucially upon the articulating power of the cadence. While his systematic investigation of different cadential types, principally the half-cadence ('imperfect', ending, on a dominant chord) and the full-cadence ('perfect', ending on the tonic chord) may seem mechanical on paper, it clearly demonstrates that without a system of cadential punctuation, the interrelation of part and whole within a movement (or even within a smaller section or individual phrase) would be meaningless. Different phrases have different functions within the whole, partly dependent upon their location, partly dependent upon their tonal function. They act as signals marking the boundaries of different regions. The interconnection of these regions and their relative significance in relation to each other is clarified by the sophisticated use of cadential emphasis.[24] All in all, Koch's description of contemporary cadential practice is a valuable starting-point in our attempts to appreciate Mozart's first-movement concerto structures (Baker, 1983, pp.3–59).

Koch's principal cadential types and their signalling of discrete functions within a movement are illustrated by the phrases ending at bar 24 (half-cadence) and at bar 189 (full-cadence) from the first movement of the F major concerto, K.459. Their functions are radically different. The first concludes a phrase that had begun with the introduction of a contrasting theme at bar 16. It resolves on to a chord of C, but without establishing that degree as a key in its own right – the continuation is unmistakably in the 'home' tonic, F. In keeping with its role as a moment of mild punctuation between thematic ingredients outlining the main key-area, this cadence does not draw attention to itself. It co-ordinates descending stepwise motion in the leading melodic part (A–G in the flute and violin 1) with ascending stepwise movement in the bass (B flat–C in the cellos and basses – and, indeed, in the left hand of the piano part if it is also fulfilling its intended continuo role here.)[25] By contrast, the cadence at bars 188–9 is far more powerful. It signals a much more important boundary than the cadence at bar 24, namely the end of the first solo (in Koch's terminology, it is a *Schlußsatz*, rounding off the second *Hauptperiode* of the first part of the movement). Technically, this strong cadence is achieved by the deliberate co-ordination of several distinct features. For instance, the preparation for the eventual perfect cadence (V–I in bars 188–9) is quite extended. Most immediately, this preparation comprises the solo phrase in triplets from bar 185 – to which the woodwind are soon conjoined – prolonged through twelve successive beats (three bars) before the concluding dominant–tonic progression. Seen on a broader scale, the entire triplet passage from bar 149 to bar 187 is a 'preparation' for the dramatic conflation of the main theme and the secondary key-area, C major, at bar 189. C major was already clearly established by bar 149 (itself marked by a perfect cadence at bars 148–9 whose force relative to that of bars 188–9 is quite weak, perhaps by virtue of the chromatic in-filling of the main melodic steps in the right hand). Mozart's intervening triplet paragraph explores harmonic space within this region, sometimes traversing chromatic sequences, and returning to a mild cadential resolution on to a first inversion tonic chord at bars 172–3 (or is this actually a half-cadence, ending weakly with a dominant chord on the unaccented 4th crotchet of bar 172?: the ambiguity is important in throwing the eventual weight of resolution on to the clinching cadence at bars 188–9).

The perfect cadence is further dramatised by means of the familiar cliché in bar 188, involving a prominent trill (on the supertonic scale-degree), lasting through the whole bar at the top of the solo texture over Alberti-bass triplet

quavers; its falling-step motion on to the tonic resolves the root-position domi-
nant-7th chord on to the new tonic, C, likewise in root-position and arriving on
the strong downbeat of bar 189. Also important here, in contrast to the earlier
cadences at bars 149 and 172–3, is the elision of the tonic resolution and the
tutti's *forte* continuation. The first beat of bar 189 is simultaneously the end of
one phrase and the beginning of the next. Juxtaposition, rather than separation,
is a fingerprint of the cadential articulation of this particular moment in the
structure, in which the previously distinct solo and tutti voices are 'fused' in
the achievement of a common tonal purpose. It is a temporal factor which,
taken together with those spatial characteristics described previously, signal
the relatively greater importance of this cadence within the whole compared to
that at bar 149.

While it is easy enough to describe some of Mozart's compositional habits
within his piano concertos from the perspective of eighteenth-century theory,
it is important to remember that the perception of a correspondence between
that theory and his practice is our perception, not a natural consequence;
indeed, such theoretical constructions were probably not in the forefront of his
mind when composing. Far more immediate in this respect were actual pieces
of music that served him well as models for his own efforts, especially in the
early stages of his career. In the next chapter, some of these models, and their
consequences for Mozart's emerging treatment of form in the concerto, will be
introduced and explored.

Notes

1. Aesthetic issues are explored at greater length in Chapter Six below.
2. The impact of this is discussed in Chapter Three below.
3. In fact, C. P. E. Bach's concertos, especially those of the 1740s, 1750s and 1760s,
    which may have been those most readily available to Koch, utilise a number of
    different structural bases in their first movements, principally the alternation of
    five tuttis and four solos and of four tuttis and three solos, the latter being that
    upon which Koch's model is grounded. For an account of Bach's schemes, and
    their relationship to contemporary North German concerto practice, see Davis,
    1988.
4. Towards the end of the entry Koch writes: 'Man vollende sich dieses scizzirte
    Gemalde und vergleich damit Mozarts Meisterwerke in diesem Fache der Kunst-
    produkte, so hat man eine genaue Beschreibung der Eigenschaften eines guten
    Konzertes' (col.354).
5. Customarily in this type of instrumental composition, concern is more for the
    facility of the player than for any particular [expressive] character. Commonly the
    whole piece consists of three movements.'
6. Such reprises are not typical of the tragic genre, although they sometimes feature
    within an extended passage for the chorus, as in Aeschylus's *The Eumenides*
    (lines 300–393).
7. This aesthetic issue is discussed further in Chapter Six.

8. For modern English editions of the relevant portions of these, see Hamilton, 1973 and Russell and Winterbottom, 1989. Though attributed to Longinus, the actual author of *On the Sublime* is unknown; see Donald Russell's discussion of the authorship in Kennedy, 1989, pp.306 foll.

9. The name for these sections is actually *stasima* ('in one place').

10. In this comedy, Dionysus is required by Pluto, god of the underworld, to judge the relative merits of the tragedians Aeschylus and Euripides. Briefly, Euripides thinks Aeschylus' choruses monotonous, because of their invariable hexameters; Aeschylus, on the other hand, thinks that Euripides' introduction of metrical flexibility is a corruption of the tragic genre. The god eventually rules in favour of Aeschylus, whose tragedies are considered to be 'weightier' than those of Euripides (partly, it should be noted, in view of their metrical consistency, suggesting that the metrical fluidity of Euripides was still regarded as something of an untried novelty). There are various English translations of *The Frogs*. That in Rogers, 1902–14, contains a useful introduction commenting in detail on the metrical aspects of these two tragedians (at pp.xxv–xxxiv). For a recent translation, see Dover, 1993, which also includes discussion of metrical characteristics at pp.10–37.

11. The passage is at lines 1403–92 of *Orestes*; for a discussion, see Webster, 1967, p.19.

12. An exception is found in the first movement of K.459 in F, in which the reprise of the opening is sounded by the soloist, preceded by a linking tutti.

13. On this topic see Davis, 1983, pp.45–61.

14. Türk's description of the concerto in the *Clavierschule* accords with Koch's outline, though it is rather more general: 'Before the solo part makes its entrance, the accompanying players perform a few periods ... which are called *ritornello* ... Also, after every solo, the accompanying instruments play a shorter or longer intervening section. After the last solo, every movement closes again with the *ritornello* or with only a part [of it]' (Haggh, 1982, iv, §27). For Türk, the solo portions were evidently of primary importance.

15. This is Koch's description of the form of a 'Symphony', but is applicable also to the solo sonata, as he notes in Koch, 1782–93, i, part iv, §108.

16. Further on Koch's conception of concerto first-movement form, see Stevens, 1971.

17. Koch was anticipated in this conception by Vogler, 1778–79, ii, pp.36–9. Abbé Georg Joseph Vogler (1749–1814) was vice-Kapellmeister at the Mannheim court and a prolific theorist; from 1786 until 1797 Kapellmeister at the Royal Swedish court; subsequently he served in a similar capacity at Darmstadt. Further on Vogler, see Clive, 1993. Vogler's advice to anyone wishing to compose a concerto is to compose a normal sonata, whose first part corresponds to the first solo of the concerto, and the second part to the second solo. Before the first part, after the second and in between the two are inserted the orchestral ritornellos (whose relative significance is perhaps disguised within Vogler's term 'Zwischenspiele'). This practice is not much different from that to be observed in Mozart's own early 'pasticcio' concerto transcriptions, K.37, 39, 40, 41 and 107/i–iii, discussed in Chapter Two.

18. Koch, 1802, cols. 354–5: '... dem Vortrage der Solostimme ein Ritornell als Einleitung vorhergehet, in welchem der Zuhörer auf den Inhalt der Solostime aufmerksam gemacht wird, und in welchem die melodischen Haupttheile des ganzen Satzes ... vorgetragen werden' (author's translation).

19. Koch, 1802, col.355: 'Das zweyte Solo ... hat die Freyheit sich unter den übrigen

verwandten Tonarten hinzuwenden ... die letzte Hälfte desselben wird jedoch in der Haupttonart durchgeführt, in welcher die melodischen Hauptheile des ganzen Satzes kürzlich wiederholt werden.'

20.   There is a consistency here between Koch's technical and generic descriptions; it will be remembered that, in the discussion of the concerto as tragedy, a distinction was also observed between the 'active' role of the actor (soloist) and the 'static' commentary provided by the chorus (orchestra), a relation articulated by metrical opposition. See also Davis, 1983.

21.   In a roundabout way such 'new themes' are covered by Koch's comments, in that they are among those 'sections of the main period' that did not have to be contained in the tutti ritornello.

22.   Three autograph scores of Mozart's piano concertos are available in facsimile: Mozart, 1964 [K.491]; Mozart, 1979 [K.491]; Mozart, 1985 [K.467]; and Mozart, 1991 [K.537]. In all of these autographs, evidence of Mozart's compositional activity may be seen, although the most obvious and radical examples occur in the case of K.491. Further comment on the compositional process revealed by these autographs is given in the respective entries in Part Two.

23.   Konrad, 1998, Skizzenblätter Skb1782d, Skb1783α and Skb1786b respectively.

24.   For a recent account of cadential organisation of first-movement concerto forms derived in part from Koch, see Berger, 1996.

25.   For this aspect of performance practice, see Chapter Seven.

CHAPTER TWO

Origins of Mozart's Piano Concertos

The 'Pasticcio' concertos, K.37, 39, 40 and 41; K.107/i–iii

Predating any of Mozart's 'original' piano concertos are several 'pasticcios', that is, concerted transcriptions of movements from solo sonatas by other composers. There are two sets of 'pasticcios', dating respectively from 1767 and 1772. The first set, consisting of K.37, 39, 40 and 41, contains arrangements principally of sonatas for piano 'avec accompagnement de violon' by four composers whom Mozart had encountered in Paris in 1764–65: Johann Schobert (c.1740–67), Leontzi Honauer (1737–?90), Johann Gottfried Eckard (1735–1809) and Hermann Friedrich Raupach (1728–78).[1] The second, K.107/i–iii, is based on three of Johann Christian Bach's solo keyboard sonatas, op.5 nos.2, 3 and 4. In each case, Mozart's practice was to insert sections of the original sonata movements as solos between 'orchestral' tuttis (also derived from the sonatas) that punctuate the outlines of the form. The resulting pattern, typical of ritornello schemes encountered in the mid-eighteenth-century concerto, is an alternation of four tuttis and three solos. In the earliest set, K.37 and K.39–41, Mozart scores the tuttis for an ensemble including strings, woodwind and horns (additionally with trumpets in K.40). In the solo episodes the strings are generally the only tutti instruments to participate, although long-held horn notes are occasionally inserted to strengthen the harmony. In K.107/i–iii, Mozart's 'tutti' ensemble consists only of a pair of violins and continuo bass, although the string writing is frequently quite full and florid.[2]

K.107/i–iii were recognised at least as early as 1800 as arrangements rather than original concertos.[3] By contrast, K.37 and 39–41 were regarded as evidence of the remarkably early development of Mozart's powers of invention until the early twentieth century. The possibility that these pieces were not wholly of Mozart's own invention did not occur to André, nor to Jahn (Jahn, 1882, i, p.63), nor to Köchel, who gave them their numbers in the first edition of his Thematic Catalogue (Köchel, 1862). They were published for the first time in the old Breitkopf & Härtel *Gesamtausgabe* in 1877.[4] Only when Théodore de Wyzewa and George de Saint-Foix began work on their magisterial study of Mozart's life and work in the early 1900s (Wyzewa and Saint-Foix, 1912–46) did doubts begin to arise. In 1909 they revealed that the second movement of K.39 was based on the first movement of Johann Schobert's keyboard sonata op.17 no.2 (Wyzewa and Saint-Foix, 1908–09a).[5] Their suspicions that yet other movements among these early concertos might be 'adaptations' rather than 'compositions' were confirmed by further study of the keyboard works of the composers encountered by the Mozarts during the Paris journeys of the 1760s: indeed, Wyzewa and Saint-Foix soon announced that they had discovered the sources of five other movements in these pieces in the published sonatas of Leontzi Honauer and Johann Gottfried Eckard (Wyzewa and Saint-Foix, 1908–09b). Finally, in the first volume of *W. A. Mozart. Sa vie musicale et son oeuvre* (Wyzewa and Saint-Foix, 1912–46), they traced four further movements in the sonatas of Hermann Friedrich Raupach. Erwin Brodsky eventually discovered Carl Philipp Emanuel Bach's 'La Boehmer' as the source for K.40's finale.[6] The model for the second movement of K.37 has only recently been discovered.[7]

The sonata models for the pasticcio concertos of 1767 are listed in Table 2.1. As can be seen from the table, Mozart was evidently familiar with Eckard's op.1 (Eckard, 1763), Honauer's op.1 (Honauer, 1765a) and op.2 (Honauer, 1765b), Schobert's op.17 (Schobert, 1765) and Raupach's op.1 (Raupach, 1765). No attempt was made in these concerto arrangements to preserve the integrity of the original sonata models. Instead these are distributed across different movements within K.37, 39, 40 and 41. For example, the whole of Raupach's B flat sonata, op.1 no.1 occurs in these arrangements, its outer movements serving for the first movement and finale respectively of K.39, and its slow movement for that of K.41. Elsewhere, only single movements of sonatas were extracted. In no case is an entire sonata reworked as three successive movements in a single concerto.

Table 2.1   Sonata models for Mozart's 'Pasticcio' concertos, K.37, 39, 40, 41

K.	1st mvt	2nd mvt	3rd mvt
37	Raupach, op.1 no.5/i	Mozart	Honauer, op.2 no.3/i
39	Raupach, op.1 no.1/i	Schobert, op.17 no.2/i	Raupach, op.1 no.1/iii
40	Honauer, op.2 no.1/i	Eckard, op.1 no.4 (all)	C. P. E. Bach, W117
41	Honauer, op.1 no.1/i	Raupach, op.1 no.1/ii	Honauer, op.1 no.1/iii

Why Mozart made these arrangements is unknown. The autographs (see below) are dated, as follows: K.37, April 1767; K.39, June 1767; K.40, July 1767; K.41, July 1767. Wyzewa and Saint-Foix believed that Mozart's encounter with the Parisian keyboard masters (especially Schobert and Eckard – in whose op.1 sonatas dynamic specifications occur for the first time in French keyboard music) was directly responsible for unlocking the boy's prodigious talent and that these pasticcios, completed some three years afterwards, were acts of homage (Wyzewa and Saint-Foix, 1908–09a). More realistically, their origin may have been prompted by the prospect of a performance at which the eleven-year-old Wolfgang could be exhibited as 'composer' and executant, probably therefore during the Mozarts' stay in Vienna in autumn

1767. Eduard Reeser offered the tempting speculation that the pieces may even have been played by the young Wolfgang at Brno, whence the Mozart family temporarily withdrew during a smallpox outbreak in Vienna in October 1767 (NMA X/28/ii, p.xii).

The presence of both Wolfgang's and Leopold's handwriting in the autographs of the four works (each entitled 'Concerto per il Clavicembalo')[8] suggests that the arrangements are not wholly Wolfgang's work. Leopold's handwriting is considerably more prevalent in these manuscripts than his son's, and includes detailed corrections of Wolfgang's notation, harmony and instrumental setting, especially in the first and second movements of K.37.[9] Wolfgang Plath's exhaustive examination of the handwriting in Mozart's autographs (Plath, 1960–61; Plath, 1976–77) has conclusively shown Mozart's J. C. Bach pasticcios to postdate those based on the Parisian repertory by some five years. Given that K.37, 39, 40 and 41 evidently represent Wolfgang's first attempts at the concerto genre, it is unsurprising that his father's help was required, especially if the pieces arose relatively quickly in the expectation of an imminent performance opportunity (in which case it would have been more sensible to present a copyist with a clearly notated and accurate text than with the uncertain script of an infant). Whereas in the autographs of K.37, 39, 40 and 41 the handwriting of father and son is freely intermixed, in those of K.107/i–iii[10] their contributions are more regularly 'layered', Wolfgang's contribution being restricted to the three string parts, his father's accounting for the remainder, including the addition of figured bass notation to the solo keyboard part, indicating the expectation of continuo realisation by the soloist in performance.[11] Plath believed that the autographs of both pasticcio sets represent a combined effort of father and son and not simply a transcription and correction by Leopold of Wolfgang's completed work (Plath, 1960–1, p.98). If this is correct, the autographs are in a sense the record of Wolfgang's composition lessons with his father (presenting, however, Leopold's answers, rather than Wolfgang's questions).

Although separated by several years, these two groups of concerto arrangements share a common approach. In each case, Mozart adds tutti passages to pre-existing sonata material by the earlier composers, creating the semblance of solo–tutti contrast typical of the solo concerto of the mid-eighteenth century (for instance, J. C. Bach's op.7 or op.13 sets of 1770 and 1777 respectively). In addition to providing light string and wind accompaniment to the solo passages taken over from these composers' sonatas, Mozart typically adds four tuttis to the first-movement sonata forms:

(1) an introduction ('tutti exposition'), based on the opening material of the model, and sometimes importing at least one other element, such as a cadential theme (K.37, K.40);

(2) a 'codetta' in the dominant key, following the first solo entry, and either

returning to the opening theme (K.37, K.39, K.40,) or else derived from secondary thematic material of the original sonata exposition (K.41);

(3)   a brief freely composed passage, leading to a 6/4 pause chord, introducing the cadenza;[12]

(4)   either a tonic repetition or adaptation of the 'codetta' passage (K.39, K.41) or else a reprise of subsidiary material from the tutti introduction.[13]

In all cases, the original order of events in the sonata model is retained, reflecting its principal modulations from tonic to dominant at the end of the first section and its modulatory sequence back to the tonic in the second half. Occasionally, as in the first movements of K.37 and K.107/iii, Mozart inserts an additional tutti into the development section, to underline the modulation scheme.[14] The overall effect is to manufacture a convincing element of solo–tutti timbral contrast, while preserving the fundamental structural outlines of the model.

Two types of sonata model are encountered in the works of these composers. In the first, all or most of the exposition material is recapitulated in the tonic, beginning with a clear restatement of the opening theme. In the second, only dominant-key material is recapitulated within the tonic towards the end. Both are developments of baroque 'binary' forms.

The particular type of sonata structure adopted affects the treatment in Mozart's arrangement to a marked degree. Raupach's F major sonata, op.1 no.5 provided the basis for the first movement of Mozart's K.37 (part of Raupach's exposition is shown in Example 2.1). It features a prominent tonic reprise of its opening theme soon after the central double-bar, following a formulaic cadential close on C. The first tutti of K.37 follows Raupach's sonata quite closely, quoting his opening theme (bars 1–11) and main secondary theme (bars 16–19). Otherwise the material, including the cadential closing gestures, is new. The first solo borrows virtually the whole of the exposition of Raupach's sonata, carefully retaining all its elements in their original sequence and resetting such textural ideas as the alternation of the piano right hand with the accompanying violin as dialogue between solo and tutti at bars 52–6 of Mozart's arrangement. The second tutti (bars 65–75) extracts material from two separate locations of the first tutti, its main theme and its scalic closing passage.[15] The following central solo is again derived from Raupach, although only bars 80–1 and 89–91 are literal quotations from the model. The reprise of the main theme at bar 92 again follows Raupach, as does the somewhat unusual key-scheme of the ensuing section to bar 129, including a return of the secondary theme from bar 16 in A minor at bar 116. The recapitulation is interrupted by a brief tutti at bars 135–8 (quoting the main theme in the tonic once more) before continuing once again with Raupach's second section from bars 139–52. The following solo concludes with new material (bars 153–60), and the closing tutti – there is no interrupting cadenza – finally brings back the

Example 2.1 Hermann Friedrich Raupach, Sonata in F, op.1 no.5 (1st movement exposition)

main secondary theme from bar 16 foll. in the expected tonic key, F major, at bars 16¹⁻⁴. The movement concludes with a return to the introductory tutti's final gesture (from bar 20 foll.), composed by Mozart, not Raupach.

By contrast, the Allegro moderato of Raupach's op.1 no.1 in B flat (the model for the first movement of Mozart's K.39) has no tonic reprise of the main theme in its second half (part of Raupach's exposition is shown in Example 2.2). As in K.37 the solo passages are taken over unaltered from the

Example 2.2 Hermann Friedrich Raupach, Sonata in B flat, op.1 no.1 (1st movement exposition)

model (save for a few octave transpositions of Raupach's passagework). But here the tuttis are far more 'interventionist'. Only bars 1–6 of the opening tutti in K.39 are taken from Raupach's sonata: the rest is newly composed, including Mozart's syncopated chromatic melody at bar 18 foll., which is reused at the end of the first movement. With only the most minimal adaptation of figuration, Mozart's bars 25–62 follow the first section of Raupach's sonata exactly. At bars 63–7 a tutti is inserted. Like the corresponding tutti in K.37, it is based on the opening theme (in the dominant). But its function here is rather different. Because Raupach's sonata has no tonic reprise of its opening material, this is the last we hear of it in Mozart's movement. Presumably, he could, had he wished, have broken up the sections of his model at some point to reintroduce the main theme as a significant tutti reprise; but he did not, possibly because he (or Leopold) recognised a different type of sonata structure in operation here. Instead, Mozart generally follows the succession of events in Raupach's sonata, in which there is no clear moment of thematic/ tonal recapitulation.[16] Mozart compensates for the lack of any defining tonic reprise by adapting the role of tutti interruptions toward the end of the movement, so that they enhance the tonal articulation in a 'progressive' way, leading gradually to a full realisation of the tonic key. The first (bars 102–5, featuring the supertonic, G minor) is based on his own new syncopated figure from bar 18 and prepares for Raupach's theme at bars 105–109 (sequentially adjacent to the tonic, B flat) far more strongly than was the case in the original sonata; the second (bars 110–13) extends material quoted from the model in bars 106– 109, hovering around the tonic and dominant minor modes, giving an added sense of purpose to Raupach's rather weak return to the tonic at this point (subtly enhanced in Mozart's transcription by the oboes and horns). Mozart's arrangement places Raupach's sonata in a broader thematic and tonal framework that is eloquently rounded off by a final tutti reprising the clear tonic cadential gestures of Mozart's own bars 18–21. It is far more than a literal quotation of a model; instead, it provides a commentary on it, reshaping and reinterpreting its originally continuous tonal and thematic procedures within the novel situation of solo–tutti contrast.

Slow movements and finales in these early pasticcios share the same basic procedure of extended quotation, the only significant deviation from the models being the addition of introductory or concluding tuttis. In K.107/i, Mozart incorporates a brief tutti into the second part of Bach's *Andante di molto* (op.5 no.2), just before the return of the secondary theme in the tonic, and towards the end he sets up a 6/4 pause chord within his closing tutti. Elsewhere, he adapts Bach's originals by thematic extension, as in the minuet and trio finale of K.107/i (Bach's op.5 no.2); here are to be found a number of additional internal phrase-repeats and the sectional alternation of tutti and solo. At times, though, as in the variation movement that forms the finale of J. C. Bach's op.5 no.3 in G (K.107/ii), the texture becomes little more than that of the familiar 'accompanied sonata' for keyboard and violin, the tutti strings contributing background figurations, ornaments and echoes. Generally, Mozart's adaptations extend the length of Bach's original movements, although the variation movement of K.107/ii is exactly the same length as the finale of Bach's op.5 no.3, and the rondo finale of K.107/iii is shorter than Bach's op.5 no.4 by twelve bars.[17]

While the sonata origins of K.37, K.39, K.40, K.41 and K.107 are plain enough, it is remarkably difficult to postulate specific keyboard concertos that may have served the young Mozart as models. Possibly he got to know some of the keyboard concertos of Georg Christoph Wagenseil during his visits to

Vienna of 1767–68 and 1773–74. Wagenseil occasionally includes a 'new theme' in the first solo and he conceives of the central development and recapitulation as an extended solo, into which the tutti intrudes only momentarily, at the reprise of the opening theme, continuing thereafter together with the soloist.[18] Both procedures were subsequently utilised by Mozart, though whether he learnt them directly (or even at all) from Wagenseil is impossible to prove. Equally impossible to state with certainty is the relationship of Mozart's early concertos to examples by local Salzburg composers, such as Anton Ferdinand Paris, Anton Cajetan Adlgasser, Michael Haydn and, of course, Mozart's own father, Leopold, all of whom composed concertos before Mozart's earliest original efforts in the 1770s. Nor should the Salzburg orchestral serenades be forgotten in this connection. These were works consisting of seven or eight movements of which roughly half were concerto movements, and were traditionally performed either at end-of-year ceremonies at the Benedictine University of Salzburg or else to celebrate important occasions such as weddings and namedays. Leopold Mozart's only surviving serenade includes a trumpet concerto as well as a trombone concerto; Wolfgang Mozart's own earliest independently composed concerto movements are found in serenades: K.63 (for oboe and horn) and K.100 (for violin).

Among composers of concertos in the mid-eighteenth-century, perhaps the most obvious influence is Johann Christian Bach, whose sonatas had served Mozart as models in the three pasticcios, K.107. The eight-year-old Mozart had first met Bach during a visit to London in 1764–65, and his compositions made a profound impact on the boy.[19] Bach's own keyboard concertos were published in London in three sets of six, in 1763 (op.1), 1770 (op.7) and 1777 (op.13). One of these sets, possibly the last (J. C. Bach, 1777a),[20] was evidently known to Mozart; his father requested that they be sent by Wolfgang from Paris to Salzburg in a letter of 13 April 1778. However, if these works were not known to Mozart prior to 1778, they appeared too late to have had any influence on all but one of Mozart's Salzburg concertos, K.365 in E flat, for two pianos. None of Bach's op.13 concertos is a 'double concerto', however, and given the special textural and structural characteristics that obtain in a concerto for two roughly equal soloists interacting predominantly with each other as well as with the tutti, Bach's set is unlikely to have been a significant influence operating in Mozart's mind during the composition of K.365. Mozart's next set of piano concertos, K.413–15, were completed during the winter–spring of 1782–83. While the first two of these share the same scoring as Bach's op.13 (allocating precious little of vital significance to the wind because of the special 'à quattro' performance designation),[21] the prospect of Mozart returning to Bach's op.13 as a model after almost five years is implausible.

For firm evidence of other keyboard concertos directly known to Mozart, we have to turn to the handful of cadenzas that he composed for his own performances of such works. Those written for the J. C. Bach 'pasticcio', K.107/i, and for the first movement of K.40 (modelled on a sonata movement by Honauer) have already been mentioned. Five more remain. K⁶626a/K.624, Teil ii, D, F, G, H and K were written for, respectively, Johann Samuel Schröter's concertos in D, op.3 no.4 (first movement), in E flat, op.3 no.6 (first movement), op.3 no.6 (second movement) and op.3 no.1 in F (first movement), and to the slow movement of a D major concerto by Ignaz von Beecke, now lost. Mozart praised Schröter's op.3 set in letters to his father of 3 and 20 July 1778. The original edition was perhaps that printed by W. Napier in London in 1774 (Schröter, 1774), although Mozart probably knew them in the edition issued by Lemenu & Boyer in Paris (Schröter, 1777).[22] These concertos were, at least, composed before K.238, K.242, K.246, K.271 and K.365, but as in the case of the op.13 set of J. C. Bach, no documentary evidence exists that Mozart knew Schröter's concertos before 1778. Consequently, they are no more likely to have been specifically influential on Mozart's concertos than were Bach's.

Mozart had encountered Ignaz von Beecke for the first time in Paris in 1766.[23] The two men subsequently met during the winter of 1775–76 when, as reported in Daniel Schubert's *Deutsche Chronik* of 27 April 1775, they participated in a keyboard 'contest',[24] a meeting which may have provided an opportunity for Mozart to discover concertos by Beecke, including the one for which he composed K⁶626a/K.624, Teil ii, K. That might just predate the composition of Mozart's K.238, K.242 and K.246, making the disappearance of Beecke's concerto – which may therefore have been an immediate model in some respects – all the more regrettable.

Aria forms as models

Arguably more influential upon the first-movement ritornello structures of Mozart's early piano concertos than any of these pieces was the aria, a forum in which the constructional principles of alternating tuttis and solos within a tonal framework of sonata form were developed and established to a considerable degree of sophistication before any of Mozart's instrumental concertos were written (Feldman, 1996; Webster, 1996). Early classical concertos, including those of Mozart's Salzburg years, demonstrate quite clear affinities to the contemporary *opera seria* aria. This relationship was recognised in contemporary theory.[25] At first sight, this seems surprising, for the *Da Capo* was poorly suited to the dynamic unfolding of a classical concerto movement, consisting, as it did, of a main section, beginning and ending in the tonic; a contrasting middle section (often in the relative minor region in the case of a major key); and an elaborately embellished repeat of the main section. Within such a structure, the forward momentum is generated by juxtaposing large, self-contained tableaux; indeed, immediately before the *Da Capo* the action is brought to a sudden halt – a dramatic device that sits uncomfortably with the rapid local interplay of solo and tutti so typical of the pacing of a classical concerto movement. A related and central musical problem within the technical and aesthetic world of classicism is the *Da Capo*'s relatively high degree of tonal stasis. As the same music is used to begin and end the aria, little tonal development within the main section is possible; moreover, as the main section must open and close in the tonic, at no fewer than four significant points in the *Da Capo* structure, the tonic key is prominently stressed. This sits uncomfortably with the classical practice of tonal progression, in which a 'home' key is established, challenged, under-mined and finally restated in a dramatic structure featuring the ultimate reso-lution of large-scale dissonance. However, by shifting the location of the middle section significantly earlier, so that its contrasting tonal function occurs within the main section – rather than being postponed until after the strong tonic cadence in the middle of the *Da Capo* – classical operatic composers (including the young Mozart, in *Ascanio in Alba* and *Lucio Silla*) were able to adapt the *Da Capo*'s archaic embodiment of baroque *Affekten-lehre* to their own more dynamic dramatic requirements – a technical expres-sion of a shift in philosophical perspective.

'Ah se il crudel periglio' from Act 2 of *Lucio Silla* (1772) provides the closest parallel between the aria and concerto genres as Mozart understood them at this stage. The aria begins with a 33-bar tutti ritornello presenting a number of discrete motives (bars 1; 3; 7; 9; 15; 25; 27; 39; 31) and tonal manoeuvres: a strong unison opening, confirming the tonic, B flat; a brief modulation to F at bars 8–9; a half-cadence on the dominant at bars 13–14; a series of cadences in the 'home' tonic, B flat thereafter, some of them suggested by the harmonic progression underlying the secondary theme beginning in bar 15, others more firmly marked, as at bars 24–5 and 32–3. The soprano (Giunia) enters at bar 34 with the main theme and a new continuation in counterpoint to the original bars 3–7 that dissolves into virtuoso display leading to the strong tonic close at bar 46. At this point there is a brief punctuation from the tutti (taken from bars 32–3) before the modulating passage based on new material, beginning from the dominant of G minor (bar 49) and moving to F *via* its own dominant (bar 55; note the chromatic rising steps in the bass, B flat–B natural–C just prior to this). The establishment of F as the new key is achieved through virtuoso scalic semiquavers that dominate from this point up to the confirming cadence in bar 70. Once again, this tonal juncture is marked by a tutti punctu-ation (bars 70–72), announcing the secondary theme from bar 15 of the opening tutti to which the soprano joins in counterpoint, leading to a half-cadence on the dominant of the dominant (bars 79–80). From this point to the end of the solo exposition, Mozart introduces a number of thematic passages whose harmonic character is purely cadential (the entire section from bar 81 to bar 106 may be reduced to linked 2- or 4-bar phrases, none of which is allowed to flourish beyond the span of a localised cadential progression). Supported by such a uniform harmonic background, the solo line unfolds into a torrent of virtuosity, leading to a cliché trill and perfect cadence resolution in the new key, F, at bars 105–106.

The middle section (elided with the resolution in the vocal part) begins with another significant tutti punctuation (bars 106–19) that draws on material from the previous tutti – bars 106–109 = bars 9–12; bars 111–16 = bars 27–32 – before diverting to F minor. The next solo entry introduces new material that roams sequentially from C minor through B flat and G (as dominant of C minor) to D and ultimately F (bar 137), at which point the material from bar 9 is recalled as a dominant preparation for the reprise at bar 141, sounded by solo and tutti together. Apart from adjustments to the modulating transition (bar 156 foll.; compare bar 49 foll.) necessary in order to ground the music within the 'home' tonic region, the reprise largely follows the same course of events as the previous solo (the secondary theme, now in B flat, returns at bar 176, again introduced by the tutti and continued by the soprano) and, following an extended passage of technical exhibitionism in the solo line, the cliché cadence with trill concludes the main part of the reprise which is rounded off by a tutti in two parts, the first coming to a fermata on a 6/4 chord (bar 217), the second, continuing after a vocal cadenza, with a return at bars 218–26 to the material of bars 25–33 which had closed the first tutti, forming a 'rhyme' with that point in the aria.

Mozart takes over many of these same procedures in the first movement of the B flat concerto, K.238 (1776). Its opening tutti (like 'Ah se il crudel periglio', lasting 33 bars) contains a variety of thematic and figurative material (bars 1; 3; 12; 17; 21; 25; 29; 32) and, after a strong tonic opening, arrives at a half-cadence on the dominant, F, at bars 16–17. From this point Mozart engineers a series of cadences in the 'home' tonic, B flat, either implicit in the secondary theme's supporting harmonic progressions or else more firmly marked, as at bars 27–8 (recalling bars 32–3 of 'Ah se il crudel periglio'). The first solo statement outlines the main theme, ending in the tonic at bar 45 and followed by a brief tutti recalling material from bars 29–30 (taken, as in the aria, from towards the end of the first tutti). New material is then introduced by the soloist commencing a transition to the dominant key, the crucial stages of which are the half-cadence on C in bar 54 and a perfect cadence in F at bars 66–7. Note too the importance of advancing semiquaver passagework in the establishment of F as the new key (the prominent 'busy' texture here is analogous to the virtuoso scalic semiquavers that dominate this section within the aria). This tonal articulation is marked by a tutti punctuation (bars 67–9), announcing the secondary theme, in turn completed by the soloist before continuing with a dominant-key presentation of the figure first sounded by the tutti at bar 21, now extended into a virtuoso flourish culminating in the cliché cadence with terminating trill at bars 86–7, convincingly marking off the end of the first solo in the dominant, F.

Themes from two different locations within the first tutti (bars 12–13; 25–33) are conjoined to form the beginning of the brief tutti separating the first and second solo sections, a procedure almost identical to that found at the corresponding point in 'Ah se il crudel periglio' (bars 106–16 of the aria derive from bars 9–12 and bars 27–32).[26] New material is presented by the soloist at the beginning of the second solo which soon dissolves into sequentially modulating progressions featuring diminished-7th chords and roving through the implicit keys of C minor, D (as dominant of the relative minor, G at bar 109 foll.) and finally G minor itself, at which point the material from bars 32–3 is recalled as a dominant preparation for the tonic reprise of the opening theme at bars 131–4, sounded by tutti and solo in combination (the solo completing the tutti phrase). Once again as in the aria, what follows is a regular recapitulation (allowing for the required tonal adjustments) of the first solo, in which mounting virtuosity towards the end leads to a cliché trilled cadence in B flat and a tutti continuation to a 6/4 fermata (bar 191), a solo cadenza and tutti peroration quoting bars 88–98. Mozart's procedure here is not quite identical to that in 'Ah se il crudel periglio', in which the final bars were taken from the end of the of the first tutti, rather than the first solo, but it is clear enough that in both aria and concerto, the tuttis closing each of these three sections are inter-related and operate as deliberate thematic and textural cross-references across the face of the movement as a whole. It is equally clear from the foregoing descriptions that the structure of the concerto movement is deeply influenced by the principles of the operatic aria, and most especially the co-ordination of tonal progression and tutti–solo contrast.

Implicit in the foregoing descriptions is a pronounced flexibility in the ordering of ritornello elements. Having presented the successive ritornello themes in a particular order in the opening tutti, Mozart feels free thereafter to select particular elements, divorced from their original surroundings, to serve as intermediate points of tutti punctuation between solo statements during the course of the movement. Mozart's application of this principle had several interesting consequences for the overall structure. Within the first aria of *Lucio Silla*, 'Vieni ov'amor t'invita' (Cinna), Mozart's radical reordering of the ritornello elements creates a dramatic opposition of solo in relation to tutti. Following the soprano's first entry (bars 30–41) there is a brief tutti punctuation, based not, however, on the second original ritornello element from bar 12, but on the much later cadential figure from bar 27. The material from bar 12 is eventually reprised, but only at bar 75, following the secondary theme in the dominant and interrupting the original succession of ideas from bars 18–29. The reordering may be represented as follows:

tutti elements: **1** (bar 1) – **2** (bar 12) – **3** (bar 18) – **4** (bar 22) – **5** (bar 27)
solo elements: **1** – **5** – [new virtuosic transition] – **3** – **2** – **4** – **5**

A similar situation is found in the first movement of K.175 (1773). The tutti elements unfold as follows:

1 (bar 1) – 2 (bar 4) – 3 (bar 7) – 4 (bar 11) – 4a (bar 15) – 5 (bar 17) – 6 (bar 21) – 7 (bar 30)

In the first solo, the sequence is substantially reconfigured:

1 (bar 33) – 2 (bar 36) – 3 (bar 39) – [new continuation] 1 (bar 46) – [new continuation] 4a (bar 63) – 5 (bar 67) – [new continuation] – 4 – (bar 83) [new continuation to V-cadence at bar 95]

Of broader consequences for the movement as a whole is the thematic reordering found in the opening Allegro of the E flat concerto ('Jeunehomme'), K.271 (1777). Within the opening tutti, the principal ritornello elements may be summarised as 1 (bar 1, the opening fanfare-like idea, shared between tutti and solo); 2 (bar 7, a cantabile continuation, leading towards the dominant chord); 3 (bar 14, a contrasting piece of rhythmic 'pointing', founded on an alternating dominant-7th–tonic pattern, re-establishing the hegemony of the tonic, E flat); 4 (bar 26, a cantabile secondary theme); 5 (bar 34, a complementary secondary theme, introducing a wider range of chordal progressions, but still firmly centred on the tonic); 6 (bar 41, *forte* rhythmic punctuation); 7 (bar 46, the first of three closing cadential figures, founded, like 5, on a progression of chords in the orbit of the tonic and only confirming their allegiance at the end of the phrase); 8 (bar 50, another cadential figure, this time much more direct in its usage of dominant and tonic chords); 9 (bar 54, again cadential, but designed to dovetail casually with the soloist's entry). Following the soloist's first presentation of the main theme (shared with the tutti, bars 63–9) the transition to B flat for the secondary theme (bars 69–88) is entirely new (a procedure found in all of Mozart's Salzburg piano concertos), elements 2 and 3 of the tutti ritornello being entirely omitted. Following the first solo's final cadence (bar 135),[27] elements 6, 7 and 8 of the first tutti return in their original order, but the distinction between tutti and solo roles is blurred here, element 7 appearing in the piano at bars 139–44, before the tutti's completion of the B flat cadence with element 8. The second solo then commences with element 2 (bars 148–58) followed by 1 (bars 158–82) and 3 (bars 182–92). A possible explanation for the omission of elements 2 and 3 in the first solo is their pending centrality within the second. If that is true, it would suggest that Mozart's plan for the movement as a whole was already clearly developed in his mind when the solo exposition was designed.

With precursors such as these in mind, it is time to examine in some detail Mozart's structural practices in the 23 original piano concertos composed between 1775 and 1791. In the next three chapters each movement-type will be treated in turn, combining historically constructed views of individual forms with analysis of Mozart's procedures encountered in particular movements. Thereafter, Chapters Six and Seven will examine the repertoire from the contrasting standpoints of aesthetics and performance.

Notes

1. For details on the possible influence of these composers' sonatas on Mozart's, see Irving, 1997, pp.21–3; also Irving, 1996. Further on the 1767 pasticcios, see Simon, 1959. Simon's interesting article contains more analytical detail on these pieces than can be accommodated here. The pasticcios are all published in NMA X/28/2, ed. W. Gerstenberg and E. Reeser (Kassel, 1964).
2. The light scoring of K.107 reflects that of J. C. Bach's own op.7 keyboard concertos (J. C. Bach, 1770b).
3. The manuscripts including the pasticcios were purchased from Mozart's widow by André in 1799; the following year an inventory catalogue of the Mozart Nachlaß was begun by André's publishing house in which the three concerto arrangements 'welche Mozart aus Johann Bachs Sonaten nahm' were itemised as nos.3–6. See Schmid, 1956.
4. Serie XVI, Band i, nos1–4.
5. Schobert's op.17 was not published until after his death in 1767, that is, at least one year after the Mozarts had departed Paris. Possibly Mozart knew Schobert's piece from a pre-publication manuscript copy or else from an anthology publication.
6. As reported by Einstein in Köchel, 1937.
7. It was revealed by Gregory Butler as the joint work of Leopold and Wolfgang Mozart in a paper read at the AMS Congress, Toronto 2000, 'The Andante K. 37/ ii: Mozart's Earliest Extant Concerto Movement'. I am grateful to Professor Butler for communicating some of his findings to me privately, prior to publication.
8. The autographs are currently in D-B, Mus.ms.autogr. W. A. Mozart 37, 39, 40 and 41 respectively. Facsimiles in NMA X/28/ii, pp.xx–xxii. The four works are bound together and are all on ten-stave Salzburg paper (K.37, 28 leaves; K.39, 27 leaves; K.40, 26 leaves; K.41, 24 leaves; Tyson, 1996, no.1), a paper commonly used by Leopold throughout the 1750s and 1760s.
9. In addition, Leopold added the titles of the works, and the tempo marks for the first and second movements of K.37 and K.41.
10. D-B, Mus.ms.autogr. W. A. Mozart 107, entitled 'Tre sonate del sgr: Giovanni Bach ridotti in Concerti dal Sgr: Amadeo Wolfgango Mozart.' Facsimiles in NMA X/28/ii, pp.xxiii–xxv. The three works are bound together and are all on ten-stave Salzburg paper (24 leaves; Tyson, 1996, no.1).
11. Leopold also wrote the titles, and the tempo marks, for K.107/i, first and second movements; K.107/ii, first and second movements (the latter duplicated by Wolfgang); K.107/iii, second movement. For a facsimile of the opening of the finale to K.107/i, see Grove, 1980, xii, p.688.
12. Examples by Mozart survive for K.40 (K^6 626a/K.624, Teil ii, C) and K.107/i ($K^6$626a, K.624, Teil ii, A and B). Judging by the paper on which they were written, all postdate the arrangements by several years, suggesting revival for some specific performances. The cadenza for K.40 (GB-Lbl, Add.Ms.47861) appears on part of a sheet that also contains a discarded sketch for a string quartet movement almost certainly associated with the 'Viennese' quartets, K.168–72 of 1773: Tyson, 1996, no.34. Those for the first two movements of K.107/i exist in two copies, one on a 1776 paper (PL-Kj, Mus.ms.autogr. W. A. Mozart 626; Tyson, 1996, no.40), the other on a 1777 paper (US-Wc, Hans Moldenhauer Collection); Tyson, 1996, no.42). Possibly they are to be associated with projected performances on the Mannheim–Paris journey of 1777–78.

13. In K.37, Mozart's final tutti reprises the main secondary theme (bars 16 foll.) in the tonic; in Raupach's op.1 no.5 the secondary theme is never brought back in the 'home' key.

14. This tutti is analogous to the 'retransition tutti' (T3) of Koch's scheme, outlined diagrammatically in Figure 1.1.

15. A feature that was to become almost standard in Mozart's later original concertos (for instance, in the first movement of K.238 in B flat).

16. The return to the tonic, B flat, at bar 94 is too weak to count in this regard, and is, in any case, followed by more developmental material that formed no part of Raupach's first section.

17. Further on the formal aspects of Mozart's pasticcio concertos, see Steinbeck, 1990.

18. For details of Wagenseil's keyboard concertos, see Scholz-Michelitsch, 1962.

19. Bach is praised in two letters from Mozart to his father in 1778 (14 February and 27 August); Wolfgang evidently used Bach's keyboard works in the course of his private teaching; and, of course, he drew on Bach's overture to *La calamità dei cuori* for the main theme of the slow movement in his A major piano concerto, K.414. There are strong similarities between Bach's op.5 no.2 and a draft of the opening Allegro of Mozart's sonata, K.284 (in the same key); see Irving, 1997, pp.24–6.

20. Almost simultaneously, this set was issued in Paris by Sieber (J. C. Bach, 1777b). This was presumably the edition requested by Leopold, which Mozart had probably discovered in spring 1778.

21. On this scoring, see the entry for these pieces in Part Two.

22. *ABC Dario Musico* (Bath, 1780), p.44 claims that Schröter wrote only the solo keyboard part, and that the simple accompaniments were composed by J. C. Bach.

23. This is mentioned in Leopold's letter to Lorenz Hagenauer of 16 August 1766.

24. See Chapter Seven, pp.129.

25. For instance, in Koch, 1782–93 and Koch, 1802, discussed in Chapter One; for Koch's treatment of aria and concerto structures, see Koch, 1802, cols.159 foll.; col.351.

26. A similar procedure is found at the analogous point in the D major concerto, K.175 (bars 95–111 bring together elements from bars 4 foll. and 21–32 of the tutti exposition).

27. By contrast with his earlier practice, Mozart decided to keep the soloist in continual play throughout this section of the movement, there being no internal punctuating tuttis before bar 135.

CHAPTER THREE

Movement Forms I: First Movements

The sonata conception

We have seen that Koch's understanding of the concerto first-movement form, though expressed in terms of alternating tuttis and solos, was measured against an underlying pattern derived from the tonal organisation of sonata form. However, it is important to remember that Koch was not actively equating concerto form and sonata form. Indeed, it would be rash to suppose that 'sonata form' had achieved sufficient stability in Koch's day to serve as a 'mould' into which the 'stuff' of a concerto might be poured. Koch's belief in the power of ritornello practice to articulate formally the opposition of tutti and solo groups, was absolute. But he observed, in addition, that the tonal and thematic practices that could typically be observed in sonatas of various kinds (be they actually solo sonatas, or symphonies, trios, quartets, quintets, and so forth) could also be found in contemporary concertos (and most especially in their solo sections), an understanding generally representative of late-eighteenth-century theoretical conceptions of the concerto first-movement form.[1] By contrast, nineteenth-century *Formenlehre* treatises tended to regard concerto first-movement form exclusively in terms of sonata form, to the neglect of its previous association with ritornello procedures. The description of concerto first-movement form given by Adolph Bernhard Marx in 1847 is typical:

> The first movement, or Allegro, is arranged so that the orchestra introduces all, or at least the most important, ideas in the principal and subsidiary parts [of the first section] entirely in the tonic, or else in the tonic and dominant (or relative major), and closing back in the tonic. Now, the solo, either alone, or supported by the orchestra (or a part of it), presents in its own *concertante* fashion the main ideas from the [principal part of the] first section, also adding new ideas of its own, and modulates, either with or without the tutti (usually the former), to the dominant, in order to present the subsidiary and closing theme, and concludes the first part [that is, the 'exposition'] together with the orchestra, wholly in the manner of a sonata-form movement, or else (usually), it leaves this closure to the orchestra alone. Now, the second section ['development'] ensues, in which the the movement's themes are worked out, mainly by alternation among the orchestral instruments against figurative passagework in the solo ... finally, the third section ['recapitulation'] unfolds according to [the] accustomed plan [that is, sonata form]' (Marx, 1847, p.439).[2]

The pattern Marx describes here is derived from a thematically rooted, tripartite sonata form, consisting of 'exposition', 'development' and 'recapitulation'

– a conception that crystallised gradually during the first half of the nineteenth century, and which attained classic expression in Marx's own theoretical writings.[3] Marx's understanding of concerto first-movement form is one in which the structure is ultimately controlled by the interaction of thematic and tonal process, within which the distinction of tutti and solo, previously so vital to theoretical explanations, has been relegated to a supporting, almost incidental, role. Even the most fundamental demarcation of tutti and solo is rationalised within sonata terms. In a sonata form, the most important thematic material is presented in a single location (the 'exposition') at the outset, modulating during its course from the tonic to the related key (usually the dominant), in which the section cadences. By contrast, in a concerto first movement, tutti and solo do not commence together, but make separate statements. Marx therefore conceives these as inter-related units within the 'first section' (equivalent to the sonata exposition). The first tutti (remaining in the tonic) is an introduction (*Einleitung*) to the first solo, which effects the expected modulation to, and continuation within, the related key. The first solo is conceived partially in terms of the preceding tutti ('Now, the solo, either alone, or supported by the orchestra (or a part of it), presents in its own *concertante* fashion the main ideas from the [principal part of the] first section'), and partially insofar as it departs from it ('also adding new ideas of its own').

This conception of a concerto first movement as a species of sonata is symptomatic of a trend observable in nineteenth-century *Formenlehre*, according to which the range of available forms is viewed hierarchically, with sonata at the top. Possibly because of a philosophical approach driven by the idolisation of Hegel, sonata form was seen as the redeeming synthesis of a previous dialectic, played out in the repertoire of Haydn, Mozart and their contemporaries, among a variety of formal patterns deriving from vocal and instrumental repertoires. The qualities observable in a sonata-form movement (in whatever genre, but most especially the symphony) were regarded by the generation of Reicha, Czerny and Marx as exemplary, and were consequently mapped on to other forms (including emergent 'ephemeral' ones, such as the Ballade and Nocturne), giving them validity by association. The treatment of other, subsidiary, forms typically follows the sonata paradigm in which a theme, or themes, are first stated, then developed in some way, creating a tension that derives as much from the interaction of contrasting themes (whose characteristics are sometimes 'gendered', as in Marx's *Die Lehre von der Musikalischen Komposition*) as from tonal opposition. The central 'argument' of the movement having been advanced, the necessary resolution of thematic and tonal conflict is assured in the recapitulation, within which the mode of discourse returns once more to thematic statement. Such a view of movement form may be regarded as a narrative (statement–conflict–resolution) that is replayed again and again within instrumental pieces. Whether this development is, or was, wholly desirable is an important question. Applied to concerto first-movement form, the sonata template arguably creates problems of comprehension where none formerly existed. In Marx's account, the status of the first tutti and the first solo in relation to the exposition of a solo sonata is ambiguous on several fronts. If the first tutti is merely an introduction, why does it present so great a quantity of the movement's essential thematic substance? Precisely what does it 'introduce', if the first tutti and first solo combined comprise the sonata 'exposition'? Might the true 'exposition' be synonymous with just the first solo?

Some of these issues will be addressed presently. For now, it may be recorded that Marx's sonata-form description proved highly influential in later Germanic approaches to concerto first-movement form. For instance, Hugo Riemann largely followed Marx's prescriptions in his famous *Musik-Lexicon* (Riemann, 1882, p.480), which describes the concerto's form as being 'that of the sonata and symphony, but with appropriate modifications' (that is, tonal modifications within the opening tutti 'exposition', which remains in the tonic). For Riemann, the concerto offered 'instead of the customary exposition and its repeat' a more concise orchestral opening, further expanded in the following solo section (Riemann, 1900, p.598).[4] The concise tutti and the somewhat lengthier solo are still conceived as related portions of a single section (the 'exposition'). Once again, this description arises from a tendency to think in 'sonata terms', irrespective of the particular conditions. The first part of a movement, before thematic 'development' sets in, comprises an exposition of those principal themes; therefore, in a concerto, the first solo (which assumes a 'presentational', rather than a 'developmental' posture) has to be included within the exposition, its identity configured in relation to the preceding tutti, of which it is an outgrowth (however different its particular thematic course). What interested Riemann above all else in these movements was their thematic and tonal processes, which were to be explained within the all-embracing theory of the sonata; the juxtaposition of unequal tutti and solo forces that they inevitably contained was a subsidiary matter.

Enshrined in print, and empowered by institutional authority, prevailing German pedagogy was readily absorbed into English musical literature at the close of the nineteenth century. That there were serious conceptual problems with these commonly held views was ably demonstrated by Donald Francis Tovey in his 1903 essay, 'The Classical Concerto', reprinted some three decades later in his famous, *Essays in Musical Analysis*. Tovey caricatured the contemporary conception of concerto first-movement form as follows:

> the orchestra gives out the first and second subject with most of their accessories, more or less as in a symphony, but all in one key, instead of the first being in the tonic and the second in the dominant; ... the solo then appears and restates these subjects somewhat more at leisure and in their proper complementary keys; after which there is a shorter recapitulation of part of the tutti in the new key, whereupon the solo again enters and works out an ordinary sonata development and recapitulation more or less in

combination with the orchestra; after which the movement ends with a final tutti, interrupted by an extempore cadenza from the solo player (Tovey, 1936; 1978, p.16).[5]

According to Tovey, this scheme 'is falsified in all its most important particulars by nearly every concerto in the classical repertoire'. The idea that the 'solo exposition' was merely a 'repetition, with considerable modification, of the first *tutti* ... divided between the principal instrument and the orchestra'[6] was a preposterous over-simplification of the truth. Tovey believed that the true situation was the reverse of that typically described: sonata principles were admitted into a ritornello framework that lay at the heart of the concerto genre. The opening orchestral section was no mere 'exposition' to be tamely repeated in a modified account by the soloist, but a necessary introduction ('a preparation for some advent'). Its prolonged tarrying in the tonic key was a purposeful adaptation of baroque ritornello practices to dynamic classical ends, for the longer the tonic key persisted, the greater the expectation of its eventual dramatic suppression *by the soloist*, personifying a conflict between the 'individual' and the 'crowd'. Subsequently, the recapitulation was no mere slavish reprise of one or other of the previous 'expositions' (adapted to the tonic), but a combination of both the previous 'tutti' and 'solo' expositions, resolving, to some degree, the tensions set up earlier by encompassing a selection of material from each within the tonic.

Tovey's purpose in 'The Classical Concerto' was to point out the inadequacy of sonata-derived 'double exposition' schemes in dealing with the essential interaction of solo and tutti in such movements. His summary of what lies at the heart of a concerto has never been bettered:

> Nothing in human life ... is much more thrilling ... than the antithesis of the individual and the crowd; an antithesis which is familiar in every degree, from flat opposition to harmonious reconciliation, and with every contrast and blending of emotion ... the concerto forms express this antithesis with all possible force and delicacy (Tovey, 1936; 1978, pp.6–7).

The concerto was that genre in which the imbalance of unequal forces was celebrated. While this had long been enshrined by the very flexibility of the ritornello design, sonata principles totally excluded this fundamental aspect. Crucially, Tovey recognised that the function of an opening tutti is not the same as a sonata exposition. Its purpose is not to define a sequence of thematic material as in a sonata (in which there would also be a tonal progression out of the home key) but to serve as a source of ideas that may be used quite freely in later sections: either entire, in their original sequence, or else selectively, recombined, fragmented, omitted altogether or partially replaced by new material. Tovey's 'modular' view of this section dispenses with the need to explain the absence of a secondary theme in the dominant. Likewise, there is no requirement to regard the first solo as a secondary 'exposition' at all, since it has no obligation to retrace the tutti's steps. Straitjacketing the actual succession of

material within the sonata 'mould' manifestly 'falsifie[s] in all its most important particulars ... nearly every concerto in the classical repertoire' since it
seeks to depict the solo's content within an inapplicable framework. The link
with the sonata was tonal, not thematic.

Tovey attempts to explode the sonata-form myth by an investigation of
Mozart's detailed procedures in the first movement of K.503 in C major. While
typically rich in illuminating digressions that occasionally threaten the continuity of his argument, Tovey's discussion achieves a great deal. He points to
the following crucial events in Mozart's 'tutti' and 'solo' expositions that are
either alien to sonata procedures or else are treated otherwise than the sonata
template dictates:

- there is no real modulation out of the tonic in the 'tutti exposition'; the
  repeated Gs at bars 48–50 are *on* the dominant, not *in* it, thus reinforcing
  the tonic, rather than opening up new tonal space, thus preparing the
  continuation in C, first minor, then major (Example 3.1a)

Example 3.1a   K.503, 1st movement, bars 48–66 (theme)

- the woodwind's C major passage starting at bar 58 is, according to
  sonata-derived interpretations, the 'second subject', eventually restated in
  the dominant during the 'solo exposition'; actually this theme is avoided
  altogether by the solo
- during the 'solo exposition', significant revision of the previous tutti
  narrative takes place; in particular, the tonic major section commencing at
  bar 26 is avoided, being instead 'continued in the minor with very dark
  colouring and great breadth of rhythm, and culminates on the dominant of
  C minor'; if, following the sonata template, the first solo section is to be
  construed as a 'solo exposition' in relation to the earlier 'tutti exposition',
  this passage should have occurred at some point soon after bar 130, but is
  in fact substantially delayed until bar 214
- following this passage, the soloist introduces a wholly new theme in E flat
  (bar 146), nowhere as much as hinted at in the earlier 'tutti exposition'
  (Example 3.1b)
- the E flat theme is not a replacement for the would-be 'second subject' at

Example 3.1b   K.503, 1st movement, bars 146–52

bar 58; its function is not overtly described by Tovey, although he seems to have regarded it rather as a (vastly expanded) transition, since he comments on the way that the chromatically inflected continuation explores new harmonic ground 'thoroughly expressive of the intention to establish the new key with firmness'[7]

- this proceeds to the entry of the actual 'second subject' (Tovey's term) at bar 170 foll.; neither has this anything to do with the material of bar 58, though it is, at least, in the expected dominant key of G (Example 3.1c)

Example 3.1c   K.503, 1st movement, bars 170–73

- the 'recapitulation' follows the course of the 'solo exposition' by omitting the material originally sounded at bars 26 foll. leading to a reprise of the piano's E flat theme from bar 324; beyond this point, though, there is considerable further adaptation, the 'second subject' being conjoined at bar 364 by the fanfare-like statement from bar 58 of the 'tutti exposition'; the scale figures of bar 26 are once again delayed (now introducing the cadenza); and the movement is rounded off with a restatement of material not heard since bars 66–90.

Tovey's great achievement here is to point out that, whereas the ritornello-inspired view of concerto first-movement form has no trouble embracing each of these procedures, the sonata-derived template is in considerable difficulty from the outset, the status of the 'tutti exposition' being especially uncertain and the applicability of almost all its terminology in doubt. His essay was widely influential in subsequent twentieth-century treatments of concerto form, among which may be singled out two accounts by Charles Rosen (Rosen, 1971; Rosen, 1980). Contrasting Mozart's flair for dramatic genres such as opera and concerto with Haydn's feeling for virtuosity within the realm of the string quartet, Rosen reminds us that

> The most important fact about concerto form is that the audience waits for
> the soloist to enter, and when he stops playing they wait for him to begin
> again. In so far as the concerto may be said to have a form after 1775, that
> is the basis of it ... Mozart's concertos are not ingenious combinations of
> traditional concerto-form with the more modern sonata allegro, but inde-
> pendent creations based on traditional expectations of the contrast between
> solo and orchestra ... and governed by the proportions and tensions of
> sonata style (Rosen, 1971, pp.196, 197).

Rosen's is a reader-orientated approach, foregrounding the obvious element of
sonorous contrast. While the basis of the form is dictated by sonata procedure
(specifically its tonal aspects), it nevertheless strongly invokes ritornello procedure. Rosen perceives the opening tutti to have an introductory function (like
Tovey), explaining it as a 'passive' section of a sonata exposition (remaining
in the tonic), followed by an 'active' section (namely, the first solo, which modulates). Likewise influenced by sonata thinking is Rosen's attitude towards the
second tutti, which has no parallel in sonata form, but which he regards as a
stabilising factor to counterbalance the modulation out of the tonic and the introduction of new themes during the first solo, at once underlining the unity of the
'passive' and 'active' sections of the exposition, and replacing the cadential
punctuation that concludes a sonata exposition at the central double bar. Rosen's
account is especially strong in that it highlights the tutti's capacity to introduce
moments of punctuation between the solos, noting the contrasting effect of the
relatively static tuttis – occasionally reprising previous blocks of material
unchanged – and the thematically and tonally inventive and evolving solos.

Subsequently (Rosen, 1980), Rosen examines concerto first-movement
form from an alternative perspective, namely the alternation of contrasting and
confirming blocks. Conceiving of the structure as shown in Figure 3.1, Rosen

R1	S1	R2	S2		R3	S3	R4
I	I–V	V		...	⇒ vi I	I	I

Figure 3.1   Model of Rosen's first-movement form

investigates (among other things) the relationship between the first tutti (R1)
and first solo (S1), noting that if R1 modulated to the dominant (as it would do
if it were the exposition of a sonata-form movement), this would disrupt the
symmetry that obtains between it and the subsequent ritornellos, all of which
hold to a single tonal area (incidentally, it would also bring it into a degree of
similarity with S1, whose modulation would then appear to replicate the tonal
pattern of the preceding tutti rather than diverge from it). By holding to the
tonic, R1's introductory character is assured and it succeeds in anticipating the
arrival of the soloist (or as Tovey had put it, 'prepar[ing] for some advent'). So
far as the function of R2 is concerned, Rosen, by contrast with his earlier treatment (Rosen, 1971), suggests three possibilities: (i) it may act as a resolution

(in V) of the solo exposition, its extension of this resolution being elided with the conclusion of the cliché trill in the piano's right hand; (ii) it may be the start of the development section, S2 being a continuation of it; or, most frequently, (iii) it may be a transition from the solo exposition to the development (beginning at S2).

Both Tovey and Rosen offer compelling and blatantly empirical accounts of concerto first-movement forms, caring little for systems, real or imagined, and unashamedly deriving from detailed observations of particular case-studies. A more systematically grounded guide is that of Daniel Leeson and Robert Levin (Leeson and Levin, 1976–77). The aim of their study was to provide a statistical model for the understanding of Mozart's concerto first-movement structures drawn from close study of a wide range of contemporary examples and considering, as well as Mozart's work, that of J. C. Bach, Boccherini, Dittersdorf, J. Haydn, K. Stamitz, Viotti and Vogler. Three fundamental principles were elaborated by Leeson and Levin: the proportioning of sections; the thematic patterns within sections; and the logic of thematic connection between sections. Their model divides Mozart's concerto first movements into no fewer than seven sections which they explain in terminology representing a fusion of ritornello and sonata types: opening ritornello; solo exposition; middle ritornello; development; recapitulation; ritornello to cadenza; and final ritornello. In turn, each of these sections is subdivided in thematic, functional and textural ways. The opening ritornello, for instance, is itself subdivided into a first theme; a modulation to the dominant degree; a confirming cadence on the dominant chord; a lyric continuation in the tonic; a *forte* closing motive, sometimes followed by a second closing motive; and a *forte* flourish, concluding the ritornello – the last three elements all being characterised by their strong cadential tendencies. Strategies for the introduction of new material in the first solo are extensively discussed by Leeson and Levin. The first solo statement, for instance, sometimes omits reference to the opening theme (which is immediately reprised by the tutti), while the previous lyric theme is frequently dispensed with, and replaced by a wholly different theme introduced by the soloist. Their scheme usefully points out that Mozart's typical practice for the middle ritornello is to end with one or more of the *forte* themes that had concluded the opening ritornello, clinching a strong cadence in the dominant key in preparation for the solo 'development'. Whereas some portions of the Leeson and Levin model highlight the ritornello-based aspects of the form (especially the contribution of fragmentation and texture contrast), others privilege the sonata-based aspects. Their account of the recapitulation, for example, arguably underplays the element of textural opposition, in favour of the demonstration of necessary tonal adjustments. While their very exhaustiveness of enquiry and demonstration lays bare the sophistication of Mozart's designs, the resulting plethora of information is so fluid in its capacity for interpretation that it is debatable whether a demonstrable 'model' emerges at all. Their purpose was not, of course, to provide a model, but to develop a statistical environment within which the authenticity of the Sinfonia Concertante itself could be tested. The precise description of different levels of segmentation within the first-movement concerto form, however, has proved a valuable guide in recent work.[8]

First-movement form

It will now be apparent that the first-movement form of a classical concerto is notoriously difficult to explain without some degree of compromise. In an important sense, it is indebted to classical sonata procedures (though its explanation as a special type of sonata is a historically grounded construction); on the other hand, there are clear resemblances to the ritornello structures of the baroque concerto. Singly, neither viewpoint offers a completely satisfying account of the form. While retaining the techniques of tutti–solo contrast offered by late-baroque ritornello practice, the concerto of Mozart's time exploits the heightened possibilities for dramatic contrast of tonality offered by the sonata. Evidently, then, the classical concerto's first-movement structure is a hybrid, and is perhaps best understood as an adaptation of an existing practice for articulating textural contrast of solo and tutti to the stylistic features of the later eighteenth century, rather than as a specifically *classical* form. While there are features of the concerto that may adequately be understood as 'exposition', 'development', and 'recapitulation', none of them equates literally to sonata practice, and it is crucial to recognise some important limitations of these terms in the concerto context:

- The 'solo' exposition differs from the preceding 'tutti' exposition in its tonal course and also in its material. Even in Mozart's earliest concertos, the soloist introduces new themes, and omits others previously announced by the orchestra. Frequently the 'solo' exposition departs significantly from the order of events in the preceding ritornello, neither deriving its material exclusively from it, nor following any particular rule.
- The end of the exposition in the sonata and in the concerto is not identical. In the sonata, it is a point of closure (in the dominant, with a firm cadence and a complete stop, typically signalled by repeated crotchet chords followed by at least one beat's worth of rests before the double bar); in the concerto it is more a point of departure, for the cadential resolution on to the dominant is elided with a tutti continuation, connecting the first main solo from the next (the 'development'). This moment functions quite differently in the two forms.
- In contrast to procedures typically found in sonata forms, Mozart's concerto 'developments' normally avoid intensive 'working-out' of

previous material. The reason for this probably has to do with the element of tutti–solo alternation, which functions most effectively in an environment featuring symmetrical phrasing. In sonata form, one of the defining features of a development section is a temporary shift away from the typically 'periodic' phrasing of the exposition towards a scansion operating at the smaller unit of the beat (or bar) rather than the phrase, reflecting the more integrated polyphonic textures normally found at this point in the movement. Usually, such a transformation in the phraseology is absent from concerto developments which retain the uniformity of scansion associated with the episodic nature of baroque ritornello practice.

• The 'recapitulation' is typically a conflation of material drawn (again in a relatively free manner) from either the 'tutti' or 'solo' exposition, normally replacing material from the tutti ritornello that had previously been omitted in the 'solo' exposition, while retaining any 'new' themes announced by the soloist; it concludes with a tutti section, breaking off with a 6/4 chord, followed by a cadenza and final tutti.

Possibly the most significant way in which Mozart reinterprets the sonata structure in his concerto forms has to do with his 'modular' handling of its thematic material. As mentioned previously, the tutti's opening ritornello is segmented, presenting several themes or figurations. Between subsequent solo entries the tutti returns with 'punctuations', reprises of material from the opening ritornello. But these are not *entire* statements. Instead, one or more elements from the ritornello are reprised, sometimes in the original order of succession, but frequently not. These punctuations occur in locations that were to become 'standard' as the classical concerto evolved. In Mozart's piano concertos they are normally found after a few bars of the first solo entry (a brief tutti, designed to highlight – by interruption – the soloist's initial presentation of the main material); following the first main solo (that is, between the end of the 'solo' exposition and the 'development'); at the beginning of the recapitulation; just before the solo cadenza; and after the cadenza. Such insertions, repeating fragments of the opening ritornello, are quite foreign to the course of a classical sonata form. To understand the first movement of a Mozart piano concerto as a sonata form ignores the vital contribution of the episodic recurrences of ritornello fragments. While the tonal course of a concerto first movement is profoundly influenced by the tonal logic of the sonata, its sectional unfolding is, in essentials, different and continues practices that were already well developed during the baroque. Important ways in which the classical concerto built upon such practices include:

• the segmentation of the ritornello, sounded at the outset by the tutti, into contrasting themes and/or figurative patterns which exploit a more varied rate of harmonic change than was typical in, say, Vivaldi's work;

- the precise co-ordination of this thematic segmentation with a more deliberate functionality (for instance, opening theme; transitional passage; cadential preparation), so that their particular succession is directional, both on a local scale, and in terms of the whole movement (for instance, a modulation to an opposing tonal region, a developmental episode, or a reprise);
- the co-ordination of this thematic segmentation with a more varied range of orchestral colour;
- heightened contrast between solo and tutti, not only in terms of their respective thematic material (as in a baroque concerto, the soloist in a classical concerto might introduce 'new' themes), but also in terms of tonal contrast (most of the significant modulations to regions outside of the tonic are undertaken by the solo);
- *timing* – this is important on several levels:
  - the entry of the soloist is considerably delayed by a substantial opening tutti (thematically segmented), typically restricted to the tonic region, after which the contrasting appearance of the solo provides both textural relief and an eventual escape from the tonic key;[9]
  - extended dominant pedals, whether in the 'home' tonic or a related key, add to a classical concerto a degree of mounting tension (and consequent expectation of a defining event) not normally associated with the baroque ritornello form; these are important in marking the key moments in the articulation of the structure, such as the end of the first solo section in the dominant, or the preparation for the tonic reprise;
  - thematic placement, for instance of a 'new' theme, announced by the soloist and coinciding with the first significant arrival in a key other than the tonic, or else the reprise of the movement's main theme coinciding with the return of the tonic;
  - the postponement of cadential material signalling the end of the opening tutti until after the soloist's cadenza, when it typically returns in its original scoring, creating a colouristic, as well as thematic, cross-reference across a large span of the movement, and enhancing the sense of finality.

The first tutti ('tutti' exposition)

Thematic variety is an impressive feature of Mozart's first tuttis. That of K.238 in B flat, for example, contains an impressive array of themes, each individually distinguished by memorable rhythmic or registral features, by articulation and by texture (bar 17 introduces a hint of rhythmic canon). Compared to his later concertos, however, this piece is relatively unadventurous in terms of texture contrast, which was to become a key element in the unfolding of tutti material. In the first tutti of K.271, in E flat, each strand of the texture has a sharper profile (especially the second violin). Following the extraordinary entry of the soloist during the opening phrase, Mozart's succession of textures is more interesting than anything found in the first section of K.238. At bar 7 is a simple theme–middle–bass layout, counterposing different rhythmic strands and articulations, into which the viola interjects briefly at bar 9 and bar 11. At bar 14 the bass and viola change function, supplanting a harmonic foundation with a motivic purpose. K.413–15 show still greater flexibility in all these aspects (for instance, bars 12–23 of the first tutti of K.413), and especially from K.449 onwards, Mozart's tuttis become far more dynamic and mobile, invigorated by an increasingly contrapuntal integration of different strands of the texture. This is apparent right from the start of K.449. Counterpoint is crucial to the unfolding of the first sixteen bars in which it is allied to a subtle process of thematic evolution. The trill figure in bar 3 acquires a cadential suffix when it is repeated in bars 5–8; transferred to the middle of the texture (and doubled in thirds by the viola) it next forms a countertheme to the first violin tune in bars 9–12, before losing its trill prefix altogether in the next phrase in which it serves as a counterpoint to the first violin tune's quaver suffix which is passed down through the ensemble. What was originally a prominent foreground motive at bar 3 has, by stages, transformed in identity and function during the course of just a few bars. Counterpoint is the framework within which this thematic technique is expressed. It plays a part at several points in the remainder of the tutti: for instance at bar 54 foll. and at bars 70–79, in the course of which Mozart inverts the bass and treble parts. Counterpoint has a special function in Mozart's tuttis. Seen against the backdrop of regular periodicity, the dominant role of canon, theme–countertheme pairings and invertibility in the first tutti of K.503 injects such a strong degree of textural contrast that these passages sit in an almost episodic relation to their surroundings.

In K.449 the bulk of the tutti activity takes place in the strings, perhaps because Mozart intended this piece to be performable 'à quattro'. The woodwind and horns provide punctuation of the phrasing and fill out the texture and dynamic by means of doublings and interior pedals; but do not make independent 'solo' or concertante contributions of any note. K.450, completed little more than one month later, revolutionises the treatment of wind in Mozart's concertos. The very opening of the work establishes two opposing choruses: wind (now expanded to pairs of oboes, bassoons and horns) and strings, each with its own distinct material, first sounded separately in alternation (bars 1–8) and then together as independent polyphonic strands (bar 9 foll.). Opposition of wind and strings recurs at bars 53–6, while further parallel polyphony is seen in bars 33–41. This colour contrast, allied to the highlighting of structure, becomes a regular feature of the first tuttis in later concertos, adding a further element of contrast to compensate for the exclusive hegemony of the tonic. The liberation of Mozart's wind writing proceeds apace in the first tuttis of K.451, K.453, K.456 and K.459, all dating from 1784. In addition to dialogue textures with the strings, concertante wind scoring, such as that at bars 64–7 of K.451, or bars 31–5 of K.453, plays an increasingly significant role in the design. K.456 is especially notable for its wind writing. In addition to the by now regular dialogue between strings and wind, Mozart entrusts the wind chorus with a complicated harmonic manoeuvre at bars 29–37, while the episode beginning at bar 39 contains a glimpse of some textures that become 'fingerprints' of Mozart's orchestral sound over the next few years: thirds in the oboes, and flute and bassoon doubled at two octaves' distance. At bars 47–51 the wind writing grows still more complex. Viewed as a whole, this first tutti places strings and winds on an equal footing. The unfolding of the structure depends on colour contrast as much as contrast of theme, and this is a feature of all of Mozart's great concertos. Arguably K.482 and K.491 display Mozart's wind writing at its most liberated. Throughout most of its first tutti the wind take the lead, exposing most of the main thematic material, sometimes at considerable length, as in bars 15–29, in which the horns play an important role. In K.491 the first tutti includes some unusually chromatic writing, in which the winds are fully engaged. There are prominent wind solos at bars 35–44 and 57–62 (both quite complex contrapuntally) and elsewhere they complement the string writing. The contrast between this scoring and that of K.238's first tutti is extreme.

The first solo ('solo' exposition)

The first entry of the soloist is, of course, a vital moment in the articulation of the structure. It follows one of two patterns: either the soloist takes up the opening material of the first tutti (for instance, K.175; K.238; K.246; K.451; K.453; K.488; K.595), or it begins with new material, immediately marking out the soloist's distinctive space, as a kind of interruption, before continuing with the original material (for instance, K.271; K.413; K.415; K.450; K.466; K.467; K.482; K.491; K.503). Moreover, new thematic material is frequently introduced by the soloist during the course of the first solo signalling the special nature of the solo part. Mozart realised early on the dramatic potential of new solo material in the regulation of structure. The transition to the secondary key-area within the first solo is an important moment of articulation in the evolving form, highlighted by the introduction of a new theme or else by a new harmonic pattern expressed through passagework in the solo part. At bar 48 of K.175 there is a completely new section preceding the entry of the second main theme in bar 66; likewise, the section beginning at bar 55 in K.238; that at bar 74 of K.242; and that at bar 77 of K.246, extending in a new direction the theme first introduced by the tutti at bar 19; and bar 69 of K.271, a new section evolving out of the main theme. In all these transitions Mozart entrusts the soloist with the crucial harmonic shift to the dominant. In the first solo of K.467 the soloist makes almost no reference to any of the previous material. Instead, from bar 91, and after only a brief nod at the 'consequent' phrase material from bars 4–7 of the first tutti, the soloist constantly evolves new themes and patterns, which function at times as a background to snatched references in either wind or strings, to the opening march tune. Apart from such fleeting references, the first solo is wholly new, proceeding independently of its predecessor.

From the textural point of view, an evolving feature of Mozart's Viennese concertos is their centring of interaction between the solo and tutti, an element highlighted by a newly liberated woodwind chorus and especially prominent in the first solos of K.466, K.467, K.482, K.491 and K.595.[10] The variety of piano and wind textures is impressive. At times the piano supplies delicate accompanying figuration over which the wind articulates the determining motivic work (for instance, K.453, bar 100 foll.; K.466, bars 88–91; K.482, bars 96–9; K.491, bar 165 foll.); elsewhere there is dialogue (K.450, bars 193–210; K.488, bars 98–114) in which the piano and wind are equal partners, complementing or even completing each other's phrases; in yet other examples, there is a growing awareness of the quasi-chamber music effect obtainable by dividing a single phrase between piano and wind, as at bars 144–53 of K.453, bars 136–40 of K.467, and bars 130–36 of K.595. On occasion the distinction between these categories is blurred somewhat, as at bars 170–87 in K.503. Here the piano initially announces a new theme (that shown in Example 3.1c) which is then (bar 178) passed to the wind, while the solo part continues with background figurative accompaniment. In K.595, beginning at bar 115, Mozart introduces the wind as a polyphonic counterpart to the soloist in a new thematic continuation, enhancing the remote key of the dominant minor by chromatic weaving around the chord of G flat.

While wind–solo interactions are a prominent feature of Mozart's first solo textures, that does not diminish the role of the strings here. Indeed, numerous memorable illustrations of the engagement of solo with strings are to be found, such as the menacing semiquaver passagework (incorporating a throbbing interior pedal point) that accompanies the syncopated strings at bars 95–108 of K.466, or the extended sections in the first movement of K.488 in which the piano's figuration is surrounded by a 'halo' of string sound, or the entire first solo of the 'Coronation' Concerto, K.537, throughout which the wind is wholly silent.[11] Texturally speaking, though, Mozart's first solos are most memorable for their colouristic qualities, in which the wind plays a vital part.

The second tutti (tutti 'codetta')

Following the prominent trill in the right hand of the piano part, with which all of Mozart's first solos end, the tutti enters briefly with a section separating the first solo from the development and confirming the newly established key. At this point reference is almost always made to themes or complete passages from the first tutti. The choice of material is impossible to categorise exactly, although there is a tendency to 'telescope' phrases from near the beginning and near the end of the first tutti. This approach is found in all of the early Salzburg concertos, K.175–K.365, and was to become Mozart's preferred design in the later concertos, all but one of which use the device. For example, K.450 takes material from bars 14–17 (the beginning, originally, of the transition from tonic to dominant), followed immediately by the material of bars 45–59 (a cadential closing figure, originally entering after a four-bar *crescendo* from *pianissimo* to *forte*, but here continuing *forte* throughout bars 137–49. Similar conjoining of material originally widely dispersed is found in several later concerto first movements: K.451 takes material from the transitional figure of bars 10–14, followed by the cadential announcement of bars 60–66 (retaining the tutti–woodwind antiphony); K.453 takes material from bars 16 foll. (the transitional figure), followed by the closing cadential idea of bars 69 foll.; K.456 takes material from bars 18–25, followed by bars 65–9 (again, a juxtaposition of previously transitional and cadential functions); K.503 takes material from bar 26 foll. (the beginning of the first tutti's protracted transition, based on an invertible combination of scalic and repeated-note patterns), followed by bars 41–50 (a sequential extension); and K.537 takes material from bar 13 foll., followed by bar 72 foll. (previously transition and cadence ideas). Interestingly, only the first four Viennese concertos follow a different course in their tutti 'codettas': K.413 and K.414 simply return to the closing material of the first solo (duly transposed); in K.415 Mozart first reverts to the opening theme, transferring it to the bass and following it with material originally from bar 17 and then the first tutti's closing passage; in K.449 he simply transposes bars 63–76 to the new key. In K.459 the development section coincides with the 'codetta', beginning immediately after the piano trill, taking over the main theme and treating it in new ways against a syncopated bass; there is texture inversion at bar 195 foll. and new modulating patterns at bars 200–210.

From this point in Mozart's concerto first movements the hegemony of sonata form over ritornello practice asserts itself with considerable force. While it is perfectly possible to regard the second main solo section as an episode, and while it sometimes proceeds largely independently of previous material (K.453, for instance), by far the majority of Mozart's central solos engage in the developmental procedures associated with sonata form. This fact determines the approach taken in the following pages which focus in the main on the developmental procedures that give shape to the second solo. Likewise, the third main solo section (preceded, in Mozart's examples, by a brief third tutti, marking the reprise of the opening theme and home key) is configured tonally as a sonata recapitulation, though, as will be shown in due course, its specific content is handled with far greater flexibility than in a solo sonata.

The second solo ('development section')

The central solos tend to be sectional rather than continuous, modulating through a range of keys (occasionally, as in K.595, traversing fairly remote territory – see below) and culminating in a conspicuous dominant preparation for the eventual return of the opening theme and key at the moment of tonal and thematic recapitulation. While there are no abstract 'templates' according to which Mozart designed his concerto developments, the division into distinct sections is always clearly articulated by harmonic markers within the overall tonal arch leading back to the tonic, or else by a change of texture in either solo or tutti. Such breaks in the texture as that at bar 211 of K.453, continuing with a section that introduces a new rhythm, a new register and a new key (C minor) are especially striking. The previous section, featuring continuous triplet quavers in the solo part, is itself divisible into at least three sub-sections: bars 184–91 (starting out from the remote territory of B flat and leading to the dominant of A minor); bars 192–202 (a transposition of bars 184–91, with chromatic extension downwards to B); and bars 203–7 (changing to triplets to semiquavers, and introducing a pedal point).

In the following discussion a number of different categories have been outlined in order to facilitate the presentation of Mozart's compositional strategies. To a degree, of course, these categories are artificial, since the beauty of Mozart's concerto developments resides precisely in the manner in which their components are co-ordinated and unfold over time.

Use of previous material

The extent to which Mozart's concerto developments refer to material previously sounded in either the first tutti or first solo is variable. In K.413 the section beginning at bar 197 clearly relates to the material originally sounded at bar 102; in K.449 the development is almost exclusively based on the motive at bar 76 foll. At bar 204 new combinations of the original theme and countertheme are presented, involving intervallic inversion resulting in contrary, rather than similar motion (cf. bars 204–5 and bar 76); in K.451, the development begins with a reference back to the passage at bars 60–66 of the earlier first tutti. Normally just one or two ideas are singled out for treatment in a development, as in K.491, which takes over at its beginning (bar 283) the new theme with which the piano had entered at bar 100, and later (bar 309 foll.) makes further references to bars 5–6 of the main subject against arpeggiated passagework in the piano part; or K.503, which makes extensive

reference to the 'second subject', arranged into new contrapuntal combinations in wind and strings from bar 261. Towards the end of this development
Mozart introduces hitherto unused imitative combinations of this element of
the main subject (bar 354 foll.). In K.456, K.488 and K.537 the development
takes over an idea previously introduced in the tutti codetta following the first
solo.

'Free' developments

Frequently Mozart's concertos have development sections based on material
wholly or largely unrelated to the previous tutti and solo sections, as in K.414,
K.415, K.450, K.453, K.467 and K.488. In these pieces the development
makes its impact by contrast with its surroundings, rather than by true 'development' of earlier material. In such cases the major factors in the continuity are
tonal progression and texture. The emphasis is firmly on virtuoso display in the
development of K.467, for example, whose harmonic structure is merely a
support for the brilliant and demanding passagework, incorporating arpeggios,
broken octaves in each hand and rows of tenths.

Tonality

- The key schemes of Mozart's developments are often fascinating, none
  perhaps more so than that of K.595 in B flat, which opens in the remote
  key of B minor (as notated – the actual tonality is technically C flat minor),
  before moving through a wide range of keys articulated by references in
  either piano or tutti to the two most important themes outlined in the first
  six bars of the movement. Several common devices are found, principally
  sequence and 'circle-of-fifths' motion. Much of K.595's development is
  controlled by 'circle-of-fifths' motion, as are those of K.450, K.456,
  K.459 and K.488, to name but a few examples. Often the 'circle-of-fifths'
  is only one harmonic stage among several within the development, as in
  K.456, in which bars 166–9 feature the device briefly before graduating to
  a broader sequential pattern (this time moving in two-bar harmonic steps),
  moving through E flat–B flat; C minor–G minor; A flat–E flat; and finally
  arriving at an extended dominant preparation (over F) heralding the recapitulation. In K.459 the 'circle-of-fifths' is rather longer (bars 217–28),
  followed by a chromatically enhanced pedal A (dominant of the relative
  minor, D) that slides unpredictably to the tonic, F at the last moment for
  the reprise at bar 247.
- Some developments contain substantial tonal digressions, as in K.413 in F
  which, beginning in the dominant minor – itself a somewhat unusual move
  – outlines the sequence V/D major–V/ G minor–diminished 7th–F–B flat–
  G minor in bars 197–217, after which the bass B flat sidesteps chromatically

upwards to B natural and C (bar 219), a key extended from this point as a chromatically enhanced dominant pedal (incorporating also a brief Adagio/ A tempo dislocation at bars 224–5) before the reprise at bar 235, beginning, like the earlier first solo, with the 'prefatory' solo before the return of the main theme in the tutti at bar 247.

- In the development of K.414 in A, Mozart incorporates an extended digression to the relative minor region. This is achieved, at bars 170–72, by an uncharacteristic progression of a dominant seventh chord, resolving the bass D natural of a 6/4/2 chord downwards to a chord of C sharp (dominant of the relative minor, F sharp), and continuing to the pause chord in bar 194 (a different inversion of the earlier 6/4/2) which here regains its expected 'dominant' function, leading, *via* a cadenza-like arpeggio, to the tonic reprise in the following bar.

- The dominant preparation for the recapitulations, which occurs at the end of all these concerto developments, is frequently enhanced by augmented sixth chords, as in K.415 (bar 188 foll.), K.449 (bar 225 foll.), K.453 (bar 217 foll.), and K.456 (bar 221 foll.). In many cases the clinching harmonic progressions from dominant to tonic are highlighted by chromatic altera-tion of the bass line (especially notable in K.449).

Textures

- Dialogue between the soloist and the tutti, so essential an element of the first solos, frequently continues into the development sections. In the first movement of K.449, for instance, the piano and tutti alternate figuration and thematic references (to the material of bar 76 of the first tutti) from bar 186; in K.451 Mozart begins his development with alternations of wood-wind motive taken from bars 64–6 of the first tutti and piano triplets; in K.488, the section beginning at bar 156 features alternation between piano figuration and a motive in the woodwind derived from the tutti's codetta at bar 143–4.

- Among the most typical development textures is that in which light thematic work, sometimes making explicit references to earlier material, appears as a 'background' accompaniment in the tutti to continuous semi-quaver passagework in the solo part, as in the B flat concerto, K.595, bars 217–42. Here, the tutti presents two significant ideas, taken from bars 5–6 and 2–4 respectively, the latter appearing imitatively in the strings (adapted) beginning at bar 225, and again in the wind, beginning at bar 235. This passage from Mozart's last piano concerto is one of his most carefully crafted examples. Similar textures are found in, for example, K.415, bars 176 foll., based on the movement's opening theme; K.456, bars 201–11, based on the closing material of the first tutti; K.459, bars 211–29, based on the rhythm of the opening theme. Elsewhere, the background orchestral material is free, as in K.414, K.450, K.453 and K.482, but the textural disposition remains the same.

Third tutti; third solo ('recapitulation')

As mentioned in Chapter One, Mozart's preference was to conclude the second solo ('development section') with a drive to the cadence featuring both tutti and solo in combination (Koch's theoretical template, by contrast, has the tutti alone in this role). Typically in Mozart's concertos the crucial moment of tonal and thematic articulation follows an extended passage of virtuosic figuration in the solo part. The actual thematic reprise normally occurs in the tutti alone[12] and conforms to its original phraseology, leading either to a full or to a half close, from which point the solo continues (K.242, K.246, K.365, K.414, K.449, K.453, K.456, K.466, K.467, K.482, K.488, K.491, K.503, K.537 and K.595). In K.175 the phrase structure of the theme is altered slightly (there is a three-bar tutti reprise, immediately repeated by the piano); in K.238 the reprise of the opening four-bar phrase is divided between tutti and solo respectively. A variant of this procedure is found in K.450 and K.451, in each of which the reprise is shared between tutti and solo (in the former the piano enters into antiphonal dialogue; in the latter it adds brilliant accompanimental semiquaver scales). Alternative recapitulatory schemes include the insertion of a solo 'episode' between the end of the development and the tutti restatement of the main theme, as in K.413 and K.415 (bars 232–47 and 200–207 respectively). In each case, the 'episode' recapitulates the new material with which the piano had originally preceded the restatement of the main theme at the start of the first solo, disturbing to some extent our perception of the exact location of the recapitulation (does it coincide with the reprise of the 'episode', or the main theme itself?). Twice, the recapitulation of the main theme appears in the piano, not the tutti. In K.271 there is a simple reversal of the tutti–solo statement at the beginning of the first solo. In K.459, uniquely, the development ends with a tutti which refers to the main theme's rhythmic properties in a six-bar modulating link (bars 241–6) preparing for a recapitulation of the main theme in the tonic by the piano in bar 247.

   Within the normal pattern of a brief tutti recapitulation followed by a solo entry, there are considerable variations in detail. The majority of tutti recapitulations last about eight bars (for example, K.453, K.488, K.537).[13] In the concerto for two pianos, K.365, on the other hand, the tutti reprises only the main theme's opening gesture at bars 205–8, after which the pianos immediately continue with a harmonically reconfigured version of the original continuation, leading into the tonally altered retransition. A similar approach underpins the beginning of the recapitulation in K.491, in which the length of the main theme is drastically curtailed (bars 362–7, followed by the solo's reworked transition). Elsewhere, the recapitulatory tutti is quite expansive (23 bars in K.467; 14 bars in K.595). In K.414, K.456, K.482 and K.488, the profile of the theme includes a balancing repeat of the opening phrase. In K.456's recapitulation, the balancing repeat occurs in the tutti, accompanied by a prominent trill in the solo; in K.482, both statement and repeat are given entirely by the tutti (after which the soloist returns); in K.414 and K.488 the embellished repeat is given by the solo.

The reintroduction of the solo part following a tutti recapitulation offers Mozart an opportunity to introduce particular combinations of tutti and solo not previously heard in a movement, and in this respect his recapitulations are far more than conventional conflations of the previous tutti and first solos. In the recapitulation of K.453 the solo's return in the middle of the second phrase (bar 237 foll.) reinforces the antiphonal contrast more strongly than at the corresponding bars of the first solo. A more dramatic textural point is made in K.503's recapitulation (bar 290 foll.). Following an eight-bar tutti, the consequent phrase is redesigned so that the piano's chords fall on the strong beats, answered now on the offbeats by the tutti, reversing the pattern found at bars 112 foll. (a situation similar in effect to the reversing of solo–tutti roles in the first-movement recapitulation of K.271). Such textural novelties are not always of merely local significance. The recapitulation of K.467 is a special case. Following an extended tutti recapitulation of the main theme (bars 274–97) Mozart reintroduces the piano as the third strand of an unfolding contrapuntal series beginning in the strings in bar 295: violin 1; violin 2; piano. This particular combination is not present at the analogous point in the first solo, although a very similar texture had previously occurred at bar 143 foll. of the first solo (this time, solo followed by strings and later woodwind, inaugurating the long preparation for the end of the first solo in the dominant). In order to highlight the re-entry of the soloist at the beginning of the recapitulation retransition, Mozart imports a texture previously associated with an entirely different location in the movement and altering the recapitulatory function of the solo part. The close stretto texture subsequently returns at bar 328, where it serves not as a parallel to the end of the first solo but as the harbinger of an introduction to the 'second subject' (bar 351), omitted from the first solo, though extensively treated during the development. All told, the recapitulation runs quite a different course from the previous first solo, a structural departure subtly reinforced by Mozart's creative approach to the reintroduction of the soloist after a tutti recapitulation. On one level, this was possibly a private indulgence, in which Mozart experimented with subtly different possibilities for the refinement of the concerto form. On yet another level, this element of 'play' may have been a concession to the public environment for which his concertos were destined, in which Mozart offered the more attentive members of the Viennese audience an alternative to their conventional expectations of this moment in the first–movement form.[14]

The recapitulation retransition

Within the recapitulation, the function of the transition is somewhat altered, compared to that of the first solo, for the tonal practices of the classical sonata form, on to which the concerto's ritornello structure is grafted, require that reprises of secondary thematic material (whether relating to original first tutti or new material first introduced by the soloist) normally occur within the 'home' tonic. At this point in a sonata structure, some means has to be found whereby the recapitulation transition (henceforth, retransition) leads naturally from a tonic reprise of the main theme at the outset of the recapitulation to a cadence preparing for that same tonic, rather than a dominant reprise (or other related key in the case of minor-mode movements). Mozart explores several ways of doing this in his piano concertos. There is no 'standard' pattern, nor is any particular practice associated with relatively early or late concertos. The simplest procedure is that found in K.246 at bars 144–52. Here, the retransition simply repeats bars 48–56 from the first solo, leading to a half-close on G which now acts as a dominant preparation for the C major continuation (in the first solo, this same cadential close had prefixed a continuation in the same key, G). In this case, no modification is applied to the harmonic course of the retransition itself; its closing cadence is merely reinterpreted in relation to what follows.

An alternative approach is to modify the retransition itself in some way. Typically, both the beginning and end of the first solo transition, along with its particular texture or passagework, are retained (involving, therefore, both solo and tutti). But by veering in the direction of the subdominant (or sometimes the supertonic in first inversion) after a few bars, Mozart can retain much of the original closing material, and especially its cadential gestures, now suitably transposed a fifth lower so as to close in the correct tonal region for the secondary theme (either that of the first tutti, or else a new theme introduced in the first solo) in the tonic. Examples of this approach are found in the first movements of K.488 and K.595. In the former, the retransition (bars 217–28) commences with the original first solo material from bar 86, but veers at bar 221 towards the supertonic, B minor in first inversion, whose bass D connects via a chromatically rising step, to E, serving as a dominant pedal preparation for the half-close on V/A major at bar 228, prior to the tonic presentation of the secondary theme. A very similar harmonic progression underlies the retransition of K.595 (bars 256–69), which incorporates falling sequential steps leading to the subdominant, E flat at bar 262–4, a procedure that transforms the harmonic context of bars 266–9 – based, as in the earlier first solo transition, on F – so that it leads convincingly flatwards to the tonic, B flat, for the reprise of the secondary theme (that is, the soloist's new theme from bar 106). In a way, this is a variant of the procedure in K.246, in that the retransition's final close is on the same cadential degree as in the first solo (here somewhat embellished), but its context forces us to recognise it as leading in a different direction.

A third possibility, one favoured by Mozart in many of the Viennese concertos, is omission in the retransition of significant portions of the original solo transition and/or its replacement with material taken from the first tutti. In this respect, Mozart was clearly influenced by the selectivity of ritornello practices and the possibilities offered in this section of the movement for creating cross-reference between tutti and solo identities. The circumstances are quite varied. Four representative illustrations are given:

- K.453: The retransition occurs at bars 242–57, and takes over tutti, rather than first solo material (that is, bars 16–31), to which the solo continuation is joined (bar 257 foll.), derived from bars 31–4 and leading into the secondary theme from the *first solo* (originally bar 110 foll.) on V/G major. Virtually all of the first solo transition is discarded. Because Mozart reverts to the transition material there is no need to alter its original tonal sequence.

- K.456: This proceeds in a very similar way to K.453, reverting at bar 249 to the first tutti transition material, abandoning that of the first solo and leading to a dominant half-close at bar 258, continuing with the secondary theme from the *first solo* now in the tonic, B flat.

- K.459: At bar 262, Mozart reprises the transition from the first solo, but omits the material of bars 93–102, skipping directly after bar 269 to the material of bars 103–6 (bars 270–73, ending with a half-close on V/F major).

- K.537: As in K.459, the retransition begins in the piano part (bar 300). Slightly unusual in that it does not commence following a firm tonic close, it follows the course of the first solo transition as far as bar 305 (cf. bars 89–94). From bar 306, however, it parallels bars 122 foll., the whole of the intervening passage from the first solo (bars 95–121) having been omitted, and leads eventually to a half-close on V/D major, reintroducing the secondary theme from the first solo at bar 312. (In the autograph of K.537, Mozart originally continued beyond bar 305 with a version of the material of bars 95–108 of the first solo transition, but then crossed it out – an interesting illustration of his 'second thoughts' in the actual process of composition.)[15]

The secondary theme

As discussed previously, the first solo frequently introduces a new theme (what would be the 'second subject' in a sonata-form view). In the recapitulation, therefore, Mozart has a choice of two candidates for 'second subject'. What principles guided his selection? If Mozart were simply to return in the recapitulation to the secondary theme first introduced in the tonic key during the opening tutti, then this would result in an unbalanced structure for two reasons: first, the new theme, marking a dramatic departure from the preceding material and establishing to some degree the soloist's special identity as distinct from the tutti, would be sounded only once, during the first solo; second, and more importantly, this strategy would leave an important block of material outside the frame of the tonic key. Tonality was of overriding importance in the context of recapitulation. Although we have seen that a sonata-influenced approach to first-movement concerto form is problematic in some respects, at this particular point in the structure the tonal principle underlying sonata form exerts itself strongly, because it is analogous to a location earlier on in the movement at which a decisive break away from the 'home' tonic was introduced. Within the framework of classical tonality that decisive event must be resolved within the tonic before the movement's close. Mozart's strategy, therefore, was to recapitulate the soloist's new theme within the tonic key, typically – but not always – continuing thereafter with a transposed restatement of the ensuing material from the first solo (which normally had also made some reference to secondary material from the opening tutti, ensuring that it was not excluded altogether and thus avoiding structural imbalance of another sort). Mozart's concertos present a fascinating array of solutions to the recapitulation of the new theme. There is no 'standard' procedure. Instead, he seems to have kept in mind only the most basic requirement of tonal resolution, considering the treatment of the new theme afresh in each piece, in relation to its own particular context.

The most straightforward strategy is that found in K.453, K.456, K.537 and K.595, in each of which the soloist's new theme is recapitulated in the tonic, leading subsequently to a tonic return of the tutti's 'second subject' (K.453, bar 261 and bar 290; K.456, bar 259 and bar 289; K.537, bar 312 and bar 348; K.595, bar 268 and bar 292). This procedure is found also in K.503 (previously discussed in the introductory section of this chapter), but here the tonality is handled with some latitude. The soloist's new theme (first sounded in the unusual key of E flat in the first solo at bar 148) is reprised still in E flat, not in the tonic, C; tonal balance is restored in this case by the continuation, leading to a tonic restatement at bar 345 of the soloist's second new theme (from bar 170), now extended and chromatically enhanced. In K.466, the tonal treatment is similar, in that the recapitulation does not at first bring material back into the tonic frame. Here, the thematic ordering (which follows that of the first solo) is the opposite of that commonly encountered: the theme sounded in the relative major, F, at bar 288 is the tutti's 'second subject', not the solo's, which occurs a little later, at bar 302 in the expected tonic, D minor.

Several of Mozart's recapitulations restore secondary tutti material not included in the first solo. In K.450 Mozart initially follows the course of the first solo, which makes no reference to the material of the opening tutti, but at bar 248 he brings in the tutti's original 'second subject'. At first sight, the recapitulation of K.459 appears to proceed according to the pattern of K.453, K.456, K.537 and K.595, restating the new theme at bar 297, followed by a secondary idea from the opening tutti at bar 335; but in the continuation the soloist reprises another secondary idea from bar 42 foll. of the opening tutti that was not previously referred to in the first solo. In K.491 the two new themes from the first solo (bars 147 and 201) are reprised in reverse order. That of bar 201 recurs at bar 391, still in the relative major, E flat, at first, but diverted in its solo restatement at bar 401 to F minor before reaching the tonic recapitulation at bar 410 of the theme of bar 147. In its tonal procedures, this is similar to the case of K.503, discussed previously, while in respect of its thematic reordering, it approximates to K.466.

At times, the recapitulation assumes a closer relationship to the structure of the opening tutti than to the first solo, as in K.414. Although there is passing reference at bar 224 to a modified version of the new theme introduced by the soloist at bar 98, its function is altered, so that it becomes a tonally modified transition (stressing the subdominant) leading to the restatement of the original tutti 'second subject' at bar 232. From this point on, the recapitulation is recomposed, leading to a statement by the soloist of another secondary theme from the opening tutti (bar 256; cf. bar 50), something that had formed no part of the first solo. In K.467 Mozart's recapitulation departs in several respects from the course of the first solo. While the new theme from bar 128 is reprised in the tonic at bar 313, the striking dominant minor chordal figure (a new element introduced by the soloist at bar 109) is omitted in the course of a modified 28-bar transition beginning at bar 295 and reprising a significant proportion of the opening tutti (taking material from bars 12–19 and bars 36–47). Moreover, the tutti's 'second subject', which is never used in the first solo, recurs in the recapitulation at bar 351. In K.482, the recapitulation exactly follows the course of the opening tutti for its first 50 bars. The theme restated at bar 314 is the tutti's second subject, now expanded to two statements, the first ending with an interrupted cadence on C minor at bar 321, and subsequently continuing from bar 330 with the new theme first introduced by the soloist at bar 152. The striking new figure in the dominant minor, sounded at bar 128 of the first solo, is wholly omitted in this reworked recapitulation.

The least common approach is that found in K.413 and K.488, in which the first solo follows the course of the opening tutti, retaining its secondary theme and continuation. In this case, the recapitulation simply operates along the lines of a sonata, bringing back the 'second subject' within the tonic key. In the case of K.488, a certain ambiguity intrudes in relation to the theme sounded by the strings at bar 143 in the dominant key. This seems like a connecting link to the ensuing development rather than part of the secondary group, although in the recapitulation it is brought back clearly within the domain of the secondary group, sounded by the soloist and immediately repeated in conjunction with the wind (bars 261–72). Retrospectively, then, this might be considered the reprise of a 'new' theme, occurring within the first solo, though introduced by the tutti, not the soloist, and having a more marginal function than any other new theme in Mozart's concertos, which is quite unrepresentative of Mozart's normal practice.

Closing strategies

Following the retransition and the modified reprise of latter portions of the earlier tutti and first solos within the tonic region, the tutti continues beyond the soloist's formulaic trill and resolution on to the tonic with a passage leading to the cadenza.[16] This relatively short tutti preceding the cadenza is typically for the whole ensemble, whose entry, *forte*, coincides with the resolution of the soloist's trill. It continues with a selection of the prominent *forte* themes from the first tutti. While there is no procedure at this point in the movement that could rightly be described as 'standard', Mozart's concertos from K.449 to K.503 display a tendency to begin this tutti with the same motive that had earlier commenced the middle tutti (again, following a trill and resolution in the solo part, this time in the dominant key). Whatever the precise order of events, the tutti culminates in a fermata 6/4 chord in the tonic, announcing the cadenza (which concludes with the familiar cliché trill and dominant-7th chord, connecting retrospectively with the tutti fermata) and finally a perfect cadence on to the tonic which closes the harmonic progression.

Following the cadenza's harmonic resolution, the movement concludes with another brief tutti. As with each section of the first-movement form, Mozart's detailed approach in the closing tutti varies from piece to piece, but he most often reprises material that had earlier ended the first tutti, as in K.459, although in K.466 Mozart draws out the *piano* ending a little with further references to the *gruppetti* of the opening bars, and in K.488 an extra cadential flourish is appended to material taken from bars 55–65. The closing phase of the first tutti normally consists of a coherent group of several discrete cadential elements, of which Mozart chooses to reprise the last two or three at the end of the movement. A variation on this procedure is found in the first movement of K.595. Following the cadenza is a chromatic passage (bars 358 foll.) that had previously occurred at bar 47 foll., a far earlier location than normal within the closing group of the first tutti – if, indeed, it can properly be regarded as part of that closing group.[17] It is separated from the eventual conclusion of the tutti by the syncopated pattern at bar 54, the digression to C flat (bar 59 foll.), and at least three further phrases, including one whose cadence initiates some local 'development' (bars 69–74), before falling into definite cadential patterns, a series of events amounting to 28 bars. In K.488 and K.491, the tutti element chosen for reprise after the cadenza – in both cases, featuring chromatic references, like that in K.595 – originally occurs significantly nearer the end of the first tutti.[18] Possibly, in K.595, a concerto that stands well outside the main chronological sequence of his piano concertos,[19] Mozart was simply trying something new.

An alternative model for the closing tutti is to follow the sequence of the middle tutti, as in K.238. Here, themes scattered throughout the first tutti are brought into a cadential sequence emphasising the dominant at bars 88–98 and rounding the movement off effectively in the tonic, B flat, at bars 192–202.[20] Unusually, in K.271 and K.491 Mozart brings in the soloist once more beyond the cadenza, continuing in each case with arpeggiated passagework right up to the final bar.[21]

Notes

1. For instance, Vogler, 1778–79, vol. i, pp.79–89 (sonata) and ii, pp.36–9 (concerto); Galeazzi, 1796, ii, p.290, the latter explicated in Churgin, 1968. Unique among eighteent-century views is that of August Frederic Christopher Kollmann (Kollmann, 1799), who specifies the concerto first-movement form as a particular application of sonata form (which he describes in his Chapter One, §11, under the rubric 'Outline of Elaborate Movements'). Kollmann's account of sonata form consists of four 'subsections' (that is, two sections, each of which is divided into two further subsections). In the 'first' subsection, the tonic key and main theme are established; in the 'second', the modulation from the tonic to the related key occurs; the 'third' modulates ('a second sort of elaboration, consisting of digressions to all those keys and modes which shall be introduced besides that of the fifth (or third)' [in minor modes]; finally, the 'fourth' is the reprise. By equating the first tutti in a concerto first movement with the 'first' [sonata] subsection, the first solo with the 'second' subsection, the second solo with the 'third' subsection and the third solo with the 'fourth' subsection, Kollmann succeeds in falsifying both the tonal and thematic outlines of the concerto, while simultaneously denying the essential element of textural contrast between tutti and solo. His description was not taken up by any subsequent strand of *Formenlehre*, although he was recommended in Gerber, 1812–14. For a penetrating review of the historical development of *Formenlehre* relevant to concerto first-movement form during the nineteenth century (to which the following discussion is indebted), see Stevens, 1974, which discusses in detail all of the principal texts involved.

2. 'Der erste Satz oder das Allegro gestaltet sich meist so, daß das Orchester zur Einleitung die sämmtlichen oder vorzüglichsten Sätze der Haupt- und Seitenpartie mit dem Schlußsätze ... durchaus in Hauptton, oder im Hauptton und der Dominante (oder Parallele) und in den erstern zurückkehrend. Nun führt das Prinzipal-Instrument theils allein, theils vom Orchester (oder einigen Instrumenten desselben) unterstützt, die Gedanken der Hauptpartie in seiner und zwar Konzertierenden Weise aus, fügt ihnen auch wohl neue Sätze zu, geht – mit oder ohne Orchester, meist das Erstere – in die Dominante, um da den Seiten- und Schlußsatz auszuführen und schließt mit dem Orchester ganz nach dem Gange der Sonatenform den ersten Theil, oder überlässt (meist) dem Orchester allein diesen Abschluß. Nun bildet sich der zweite Theil, in dem die Melodie der Sätze meist von wechselnden Orchesterinstrumenten gegen die Figuren und Passagen der Prinzipalstimme durchgeführt wird ... endlich gestaltet sich der dritte Theil nach bekannte Form ...'

3. For instance, Marx, 1845 is devoted substantially to sonata form as observed in the instrumental works of Beethoven. The origin of Marx's tripartite division of sonata form is complex, and beyond the scope of this section. Possibly it developed from Czerny's German translations of the theories of form advanced in Reicha, 1826, published in Czerny, 1834. Reicha had famously characterised the sonata form as the 'grande coupe binaire', stressing its historical derivation from the binary pattern. Nevertheless, within his scheme, thematic functions were assigned a far greater prominence than had obtained in the writings of Koch, and this began to highlight a tension between a bipartite tonal conception and a tripartite thematic conception, within which thematic *development* is crucial. Such was the perceived importance of the element of thematic development following the exposition of the main themes that it began to acquire an independent status within the structure of a movement as a whole – a development *section* sandwiched between the initial thematic presentations and their reprise towards the movement's close. Within Reicha's 'grande coupe binaire', there lurked a three-stage pattern of exposition, development and recapitulation, a pattern that was to become the norm for nineteenth-century understandings of sonata form, in whatever genre. Reicha, 1826, ii, p.240, classifies the development's various functions under several headings: the development of melodic ideas already heard in the exposition; their fragmentation; their presentation in new environments; their novel combination with other material; and the revealing thereby of unexpected facets of those familiar melodic ideas ('Développer ses idées, ou en tirer parti (après les avoir faits précédemment entendre), les présenter sous différentes faces, c'est les combiner de plusieurs manières intérresantes, c'est enfin produire des effets inattendus et nouveaux sur des idées connues d'avance'). 'Development' here is exclusively to do with thematic manipulation; note that this is also true in Marx's discussion, quoted above ('Nun bildet sich der zweite Theil, in dem die Melodie der Sätze ... durchgeführt wird').

4. 'An Stelle des zweimaligen Vortrags der Themen tritt der knappe Vortrag derselben durch das Orchester mit volgendem erweiterten durch das Soloinstrument.'

5. Note that this template is Tovey's own conflation of what he presumably took to be the variety of generally held views (he cites no specific theoretical literature).

6. As claimed in the article 'Concerto' in the first edition of *Grove's Dictionary of Music and Musicians* (London, 1879), pp.387–9. The article is by Ebenezer Prout (1835–1909), one of the most prolific musical theorists of his age. Prout later wrote that 'a very important modification of the sonata form is that to be seen in the first movement of the concerto, as treated by Mozart, Beethoven and their contemporaries' (Prout, 1895, p.203).

7. To what extent the term 'transition' fits comfortably with Tovey's specifically ritornello-influenced view of the concerto first-movement form may be disputed. It seems to be a subconscious relic of sonata thinking that is so difficult to expunge from the historically conditioned – even canonically sanctioned – understanding of the form. Interestingly, Tovey largely reverts to sonata terminology beyond his consideration of the brief tutti following the 'solo' exposition', possibly because from this point in his discussion he was at pains to explain the significance of the tonal procedures pertinent to the 'development' and 'recapitulation' above all else.

8. Another, slightly different approach to segmentation, influenced by Leeson and Levin, is that outlined in Küster, 1991. Küster identifies 15 'Ritornellzonen' whose characteristics are explained at considerably greater length than in Leeson

and Levin and are applied across the whole range of Mozart's concerto first movements. Grayson, 1999 applies the Leeson and Levin model in his analyses of the first movements of K.466 and 467.

9. Unusually in the first movement of K.449 the opening tutti includes an actual modulation to the dominant key (confirmed by thematic statements within that key).

10. The significance of the quintet for piano and wind, K.452 in this development should not be forgotten. Its first movement demonstrates Mozart's command of a variety of different possibilities for integrating the 'soloist' and the winds, resulting in a sophisticated unfolding of accompanimental and dialogue textures, for instance at bars 29–41 of the first movement. The structure of the 'second subject' (stated at bars 43–50) depends crucially upon the element of complementarity between the piano and the wind group, bars 47–50 reversing the polarity of bars 43–6 with phrases initially taken by the piano now being claimed by the wind (and vice versa), resulting in an engaging symmetry not simply of phrasing but of instrumental roles.

11. However, it is probably not safe to infer much from this example, since, in so many respects, the autograph score is deficient in detail. Much of the piano's left-hand stave was left blank (it was filled in subsequently in André's first edition), and it seems unlikely that Mozart really intended the winds to remain unheard for over 230 bars (they drop out again for much of the recapitulation). Further on this, see the entry for K.537 in Part Two.

12. Once more, a departure from Koch's theoretical prescription, which allocated this function to the soloist.

13. The apparently diminishing significance of this third tutti within the overall scheme of the movement was acknowledged by Koch in the *Musikalisches Lexicon*; see Chapter One, p.9.

14. On 'listening strategies' that may have been applied to the concertos by contemporary audiences, see Chapter Six.

15. This is addressed further in the entry for K.537 in Part Two.

16. Cadenzas and *Eingänge* are treated separately in Chapter Seven as a special case of the art of improvisation and embellishment in performance.

17. For an account of the textual ambiguities of this passage, see the entry for K.595 in Part Two.

18. In K.491 the closing section (in which, unusually, the soloist participates) is labelled 'Coda' in the autograph.

19. Spanning K.449 (9 February 1784) to K.503 (4 December 1786); K.537, though dated 24 February 1788, may well have been begun in mid-1787, according to the evidence of its watermarks (see the entry for this piece in Part Two), and is thus perhaps not so isolated from the earlier series as might be supposed.

20. An identical procedure is found in the first movement of the concerto for three (two) pianos, K.242 (cf. bars 122–35 and bars 252–65).

21. Possibly the latter example influenced Beethoven in his C minor concerto, op.37, in which the piano also returns in the closing bars of the first movement in similar figural and harmonic contexts.

CHAPTER FOUR

Movement Forms II: Slow Movements

Character

With the remarkable exception of K.271, slow movements within the Salzburg concertos display an uncomplicated innocence, plumbing no remote depths of feeling. The opening theme of K.238's Andante un poco adagio perfectly personifies the *galant* style of J. C. Bach (Example 4.1).[1] Supporting its gently lilting scansion is a succession of varied rhythms, dotted at first, within what feels like a long upbeat, and soon giving way to that epitome of *galant* idiom, the triplet. Precisely notated details of articulation, in both themes and accompaniments (combining here both *sordino* and *pizzicato*), contribute essentially to the idiom. This movement, composed in January 1776, reveals a style-conscious young Mozart. But whereas his later slow movements evoke a spirit of timelessness, this one is frozen in its time – unmistakably current (that is, *galant*), charming, but without any deeper significance. It lacks an expressive dimension that the mature lyricism of the later Viennese concerto slow movements possess in such abundance: that is, a mobility of meaning that allows us to interpret their characteristics in a variety of different ways. The same could be said of the slow movements of K.242 and K.246, though in the latter, there is a greater imagination in the interrelationship of soloist and orchestra and hints of a deeper intensity of purpose in the phrase beginning at bars 94–5.

The C minor Andantino of K.271 (January 1777) is of quite a different order. Its confident embracing of the *Empfindsam* idiom rests upon two significant technical advances: first, in Mozart's command of declamatory melody, typified by the intervallic and rhythmic profile of the first solo phrase; and second, of expressive chromatic harmony, enhanced by careful placement of *fp* markings, slurrings and the muting of the violins. (Both aspects are reinforced in the two cadenzas that Mozart composed for this movement.)[2] Some of the technical manoeuvres through which Mozart achieves his powerful expressive effects are borrowed from the syntax of *opera seria* recitative, most obviously the tutti phrase, bars 11–16, ending with the typical closing formula of an unsupported falling fourth (in the first violins), concluded by a perfect cadence (Example 4.2). At the beginning of

Example 4.1   K.238, 2nd movement, bars 1–7 (theme)

Example 4.2 K.271, 2nd movement, bars 11–16

this phrase the harmonies are enhanced by Neapolitan inflection, giving way as the cadence approaches to chromatic diminished-7th and augmented-6th chords allied to a 'foreshortening' of the rhythmic scansion in the lower strings (bars 13–14), marking with impeccable timing a climax of intensity at the tutti's close. Careful attention to such *minutiae* of expression at the level of the phrase is one dimension of this movement. At the opposite end of the scale is its sheer spaciousness, which emanates partly from an evolving relationship between solo and tutti. Mozart signals the special nature of this relationship from the very first solo entry which presents not the main theme, but a descant to it (as before, the theme itself is sounded canonically in the strings). Thereafter, he continues not with the expected solo counterstatement, but with a two-bar link into the secondary theme in E flat at bar 25. At the equivalent moment in the reprise (bar 74 foll.), this relationship is slightly altered: the main theme is stated unaccompanied by the solo, after which the texture of bars 17–23 returns exactly. Further instances of the unfolding discourse between solo and tutti are not hard to find. One concerns the cadential phrase at the end of the first tutti (bars 11–16). As in a first-movement ritornello form, this passage returns periodically as a 'punctuation' during the course of the movement, at bars 48–53, bars 109–16 (extended) and finally at bars 126–31. Beyond the initial appearance, however, this cadential marker is sounded not by the tutti alone, but unusually in combination with the solo. Moreover, each subsequent presentation couples the solo and tutti in a slightly different way, each 'refrain' being a 'variation' of its predecessor in a process of continual transformation. By the end of the Andantino, the solo part has taken over all but the first four beats of this phrase. A third way in which this movement penetrates far beyond the range of contemporary *galanterie* is in its handling of tonality. The reprise of the secondary theme from bar 25 at bar 84 restates the relative major, E flat at first, throwing the ensuing deviation to C minor into sharp relief and pointing up the expressive contrast of minor and major modality, both locally and 'structurally' (in relation to the complementary passage in the first solo). That contrast is achieved not only by harmonic means but also through subtle changes to interval patterns within the filigree embellishment which assumes a strangely ethereal character at this point in the movement (bars 87–100 especially). All in all, this Andantino is an amalgam of characteristic and structural influences from several different directions that speaks with a voice more eloquent than any of the earlier Salzburg concertos and foreshadows the depth of utterance that characterises the concertos of the following decade.

The Viennese concertos tread a broader expressive path than any of their predecessors. Sudden turns to a darker emotional side are found in the slow movements of, for instance, K.453 (bar 35 foll.), K.459 (bar 57 foll.) and K.467 (bars 10 foll., and 66 foll.), which range from the declamatory to the merely reflective, while that of K.488 (uniquely, for Mozart, in the key of F sharp minor) retains something of the atmosphere of a lament throughout, not only by virtue of its siciliana *topos* (which had been used for this purpose since at least the time of Vivaldi)[3] but also in its melodic and harmonic language, emphasising frequent chromatic part-movement, accented appoggiaturas (in the solo phrases beginning at bar 28, for instance), suspensions (particularly in the tutti's first phrase, reinforced by the woodwind scoring, and again at bar 80 foll.) and Neapolitan harmonies (introduced for the first time by the piano in its opening phrase, bars 9–10). Command of colour is important in conveying these expressive effects. Most especially, Mozart's mixing of orchestral timbres is masterly. Among the many passages of this kind that are to be found in the Viennese concerto slow movements are those at K.453, bar 64 foll., K.467 (applying mutes to the strings throughout, and involving many poignant woodwind phrases, for instance, that beginning at bar 44), K.488, bar 84 foll., K.482, bar 125 foll., K.491, bars 20 foll. and 42[3] foll., K.503, bar 17 foll. (especially the handling of the bassoon, separated from the first violins by two octaves) and K.595, bar 103 foll., a passage in which Mozart originally notated the left-hand piano part an octave higher (forming parallel fifths with the tune in the violin – actually the bass-line at this point).

Beautifully shaped melody is by far the most prominent feature of the slow movements in Mozart's piano concertos, one which has doubtless contributed in large part to their widespread popularity. An outstanding illustration of this is the secondary theme of K.466's slow movement. Introduced by the soloist, it proceeds in an unbroken line from bar 40 to bar 68 where the opening theme recurs. Within its span are many of the quintessential qualities of a Mozart concerto slow-movement theme (Example 4.3):

- it proceeds in a series of four-bar units;
- its texture is exclusively theme and accompaniment (in this case, light quaver throbbing from the strings) and separated in register from the accompanying instruments;
- its underlying basis is simple – much of it could be reduced to scales and arpeggios (its first four bars, for instance);
- the harmonic pace is slow and uniform, sometimes structured by sequence (bars 52–5);
- the basic melodic line is overlaid with fairly sparse embellishment, though this is tellingly placed (bars 51, 56–7, 59, 69), sometimes resulting in temporary dissonances against the bass-line (bars 63–6);

Example 4.3 K.466, 2nd movement, bars 40–68 (theme)

- some phrases have a notated 'accelerando': the first phrase moves through smaller note-values during its course, for instance, giving a quite pointed sense of direction to the theme;
- elsewhere, the notated accelerandos are co-ordinated with the tonal design: bars 57–60 are characterised by a sudden flurry of rhythmic activity, marking the transition from chromatic outburst to diatonic resolution (after which the activity relaxes once more).

This is the only movement among the concertos actually entitled 'Romance' by Mozart.[4] The romance was identified as a particular type of slow movement by Koch:

> In more modern concertos, however, instead of the customary adagio, often a so-called romance is composed. This has a definite character, which one can best get to know from Sulzer's description of the romance in poetry ... 'Nowadays', says Sulzer, 'the name is given to short narrative songs in extremely simple and somewhat antiquated tone of the old rhymed romances. Their content may be a passionate, tragic, amorous, or even merely entertaining narrative ... Ideas and expression must be of the utmost simplicity and very naïve.' This composition usually takes the form of a rondo (Koch, 1782–93, i, part iv, §126; Baker, 1983, pp.212–13).[5]

Koch's summary, and especially his recourse to analogy, is irritatingly loose. He begins by comparing the romance to a specific tempo (Adagio). The equation of a 'definite character' with a tempo is suggestive, but not conclusive. Does Koch mean that the more modern romance was associated with the portrayal of a characteristic *Affekt* whose appropriate realisation was in a tempo somewhat quicker (or slower) than the norm?[6] As to the romance's 'definite character' itself, the quotation from Sulzer makes it clear that the poetic romance is a *narrative* genre characterised by identifiable stylistic aspects (which he lists). While Koch's focus in this analogy is apparently on the 'characteristic elements' of the romance ('this has a definite character, which one can best get to know from Sulzer's description of the romance in poetry'), the fact that these elements are directed, in a poetic romance, towards the production of a specifically narrative result raises an important side-issue: by making an analogy between the musical romance and its poetic counterpart, did Koch mean to suggest that 'romances', as found in concerto slow movements, were themselves 'narrative'? Might Koch have been attracted to Sulzer's description of the poetic romance because he himself envisioned a specifically narrative quality within slow movements of the 'romance' genre? Consequently, might the dramatic outburst of the G minor episode in the 'Romance' of Mozart's K.466 be construed as the middle stage of a 'story being told' by that movement as a whole? Unfortunately, Koch does not expand upon his analogy, either with regard to 'character' or 'narrativity', leaving the question open. The possibility of musical narrativity in instrumental music is one which lies beyond the scope of this study,[7] although its immediate historical context for the slow movement romance may be briefly sketched here.

The dominant tradition of eighteenth-century music criticism privileged vocal music above instrumental. Music was, like all the arts, an imitation (*mimesis*) of nature, and from this philosophical stance it drew its justification. Without a text, however, music was unable to represent anything concrete, especially a sequence of events. This collective viewpoint attained its classic expression in Charles Batteux's widely circulated and translated treatise, *Les Beaux-Arts réduits à un même principe* (Batteux, 1746).[8] Moving forward from such opinions, Sulzer's *Allgemeine Geschichte* explicitly acknowledges the capacity of instrumental music to represent emotional states, though perhaps not in so clearly focused a manner as vocal music. Furthermore, Sulzer recommends that the composer of a concerto (or other instrumental work), in order to compensate for the lack of a referential narrative context enjoyed by the composer of an overture to a play,

> would do well to imagine some person, or a situation or passion, and exert his fantasy to the point where he can believe that this person is ready to speak. He can help himself by seeking out poetry that is pathetic, fiery, or tender in nature, and declaim it in an appropriate tone, and after that sketch out his composition following this sentiment (Baker and Christensen, 1996, p.96).

Presumably Sulzer's premise was that the lofty sentiments induced by such contemplation could be translated into musical terms by means of the doctrine of the affects, which still enjoyed widespread acceptance and validity in German musical theory of the later eighteenth century.[9] But that is not the same thing as a theory by which narratives may be either embedded in musical compositions or subsequently recognised by criticism. While the representation of 'feelings' (*Empfindungen*) was assumed in some critical reviews of C. P. E. Bach's sonatas (and occasionally also in Mozart's) during the 1780s (Morrow, 1997, pp.126–9), it was not until the early nineteenth century that there arose a critical tradition that imputed a narrative quality to instrumental music. One early illustration of this trend actually refers to a work by Mozart. In his 1806 *Cours complet d'harmonie et de composition*[10] Jérome-Joseph Momigny attempted to convey the expressive qualities of the first movement of Mozart's D minor string quartet, K.421, in overtly narrative terms. Momigny even invented a text which he applied to the movement in order to clarify the precise sequence of affective states he believed lay hidden in it:

> I believed that the sentiments expressed by the composer were those of a lover on the point of being abandoned by the hero whom she loves; *Dido*, who suffered such a misfortune, came immediately to my mind. Her lofty station, the ardour of her love, the familiarity of her misfortune, all these persuaded me to make her the heroine of this subject (Momigny, 1806, i, p.371 – author's translation).[11]

For Momigny, Mozart's music clearly evoked a train of narrative thought, which could be brought alive by adaptation to a suitable programme (chosen to represent the reaction of the critic, of course, rather than any quality demonstrably inherent in the music itself). The first movement of K.421 encapsulated for him a particular set of sentiments; it could be 'read' as a story.

So if Koch was indeed imputing a 'narrative' quality to the unfolding of a slow movement 'romance', he would have been anticipating a strand of early nineteenth-century criticism, rather than reflecting contemporary aesthetic theory. It remains doubtful, given the historical situation of the *Versuch*, that Koch had any such elaborate scheme of narrativity in mind in relation to concerto slow movements. Insofar as Koch envisaged the possibility of a musical narrative – whether in slow-movement romances or elsewhere – this probably lay in the logical interrelations between melodic and phrase constructions that he treats in extended detail in Part Three of the *Versuch*.[12]

Questions of narrative content apart, the Koch–Sulzer description of the romance nicely captures the character of the slow movement of K.466, and also of K.491, K.537 and K.595 which share very similar traits. They each begin with the piano alone, presenting melodic ideas 'of the utmost simplicity and very naïve' (immediately repeated by the tutti). All are rondo forms, conforming to Koch's closing recommendation, the sectional episodic contrast allowing for the balancing of a range of 'definite characters' within the whole. Their episodes always introduce contrasting new material and scarcely any attempt is made in them to engage in thematic development, a technique that would threaten the prevailing aura of 'simplicity'. Contrast tends to be between sections rather than within them: internally, themes and episodes maintain a single *Affekt*, a practice

that lends these romances a quite 'artificial' nature, especially when set alongside the generally dynamic successions of *Affekt* so characteristic of late classic
style. In Sulzer's parlance, such movements assume an 'extremely simple and
somewhat antiquated tone'. The central episode of K.466's slow movement
offers the most extreme emotional contrast among the slow-movement
romances. Its energetic sextuplet semiquavers, *forte*, sweeping across almost
the entire range of the keyboard, its chromatically descending bass-lines and its
surging wind counterpoints conspire to shatter the tranquillity of the preceding
section. This striking emotional outburst may justly be termed 'passionate', even
'tragic', to adapt two of Sulzer's categories to the particular case.

Slow-movement structures: overview

Structurally, the slow movements are extremely diverse, although they rely on
just a handful of basic types. Most of the slow movements are influenced
tonally by the sonata principle, in which secondary material originally introduced out of the tonic key is eventually recapitulated within it towards the end
of the movement. Several (for instance, those of K.175, K.242, K.459, K.488
and K.503) demonstrate clear sonata-form tendencies. The first two of these
have quasi-development sections (that of K.175 consists of an extended dominant pedal), while the rest separate the 'exposition' from the 'recapitulation'
by means of a short linking passage, leading to a cadence on the dominant
before the return of the main theme. Particularly influential are ritornello structures imported from the operatic aria, though applied in such a wide variety of
ways that it is impossible in this chapter to do anything other than list a few
representative examples of Mozart's procedures. Episodic (rondo) forms are
frequently found, as in K.466, K.491, K.537 and K.595. Two slow movements,
K.450 and K.456, are variations. Uniquely among the piano concertos, K.482
has a slow movement that is a hybrid of rondo and variation. The main theme
(bars 1–32) is immediately restated in a decorated version by the solo (variation 1); episode 1 (bars 64–92) features woodwind and horns; this is followed
by further decoration of the main theme by the solo (variation 2); episode 2
(bars 124–44) is an extended dialogue for the flute and bassoon with string
accompaniment; in variation 3 of the main theme (bars 144–85) the dialogue
texture is retained, the soloist providing (usually) cadential responses to the
tutti, giving way to echoes from bar 166, extending the harmonic range of the
original pattern of bars 21–7 and dissolving into a coda (bars 185–213).

Ritornello ('aria') forms

The opening tutti sections of those slow movements in 'aria' form typically
contain several distinct thematic ideas and Mozart handles these quite freely,

according to no set pattern. During the course of the movement one or more of these distinct ideas will be separated from its original context and briefly reprised, standing in place of the whole of the original statement. It is as if Mozart regarded the individual ideas as 'prefabricated' units or elements, to be transplanted to new contexts at will. The principle was imported to the Viennese concerto slow movements from operatic arias and before discussing its application in the concertos, it will be as well to examine its use in one of his recent operas, Ilia's aria 'Zeffiretti lusinghieri' from Act III of *Idomeneo* (1780–1).

The opening tutti ritornello contains several distinct ideas: (**A**), bar 1; (**B**), bar 5; and (**C**), bar 9. Ilia's first phrase ('Zeffiretti lusinghieri, deh volate al mio tesoro') repeats (**A**) and (**B**) in succession before introducing new material, principally (**D**), bar 30 ('e gli dite') and (**E**), bars 37–8 ('Zeffiretti lusinghieri' again), the former modulating into, the latter actually in the dominant key, B major. Following what amounts to an episode within the ritornello interpretation of this structure, or else a 'second subject group' within a sonata interpretation, there is a return to theme (**C**), transplanted to the dominant, but retaining its cadential function (bar 52 foll.). Once the cadence has arrived, however, theme (**E**) returns (bar 60, stated by the tutti, not solo), followed by a reworking of (**B**) as a countertheme to Ilia's new phrase ('E voi piante, e fior sinceri che ora innaffia il pianto amaro') commencing at bar 66 (a quasi-development section). The 'recapitulation', telescoping the 'tutti' and 'solo' statements of the opening ritornello, starts at bar 82, in which themes (**A**) and (**B**) return in the original sequence (though (**B**) retains the revised form of bar 66); (**C**) is omitted at this stage, however, allowing (**D**) and (**E**) to be restated within the tonic, so that this passage (bars 94–107) functions much like the tonic recapitulation of the 'second subject group' in a sonata form. When (**C**) finally recurs, it does so right at the end of the aria as a culmination (bar 116), though Mozart is not quite finished with (**E**), with which the piece actually ends (bars 124–30) – its function significantly altered from 'contrasting theme' to 'concluding cadence'. In this hybrid between ritornello and sonata the 'modular' flexibility with which Mozart treats individual phrase-elements in building a structure is remarkable. See Figure 4.1 for a diagrammatic representation.

Theme:	[ABC]	AB	D	E	[C]	E*	[B]	[AB]	DE	[C]	E
Key:	I	I	V		V		V	I	I		I
Bar:	1–17	18	30	37	52	60	66	82	94	116	124

[tutti ritornello elements in square brackets]
* = a tutti statement of the solo theme

Figure 4.1 'Zeffiretti lusinghieri': Overview of aria structure

Similar principles obtain in some of the concerto slow movements; three are examined here: K.414, K.453 and K.467. In the Andante of K.414 the opening tutti contains four principal ideas: (**A**), bar 1; (**B**), bar 9; (**C**), bar 13; and the cadential phrase, (**D**), bars 16–20, all within the tonic, D major. While the piano begins with a reference to (**A**), it continues with a new theme (**E**) at bar 29, modulating to the dominant in which key themes (**B**), (**C**) and (**D**) of the original tutti ritornello are reprised in order (bars 37–57, concluding with a tutti restatement of (**D**) after the trill, rather as in a first-movement ritornello structure). The central episode effectively functions as a development, taking up the closing part of (**D**) at bar 57 and subsequently (bars 62, 67–72). Following an *Eingang* ('lead-in' – Mozart provides two examples), (**A**), (**B**), (**C**) and (**D**) follow as in their original sequence – now in the tonic region, omitting the transitional (**E**) – and functioning, as in the corresponding section of 'Zeffiretti lunghieri', as a 'recapitulation' (bars 74–98), tonally influenced by the sonata; after the cadenza, the Andante concludes with a tonic restatement of element (**D**) from the opening ritornello (with slight harmonic modifications). Diagrammatically, this thematic/tonal succession may be represented as in Figure 4.2.

Theme:	[**ABCD**]	**A**	**E**	**BCD**	[**D***] *Eingang*	**ABC** Cadenza	[**D**]
Key:	I	I		V		I	
Bar:	1–20	21	29	37	57	74	99

[tutti ritornello elements in square brackets]
* a quasi-development, utilising theme (**D**) and modulating through related keys

Figure 4.2   K.414: Overview of slow-movement structure

In this movement there is very little new material besides that outlined in the ritornello, although the ritornello-like handling of element (**D**) is similar to that of the new theme, (**E**) in 'Zeffiretti'. The ritornello structure of K.453's Andante is more complex. Again, it consists of four themes and these recur, sometimes individually, sometimes in combination, later in the movement. Diagrammatically, its thematic/tonal succession may be represented as in Figure 4.3. This structure intermingles the new theme (**E**), introduced at bar 35, with reprises of ritornello material and the three appearances of element (**D**) from bar 25 at the end of the opening tutti (tonic); a dominant-key entry in the middle and a concluding, tonic, presentation at the end of the movement.

Theme:	[**ABCD**]	**A**	**E**	[**B**]	**D**/[**D**]	[**A**]	**F**	**A**	**E**	[**BC**]	Cadenza	[**A**]	**D**
Key:	I		I	v	V V		I	ii	I	IIIb I		I	I
Bar:	1–29		30	35	42 54		64	69	90	94 103		123	130

[tutti ritornello elements in square brackets]

Figure 4.3   K.453: Overview of slow-movement structure

Another hybrid structure is illustrated in the famous Andante of K.467. It too combines features of sonata and ritornello, though here the two are more widely separated: the tonality is that of a sonata in which the recapitulation of the opening theme occurs in the wrong key (here, A flat major, the flattened mediant); thematically, the recapitulation is quite irregular, mixing up the order in which one would normally expect themes to occur in a sonata form, but quite typical, as we have seen above, of Mozart's flexible, 'modular' handling of the ritornello principle. The orchestral ritornello, bars 1–22, contains four contrasting thematic elements (remarkably diverse in their expressive character, but held together by the throbbing triplet patterns) at bars 1–7 (**A**), 8–11 (**B**), 11–16 (**C**) and 17–22 (**D**). New ideas are introduced by the soloist at bars 37 (**E**) and 62 (**F**). Within this ambiguous structure, theme (**E**) might be regarded either as a 'second subject' within a sonata conception, or else as an interruption of a restatement of the ritornello (**AB E CD** in Figure 4.4). Probably the latter interpretation is correct, since this theme is never reprised. The assemblage of thematic elements in this movement is relatively loose, especially as regards the ordering of individual ritornello elements towards the end, although the identity of these is always clearly retained. The thematic/tonal structure is diagrammatically represented in Figure 4.4.

Theme:	[**ABCD**] **AB**	**E**	**CD**	**F**	**C** (developed)	**A**	**C**	**DB** coda (bars 99–104)
Key:	I	I	vi	V	IV	modulating	IIIb V/I	I
Bar:	1–22	23	37	45	62	66	73	82 88

[tutti ritornello elements in square brackets]

Figure 4.4   K.467: Overview of slow-movement structure

Episodic (rondo) forms

As mentioned above, K.466, K.491, K.537 and K.595 conform to the extended episodic structure of rondo. In each case the soloist begins alone. For all their melodic sophistication their form-schemes are extremely simple and rely for their effect on contrast between a succession of self-contained sections. The contrast between sections may be primarily melodic in character, as in K.537, textural, as in K.466 (featuring a turbulent minor-key central episode) and K.491 (which creates continuity by opposition of different instrumental colours), or else harmonic, as in K.595 (whose central episode incorporates a modulation to the remote key of G flat). In K.466 Mozart returns to the opening theme no fewer than seven times after its original statement. In the other three rondos his structure is rather tighter. In K.537, for instance, the repetition of the opening section within what is effectively a ternary design is 'telescoped', the tutti's reprise of bars 1–8 being omitted after the piano's restatement at bars 72–9 (instead, the piano continues, alone, with the phrase originally heard at bar 17). In K.491 and K.595 the concluding section of the rondo is marked by the introduction of a new theme (in the former, there is a full-blown coda, bars 78–89; in the latter the cadential theme is sounded by the piano at bar 122).

The individual sections within the rondos are quite varied in construction. Within the middle episodes of K.466 and K.491, there is a binary division (A–A′–B–B′, in which the superscript prime denotes a decorated reprise); at this point in K.537 and K.595 the section is 'through-composed', hinting at some of the melodic procedures of a sonata development. In K.537 and K.595 the ritornello principle makes itself felt to a limited degree in that there is a return, towards the end of each movement, to tutti material which formerly rounded off an earlier section (always, this occurs within a cadential context). The passages in question are K.537, bar 36 foll., repeated at bar 99 foll.; K.595, bar 32 foll., repeated at bar 110 foll.

Variations

Variation sets appear surprisingly infrequently in Mozart's piano concertos. The variation genre offers a concerto composer ample opportunity for setting off the soloist against the orchestra: the soloist stands apart from the tutti in that its function is to glamorise by means of charming and sometimes exciting decoration of what the tutti states plainly (at least, at first). Nevertheless, only two slow movements are variation sets, those of K.450 and K.456. Variations are not the special preserve of slow movements, of course, but there is an important distinction in character to be observed between slow-movement variations and variation finales such as are found in K.453 and K.491. Admittedly, the fundamental techniques are the same. Whether in slow movement or finale, a potentially chaotic perpetual evolution of ornamental display out of 'pure' melody is grounded semantically by a controlling phrase and cadence pattern beneath (typically, the structure is binary); the continuity derives from a satisfying balance of conflicting dynamic and static dimensions. Yet the results in each case are radically different. Whereas in concerto finales, Mozart uses variation techniques to emphasise the element of virtuosity (as a climactic feature, crowning the work as a whole), in the slow movements, variations serve a different, expressive, purpose. In finales, the dynamic–static conflict becomes a contest in which the figurative surface seeks to escape from the confining centre, propelling the music forwards, revelling in the release of 'centrifugal' energy that gives it meaning. By contrast, in the slow-movement variation species, the embellishment takes on a searching, introspective quality, drawing coherence instead from within the limitations of the frame. As the movement unfolds, it writes a commentary on itself.

Technically, this is achieved by defining an environment in which the 'free' melodic and 'confined' harmonic aspects meet. Chromaticism is just such an environment. Within the slower tempo of an Andante or Adagio, the ear can assimilate a greater complexity of harmony, and it is this factor that Mozart exploits to such telling effect in the slow-movement variations. The harmonic underpinning of the theme in K.456's Andante un poco sostenuto is at first almost entirely diatonic, though it is chromatically enhanced in bar 3 by an augmented-6th chord, articulating the resolution on to the dominant at the end of the opening phrase. Chromatic harmonies become more prominent during the theme's second section, animating the polyphonic texture in the strings from bar 14 and lending definition to the tonic resolution at the close. In the subsequent variations, Mozart conforms fairly strictly to the harmonic pattern established at the outset,[13] the only significant departures adding further to the chromatic 'gloss' upon the diatonic basis (for example, the chromatic passing crotchets in the bass at bar 44). What seems to be emerging harmonically is a gradually unfolding environment in which chromatic chords are applied 'strategically' as a *topos*. For Girdlestone, this movement is 'the story of an emotional experience full of anguish ... [expressing] despair carried almost to a point of physical suffering ... complete hopelessness ... utter disillusion ... seldom equalled by the passionate and feverish cries of Romanticism'.[14] For Hutchings, it displays 'the whole technique of grief'.[15] Exactly what the association of the chromatic *topos* might be is not the central point here. What is remarkable is that its topical association is paralleled in the allied treatment of melodic embellishment, which also relies heavily on chromaticism for its detailed continuity at every stage, bringing it into a close unity with the harmonic dimension. The meeting of melody and harmony in a chromatic 'middleground' results in a consistency of expressive purpose nurtured by its repetitive yet evolutionary context (the variation structure), a remarkable homogeneity of content and form.

That homogeneity is further enhanced by other 'middleground' features such as dynamics, accentuation, texture and colour. All have a 'reflective' rather than 'exhibitionist' status. The precise accentuation of the theme, along with its dynamic values, enhances the oscillation between diatonic and chromatic conditions. Mozart's application of texture and colour here likewise suggest stasis, rather than dynamic evolution away from the centre. Alternations of piano, strings and wind (for instance, at bars 42–84) merely provide a space for the theme to inhabit – however resourcefully – rather than contributing a 'developmental' aspect to the progress of the movement as a whole. Such alternations of texture and colour are illuminated more prominently in the Andante variations of the slightly earlier K.450. From the outset, the binary-form theme (**a–a'–b–b'**)[16] and the two ensuing variations are presented as a series of regular periodic alternations between strings and piano, later implicating the wind. No attempt is made to 'escape' these parameters: the variation structure is one of reflective stasis, in which, once again, the successive overlaying of chromatic melodic embellishment in the ornate solo part merges with the equally chromatic inflections of the underlying harmonic profile. Contrasting 'blocks' of instrumental colour mark out the Andante's structural boundaries (see Figure 4.5).

Theme:	**a** (bar 1)	**a'** (bar 9)	**b** (bar 17)	**b'** (bar 25)
	strings	piano	strings	piano
Var.1:	**a** (bar 33)	**a'** (bar 41)	**b** (bar 49)	**b'** (bar 57)
	strings/piano	piano	strings/piano	piano
Var.2:	**a** (bar 65)	**a'** (bar 73)	**b** (bar 81)	**b'** (bar 89)
	piano [+ strings	piano + wind	piano [+ strings	piano + wind
	(bar 69)]	and *pizz.* strings	(bar 84)]	*pizz.* strings

coda: alternates strings + wind with piano in two-bar units (bars 101–9); thereafter piano + wind
(bars 109–11) and piano + strings + bassoon (bars 112–13)

Figure 4.5   K.450: Overview of slow-movement structure

Notes

1. The Andante grazioso of K.414, whose form is analysed below, actually uses a theme of Bach's, from his contribution to Galuppi's opera, *La calamità dei cuori*, published separately in Bach, 1770a.
2. See the entry for K.271 in Part Two.
3. See, for instance, the third movement of his concerto in D minor, op.3 no.11 for two violins.
4. A sketch for the theme of the slow movement of K.537 is entitled 'Romance', but this designation did not subsequently appear in the autograph manuscript; see the entry for K.537 in Part Two.
5. For Sulzer's description see Sulzer, 1771, article 'Romanze', vol.iv, p.544.
6. The Romance of K.466 has no separate tempo marking, but is normally played larghetto, rather like the slow movements of K.491, K.537 and K.595 (only the last of which was marked larghetto by the composer).
7. On the problematic aspects of narrativity in music, see, for instance, Nattiez, 1990, Newcomb, 1984 and Rink, 1998.
8. Further on the infiltration of the predominantly French tradition of *mimesis* in the arts into German letters, see Hosler, 1981, pp.1–13. Some contemporary aesthetic trends are considered further in Chapter Six.
9. Bach, 1753 considers the representation of affects in music in detail; see Mitchell, 1949, pp.147–66. Elsewhere in the *Allgemeine Geschichte*, Sulzer notes that 'Every composition, whether it be vocal or instrumental, should possess a definite character and be able to arouse specific sentiments in the minds of listeners' ('Ausdrück in der Musik', vol.i, p.273; Baker and Christensen, 1996, p.53).
10. The sections devoted to Mozart's quartet are vol.i, pp.307–82; vol.ii, pp.387–403; vol.iii, pp.109–56 (an extended musical example).
11. The text appended to Momigny's annotated score in vol.iii of the treatise begins 'Ah! quand tu fais mon déplaisir, ingrat, je veux me plaindre, et non pas t'attendrir.'
12. Discussed in Chapter One, pp.12–14, and Chapter Six.
13. That is, allowing for the modal transformations of the *maggiore* statement incorporated at bars 126–59 and the closing coda from bar 180.
14. Girdlestone, 1958, p.270.
15. Hutchings, 1948; 1998, p.44.
16. In which a' and b' are varied internal repeats of the **a** and **b** portions of the theme.

CHAPTER FIVE

Movement Forms III: Finales

Koch's relatively perfunctory description of the concerto finale includes a catalogue of the principal types:

> The last section of the concerto is either an allegro or a presto. It may take the form of the first allegro, or an ordinary rondo with very amplified episodes, or variations on a short melody consisting of two sections (Baker, 1983, p.213).[1]

By far the majority of Mozart's piano concerto finales are rondos. Possibly because they have so often been regarded as formulaic, they have commanded considerably less attention than first movements. In fact, rondo 'templates' offer great scope for invention.[2] There is certainly no such thing as a 'standard' Mozart rondo finale; although it is relatively easy to understand the general outline of such finales in relation to one or other model of alternating refrains and episodes (providing textural, thematic and tonal contrast), their detailed execution frequently departs from the 'mould'. One instance of this is the relative freedom with which Mozart handles the thematic ordering of his refrains, as in the finale of K.467, where the reprise beginning in the solo part at bar 178 substantially reconfigures the original sequence of events: in the original refrain, subsidiary elements follow the opening theme (**a**), at bars 28 (**b**), 34 (**c**), 41 (**d**), 46 (**e**) and 52 (**f**); in the first reprise, this is re-ordered (**a**)–(**d**)–(**c**)–(**b**)–(**c**), themes (**e**) and (**f**) being omitted. Considerable variety is also found in the profile of successive returns of themes or episodes. In no case in Mozart's piano concerto finales is the reprise of a refrain or episode literally identical with a previous or original statement. There is always some element of variation, be that a localised embellishment of a melody (as in the reprises of the main finale theme in K.488, whose ending is subtly recast each time), or a rescoring of themes upon their restatement (as in K.503, which begins with a tutti statement, but whose reprises are sounded by the solo). Two broad types are encountered in the concerto finales: episodic rondo forms ('simple' rondos and 'sonata' rondos) and variations. They are discussed in that order here.

Rondo structures (whether 'simple' rondos or 'sonata' rondos) unfold as an alternating succession of refrains and episodes. The refrain consists of both a solo and a tutti element. Either solo or tutti may begin. Within solo openings, several schemes are found. One possibility (for example, in the finale of K.488) is an entirely unaccompanied solo statement of the main theme, normally consisting of a rounded phrase, or balancing pair of phrases, ending after 8 or 16 bars with a clear cadence in the tonic.[3] Alternatively, there may be light tutti accompaniment, as in K.238, K.450 or K.456. A variant of the solo opening is a more extended statement as in K.459, a 32-bar section shared antiphonally between solo and tutti, or K.482 (a 41-bar opening, structured **A–B–A**). The tutti which immediately follows continues in the manner of a first-movement ritornello, that is, with a relatively extended paragraph (for tutti alone) containing a succession of several themes or figurative patterns,[4] concluding with a clear cadence. In subsequent appearances of the refrain, which always begin with a solo statement (occasionally decorated in some way), the tutti is reprised either completely or more often incompletely, reflecting the selectivity inherent in ritornello designs, touched on in Chapter Three. Also as in first-movement ritornello practice, elements from the opening refrain that are omitted in intermediate recurrences are sometimes brought back in the final refrain, contributing to the sense of a grand peroration. In the final refrain, following the solo statement, solo and tutti combine, with the piano sometimes taking over one strand of an antiphonal texture originally shared between sections of the tutti (K.459), or contributing new strands (K.482). By comparison with first-movement ritornellos, the idiom of the opening rondo refrain in concerto finales is normally far more closely related to the simple repetitive melodic, rhythmic and cadential schemes of the dance, and often disposed in something approximating to the sectional divisions and sub-divisions of a binary form, sometimes emphasised by antiphony between piano and tutti, or strings and woodwind. At the outset, the phrasing holds to four-bar and eight-bar symmetry, but towards the end this is sometimes fractured by irregular groupings (in K.488 and K.595, for instance). Such an unpretentious opening gesture exerts an influence over the finale as a whole, establishing an expressive norm and a consequent set of expectations for the unfolding of the structure. In comparison to first-movement ritornellos, those of finales aim at a straightforward mode of discourse, predictably periodic and tuneful (which is not to say disappointing in quality), and characterised by melodic statement and counterstatement, rather than thematic development. This is, of course, a generalised picture. Mozart's finales are certainly no lightweight supplements to the more dramatic and expressive preceding movements, nor is the quality of their discourse inferior to that of first movements by virtue of the accessibility of their musical language. It may be objected that the nature of the first-movement ritornello advanced here, and against which the characteristics of a rondo-finale ritornello are opposed, is one unduly and anachronistically influenced by nineteenth-century prescriptions of form, in which a continually unfolding musical 'argument', founded on thematic development, is taken as an exemplar, in relation to which other formal procedures are measured (to say nothing of the insidious value judgements inherent in such a model). This much is acknowledged, although the obvious exception to the general description, the finale of the D minor concerto, K.466, proves the rule to some extent.

Some finales, including K.365, K.414, K.451, K.467 and K.503, begin with tuttis. In such cases, the tutti is effectively synonymous with a ritornello, leading to a tonic cadence followed by the initial solo statement with contrasting material at the start of the first episode. Again the procedures vary in detail. Whereas the tutti ritornello K.503 unfolds in the manner of a segmented first-movement ritornello, those of K.365 and K.451 are more 'patterned' (**A–A'** and **‖: A :‖: B :‖**, respectively), whereas that of K.467 involves a solo interruption of the tutti ritornello.

'Simple' rondos

Among Mozart's early Salzburg piano concertos, all except one, K.365 for two pianos (composed somewhat later than the rest), conclude with 'simple' rondos – that is, rondos whose alternation of refrains and episodes is not so closely regulated by the tonal outlines of a sonata form, although towards the end of a movement material from an earlier episode is partially recapitulated in the tonic key. These finales are characterised by polythematicism, simplicity of harmony, texture and phrasing, and frequent repetition of material from phrase to phrase (solo answered by tutti).

The rondo in its simplest form is illustrated by the Menuetto finale of the C major concerto, K.246 (April 1776). It begins with an eight-bar solo phrase immediately answered by the tutti which adds a counterbalancing phrase (bars 16^3–24) and a closing cadential idea whose repeated quaver Gs are taken up by the solo in the following phrase. At first the status of this new phrase is ambiguous (a continuation of the refrain, or the beginning of the first episode?), although in retrospect it becomes clear that it belongs to the first episode as it marks the beginning of a transitional modulation to D major (V/G major), introducing a second episodic theme in octaves between the hands at bar 39. This episode is notable for its thematic multiplicity. Another theme appears in bar 46, containing a broken chord element that is taken up in a cadential extension at bar 58, leading to a long dominant pedal, preparing for the return of the main theme at bar 84. This restatement is an exact one and leads, through a two-bar link, to the central episode in the relative minor at bar 113. Like the refrain, this is characterised by statement and answer phrasing (at the opening, for instance) and is a binary form, modulating to the dominant, E, at bar 136 (introducing a new theme in the minor at bar 139) and returning to A minor with a reprise of the opening idea at bar 151. Towards the end of this central episode is a reinterpretation of the repeated quaver idea from Episode 1 at bar 176, eventually giving way to semiquaver passagework and a cadenza preceding the third (curtailed) refrain (bar 194). Episode 3 begins with a further development of the repeated quavers, now in a contrapuntal setting (bar 209); a new theme follows over a triplet accompaniment; and, from bar 227, Mozart recapitulates within the tonic a sizable portion of material from Episode 1, retaining the thematic sequence exactly. The movement concludes with a modified refrain (including some minor harmonic refinements at bar 277 of the solo part) that imports the triplet quaver texture from Episode 3. Altogether, this is a formulaic, though charming, structure, unfolding in predictable paragraphs, each with its own uncomplicated character. It is notable for its separation of material between sections, rather than its broader integration.

A more elaborate example of the rondo finale is that of the E flat concerto, K.271, written in January 1777. It too alternates statements of a refrain with contrasting episodes, but is of far more extensive proportions and a broader expressive range. The refrain begins with an unusually long passage for the soloist (34 bars) answered directly by the tutti, whose continuation modulates into the new key (in Mozart's later sonata rondos, it is typically grounded in the tonic, the transitional function being subsumed into the first episode). Episode 1 exploits contrasting registers of the solo instrument (exploiting cross-handed textures) and introduces light chromaticism, leading to a second theme at bar 83 (extended in light counterpoint in the tutti beneath bravura quavers). Episode 1 is separated from the ensuing refrain by the first of two *Eingänge* in this movement. When it finally arrives, the refrain's solo opening is retained intact, followed by a much curtailed response from the tutti, shifting to V/F minor at bar 196, alternating solo and tutti phrases at the beginning of the central episode and continuing with a sequential restatement up a tone (V/ G major) and subsequently V/C minor, V/B flat major and V/A flat major, dissolving into a Menuetto in A flat (bars 233–303) which constitutes a self-contained middle portion of this central episode. In terms of tempo, key, time-signature, phraseology and texture, this is in striking contrast to all that surrounds it. It is a binary form (in which the written-out repeats are accompanied by the tutti) featuring reprise of the opening theme in A flat during its second part, concluding with a chromatic extension (bars 292–303) and second *Eingang*, before the second return of the energetic opening refrain, this time dramatically curtailed, dovetailing solo and tutti. The third episode, beginning at bar 325, combines elements of the preceding two episodes. It opens with a quotation from bar 196 (the beginning of Episode 2), with sequential extensions now remaining within the orbit of the tonic, but then switches at bar 344 to material from Episode 1 (originally bar 71 foll., but transposed towards the home key). Finally, beneath a high B flat trill in the right hand of the solo part, the tutti reintroduces the main theme, *pizzicato*, and answered by the solo, thus reversing, in foreshortened form, the original sequence of events at the close of the piece which concludes with a further reinterpretation of the opening melodic notes as a V–I cadence.

Sonata rondos

In a sonata rondo, the alternating scheme of Refrain and Episode is regulated by the tonal thinking of sonata form, insofar as material in the first episode is recapitulated towards the end of the movement in the tonic key. In outline, the sonata rondo template is as follows:

A	Refrain (I)
B¹	Episode 1 (I–V)
A	Refrain (I)
C	Episode 2 (variable key; sometimes relative minor; typically modulating)
A	Refrain (I)
B²	Episode 1 (I)
A	Refrain (I)

A clear illustration of this scheme is provided by the finale of the D major concerto, K.451. Following the opening symmetrical binary-form theme (bars 1–16) there is a transitional section beginning in octaves and continuing with a solo flourish that moves sharpwards, preparing for the new theme in the dominant at bar 55 (tutti) and its solo restatement, extended in virtuoso semiquaver passagework and ending with a chromatic lead-in to the main theme of the refrain at bar 104, now shared between solo and tutti. The central episode (bars 135–214) introduces a further theme, this time in the relative minor, continuing with a reference to the theme of Episode 1 at bar 157, incorporating modulations initially to G, E minor and C, from which point a more chromatic harmonic sequence, supporting imitative fragments of the main theme in the wind, extends gradually towards the tonic reprise of the main theme at bar 214. The remainder of the movement comprises an embellished statement of the refrain (bars 214–45) followed by Episode 1, now transposed to the tonic and dissolving in a cadenza (which, in addition to bravura scales and arpeggios, makes fleeting canonic allusion to Episode 1). The finale concludes with a $\frac{3}{8}$ coda which refers briefly to both the main theme and Episode 1.

It would be a mistake to regard Mozart's sonata rondo finales as conforming to a strict 'model', however. The sonata-rondo template was developed in the nineteenth century in order to describe the ambiguous structures found in some of Beethoven's finales (for instance, that of the 'Pathétique' sonata, op.13) in which the thematic unfolding followed the statement–episode pattern of the rondo, but was regulated by the tonal operations of sonata form to such an extent that the material of the refrain and first episode (**A** and **B** in the above template) functioned as if they were 'first subject' and 'second' subject' respectively within a sonata exposition, the only significant deviation from sonata form being the return of the 'first subject' (**A**) prior to the second episode (**C**).[5] In practice, there is considerable variety in the precise organisation of refrains and episodes in Mozart's concerto finales. Whereas in K.450, 451 and 467 the opening refrain (**A**) returns between the central episode (**C**) and the tonic reprise of Episode 1 (**B**²), in other cases (K.459, K.466, K. 488,

K.595), Mozart substantially delays its return until a much later stage in the movement, decoupling its thematic and tonal functions. The return of the tonic key is now associated with the restatement of subsidiary material (the first episode, $\mathbf{B^1}$), the role of the refrain theme becoming confirmatory, in the manner of a coda:

A	Refrain (I)
$\mathbf{B^1}$	Episode 1 (I–V)
A	Refrain (I)
C	Episode 2 (variable key; sometimes relative minor; typically modulating)
$\mathbf{B^2}$	Episode 1 (I) (incorporating tonally and thematically modified retransition)
A	Refrain (I) (typically curtailed, functioning as a coda)

In this design, there are only three statements of the refrain instead of four, and the postponement of the final appearance markedly enhances the sense of culmination towards the end of a movement (indeed, of the work as a whole) since the long-expected return of the opening theme further reinforces its tonic closure. In the finale of K.466, for instance, there is no tonic return of the main theme following the 'developmental' central episode of bars 196–270, roving through A and G minors before re-establishing the tonic, D minor, from bar 240. Instead, from bar 271, Mozart reintroduces the secondary theme-group (first stated at bar 92 foll.) which persists until the cadenza. The main theme does not recur until bar 346, its effect now transformed: it no longer operates within a weighty network of ritornello themes as it had done previously but is radically curtailed, breaking off after just eight bars on a diminished-7th chord, dovetailing with one of the 'secondary group' themes (from bar 139), now translated into the tonic major as a substantial coda culmination.

Joel Galand (Galand 1990) has offered an interpretation of this species of sonata-rondo structure that highlights its similarity to expanded binary form:

$$\mathbf{A \ B^1} \ :\|: \ \mathbf{A} \ ... \ \mathbf{B^2}$$

in which the restatement of **A** in the dominant key (or other related key) after the central double-bar is linked to $\mathbf{B^2}$ (the tonic reprise of subsidiary material from the first section) by connecting tissue of episodic or 'developmental' character. By omitting the restatement of the refrain (**A**) of a sonata rondo prior to the 'recapitulation' of the first episode ($\mathbf{B^2}$), the sequence of refrains and episodes becomes $\mathbf{A \ B^1 \ A \ C \ B^2}$ (coda = **A**). The derivation of sonata form from this binary-form model has long been acknowledged, but the relationship between sonata rondo and binary form, developed at length by Galand, is less obvious, though striking (see Figure 5.1). Viewed in this way, the central episode (**C**) of

(a) Sonata-rondo forms
$$\mathbf{A} \quad \mathbf{B^1} \qquad \mathbf{A} \quad \mathbf{C} \quad \mathbf{B^2} \, (+ \, coda = \mathbf{A})$$
key: I   V   I – I

(b) Binary forms
$$\mathbf{A} \quad \mathbf{B^1} \; :\|: \quad \mathbf{A} \; \text{---} \; \mathbf{B^2}$$
key: I   V   V – I

Figure 5.1 Comparison of sonata–rondo and binary form (following Galand's model)

the sonata rondo is to be equated with the extension (---) that connects **A** and **B²** after the double bar within the binary form. This passage is similar in function and character in each form, typically modulating to a relatively remote point, from which a tonic return is engineered. The most obvious dissimilarity here is the tonic reprise of **A** between **B¹** and **C** of the sonata-rondo scheme, as opposed to the dominant (or other) statement of the opening theme after the central double-bar within a binary form. Galand notes, however, that the binary form itself existed in many subtle variants during the second half of the eighteenth century, and cites examples by Haydn (Galand, 1990, pp.124–8) in which a dominant-key statement after the double-bar is immediately answered by another in the tonic, followed by developmental material linking eventually to a 'recapitulation' of the subsidiary material from the first section (now in the tonic).[6] Galand's claim is that 'Mozart's binary rondos are not pieces in which the third return of the refrain has been removed from a normative [**ABACABA**] sonata-rondo, as is often contended. Mozart is not abbreviating a rondo form, he is expanding a binary structure.'

Comparison of Mozart's finales against the 'standard' template of sonata-rondo form reveals an appealing variety of approaches. An especially inventive case is the rondo finale of K.449 in E flat. Within its opening refrain are two principal themes: the first stated in combination with a legato counter-theme which further highlights the angularity of the first violin line; and the second over a dominant pedal in the viola; the refrain ends with a return to the character (and something of the shape) of the main crotchet theme of bar 1, closing firmly in the tonic. From this point, the solo takes up the main theme (repeated in embellished form at bar 40) and proceeding to the dominant, from which point Episode 1 begins (bar 63), not, however, with a new theme, but with the second refrain theme, continuing in striking new textures (involving hand-crossing from bar 71) and interrupted by a dominant-key appearance of the movement's main crotchet theme, in a quasi-fugato texture, at bar 90. This turns out to be only a punctuation within Episode 1, which continues with virtuoso writing, a new syncopated idea (bar 118) and an extended dominant pedal, leading back to the true refrain at bar 136 (in which, as at bar 40 foll., the right hand of the piano part sounds an embellishment of the theme simulta-neously with its 'plain' form in the violins). This, as is often the case in

Mozart's rondos, is a curtailed statement, in which only the main theme (and not the secondary material from bar 16) is reprised. The intrusion of main theme into Episode 1 is unusual in Mozart's practice: normally any episodic references to the main theme occur within the central episode, which sometimes serves a developmental function, analogous to that section of a sonata-form movement). In K.449, the central episode first introduces a new theme in the relative minor, soon followed (bar 165) by the main theme, once again stated as a quasi-fugato, but this time continuing, to the contrasting accompaniment of quaver figuration in the piano part, until bar 190, from which point there is a long preparation for the next refrain (bar 218). This is followed not by the expected tonic statement of Episode 1, but by the opening of Episode 2 (in the tonic), and only slightly later (bar 246) by the syncopated theme from bar 118. Nor is the key-scheme straightforward. The syncopated theme continues into remote chromatic territory (D flat minor at bar 258), before side-stepping chromatically to a fermata on the dominant, B flat, at bar 268. From here to the end of the movement is a final restatement of the refrain, now incorporating both its principal themes, in $\frac{6}{8}$, closing with dialogue between the solo and tutti. All in all, K.449's finale is one of Mozart's most original applications of the sonata rondo structure, in which the expected *separation* of thematic and textural function between refrains and episodes is replaced with deliberate thematic *integration* (in an unpredictable sequence), and an engaging combination of dance-like and contrapuntal idioms.

All three of the earliest Viennese concertos, K.413–15, contain sonata-rondo finales, but in each case the structure is significantly different. In K.413, the recapitulation of Episode 1 (originally in the dominant, C) occurs in the unusual key of F minor. The finale of K.414 is notable for its thematic multiplicity – a point highlighted by the absence of the main theme throughout much of its length. While it is reprised after the first episode (bar 91), it is not heard again until after the cadenza (at bar 197), and then only after the reprise of the theme with which the soloist originally entered at bar 21. In the finale of K.415 the opening refrain is punctuated by a highly expressive $\frac{2}{4}$ arioso section, Adagio, in the tonic minor, hinting at an emotional world far removed from the previous, rather perfunctory material. From bar 64 there is a return to the opening theme, and the refrain achieves its tonic closure at bar 72. Episode 1 is largely based on a secondary theme from the refrain (from bar 30), leading, *via* a cadenza, to a restatement of the main theme at bar 123, and a tightly worked central episode (bars 139–80), based almost entirely on this theme, which is subjected to development by fragmentation of its opening phrase, presented in dialogue between upper and lower strings. Subsequently the material of Episode 1 is substantially modified. Its opening is omitted, replaced by a quotation at bar 180 of the music of bars 18 foll. from the refrain, and a brief flatwards modulation, before continuing at bar 192 with a modified version of the material from bars 101 foll. of the first episode. This passage breaks off at bar 215, heralding a return to the C minor Adagio (now with additional embellishment in the right-hand line and a *pizzicato* accompaniment from the strings) and a final modification of the opening theme, ending *pianissimo*.

The interruption of rondo finales by sections in a different time-signature, tempo and sometimes mode is not unique to this work. Both the E flat concertos K.271 and K.482 incorporate such sections as middle episodes.[7] Mozart's intention was doubtless to heighten the degree of contrast that an episodic rondo structure could contain, but may also have been influenced by a sophisticated awareness of the rhetorical function of interruption. The sheer surprise of the onset of material which, in the case of K.482, appears at first to be a separate slow movement creates a degree of uncertainty, perhaps even temporary anxiety as regards a movement's continuity, creating, in its turn, a tension whose release greatly enhances the structural effect of the inevitable thematic (and especially tonal) reprise. K.482's Andante cantabile (beginning at bar 218 of the finale) stands apart from the surrounding material not merely by virtue of its slower tempo, its time-signature, its key (A flat) and its new thematic material, but principally by virtue of its soloistic woodwind writing, alternating in dialogue with the solo piano and string accompaniment and consequently creating the episode's internal form.

Several aspects of the sonata-rondo design merit more detailed consideration. These are the design of the refrain (the nature of its material and treatment); the design of Episode 1 (number of themes; degree of contrast with refrain and tonal plan); the design of the central episode (in particular, its relation to the themes of the refrain); and strategies for the retransition and concluding refrain.

Refrain design

One of the few detailed observations made by Koch in his description of rondo design in concerto finales is that 'it is more usual that the solo part performs the rondo theme first, before it is repeated as a ritornello by the orchestra' (Baker, 1983, p.172, note 50).[8] In general terms, this description equates to Mozart's preferred strategy, which was to alternate solo and tutti in the opening section. In K.537 the solo and tutti alternate symmetrically with harmonically rounded-off phrases in the pattern **a a b b**, but Mozart's more usual practice is to follow the soloist's opening statement with a more extended tutti, sometimes of considerable length, and involving variety of texture and scoring, as in bars 9–61 of the finale of K.488, which contains, in addition to the repeat of the main theme, several extra ideas and introduces elements of counterpoint at bars 16–17 and 32 (the latter showing invertibility), and antiphony of string and wind choruses at bars 16–32, which amounts to a middle section within the ritornello component of the refrain. While Koch's model opening of solo answered by tutti accounts for most of Mozart's concerto finales (K.466, K.488 and K.595, for instance), it is by no means the standard pattern. In the finales of K.365 for two pianos, K.413, K.414, K.449, K.467 and K.503 the tutti begins, normally with quite an extended ritornello, following which the solo normally introduces the contrasting material of Episode 1 (though in K.467 it repeats the opening theme). Moreover, there are significant variants on the solo–tutti pattern, as in K.459, in which each phrase of the opening theme is stated first by the soloist, and answered by the tutti, before the more extended tutti continuation and K.451 (discussed above), in which the tutti states a rounded binary-form period before the entry of the piano. The finale of K.595 begins according to Koch's model, but the tutti simply repeats the opening phrase before the soloist re-enters with a contrasting theme on the dominant.

In those concertos beginning with a solo statement, the phraseology is frequently straightforward, as in K.482 and K.488, each featuring an eight-bar theme (4 + 4), answered immediately by the tutti. The other main type of opening (tutti) normally involves a ritornello comprising two or more themes, as in K.467. K.503's opening ritornello offers a particularly majestic design which migrates through three sharply contrasted idioms (contredanse, march, and quasi-fugal counterpoint – the latter touching on the minor mode in a fore-taste of the tonal digressions of the finale's central episode) before ending with a fanfare-like tonic close. The contrast of this highly sophisticated ritornello with the opening of the earlier C major concerto, K.246, examined at the beginning of this section, could hardly be more pronounced. In K.482, the ritornello follows an overall ternary (A–B–A) pattern within which the solo entry at bars 34–41 is a quasi-episode, giving way to a reprise of the main idea at bar 34 (the 'true' first episode follows at bar 51).

A recurring characteristic of Mozart's refrains is the clear segmentation of closing material. Sometimes this is distinguished by a sudden and decisive change of texture, as in K.466; elsewhere it is separated from the opening material by an intervening passage (as in K.459, in which the opening solo–tutti alternation develops into a fugal continuation before closing cadential gestures arrive). In taking such an approach, Mozart was importing a feature more familiar from the ritornello design of his concerto first movements (themselves possibly informed by sonata-form expositions in which segmentation of discrete functional areas aided coherence). Such similarity of procedures argu-ably strengthens Joel Galand's contention that rondo and concerto first-move-ment form are not so much different forms as different ways of representing the underlying 'extended binary' form to which both are fused.

Episode 1

The principal function of this element of the rondo structure is to create contrast with the refrain. Often there are two striking themes, as in the first episode of K.466's finale, which opens with a new idea in D minor (bar 63) and modulates sequentially to F minor (bar 92), at which point a second contrasting theme is introduced.[9] The first episode of K.467 is likewise poly-thematic, incorporating new material at bars 58, 82 (based on the main theme), 110 and 154.[10]

In addition to its role as a provider of thematic contrast, Episode 1 carries the important function of modulating out of the main key. Immediately following the new theme, therefore, is a transitional passage in which Mozart normally shifts to the dominant of the dominant, as in K.467 (achieving D major at bar 108, as a preparation for the secondary woodwind theme in G). The same tonal scheme appears in the first episode of K.503 (bars 32–113), modulating from C to D (bar 66), followed by an extended pedal D, heralding the arrival of the secondary theme in G at bar 75. Within these segmented episodes there is a precise co-ordination between tonal and thematic events. The modulation to the dominant of the dominant is frequently a long one, moving within a fairly slow and uniform harmonic rhythm supporting brilliant passagework in the piano part but carefully avoiding too clear a thematic focus so that, once the dominant has been properly established, there is every justification for a new theme. While Mozart's episodes may appear to present a bewildering variety of themes, these are deliberately 'timed' to actively assist the progression of the rondo structure. In Episode 1 of K.482, for instance, there are several subsections, each characterised by its own theme or texture and each contrib-uting to the shift from E flat to B flat:

- bars 51–72 featuring woodwind solos (no piano);
- bars 73–127, new theme, stated by piano, dissolving in brilliant figuration, and modulating to F at bars 105–6 from which point F acts as a preparation for the dominant, B flat (bar 128); note that the strategic moments in this long modulation (for instance, the B flat pedal at bar 99 and the arrival on F at bar 106) are both marked by entries of the woodwind;
- secondary theme in the dominant, B flat (bar 128 – solo, repeated by wind with piano accompaniment from bar 136);
- second 'brilliant' passage (now with string accompaniment), introducing chromaticism from bar 157 and leading to a 'home' dominant preparation (on B flat) for the return of the main refrain theme at bar 182 in E flat.

The central episode

Two basic types are found: those in which there is actual development of earlier material (principally from the refrain), and 'free' episodes, introducing further new material. Clearly, 'developmental' types (such as K.466 and K.595 – which ranges widely through remote keys) need not wholly eschew new material and, as a foil to detailed workings-out of one or more principal themes, Mozart always presents contrasting material, frequently giving the soloist brilliant passagework as a background to the main motivic work. Brilliant passagework is common to central episodes of all the concerto finales, some of the most spectacular being found in K.450, K.451 and K.456.

The most frequently found key for the central episode is the relative minor, although there are alternatives: the subdominant in K.450 and K.482 and, unusually, the flat supertonic, notated as B minor in the B flat concerto, K.456, beginning at bar 171 and approached by means of an enharmonic reinterpretation of a dominant-7th chord, G–B–D–F, within C minor as an augmented-6th chord resolving in the bass to F sharp (bars 165–7).[11] Typically the central episode migrates to at least one other related key during its course (frequently by means of sequential motion).

An example of the 'developmental' type is the central episode of K.467's finale. It begins with a developmental link built from the cadential theme originally sounded in the tutti at bar 34 foll., which recurs at bar 219 (following a refrain restatement) and continues into A major *via* a couple of deflected cadences. Most of the rest of this episode is dominated by statements of the main theme, featuring dialogue between the solo and the woodwind. Fragmentation of the grace-note termination follows at bar 266 (in A minor) and this suffix pattern is reconstructed as a motivic prefix in the next phrase (over quaver chords), modulating to F (bar 277), a significant moment in the episode's tonal progress that is co-ordinated with yet another stage in the development of the main theme. From this point, its chromatic prefix is singled out recalling a similar treatment found earlier at the end of the opening refrain (at bar 41 foll.). However, whereas at that point the fragmented chromatics appeared in close stretto within the higher woodwind, in this episodic reformulation it supports a more leisurely modulating dialogue between the piano's left hand and the wind. At bar 289 the motive is reduced to just its last four quavers, and becomes grounded on the dominant (G), preparing for the return of the main theme at bar 314 (quietly ushered in by a transposition of bars 233 foll.). While virtuosity is an important feature here (especially following the move to F major), the episode's principal characteristic is motivic: almost every bar of this central episode is derived from the material of the refrain and is as tersely constructed as many a first-movement sonata form, revealing previously unexplored aspects of the main themes.

At the opposite extreme is the central episode of K.488, which makes no reference to previous ritornello material. Instead, it introduces two important new themes, in F sharp minor (bar 230) and D major (bar 264). The first is organised as an **A–B–A–B** structure, with statements of the principal descending scale in the solo part at bars 230 and 246 (A) alternating with a contrasting legato wind chorus. The 16-bar D major theme, constituting the second section of this episode, brings the solo and tutti into closer thematic relationship. Its binary structure is **A, A'**; **B, B'**, in which A is the first half, ending on the temporary dominant (here, A major), and **B** is the second half, regaining the temporary tonic (D major). Each half of the theme is begun by the wind (accompanied by the solo) and repeated, embellished, by the soloist (accompanied by the strings). The continuation, from bar 293, leads to an enhanced dominant preparation for the expected return of the refrain in A major, but, in fact, what follows, at bar 312, is a recapitulation of Episode 1. Mozart delays the return of the main theme until bar 441, where it is extended as a coda, featuring also a return of the central episode's D major theme (now over a tonic pedal from bar 480).

A central episode whose organisation falls mid-way between these two extremes is that in the finale of the B flat concerto, K.450. It begins with new material in the subdominant, E flat (bar 141), featuring hand-crossing in widely separated registers of the keyboard in a vigorous sextuplet texture with fleeting support from the strings. At bar 168, however, Mozart reintroduces the main theme (still in E flat) in the oboe, alternating with the right hand of the solo part; transfers it to the bass (bar 180); inverts the texture, setting it against running semiquavers (bar 186); returns to the oboe–piano dialogue (bar 200 foll.); and finally fragments the thematic suffix (bars 205–9) before closing into the recapitulation of the main theme at bar 210. In addition, there is a brief hint of the earlier chromatic scales from bar 76 foll. of Episode 1 (at bars 192–9). Altogether, then, this central episode looks both ways: retaining a strong element of integration with previous thematic specifics, while contributing new elements to the form of the movement as a whole.

The retransition and conclusion

Towards the end of a sonata rondo, tonal adjustments are necessary (as in any sonata-influenced form) in order to resolve the movement convincingly within the 'home' key. This means that, as in a first-movement recapitulation, material in the first episode that had modulated into remote regions is reprised within the tonic frame, preceded by an adjusted transition (the 'retransition') as in K.467, bar 333 foll.

Mozart's strategies for the recasting of the first episode's original transition out of the 'home' key are varied indeed (Galand, 1990, pp.273, 292, 294, 299–302). In K.466 and K.537 the solo theme that originally opened the first episode is substantially extended in a quasi-developmental manner, replacing the earlier transition so as to confirm the tonic key. The finale of K.414 achieves something similar. Following the refrain (bars 87–107) Mozart sets a linking episode in the subdominant, beginning at bar 108, this time leading not to a restatement of the first episode's theme (originally bar 21), but directly to the transitional material; the solo theme that originally opened the first episode is here postponed until after the cadenza (bar 182). The finale of K.595 offers a different solution to the retransition, reprising the refrain's main theme in the subdominant (bar 182), continuing at bar 188 with antiphonally situated thematic developments of the main theme's consequent phrase (bar 186), predominantly in the minor mode, and eventually settling on a dominant (F) pedal before the return in the tonic of the first episode's principal theme (bar 204). The extension beyond this point is once more to F (bar 217; cf. bar 78); but this time F is treated as V/B flat, rather than a new key, confirming instead the tonic, B flat. In the finale of K.459 the original opening theme of the first episode is omitted altogether. Beginning at bar 289, Mozart recasts part of the opening refrain (which had included a protracted fugato commencing at bar 32), the beginning of the first episode and the transitional material (lasting until bar 165) as an extended secondary development section, founded primarily on the fugato theme, but incorporating also fragmented references to the movement's opening theme. In K.488 Mozart combines modal opposition with antiphony and a reworking of the original order in which the episodic material occurred. Following the soloist's restatement of the main theme of the first episode at bar 312, the upper winds answer it in the tonic minor, limiting the tonal orbit, before turning in bar 330 to a presentation in the tonic major of the secondary theme originally sounded at bar 106 of the first episode (omitting any reference to the previously intervening material of bars 77–105). This too is repeated in the opposite (minor) mode by the soloist (bar 338), developing in the continuation the rising diminished-5th figure of bar 343 over a chromatically inflected bass line eventually arriving at a dominant (E) pedal in bar 359, before launching (bar 363) into a tonic reprise of the arpeggiated passagework of bar 151. In the finale of the B flat concerto, K.456, Mozart experiments with the potential of a remote tonal region to function as a strong harbinger of tonic return. At bars 171–209 he inserts a passage in the flat supertonic key (notated in B minor, but properly in C flat minor) between the refrain and the reprise of the first episode, pitting thematic work in the winds against virtuoso arpeggiations in the solo piano. Thematically it is based on the stepwise ascending 5ths figure from the last two bars of the preceding refrain (bars 145–62). From the tonal point of view, the flat supertonic is initially tonicised by virtue of a stepwise ascending bass progression between B and its dominant relation, F sharp (bars 171–9, repeated in embellished form by the soloist in bars 179–87), and subsequently (bars 187–95) conducted *via* rapid sequential movement through E minor and D minor, to the 'home' dominant, F (bar 195), approached *via* its upper neighbour, G flat, and the 'home' supertonic, C. The reprise of the theme that had originally opened the first episode arrives at bar 209 (from which point it serves as the retransition, confirming the tonic, B flat).

Following the recapitulation of all the relevant secondary material within the frame of the tonic, the final statement of the refrain, sometimes preceded by a cadenza, combines solo and tutti beyond the initial thematic statement, normally concluding with the same material as had earlier concluded the opening refrain and, as in the first-movement 'ritornello' structure, its long postponement acts as a signal of imminent closure. The concluding refrain typically involves a certain amount of adaptation of either the material or its setting. In K.459, following Mozart's own cadenza (which treats the fugal ritornello theme and the main theme in reverse order) the final refrain reprises the antiphonal texture of the opening 16 bars (now with triplet accompaniment), skipping immediately at bar 470 to the subdominant-coloured ritornello codetta (not heard since bar 98). The original alternations between strings and wind are replaced at the end of the movement by prominent opposition of piano and tutti, initially in eight-bar phrases, but progressively fragmenting – eventually to groups of just four quavers – before the arrival of the final cadence. Variations on this fundamental pattern include the final refrain of K.503. As in K.459, there are textural alterations: the final refrain begins with the solo rather than tutti, replacing the string–woodwind alternation of bars 1–24 with antiphonal division between solo and tutti. But at bars 331–74 there is a substantial interruption of the original ritornello sequence, amounting to a structured insertion between the original bars 1–24 and 24–32 (subdivided bars 331–44; 344–57; 357–74), and introducing solo passagework that becomes increasingly virtuosic as Mozart prepares for the movement's conclusion. At bar 374, the codetta from the original tutti ritornello finally returns (cf. bars 24–32), its climactic effect enhanced by substantial postponement. Restructuring by insertion also characterises the final refrain of K.488 (bars 441–524). This proceeds by close analogy with bars 1–61 (solo statement, followed by tutti ritornello) as far as bar 480, at which point there is a solo interruption, quoting the new theme introduced at bar 175. From bar 496 the reprise returns to the outline of the ritornello. Probably the quotation was felt by Mozart to be necessary for the sake of tonal balance (resolving a prominent episodic theme within the frame of the tonic, A major), an interpretation reinforced by its subtle subdominant weighting. In K.467 only the material of the ritornello's first section is reprised (bars 425 foll., solo first, then solo and tutti combined), capped by a final antiphonal flurry of the original bars 7–8 and closing tonic chords. In K.466 the reprise of the tutti ritornello's codetta precedes the cadenza (bars 337–45). Afterwards, the expected refrain is represented by only a brief reprise of its opening arpeggiated phrase (bars 346–53), dissolving on a diminished-7th chord followed by a substantial D major coda, based on the theme first introduced by the woodwind at bar 139.

Variations

While the previous discussion of rondo and sonata-rondo finales has concentrated mostly on structural features, that is not to diminish the significance within these types of movement of virtuoso display. Passages of bravura display account for prolonged sections of these finales and were clearly a major factor in their appeal to a contemporary audience which delighted in brilliance of effect, especially at the keyboard. Brilliant passagework is likewise a central element of finales in the variation genre, of which there are just two examples: K.453 in G and K.491 in C minor. It is perhaps a little surprising that Mozart wrote only two variation finales among the piano concertos, given the opportunity that this type presented for displaying his prodigious talents not only as a keyboard performer, but also as a skilful inventor of contrasting textures.

Sets of variations, often based on operatic arias, remained a popular 'concert' genre throughout the later eighteenth century and into the nineteenth. Mozart frequently played his own examples for solo piano in public concerts. The ability to invent exciting variations on a theme provided him with an instant entrée to Viennese concert life. At a public concert on 23 March 1783, for example, he improvised on 'Les Hommes pieusement' from Gluck's opera, *La Rencontre imprévue* (in the composer's presence) to loud acclaim. This set subsequently became extraordinarily popular with Viennese audiences – and aspiring keyboard players – under its German title, 'Unser dummer Pöbel meint' (K.455). Mozart's variations were very popular with Viennese publishers. For instance, on 14 September 1785 the important Viennese music dealer, Johann Traeg (1747–1805), announced in the *Wiener Zeitung* that he had good-quality manuscript copies of Mozart's keyboard variations, K.455 (on 'Unser dummer Pöbel meint'), and of K.359 and K.360, on French tunes, for violin and piano, composed probably just about the time of Mozart's move to Vienna in 1781. Typically in these solo sets, the phrase and harmonic structure of the theme is preserved intact but at times the amount of figurative embellishment becomes so prodigious that it is difficult, and sometimes impossible, to detect the original theme. While we may find the quality of embellishment detracts from the overall structural integrity, it is important to bear in mind that it was precisely their ephemeral, 'showy' effect that so appealed to the taste of the Viennese public for which Mozart was writing. Virtuosity takes centre stage in the concerto variations, too. Such dazzling passages as bars 56–64 in the finale of K.491 are possible largely because of the careful choice of theme. In its initial presentation the theme underlying these variations is quite 'plain', proceeding in crotchets and lacking melodic or rhythmic embellishment, though with a distinctive phrasing. It also moves at a slow and steady harmonic pace, highlighting the augmented-6th chord in bar 3. All of these factors leave room for later amplification within the prevailing 8 + 8-bar binary framework by means of exciting scale passages and contrasts of instrumentation and texture. In an important sense, the form of a set of variations is to be appreciated as a goal-directed process in which the original statement is successively paraphrased.[12]

While each individual variation retains a single character, taken together as a whole these deliver an overall expressive range as wide as any rondo finale. Two types of variation are found. In Variation 1 the notated repeat-marks are simply retained as in any straightforward binary form. Thereafter, though, Mozart introduces a series of 'double variations', in which tutti and piano embellish each half of the binary theme alternately. In Variation 2, for instance, the wind alone present a version of its first half which is immediately decorated by the piano (bars 40–48); the second part of the theme is organised in the same way. In Variation 3 the roles are reversed: the piano (alone) leads off, recasting each half of the theme as a march, answered alternately by the tutti. Variation 4 turns to the flat submediant, A flat (though retaining the basic outline of the theme and its phrase-structure), highlighting the woodwind once again in its presentation of the **A** and **B** strains of the theme, to which the piano and strings reply (the right-hand solo part becoming progressively more ornate as the variation unfolds). A further contrast of texture emerges in the next variation which begins with rigorous counterpoint, giving way, at bar 137, to gushing semiquavers – a pattern repeated in the theme's second half (bars 146–64), in which the phrase-structure is extended for the first time, leading to a serenade-like statement by the woodwind in the tonic major, alternating, as in Variation 4, with the piano and strings. At bar 201, Mozart returns to the tonic minor for a particularly virtuosic statement (without the repeats). The final variation begins with an unaccompanied solo statement (once again without repeats, and now translated into $\frac{6}{8}$) and continues with a coda which is basically an extended development of a cadential progression, D flat–C, stated repeatedly by both soloist and wind. In a sense, this coda assumes the character of a development section, in that it works out an implication of the prominent chromatic 6th chord in bar 3 of the theme (now reinterpreted as 'Neapolitan 6th').

Probing a little further beneath the surface, we may observe some ways in which this variation finale operates as a kind of episodic structure. Once the piano has entered, the manner of continuity is predominantly that of bravura display. There are, however, two exceptions to this, Variations 4 (bar 96 foll.) and 6 (bar 164 foll.). In relation to the virtuosity that surrounds them, these relatively calm variations assume something of the status of 'episodes' within the whole structure. For example, Variations 2 and 3 reverse the order of solo–tutti entries within the 'double-variation' pattern and can be seen as a 'pair' of statements. This is followed by a more reflective statement in which subtle instrumental colour and delicate embellishment play important roles. The energetic left-hand figuration in the varied repeats of Variation 5 recalls the left-hand triplets in the march-like Variation 3. The woodwind scoring, embellishment and major mode of Variation 6 refer back to Variation 4. In Variation 7, Mozart returns to the vigorous semiquaver passagework characteristic of Variation 1. All in all, the finale hangs together by means of a sophisticated network of cross-references that embrace as wide an expressive range as any of the rondo finales.

Similar principles of contrast and continuity obtain in the other variation finale, that of the G major concerto, K.453. Once again, it is the construction of the theme and its harmonic basis that determine the nature of the subsequent treatment. In each half of the 8 + 8-bar binary theme, the leisurely harmonic pace of the leading phrase (moving on the bar and half-bar) is followed by a more hectic cadential approach (crotchet chord-changes). Such counter-pointing of different momentums is one factor underlying the humorous character of this movement and is exploited to comic effect at several points, for example, at bars 149–52. Except for the first variation the successive state-ments are of the 'double variation' type. Several contrasting techniques are employed, including melodic decoration (Variation 1), triplet embellishment as a 'moto perpetuo' accompaniment (Variation 2), texture contrast, alter-nating a contrapuntal wind statement and a theme and Alberti-bass response from the piano (Variation 3), a syncopated texture, reminiscent of species counterpoint (in which the piano's syncopations are at the level of the quaver, creating the effect of 'diminution' by comparison with the preceding tutti phrase), and injecting an element of harmonic chromaticism into what has hitherto been a purely diatonic movement, and a final statement pitting virtuoso orchestral high-jinks against the unaccompanied solo, melting into a formulaic cadence on the dominant at bars 169–70.

What follows is a presto coda in comic manner, slightly longer than the preceding theme and variations combined. It bears no relation at first to the theme or its harmonic background, featuring instead elements transplanted from the world of an *opera buffa* finale: driving pedal points and punctuating fanfares, sudden interruptions (bar 221), resumption of hectic activity, expressed in stretto entries over pedal points (bar 233 foll.), yet further inter-ruptions and continual breathless interplay of textures between soloist and tutti, which here assume (metaphorically) the function of *dramatis personae* on the stage. Characterisation is as vivid in this coda as in any operatic finale (for example, the woodwind interjections from bar 224). At bar 248 the main theme finally recurs and remains in view until it dissolves, exhausted, into pieces at the very end.

When this concerto was composed in April 1784, Mozart had not yet made his reputation as the author of *Le nozze de Figaro*, although the language of its last few pages is not far from that of the end of Act II of the opera. Clearly, Mozart was already sensitive to the techniques of the *opera buffa* finale at this stage. But this is a concerto, not an opera, and the appearance of clearly recog-nisable elements of a *buffa* finale at the end of an instrumental concerto amounts to generic transplantation. Why does this work here? Possibly, the answer (or a part of it) lies in its relationship to the construction of the preceding variations. In contrast to those of K.491, the successive variations in

K.453's finale do not link into 'sub-groups' – indeed, there are only four variations – but proceed as an 'open-ended' chain of highly individual statements,
focusing principally on different techniques of melodic elaboration. The first
strong moment of articulation in this succession is the elaborately introduced
dominant fermata at bar 170, which simultaneously implies a break in the
established pattern of self-contained 16-bar binary units and demands a continuation of a rather different order. What follows is a counterbalancing coda in
which the phrase spans finally break free from the previous segmented rigidity,
while retaining something of the characteristic element of colour contrast
(alternating strings with a horn and bassoon fanfare at the opening, for
instance). The structure of the *buffa* section is basically **A–A'–B–B**:[13] a binary
model, identical with that of the theme itself, and which doubtless plays a part
in making this coda hang together with the preceding variation-chain. But its
grand sweeps operate across a much broader range than the 8 + 8-bar pattern
of the theme (**A** = bars 171–93; **B** = bars 222–72 – each followed by a varied
reprise). All in all, the *opera buffa* gestures provide a satisfying stylistic and
structural complement to the earlier variations and a fitting conclusion to one
of Mozart's most genial movements.

Notes

1. Koch's comment that the finale 'may take the form of the first allegro' is ambiguous. While he appears to be describing the full-blown ritornello design of
   first-movement concerto Allegros, it is possible that he simply means that the
   usual episodic rondo form of a finale is sometimes influenced by the tonal design
   of the first movements, since he immediately goes on to contrast this type with the
   'ordinary rondo', whose tonal design is freer. In such a case, he would presumably be referring to what we recognise as 'sonata-rondo' form.
2. The most extensive treatment of Mozart's rondo procedures is undoubtedly
   Galand 1990, to which the present chapter is partially indebted.
3. Other examples: K.246, K.271, K.415, K.466, K.537, K.595.
4. And, in the case of a simple solo opening, starting with a restatement of the main
   theme.
5. For a summary of nineteenth-century theories of the sonata rondo, see Cole 1969.
6. This sequence of events is one example among several that became popularly
   known as the 'false recapitulation', and was associated particularly with Haydn.
7. The device is found also in Mozart's violin concertos, for instance, the G major,
   K.216.
8. Koch regards the ritornello as the tutti section following the opening solo statement; it is a separate component within the refrain – one from which only selected
   elements are reprised later on – and not to be confused with the refrain itself (that
   is, the entire opening section before Episode 1).
9. At bar 73 foll., Mozart briefly recapitulates the main theme of the finale – an
   unusual procedure within the first episode (although it is encountered also in the
   corresponding section of K.467). Philip Radcliffe believes that this section is still
   part of the opening refrain, for he states that the D minor theme at bar 63 'is soon

brushed aside by the main theme, which leads to what proves to be the first episode in a sonata rondo. It has two contrasting elements, an agitated theme in F minor, and a very gay one in F major' (Radcliffe, 1978, p.50). Alternatively, the full tonic closure at bar 62 could be felt to mark the end of this refrain, the first episode commencing with the solo theme in the following bar, and the quotation of the main theme being an 'insertion' within this episode. Whatever the interpretation, this episode is certainly generous in its presentation and subsequent use of new material, for the F major theme at bar 139 recurs in the recapitulation (bar 302) and is the main inspiration for the coda (in D major).

10. Other examples: K.450, K.482, K.488, K.503 and K.595, which reintroduces the main theme in the dominant minor at bar 94 as part of the preparation for the new key.

11. Also unusual is the retention of two time-signatures, simple and compound duple, simultaneously from bar 179. The finale of the oboe quartet, K.370, provides another instance of two simultaneous time-signatures.

12. The linguistic metaphor is deliberate. Insofar as each successive variation of an 'original' statement is a refinement of it, an adjustment of its form, the variation set functions analogously to one of the elements of oratory, the *trope*. As will be explained further in Chapter Six below, rhetorical models for the understanding of music were widely acknowledged in eighteenth-century theory. A *trope* belongs within the rhetorical category of *elocutio* (best understood as denoting the stylistic refinement of a speech or a piece of prose). Each variation in a set of variations is a *trope* of the original statement of the theme. Further on rhetorical models for variations, see Elaine Sisman, 1993 *passim* and Irving, 1997, pp.135–41. For a recent rhetorical interpretation of variations in Mozart's piano concertos, see Sisman, 1996.

13. **B** incorporates the reprise of the main theme; **B'** varies the reprise, introducing subdominant colouring towards the end of the movement, along with some novel reformulations of the main theme itself.

CHAPTER SIX

The Listener's Perspective

I: Ways of listening: 'kenner' and 'nichtkenner'

On 28 December 1782, Mozart wrote to his father about the progress of his 'freelance' existence in Vienna, incidentally mentioning his work on three new piano concertos, K.413–15:

> There are still two concertos wanting to make up the series of subscription concertos. These concertos are a happy medium between what is too easy and too difficult; they are very brilliant, pleasing to the ear and natural, without being vapid. There are passages here and there from which connoisseurs alone will derive satisfaction; but these passages are written in such a way that the less learned cannot fail to be pleased, though without knowing why.[1]

This is surely one of Mozart's most famous statements about his own music. He seems to be distinguishing between two different *ways of listening* – to both of which his three new piano concertos, K.413, 414 and 415, issued publicly by subscription early in 1783, were simultaneously addressed. On the one hand, there is the way of listening identified with the 'kenner' (connoisseurs); on the other, there is an alternative way of listening identified with the 'nichtkenner' (the less learned). On one level, Mozart's comments suggest an overt élitism, distinguishing an exclusive class of sophisticated listeners ('kenner allein') who could follow his musical argument, from another whose receptive powers were merely passive ('nichtkenner damit zufrieden seyn müssen, ohne zu wissen warum'). He is defining a cultural hierarchy within which his new concertos were situated.[2]

What might the characterising features of 'kenner' and 'nichtkenner' have been? The former were surely listeners possessed of a capacity for understanding the inner technical functions of music which included such aspects as periodic phrasing, harmonic and tonal design, modulation schemes, formal strategies, motivic development and so on. Among the 'connoisseurs' to which Mozart's three concertos, K.413–15, were addressed were those members of the Viennese aristocracy educated in musical matters through the study of treatises such as Johann Friedrich Daube's *Der Musikalische Dilettant; eine Abhandlung der Komposition* (Daube, 1771; Snook-Luther, 1992) – a textbook specifically designed to provide amateurs with a detailed acquaintance of the elements of *galant* musical styles. Specific matters that Daube highlights in his treatise that may be interpreted as 'filters' through which the increasingly complex chamber and orchestral music of the later eighteenth century might be mediated and made accessible to the 'dilettante' listener include:

- a reductive harmonic system somewhat similar to that of Rameau (but independently derived; see Snook-Luther, 1992, pp.9–10) in which all the chords in a composition can be understood in relation to the controlling tonic, dominant and subdominant triads
- a melodic system that related ornamental passagework (for instance, flurries of semiquavers in the 'brilliant' style) to controlling pitches extracted from the three controlling triads (and typically arriving on stressed beats of the bar) by means of a clear distinction between 'harmony notes' and 'non-harmony notes' (passing-notes and so forth)
- a clear description of three characteristic styles of music (church, chamber and theatre) and their affective qualities (including prominent attention to texture and orchestration)
- an equation of 'beauty' with symmetry, especially as expressed through phrase structure

Armed with such an interpretive background, the amateur concert-goer in late-eighteenth-century Vienna could conceivably have made a good deal of sense out of, say, the first movement of Mozart's A major concerto, K.414, appreciating the functional inter-relationships of its chord progressions; its reliance on melodic passing notes (in bars 5–8, for instance, which could be conceived of as an 'answering phrase' to the opening, balancing not only in length, but by complementing the overtly triadic melodic flow of bars 1–4 with stepwise motion introducing some 'non-harmony' notes resolving against the harmonies beneath, and later some quaver passing notes); and, following a repeat of the opening theme, a sudden textural shift from the prevailing 'cantabile style' to 'brilliant style', featuring rushing semiquavers in the first violins (similar, in fact, to an example in A major in Daube's treatise (Snook-Luther, 1992, pp.95–6)).

In addition to these matters, the chapters of Daube's treatise cover simple chordal harmony, part-writing, descanting over a bass, counterpoint in two, three and four parts, variation, imitation and canon and various fugal practices, all copiously illustrated with musical examples. 'Kenner' educated in such a way were conditioned to appreciate Mozart's concertos according to recognisable *codes* that could be learnt and applied. The 'kenner' derives pleasure in the discovery of a 'fit' between Mozart's concertos (or, at least, in 'certain passages') and a book-learned exemplar enshrining contemporary pedagogy. Contrasting with this 'way of listening' is the 'unknowing' response of the 'nichtkenner' who enjoys 'certain passages' in Mozart's concertos 'without knowing why'. In place of a 'technically literate' response is one of a different kind, aesthetic rather than analytic, more a reaction to events on the musical surface than to intricate relations of parts and wholes.

An example may help to sharpen this distinction. Among the features that would engage the attention of a 'kenner' listening to the first movement of

K.415 is the design of the first solo relative to the preceding tutti. Rather than simply replicate the earlier sequence of thematic events, Mozart introduces a new theme for the soloist at bar 93 (preceded by a transitional modulation to the dominant region). Its continuation from bar 108 includes a quotation of the material of bar 32 foll. newly adapted to an exciting virtuosic texture incorporating a strand of continuous semiquavers (bar 112 foll.). Towards the end of the solo section is a greatly extended version of the tutti's earlier cadence approach at bars 52–7 (cf. bars 133–48). The 'kenner' would have appreciated the important role of chromatic harmony underpinning this extension, especially in relation to the predominantly diatonic character of the music up to this point. He may also have noted an interesting constructional feature of the tutti's continuation from bar 148. Here, Mozart reprises the movement's opening theme, leading eventually to a reaffirmation at bars 157–9 (in the dominant) of the cadence from bars 57–9. His quotation of the main theme at this point is quite unusual, however, for it is neither the end of this section nor the beginning of the next, but a strategic interruption inserted between the two stages that formerly made up the closing cadence of the first tutti, *viz.*:

first tutti, closing cadence: (i) bars 52–7; (ii) bars 57–9
first solo, closing cadence: (i) bars 133–48; [main theme insert] ; (ii) bars 157–9

Seen in relation to the opening tutti, the first solo is a thorough-going recomposition of its thematic and tonal premisses, in part referring to it, in part reacting against it, resituating even its most important aspects in novel environments. In contrast to such constructional subtleties is a 'popular' dimension open to the 'nichtkenner', including the march-like character of opening theme, the exciting orchestral colours, the sheer element of display in the solo part, exploring a broad spectrum of keyboard textures and registers and, not least, the 'catchy' rhythmic syncopations that come to the fore in the closing cadential sections.

Mozart's identification of different categories of listener, and specifically his suggestion that he sought in his music to accommodate both 'kenner' and 'nichtkenner', invites us to examine the different technical and stylistic perspectives from which such contemporary listeners may have appreciated his piano concertos. This ground is explored in the first part of this chapter, following which attention is turned to some of the broader intellectual and philosophical environments within which his concertos were situated.

'Kenner'

The difficulty of Mozart's music, and the capability of an audience to deal with its demands, were interestingly treated by Adolph von Knigge in the

Dramaturgische Blätter (Hanover, 1788) in relation to *Die Entführung aus dem Serail*, a work contemporary with Mozart's first Viennese piano concertos:

> The knowledgeable [that is, those with some formal musical training] feel the worth of these [intricately scored and harmonically complex] passages, but for popular utterance they are of no use. The same occurs with the pile of modulations and numerous enharmonic movements ... partly because the resolutions alternate too quickly with the discords, so that only a skilled ear can pursue the harmonic process (Robbins Landon, 1991, p.387 – translation slightly adapted).

It is interesting that this reviewer should remark that only those with a formal musical training could adequately follow Mozart's harmonies. He does not speculate on the effect that Mozart's music might have had on the rest of an audience, but his comment implies that the audience was composed of patrons of mixed musical abilities, relatively more or less musically literate. Plainly, doubts about various of Mozart's more recherché passages had been raised – why, otherwise, would the issue of accessibility have been addressed? One strand of contemporary critical opinion evidently felt that Mozart's music was 'élitist' because it did not fall into straightforward keyboard patterns and predictable phrase lengths. A couple of examples readily suggest themselves. First, the very opening of the C minor concerto, K.491: *piano*, unison, featuring a questioning diminished-7th interval as a suffix, which is instantly separated off and sequentially repeated a step lower, thus obscuring, rather than clarifying, the tonality at the outset. This is hardly conventional harmonic usage, added to which the irregular, asymmetrical phrasing confounds expectation still further. Perhaps Knigge was right, and 'only a skilled ear can pursue the harmonic process'. Secondly, the B flat concerto, K.595: the first-movement development section swerves into the remote territory of B minor (enharmonically, C flat) for a statement of the main theme by the soloist, followed by dislocated fragments of the dotted answering phrase in the orchestra (adapted here to diminished-7th harmonies) and some connecting tissue leading to a restatement of the whole pattern in C. The subsequent harmonic progressions, although largely periodic in scan, and at times tending towards circle-of-fifths motion, is actually rather difficult to follow. Within the development as a whole, E flat is quite a significant key-area: it initiates the woodwind dialogue based on the main theme's triadic prefix (turning to the minor at bar 207), and later coincides with the diversion to G minor at bar 217 (supported by arpeggiaic piano figuration), following the section elaborating the main theme's dotted suffix. In the long term, E flat's function is perhaps as an upper-neighbour tone to D, from which, beginning at bar 231, Mozart slips chromatically back into the reprise. While the texture (foreground piano figuration supporting motivic woodwind dialogue) is familiar in Mozart's concerto developments, this particular tonal grounding is less so.

Pre-eminent among the compositional techniques appreciated by Viennese connoisseurs was counterpoint. Counterpoint was the mode of musical discourse associated with sacred vocal music, the genre which occupied the highest position within the eighteenth-century scale of cultural values. Mastery of this craft was essential for any composer operating within the prevailing system of ecclesiastical and court patronage. Fugal composition was a keen interest of one of Mozart's staunchest Viennese patrons, Gottfried van Swieten. On 10 April 1782 Mozart explained to his father that 'I go every Sunday at twelve to the Baron van Swieten, where nothing is played but Handel and Bach. I am collecting at the moment the fugues of Bach – not only of Sebastian, but also of [Carl Philipp] Emmanuel and [Wilhelm] Friedemann. I am also collecting Handel's.' Van Swieten owned a substantial collection of music by Bach and Handel, including many fugal pieces, and Mozart recounted to his sister on 20 April 1782 that he had been allowed to borrow some of van Swieten's copies for study purposes: 'When Constanze heard the fugues, she fell in love with them. Now she will listen to nothing but fugues, and particularly (in this kind of composition) the works of Handel and Bach.' Counterpoint was clearly a style of composition highly favoured among 'connoisseurs', such as van Swieten, who had studied composition with Johann Philipp Kirnberger in Berlin during his tenure as special ambassador to the Prussian court between 1770 and 1777. Mozart lost no opportunity to exploit this fact in the design of his concerto movements. While the melodically driven *galant* idiom is dominant, producing an elegant ebb and flow of symmetrically balanced phrases articulated by clear cadences, the texture is not infrequently shot through with thematic inter-connections between the parts. In the finale of K.414 this manifests itself as a light dialogue between the piano and the violins in the D major episode beginning at bar 108; somewhat more pointed is the relation between the violins at bars 106–14 in the finale of K.413. Among the most thoroughly integrated textures in these concertos are those found in the opening Allegro of K.415, whose tutti exposition sets the contrapuntal tone from its very first phrase, second violins imitating the firsts at two bars' distance at the unison. Canon infiltrates the solo part at times, too, for example at the beginning of the development (bar 160 foll.). Nevertheless, it is clear that such contrapuntal procedures are situated within a broader frame of periodicity, and not *vice versa*. While the inclusion of fugal textures may have been perceived as allusions to the compositional practices of a previous era, they remain no more than that; their function is to provide an enhanced degree of cross-reference among the polyphonic strands within the apparently simple theme-and-accompaniment textures of contemporary classicism – a means to an end, not an end in itself.

This fusion of periodicity and counterpoint is a recurring feature of Mozart's later concertos. A superb example is the finale of K.459 in F (December 1784). Beginning as a straightforward contredanse, enlivened from time to time by engaging syncopations and featuring frequent echo effects between solo and tutti, the dance idiom gives way to extended fugato passages at bars 32–65 and 288–352, latterly with the fugato theme as a counterpoint to virtuoso semi-quaver figuration compassing much of the keyboard – a texture recurring at bar 416 foll. In this finale, counterpoint carries a structural responsibility: in its topical contrast to the regular periodicity of the surrounding contredanse, it defines the form. A somewhat different approach, in which counterpoint is rather more closely dovetailed into its surroundings, is found in K.503 in C major (December 1786). In the first movement, the opening tutti exposition includes a rigorously organised passage (bars 18–44) featuring a highly charged quaver motive that is at first imitated between the violins before receding into the background somewhat, as a countertheme to the rushing scale patterns that infuse the ensuing transition to the secondary theme in the dominant (itself rhythmically influenced by the preceding material). In this case, counterpoint is an increasingly vital element in a progression through different topics, from march (bar 1), to learned style (bar 18), to brilliant style (bar 26).

Counterpoint is considered in just about every music theory text of the period. Austro-German music theory had reached a high point in the eighteenth century. It plays a substantial part in the textbooks of, for instance, Heinichen, Fux, Mattheson, Riepel, Kirnberger, Daube, Forkel and Koch.[3] Among the pages of these works are considerations of two-part, three-part and four-part counterpoint; composition in five and more parts (including contrapuntal rela-tion of the voices); imitation, canon, invertible counterpoint and fugue. In an age in which counterpoint was largely replaced by elegant melody and accom-paniment as a key element of musical style, the continued concentration on counterpoint within theoretical texts is surprising. Relatively few texts deal at length with the element that made perhaps the most immediate and long-lasting impact on the contemporary listener, namely melody.[4]

For many eighteenth-century theorists, melody was a crucial element in the conception of musical form, but one that was of primarily local significance, influencing the immediate continuity of the structure, rather than creating its large-scale coherence. From the listener's point of view, appreciating this localised continuity meant understanding the ways in which melodies were constructed. Several of the treatises on melody (those by Riepel, Kirnberger and Koch) explain these procedures in great detail. The methods that they outline provide possible points of contact between Mozart and his audience, channels of melodic communication through which he sought to 'speak' to his listeners. What Riepel, Kirnberger and Koch have in common in their respec-tive treatments of melody is the concept of subdivision. Various punctuation points are possible within classical themes and these are achieved by melodic and harmonic points of termination, in addition to rhythmic profile. Koch, whose writings are roughly contemporary with the final decade of Mozart's creative life, classifies in bewildering detail the organisation of melodies into phrases and periods of varying length. His theory builds upon that of Riepel (whose pioneering work in melodic analysis Koch praises) in that the basic unit considered is the four-bar phrase, from which Koch rigorously pursues the possible linkages, large and small, both internal and external. Symmetrical patterns of continuity are fundamental to his scheme and provide a general vantage point from which the melodic art of the classical period could be judged by an audience.[5]

Johann Philipp Kirnberger's *Die Kunst des reinen Satzes in der Musik* (Kirnberger, 1771–79) explains how periodisation of melodies is defined by harmonic cadences:

> Chords are in music what words are in language. Just as a sentence in each consists of several words that belong together and express a complete idea, so a harmonic sentence or period consists of several chords that are connected and end with a close [cadence]. And just as a succession of many sentences constitutes an entire speech, a composition consists of a succession of many periods (Thym and Beach, 1982, p.109).

Within this periodic scheme, two or more bars can be felt as a component of a (normally four-bar) phrase; together these components exhibit a higher-level rhythm – the phrase 'breathes'; two or more phrases can be felt as a sentence, which 'breathes' on a still higher level; two or more sentences can be felt as a paragraph, 'breathing' on a still higher level; and so on. The internal divisions of phrases are analogous to different levels of punctuation in written (or spoken) prose – commas, semicolons, colons, full stops; the successive phrases are likewise analogous to sentences in prose, which are subsequently grouped together in paragraphs. This model attempts to establish order within a potentially unwieldy and prolonged melodic line, comprehending the whole in terms of its constituent parts. Such an approach is widely applicable within the melodic realm of Mozart's piano concertos.

Numerous illustrations suggest themselves. One reason for the remarkable early popularity in Vienna of the new rondo finale, K.382, to the D major concerto K.175, to take just one memorable theme, is perhaps its appealing regularity of phrasing, making it a fitting subject for virtuosic variations. The theme itself (Example 6.1) is in binary form, each section of equal length (eight bars). The first half is subdivided in a balancing 4 + 4 structure; each of these shorter phrases is itself subdivided into two segments, so that bars 1–2

Example 6.1   K.382, bars 1–8 (theme)

link together sequentially, while bars 3–4 lead to a half-cadence on the dominant. A repeat of the opening sequential pair is followed by a tonic cadence at the end of the first section. The second half is likewise subdivided into two four-bar phrases, the first, bars 9–12, consisting of two segments, linked by simple repetition, the second a straightforward reprise of bars 5–8 (balancing the first section's closing cadence). This structure, equating nicely to Kirnberger's models of 'phrase-rhythm' outlined above, may be traced in each of the movement's successive variations. Clearly, there is more to the appreciation of such a 'phrase-rhythm' than the mere ability to count beats or bars. The internal design of phrases depends at least as much on spatial as on temporal considerations. Identifying the precise repetition of phrases or phrase-elements in K.382's theme is as important as perceiving that each half of the temporal structure is in a symmetrical balance. Awareness of relatively strong and weak stress patterns also plays a part in understanding the whole: perceiving these dimensions together is what ultimately reveals this movement's charm in performance.

Joseph Riepel's discussion of melody is strongly grounded in periodic symmetry. His preference for balancing two-, four-, eight-, 16- and 32-bar phrases, sentences, or paragraphs is unmistakable, a norm against which irregularities such as three-, five-, or seven-bar phrases appear as anomalies in need of regularisation (Riepel, 1755, pp.36–71 *passim*). According to Riepel, the natural preference was for symmetrical, balanced phrases in units of two or four bars. Examples in the Mozart concertos abound. Among the more well-known are the opening first-movement themes of K.414, K.459, K.467 (with repetition of the second segment) and K.537; the slow-movement themes of K.413, K.451, K.488 and K.595; and the finale themes of K.450, K.453, K.456 and K.491.

Riepel's account includes painstaking study of internal subdivisions of the phrase (*Absatz*; the term he employs for such subdivisions of the whole *Absatz* is *Einschnitt*), primarily according to its cadential goal, either tonic (*Grundänderungsabsatz*) or dominant (*Quintänderungsabsatz*). (Some of these concepts are implicit in the brief analysis of K.382 above.) Subdivision of a phrase is explained in detail (2 + 2 bars; 4 + 4 bars, and so on), as well as the symmetrical balance of phrases to form larger continuities (4 + 4 bars, for instance). He nevertheless devotes some attention to the construction of irregular groupings, up to as many as nine bars (which he regards as being an aggregation of a four- and a five-bar group). In Riepel's view any local irregularity (a five-bar phrase, for example) was best 'smoothed out' by repetition, resulting in a larger symmetry (5 [= 3 + 2] + 5 bars, and so on). The three-bar phrase which opens the E flat concerto, K.271, for instance, is immediately echoed by another of the same length, and in this sense, Mozart fulfils Riepel's theoretical prescription perfectly. In fact, Riepel's textbook was possibly owned by Leopold Mozart, who refers to his ownership of a book by Riepel in a letter of 11 June 1778.

Phrase extension resulting sometimes in irregular phrase-lengths is achieved, according to Riepel, by several means, including sequential repetition, interpolation of a phrase-segment within an otherwise regular phrase, and repetition of cadences. These types of phrase-extension are common in Mozart's concertos, both before and after his domicile in Vienna, and while his designs go far beyond any of the simple textbook examples of contemporary theorists in their sophistication, these texts provide valuable conceptual models against which contemporary listeners would perhaps have judged Mozart's melodic style.[6]

An early example of the extension of a phrase by internal repetition is seen in the Andante of K.246. It opens with a regular eight-bar phrase (Example 6.2), symmetrically balanced as two phrases, each of four bars. In the first

Example 6.2   K.246, 2nd movement, bars 1–8 (theme)

phrase, the main subdivisions are all clearly marked by melodic and harmonic punctuations in bars 2 and 4 (each of these segments is an *Einschnitt* within the four-bar *Absatz*). The following four bars evolve continuously, without internal punctuation – that is, unless one views this four-bar phrase as a succession of four single bars, a possibility reinforced by the scoring: imitation of the first violins by the seconds at bar 6; addition of woodwind at bar 7; cadence in bar 8. The ensuing solo immediately alters this original pattern. Its opening phrase is ten, not eight, bars long, and the extension is achieved by internal repetition of its third and fourth bars (bars 25–6 are repeated at bars 27–8), creating a six-bar leading phrase. After this, the semiquaver pattern of bars 5–6 is abandoned altogether, replaced by a new cadential approach in which the harmonic termination on F in bar 30 is echoed by the orchestra, overlapping the piano part in bars 31–2. In the recapitulation, something of the original symmetry of this theme is restored. Mozart telescopes the tutti and piano entries here, and while the piano's repetition is retained this now follows on from a quotation of the whole of the first four bars of the tutti theme, leading to a balancing 4 + 4-bar scheme, followed by the altered cadence from bars 29–31: a 12-bar unit in all.

Phrase extension by repetition, or elaboration, of a cadence is found in the Adagio of K.242 for three pianos. In bar 2 there is a firm tonic cadence, repeated in a different melodic guise in the following bar. The continuation is a regular two-bar phrase, creating an irregularity (five bars) that is to some extent smoothed out in the next phrase, also a five-bar structure, cadencing in bar 10 and subdivided 2 + 3 (= 1 + 1 + 1) bars, the articulations being rein-forced by the oboes' *piano* echo of the violins at the end of bar 8. This much is in keeping with Riepel's prescriptions for irregular phrase-building, since the opening five-bar irregularity is balanced by a phrase of the same irregular length, and creating a broader sense of symmetry. However, the cadential punctuation at bar 10 of K.242's Adagio is light, and proceeds for another two bars (again featuring some internal melodic repetition) to a tutti conclusion at bar 12.

Symmetry between successive irregular phrases is also present at the very beginning of the same concerto, though here Mozart applies Riepel's guide-lines to a still higher level of phrase rhythm. The march-like dotted motive, *forte*, covers the first three bars, and is answered by a six-bar cantabile phrase, *piano*, in minims, creating a significant proportional imbalance between successive units, one-third–two-thirds.[7] However, Mozart repeats the whole scheme, resulting in the semblance of symmetry within the larger paragraph, bars 1–14. That Mozart did not always adhere to such theoretical prescriptions is shown by the scansion of K.175's Andante ma un poco adagio, in which the opening three-bar theme creates an imbalance never subsequently resolved; likewise, K.238's Andante un poco adagio answers an initial seven-bar tutti phrase (3 + 4 bars) by an eight-bar solo, itself irregularly divided (3 + 3 + 2 bars).

Such irregularities of phrasing, particularly when left unadjusted to the clas-sical norm of periodic regularity, affect the phrase-rhythm on quite a broad scale, lending movements in which they occur a certain 'prose' character, in contrast to an expected 'poetic' scansion. One instance, among several that could be cited, is the fate of the new theme that occurs immediately after the solo exposition in the first movement of K.488 in A. Mozart draws attention to it by contrasting its steady cantabile flow (presented by the strings only) with the more hectic cadential articulation of the preceding bars. Initially, the new theme lasts six bars, featuring increasing imitative interplay of a dotted rhythm and a gradual speeding-up of the harmonic rhythm of the opening, but is expanded to seven when the piano takes it up in decorated form at the begin-ning of the development immediately afterwards. When this theme recurs just before the cadenza the six-bar phrase (now announced by the soloist) is actu-ally contracted to five on repetition.

Koch's extensive treatment of melodic organisation, touched on in Chapter One, builds on Riepel's work. He discusses a wider variety of ways in which phrases could be built from symmetrical two- or four-bar units, and ways in which either these phrases or their component units could be extended by repe-tition of several kinds. On a simple level, no doubt, these were the criteria within which melodies were assessed empirically by a player (for instance, of a first violin part in a Mozart piano concerto, which typically presented all or most of the main themes). It is a relatively straightforward matter to relate the melodic course of the opening paragraph of the B flat concerto, K.238 (1776), to the theoretical models of Koch.[8] Bars 1–4, for example, present two symmetrical two-bar units, the first ending with a half-cadence on the dominant note, the second returning at its end to the tonic, though weakly (over a first inversion chord). The continuation (bars 5–12) offers an example of a type of phrase-extension specifically described by Koch in which an otherwise symmetrical phrase structure (bars 1–4; bars 5–8) is elaborated by varied repetition in bars 9–12, in which the melodic and harmonic profile are diverted at the cadence approach, rounding off the paragraph convincingly in the tonic, B flat. However, the parallel between theoretical template and practical realisation soon breaks down, even within this relatively early work. The answering phrase-unit (bars 3–4) is subtly anticipated by a quaver upbeat, rather than lamely duplicating the previous pattern. In the ensuing phrase, the melody pursues a developmental course on at least two levels: in bar 5 its first note, E flat, co-ordinates squarely on the beat with the supporting C minor harmony; on the first beat of bar 6 an accented passing-note has been added (quavers B flat–A, over a chord of F); by the start of bar 7 this dissonance has become chromatic; rhythmically, too, it evolves towards a peak of activity in bar 7 (no two successive bars share the same pattern).

Beyond the most generalised condition, however, the resemblance between eighteenth-century melodic theory even at its most sophisticated, and Mozart's actual practice, breaks down. While the opening of the first of the Viennese concertos, K.414 in A, proceeds in a 'theoretically approved' series of balanced phrase successions, their unfolding presents a dynamically varied profile quite beyond the scope of Koch and his contemporaries to explain in anything other than local terms. Whereas bars 1–4 and 5–8 are symmetrically ordered, the two phrases are of quite different scansions, the latter counterbalancing its predecessor's characteristic square-cut with consistent syncopation. The balancing period (bars 9–12; 13–17) groups together two phrases of radically different kinds, answering the reprise of bars 1–4 with a phrase consisting of sequential repetitions of a single quaver figure from bar 13, and extended by a bar (a possibility discussed by Koch), and resulting in an overall balance for the paragraph as a whole of 8 + 9 bars. Later in this tutti, the phraseology returns to a more 'predictable' form: that beginning in bar 50 is reducible to two balancing phrase-units, the first ending with a half-cadence (bar 54), the second corresponding very closely in its intervallic and rhythmic profile. Individually, then, these phrases are explicable within the terms of Koch's treatise. But their aggregated contribution within the unfolding momentum of this tutti section is not. The sequence of phrase-types proceeds according to no obvious textbook prescription and perhaps belongs outside of theoretical formulation. All told, comparisons between Mozart's melodies and contemporary theoretical models prove little besides his ability to transcend them.

'Nichtkenner'

While underpinned by technical characteristics such as counterpoint, melodic design and periodicity that were basic to the musical understanding of the erudite 'kenner allein', Mozart's piano concertos also contained a range of more immediately appreciable qualities that would have impressed themselves more firmly on the ears and minds of the 'less learned' (Mozart's 'nichtkenner'). Central to the wide popular appeal of these works is the solo part, and especially its virtuosity, a factor highlighted in contemporary reviews of Mozart's concerts that comment on his brilliance not simply as a composer, but also as an executant of his own concertos.[9] Mozart himself acknowledged the difficulty of some of these works, as he noted in a letter to his father on 26 May 1784: 'I cannot choose between [K.450 in B flat and K.451 in D]. I regard them both as concertos which are bound to make the performer perspire. From the point of view of difficulty the B flat concerto beats the one in D.' While Mozart is dealing with technical demands here, it should be remembered that difficulty for the player equates to an exciting experience for the audience. In the first movement of K.450, the virtuosic character of the solo part is established from the outset. The soloist's first entry does not take up the woodwind's opening double-thirds motive in quavers, but commences instead with preparatory scale-flourishes in semiquavers, serving to 'warm-up' the player's fingers at the start of this exacting movement, in which the soloist's contribution of exciting running passagework is proportionately very high. More impressive than the sheer number of notes in this section (indeed, in the movement as a whole) is the degree of technical difficulty (and associated audience excitement) stemming from its rapidly shifting textures. From its entry in bar 59, the solo part is constantly active until the end of the 'solo' exposition at bar 137. Its first section is based on scalic patterns in the tonic key (bars 59–70), in single lines at first, but climaxing in parallel tenths at the cadence approach, the right hand ascending almost to the top of the fortepiano's range. Next comes a passage in double thirds (bars 70–78), followed by the restoration of semiquaver motion, dissolving in a descending cascade of triplet arpeggios spanning five octaves (bars 84–5). Broken octaves characterise the following section, antiphonally arranged in contrary motion and exploiting widely separated keyboard registers (bars 96–102). In the remainder of the 'solo' exposition Mozart continues to explore the contrasting qualities of treble and bass registers, introducing patterned arpeggios in the right hand over alternating tonic and dominant chordal support (bars 112–15); a more animated pattern, passing from left hand to right hand on alternate crotchet beats above a minim rate of chord-change (bars 116–17); a three-part contrapuntal texture featuring suspension resolutions over a running semiquaver bass, widely separated at first, but steadily converging before dissolving into rows of closely spaced semiquavers (bars 119–24); a continuation inspired by the intervallic shape of bars 122–3 but expanded in amplitude and transferred to the treble register (bars 126–9); and a conclusion founded on broken chords spread out over virtually the whole range of the fortepiano, switching between left-hand triplets (bars 130–2) and right-hand semiquavers (bars 133–4). These keyboard textures unfold as a breathtaking torrent of activity that could not have failed to impress the public. Within the movement as a whole, occasional moments of delicacy, such as those at bar 103 foll. and bar 216 foll., sit between extensive passages of almost unrelieved semiquaver or triplet motion, and are noticeable not so much in themselves as for the temporary ruptures they create in the prevailing flow.[10]

While the level of technical difficulty in Mozart's concertos is not that of a Liszt, Brahms, Tchaikowsky or Rachmaninov concerto, there are unmistakable points in the course of their outer movements (and, in the case of K.466, the slow movement) at which the contribution of the soloist attains remarkable prominence over an extended stretch of time. One thinks of passages such as the first solo in the finale of K.503 (bars 32–121), or bars 65–130 in the finale of K.595. In both these extracts the role of the soloist is to provide dazzling foreground display, supported by the rest of the ensemble (it is remarkable that the harmonic underpinning in many such cases is relatively simple and uniform – even predictable, as in the first-movement development of K.488, bars 170 foll., which merely marks out a circle of fifths, preparing for the reprise). Frequently, virtuosity in the solo part may be aligned with the representation of a specific topic, the so-called 'brilliant style' consisting principally of extended semiquaver or triplet quaver runs, sometimes for the right hand with simple accompaniment beneath (as in K.453/iii, Variation 2 or K.503/i, bars 126 foll.); elsewhere for both hands simultaneously (K.467/i, bars 148 foll.; K.503/i, bars 189–202). Often such extended patterns turn out to be sequential in design, as in the transition from first to second subject in the solo exposition of K.488's opening Allegro (bars 87 foll.). Most frequently, the semiquaver runs consist of single lines, rather than doubled thirds, sixths or octaves; while Mozart often employs thirds (or tenths) between the hands in short bursts (as in the reprise of K.488's first movement, just after the statement of the main theme), he avoids excessive use of parallel scales. Indeed, he derides precisely this fingerprint of Clementi's piano writing in a letter to his father of 7 June 1783: 'as compositions, they are worthless. They contain no remarkable or striking passages except those in sixths and octaves … [producing] an atrocious chopping effect and nothing else whatsoever. Clementi is a *ciarlatano* … he has not the slightest expression, or taste, still less, feeling.' For Mozart, textures of this type evidently represented empty virtuosity, existing merely for its own sake. While superficially no less exciting for the listener than his own virtuosic passagework, such showmanship is musically far less inspired, amounting to nothing more than a surface veneer overlaid onto a work whose inherent qualities were in themselves rather limited. By contrast, the virtuoso character of Mozart's piano concertos is typically more 'integral' to the particular work, proceeding from within the musical argument itself, as in the case of K.491 in C minor (1786), the autograph of which reveals that in many of the most sparkling semiquaver passages, Mozart had at first indicated the solo part as a bare outline sketch, notating the precise shape of the patterns only at a later stage once the progress of the harmonies had been fixed.[11] That dimension of K.491 perceived by the listener as 'virtuosity' is by no means a superficial façade, external to the work itself, but a vital element of its structure, representing at the surface level the underlying harmonic discourse.

Mozart's public presence as a talented executant of his own virtuosic keyboard concertos was clearly an essential factor in their early popularity. Almost equal in importance, though, was their memorable orchestration. The relatively easy availability of woodwind and brass players in Viennese concert life (at least, as compared to his previous situation in Salzburg) led Mozart to exploit possibilities for larger and more colourful ensembles. In a work such as the C major concerto, K.503, the inclusion of a flute, trumpets and timpani appears to signify an altogether grander conception of the genre. Its opening theme is 18 bars long, the tutti exposition in total 90 bars, the entire first movement 432 bars. In its developmental processes it is likewise expansive, incorporating extended passages of motivic evolution and including modulations to relatively remote areas such as E flat (the relative major of the tonic minor degree). Within such a framework the occasionally returning punctuations of the trumpets and timpani produce a fine effect. K.503 is an overtly theatrical piece, making a grand statement in a public forum. It is a work designed to make its Viennese audience sit up and take notice, partly by virtue of powerful sonority, partly insofar as this sonority is allied to a structural purpose.

Such a grand orchestral conception was quite new in Mozart's concerto output. In the concertos of the Salzburg years his typical orchestral forces had been strings (the bass line conventionally reinforced by one or two bassoons, to judge from the surviving orchestral materials for these pieces found in the Library of St. Peter's, Salzburg, which normally include a separate bassoon part, even where none is prescribed in the autograph score),[12] along with pairs of oboes and horns. In K.175 (cannily revised in the early 1780s, specifically in order to appeal to the Viennese public) and K.415 this scoring is supplemented by an additional pair of trumpets, and timpani.[13] From 1784, however, Mozart's use of the orchestral woodwind grew considerably in sophistication. K.450 in B flat requires only the standard wind complement of two oboes, two bassoons and two horns (a flute is added in the finale), but utilises them in ways previously unimagined. The very beginning of the work celebrates the woodwind's independence, treating them as an integrated 'block' of sound, antiphonally set against the strings, whose initial contribution is mere accompaniment to the newly liberated wind. Dialogue between the wind and piano persists throughout the movement, indeed, is one of its principal articulating features: it underpins the closing material of the tutti exposition (bars 53–9), and the recapitulation replaces the opening alternation of wind and strings by wind and piano at bar 196 foll. Whereas in the first movement Mozart employs the wind as a block, the finale is notable too for its handling of individual colour: for instance, the flute from bars 76–86 (an extended pedal followed by delicate chromatic doubling), and oboe (bars 199–210, in a trio with piano and flute).

Mozart was plainly satisfied by the inclusion of the flute in K.450's finale: he included one from the first bar of K.451 in D and retained one at the top of the woodwind group in all of his subsequent piano concertos. The woodwind group's precise formulation was to remain variable, however. In K.482 the oboe pair is replaced by B flat clarinets; the original conception of K.488 included oboes, as may be seen from the first page of the autograph (now in the Bibliothèque Nationale, Paris), but these were subsequently replaced by A clarinets;[14] the C minor concerto, K.491, includes both oboes and clarinets; the last three concertos revert to oboes. To some extent, choice of instrument depended on choice of key. Classical clarinets have considerably less keywork than their modern counterparts and in Mozart's day worked best in B flat and A majors and their close relatives; F major, G major and C major were relatively less comfortable, and the clarinet is not found in K.453, K.459, K.467 and K.503. Functionality of key was more of an issue in the selection of crooked trumpets, usable only in the keys of B flat, C, D, E flat and F (and their relatives). Clarinets and trumpets appear together only in K.482 (E flat) and K.491 (C minor). For all these limitations the wind and brass combinations in Mozart's Viennese concertos from K.450 onwards are one of their most endearing qualities and must have struck contemporary listeners with remarkable force. Memorable illustrations include the frequent alternation of piano with woodwind throughout K.453; the opening paragraph of K.482 (especially the horn suspension chains); the slow movement of K.488 (in the unusual key of F sharp minor, possibly selected precisely in order to exploit certain colour characteristics of the clarinets); the ghostly reprise of the main theme at bar 103 in K.595's Larghetto, enhanced by peculiar unison colouring of flute and piano; the block chordal writing throughout much of the finale of the same work.

II: Channels of communication: rhetoric

Within what kind of aesthetic, theoretical and philosophical contexts would Mozart's piano concertos have been understood in his own day? Although he himself wrote no theoretical textbooks, his work did not take place in a theoretical vacuum. His output was accessible to contemporary listeners only because it operated within then-current conceptual frameworks of musical understanding, whether consciously rationalised or passively sampled. It is the purpose of this section to introduce some of these issues, beginning with a brief discussion of the relation of Mozart's melodic writing in the piano concertos to contemporary melodic theory, before turning to a broader consideration of the intellectual contexts within which the creative process may have been understood in Mozart's day.

Textbooks on music theory, providing detailed discussion of compositional matters (such as melodic construction, touched on in the previous section), catered to one quite specialised constituency of later eighteenth-century intellectuals. Important though it was in its own right, this kind of theoretical activity was part of a wider intellectual debate concerning the fine arts emanating in part from recent products of contemporary French philosophy, as embodied above all in the *Encyclopédie*. The writings of the *philosophes* were well known in German-speaking lands through translations of Hiller, Marpurg, Gottsched and others (see below) and soon found their way into classic German texts such as Johann Georg Sulzer's widely influential *Allgemeine Theorie der schönen Künste* (Sulzer, 1771).[15] Mozart himself had been educated within a household in which the intellectual traits of emerging Enlightenment philosophy were highly prized. His father, Leopold, was a passionate advocate of learning. He had attended the Gymnasium and the Jesuit Lyceum in Augsburg, and his university education at Salzburg included law, in the course of which he must have gained a detailed knowledge of the ancient and noble art of rhetoric.[16] He was a subscriber to Grimm's *Correspondence littéraire* and owned a number of music theory books. Before writing his famous treatise on violin-playing, *Versuch einer gründliche Violinschule* (Augsburg, 1756), Leopold had devoted himself to intensive study of a number of theoretical textbooks, including up-to-date writings of the German rhetorician and lexicographer Johann Christoph Gottsched, as revealed by letters he wrote to the Augsburg publisher, Johann Jakob Lotter, on 9 June and 28 August 1755.[17] Gottsched's influential *Ausführliche Redekunst* (1736, and many later reprints) derived from ancient classical traditions of rhetoric dating back ultimately to the writings of Cicero and Quintilian. Rhetoric was the art of persuasion, operating by means of a series of conventions understood by both speaker and listener. According to such conventions, an argument (be it verbal or, by analogy, musical) could be presented in a coherent way. Rhetorical conventions included not only the *figurae* well known to baroque orators and musicians, but structural matters too – principally the relation of parts to the whole – the careful organisation of which required skill on the part of the speaker (or composer). An orator's success or failure in persuading his audience of his case rested upon his command not only of the material itself but also of the conventions for presenting it. The same was widely held to be true in musical matters.

Rhetoric was widely discussed in eighteenth-century musical literature and proved an enduring and influential conceptual tool.[18] Johannes Mattheson specifically likened music to the arrangement of ideas in a speech:

> The disposition [*dispositio*] of a piece of music differs from the rhetorical layout of a speech merely in its relevant material [*objecto*]. So, it must follow the same six partitions that are typically required of the orator, namely the introduction, narration, proposition, proof, refutation and conclusion, otherwise known as *exordium, narratio, propositio, confirmatio, confutatio*, and *peroratio* (Mattheson, 1737, p. 128 [author's translation]).

This framework was likewise central to the thinking of Johann Nikolaus Forkel (Forkel, 1784, pp.31–2; Forkel, 1788, i, p. 24), according to which musical composition was a kind of 'oration in sound' consisting of three stages: *Erfindung*, the creation of basic ideas (themes, for instance); *Ausführung*, the planning of a movement (for example its subdivision into sections of a recognised form, such as sonata form); and finally *Ausarbeitung*, the working-out of surface detail (including the embellishments, or *figurae*, so beloved of baroque composers). Such was the rhetorical system of conventions within which composers of Mozart's time worked (or, at least, according to which their music was understood by some theorists).

These basic subdivisions are indicated also in the writings of Sulzer and Koch. Additionally, Sulzer inserts the separate categories of *Entwurf* (sketch), *Anlage* (layout), *Form* (form) and *Plan* (plan) between the *Erfindung* and the *Ausführung* of Forkel's scheme (here termed *Anordnung*), though it is clear that their technical characteristics are merely supplementary, and do not materially alter the relative significance of *Erfindung* and *Ausführung* (Sulzer's final stage of elaboration is still termed *Ausarbeitung*).[19] As is typical elsewhere in his treatises, Koch refers in detail to the work of Sulzer, whose description of the creative process he fundamentally accepts, though he lists the successive elements as *Erfindung, Entwurf, Anlage, Anordnung, Ausführung*, and *Ausarbeitung*. In practice, this reduces to just three essential stages beyond the initial inspiration: 'plan', 'realisation' and 'elaboration.' Koch's summary of these stages, quoted from Sulzer, is as follows:

> Every great art work is the result of a three-fold process: the plan [*Anlage*], the realization [*Ausführung*], and the elaboration [*Ausarbeitung*] … In the plan, the overall design of the work, along with its sections is decided upon. The realization gives each of these sections its own characteristic form, while the elaboration works out and ties together the smallest parts [for instance, harmonic details].[20]

For Koch, the *Anlage* comprises the principal material of a composition, melody and harmony being considered as complementary aspects of a unified conception. He illustrates this by an analysis of an aria, 'Ein Gebet um neue Stärke', from *Der Tod Jesu* by Carl Heinrich Graun (c.1704–59), in which he presents, first, his own notated *Anlage*, containing what he considered to be the aria's main material, and secondly, Graun's aria, with supporting commentary (Baker and Christensen, 1996, pp.163–75). Evidently, Koch's hypothetical *Anlage* contained everything necessary to proceed with the technical work of composition: 'In my judgement ... no more, no less, could be considered the plan of this aria' (Baker and Christensen, 1996, p.164). That would seem to locate the *Anlage* early on in the creative process and within the shadow of *Erfindung*, as Koch's further discussion confirms:

> [The *Anlage*] should contain the main ideas of the piece already connected with one another which together present themselves to the composer as a complete whole, combined with its principal harmonic features ... The composer *working in the fire of imagination* [emphasis added] may be fortunate enough to invent the main ideas of his piece directly in such an order and connection that [they] appear to him as a complete whole' (Baker and Christensen, 1996, p.161).

Beyond the *Anlage*, everything was part of the subsequent rhetorical stages of realisation or elaboration.[21]

As discussed in Chapter One, Koch's understanding of the *Anlage* of a concerto referred in particular to the mapping out of the first solo section, a state of affairs that does not reflect Mozart's normal practice as revealed in his autograph scores. At the level of the phrase, however, Koch's description of plan, realisation and elaboration is generally acceptable as a conceptual model that contemporary listeners may have recognised and applied to their experience of Mozart's concertos. An application of Koch's 'three-fold process' to a single musical phrase is illustrated by Example 6.3. Line (a) is a hypothetical *Anlage* representing bars 170–178 from the first-movement development of K.488. The *Anlage* (a) is a harmonic pattern (sequentially structured as a 'circle of fifths'); the *Ausführung* (b) realises this as a canonically imitating woodwind dialogue over a bass; the *Ausarbeitung* comprises the specific rhythmic and intervallic content of the wind parts and the patterned semiquaver runs contributed by the solo piano. Example 6.4 applies the same hierarchical patterning to bars 38–41 in the Larghetto of K.595. Line (a) is the hypothetical *Anlage*; the *Ausführung* (b) realises the harmonic content of that cadentially directed phrase as a three-part contrapuntal texture in the string parts (main theme at the top, flowing semiquavers in the middle, harmonic punctuating chords beneath). The actual rhythmic and intervallic shapes of the two highest strands of the texture (along with refinements of articulation and dynamic level) are features of the *Ausarbeitung*.

While the rigour of Koch's rhetorical model has a certain appeal, its highly systematic nature, separating *Anlage*, *Ausführung* and *Ausarbeitung* (closely approximating to the rhetorical terms, *inventio*,[22] *dispositio*[23] and *elocutio* found in the classical treatises of Cicero and Quintilian – terms actually appropriated by Mattheson in the extract quoted previously), encourages us to view

Example 6.3a, 6.3b K.488, 1st movement, bars 170–178: relation of simple and figured versions

the genesis of a musical work in rigidly separated stages: first the invention (the stuff of 'inspiration'), next the technical work of composition, in which the 'fleshing out' of these initial ideas was achieved by means of large-scale tonal planning, articulated by structurally defining cadential divisions, periodic phrasing, sequence and so on. Mozart's legendary fluidity seems difficult to reconcile with such a scheme. However, it is important not to take the above structure too literally. Presentation of the creative process in successive stages according to well-known rhetorical models surely derives from a pedagogical concern for clarity of exposition. In a lecture or in a textbook, ideas have to be presented *successively*, the complete picture only emerging in the reader's mind from retrospective consideration of an ordered sequence of concepts. So far as rhetoric is concerned, there is a danger of conveying the impression that, for example, the *inventio* is a stage in the creative process that is wholly separate from the *dispositio*, simply because all rhetorical textbooks discuss the

Example 6.4a, 6.4b   K.595, 2nd movement, bars 38–41: relation of simple and figured versions

two conceptual levels in different chapters, even different books. This had to be the case, of course, purely because of the medium of conveying the information. Authors of rhetoric manuals constructed their texts in such a way as to ensure that a student of rhetoric had a thorough grasp of the distinct elements of *inventio* before proceeding to the techniques appropriate to the *dispositio*. This all makes good pedagogic sense, but can blind us to the fact that a trained orator (having absorbed the prescriptions of theoretical treatises over many years of study) would conceive several different elements of his speech *simultaneously* – particularly in an extemporisation. Writing a textbook on how to do that, though, is an entirely different matter. Here the disparate elements that together make up an oration need to be presented to the student separately in order to avoid confusion.

There is no reason to suppose that the situation is any different in rhetorically inspired treatments of musical composition, which is why eighteenth-century traditions of musical rhetoric culminating in the writing of Sulzer and Koch outline the creative constructs of *Erfindung*, *Entwurf*, *Anlage*, *Ausführung* and *Ausarbeitung* separately in a strictly ordered succession. A composer, on the other hand, would have conceived of elements of several rhetorical stages simultaneously. Evidence that this was so can be gleaned from the autograph scores of Mozart's piano concertos, which, as noted previously in Chapter One, were also *composing* scores. Careful study of the handwriting, ink colour and nib thickness within Mozart's autographs sometimes betrays separate stages of work. In the first tutti of the 'Coronation' concerto in D, K.537, for instance, separate stages of writing are clearly detectable within the autograph, distinguished by contrasting combinations of ink shade and nib thickness: some staves display a fairly broad nib and a relatively light brown ink; others a thinner nib and darker brown ink.[24] This 'archeology' of Mozart's autograph is not, however, to be interpreted as evidence of successive 'rhetorical' stages in composition. If the opening passage of K.537 had literally evolved according to the autonomous stages of *Erfindung, Entwurf, Anlage, Ausführung* and *Ausarbeitung* then one would expect to be able to recover those distinctive stages from the detectable differences in ink colour and nib thickness within individual strands of the texture. The *Anlage*, containing, according to Koch, 'the main ideas of the piece already connected with one another which together present themselves to the composer as a complete whole, combined with its principal harmonic features', would be represented in Mozart's composing score as an *Entwurf* exhibiting a distinctive 'complex' of ink shade and nib thickness. The precise details of rhythmic and intervallic profile, subtle turns of semiquaver passagework and refinements of articulation, apparently conceived at the later rhetorical stages of *Ausführung* and *Ausarbeitung*, would exhibit different 'complexes' to be associated with those later stages of work. Consequently, individual strands of the polyphony – the first violin line, for instance – would inhabit 'patchworks' of ink-shades and pen-widths, reflecting the accretions associated with each successive rhetorical stage of work. Of course, such distinctions are not found. Instead, the principal theme, including all of its refinements, is written throughout in a single ink shade using one nib, reflecting a single phase of creative activity. The different phases of writing detectable from the ink and nib patterns relate to Mozart's practice of writing the leading parts first (in the relatively light brown ink, in the case of K.537) and adding the subordinate parts, such as interior accompaniments, later on (in the darker brown ink). So while there is an important distinction to be drawn between 'leading parts' and 'subordinate parts' combining to form the texture as a whole, within any single strand Mozart's inspiration evidently contained several elements bound together – melodic, harmonic, rhythmic and so on – exactly as one would suppose of an experienced composer. The apparent rigidity of rhetorical systems of thought therefore turns out to be, at least in part, a function of the medium of its expression, rather than of the message itself, and is certainly not to be construed as a fault undermining the relevance of rhetoric in a musical situation. Within carefully considered limits, a rhetorical framework continues to have significance in relation to eighteenth-century understandings of Mozart's music.

Actually, the blurring of distinctions between different categories of rhetoric was always implicit in the classical treatises as, for instance, in Quintilian's discussion of *inventio* (*Erfindung*) which dwells upon the relationship between invention and judgement. Quintilian advises the student of rhetoric that 'it is necessary first to invent and then to exercise our judgement' (Butler, 1989, III.iii; c.f. Hubbell, 1976, I.xiv.19; Caplan, 1989, I.ii.3; I.iii.1). The merging of these two processes is especially pertinent to a consideration of melodic functions in music: does a composer first 'invent' a theme and then work it out? Or does experience teach him only to invent themes that he knows will prove suitable for the kind of treatment he already has in mind within a particular piece? Probably, a musical theme was not simply devised as a 'thing in itself' but with a view to what it might become during the course of the piece or movement, including, for instance, its potential for development, and for combination with other themes. Within the first movement of the C major concerto, K.467, for instance, there are several illustrations of the latter tendency. Its striking march-like opening idea could hardly be more sharply defined and yet, during the course of the tutti exposition, it assumes a range of contrasting characters. Mozart clearly designed it to function in this way. His adaptations are quite numerous. In the transitional passage commencing at bar 12, the theme is transferred to the bass as a counterpoint to a new legato idea in the upper strings and winds; the closing tutti exposition passage (bar 36 foll.) transforms the march theme to an imitative context, the entries piling up as in a fugal stretto; its return at the beginning of the solo exposition (bar 80) places it as an accompaniment to a prolonged trill, heralding the soloist's entry; later, at bar 143, the imitative setting from bar 36 is recalled (now shared between solo and tutti) and continuing from bar 148 in a new way, the first four notes of the march theme being separated off from the remainder and divided alternately between lower and upper strings, providing a harmonic 'cushion' for the soloist's gymnastics. At bar 328 foll. (the tonic reprise of this section) the march theme is yet again adapted, by the telling restoration of its closing *gruppetto* in the bassoon. In this case, thematic *Erfindung* is not something fixed and immutable, but a 'trace', capable of colouring a broad spread of contrasting environments within which it is set.

Thematic *inventio* (*Erfindung*) carries especial significance in the development section of a sonata-form movement. The potential of a theme for later 'working out' profoundly affects the content of Mozart's developments, as illustrated by the first movements of the A major concerto, K.488, and the C minor concerto, K.491. In K.488, the development makes no reference to exposition material; instead, Mozart structures his development on a new idea introduced at bar 143. Evidently, he felt that the cantabile melody with which the concerto opens was not suitable for extended development. The situation is wholly different in K.491, in which the development is based almost exclusively on elements of the principal subject. Within the development the theme's main intervallic and rhythmic elements are placed in novel contexts, undergoing true 'development': for instance, at bar 309 foll. the theme's secondary phrase is set in dialogue between the wind and strings, the solo piano providing a scalic 'filler'.

At the opposite end of the rhetorical spectrum was the *elocutio* (Forkel and Koch's *Ausarbeitung*), the level at which the detailed melodic, harmonic and rhythmic profiles of a phrase were shaped. *Elocutio* was regarded as the pinnacle of the orator's art and was considered at length in all the major rhetorical texts of classical antiquity. The technical means by which the surface of a prosodic or poetic structure was refined by stylish adornment included *figurae*, decorous figures of speech which enhanced the appeal of an argument through the application of sophisticated language.[25] Musical *figurae* were likewise fundamental to the craft of eighteenth-century composition and improvisation.[26] They were considered at length by many eighteenth-century theorists, including Mattheson, Spiess, Scheibe and Riepel, whose writings were well known to Leopold Mozart.[27] Such figures were primarily a means of localised melodic decoration, used to 'heighten' the language and so 'move' and persuade the audience.[28] But they could also be applied progressively, in which case they affected the structure of a piece (therefore overlapping with the function of the rhetorical *Ausführung*), as acknowledged in Forkel, 1788 (vol.i, pp.53 foll.). An example of such 'structural' ornament, operating at the level of *Ausarbeitung*, is found in the Larghetto of K.595, mentioned previously. The phrase considered in Example 6.4 returns towards the end of the movement (bars 116–19). Bars 119–22 repeat this phrase, transferring the semiquavers to the piano (incorporating an extra contrary-motion strand) and offering additional layered decorations in the wind (especially bassoon and horns). In relation to the preceding phrase, this variation is a further stage of *Ausarbeitung*, and thus a 'localised' ornament. But it also exercises a commentary on bars 41 foll., one whose impact is all the more forceful for Mozart's skilful timing: he reserves the most developed form of ornamentation for the end of the movement, so that, retrospectively, the listener senses bars 119–22 as the furthest stage in a measured progression from simple to complex presentations of this idea. If this element of 'progression' is interpreted, in turn, as a structural counterpoint to the 'static' successive presentations of the Larghetto's main theme (for which no embellishment is notated), then that is further confirmation that, in the hands of a composer of Mozart's originality, rhetorical frameworks of understanding, in which *Erfindung*, *Ausführung*, and *Ausarbeitung* are apparently rigidly separate categories, are liberating starting-points, not straitjacketing templates.

III: Frameworks of understanding: aesthetic and philosophical contexts

Identifying the distinction between a 'pedagogical' framework, in which the creative process may be understood as part of a rhetorical sequence of

Erfindung followed by a separate *Ausführung*, and a more holistic conception in which ideas and treatment are less obviously divisible, has important resonances within the emergent discipline of aesthetics during the later eighteenth and early nineteenth centuries, namely the shift from Aristotelianism towards neo-Platonism, a context of fundamental importance to the compositional background to Mozart's concertos. The former takes as its starting-point Aristotle's *Poetics*, a book whose centrality to literary criticism extended well into the eighteenth century (Russell and Winterbottom, 1989, pp.51–90). Actually the *Poetics* is a series of lectures explaining in considerable detail various types of tragic and epic plot, along with strategies for developing elements within those plots that borrow heavily from the techniques of rhetoric known as *dispositio* ('arrangement'). It is within this tradition of appeal to exemplars that the rhetorical textbooks of Gottsched (sought out by Leopold Mozart) are situated, for example.

The rhetorical approach of Aristotle's *Poetics* demonstrably encroaches on musical criticism during the late eighteenth century. It is the background to the oft-repeated remark of Joseph Haydn about Mozart's six 'Haydn' quartets (1782–85, contemporary with the main period of concerto composition) which Leopold Mozart reported in a letter of 16 February 1785, to his daughter, Nannerl: 'H: Haydn sagte mir: ich sage ihnen vor gott, als ein ehrlicher Mann, ihr Sohn ist der größte Componist, den ich von Person und den Nahmen nach kenne: er hat geschmack, *und über das die größte Compositionswissenschaft* [italics added]'. Haydn apparently believed that Mozart possessed two complementary attributes, taste ('Geschmack') and compositional technique ('Compositionswissenschaft') since his formulation, as reported by Leopold, separates the two: 'er hat geschmack, und über das die größte Compositionswissenschaft' ('he has taste, and moreover, the most profound knowledge of composition'). This sounds like a construct according to which the creative process consists of at least two related but distinct stages, the second of which (technique) builds a piece of music out of the materials suggested or approved by the first (taste): Mozart first exercised his taste in selecting musical ideas for the subsequent generation of a piece according to the techniques of composition (of which Haydn believed he possessed a 'profound knowledge').

In contrast to the formalistic, 'rule-based' philosophy of the Aristotelian criticism, later-eighteenth-century critical thinking developed an interest in the writing of Plato, which foregrounds instead the rhetorical *inventio* as the object of aesthetic attention. Whereas some strands of eighteenth-century intellectual writing (Mattheson, Gottsched and Forkel, for instance) had strongly promoted the technical discipline of rhetoric, in which – as explained in the preceding section – inspired ideas residing in the *Erfindung* were rationalised according to the conventional processes of *Ausführung* and *Ausarbeitung*, such descriptions as the following leave little doubt as to the emerging neo-Platonic predominance of the intuitive over the technical:

Taste [Geschmack]. Taste is really nothing other than the capacity to sense beauty, just as reason is that which is true, perfect and just, and morality the capacity to feel that which is good ... Beauty pleases us not because reason finds it perfect, or our moral sense finds it good, but because it flatters our imagination by presenting itself in an attractive, pleasing form. The inner sense by which we may enjoy this pleasure is taste ... taste is something real in our soul to be distinguished from other faculties. Namely, it is the intuitive capacity to recognize beauty (Baker and Christensen, 1996, pp.48–50).

Neo-Platonism accorded a higher place to the less tangible introductory concept of 'inspiration' or 'genius'. For instance, in Plato's *Phaedrus*, Socrates's second speech deals with types of 'divine madness' by which man is, from time to time, possessed. He believed that such madness was of great benefit to the true poet:

The third type of possession and madness is possession by the Muses. When this seizes upon a gentle and virgin soul it rouses it to inspired expression ... But if a man comes to the door of poetry untouched by the madness of the Muses, believing that technique alone will make him a good poet, he and his sane compositions never reach perfection, but are utterly eclipsed by the performances of the inspired madman (*Phaedrus*, §§244–5; this translation from Hamilton, 1973).

In *Ion*, Socrates attempts to explain the rhapsode Ion's ability to speak well on any Homeric subject, but only indifferently on other subjects, in the same theoretical terms of 'possession', as a 'divine force' rather than mere technique: 'a poet ... cannot compose until he is possessed and out of his mind, and his reason is no longer in him ... it is not art but divine inspiration that enables them ... their utterances are the result not of art but of divine force' (*Ion*, 533–4; this translation from Russell and Winterbottom, 1989).

The concept of 'possession' by the Muses was considered at length by Charles Batteux in *Les Beaux-Arts réduits à un même principe* (Batteux, 1746).[29] Batteux's writing, in this respect, may be regarded as transitional between the Aristotelian and neo-Platonic critical worlds. Batteux describes this state of 'possession' as 'enthousiasme' noting that the creative artists 'lose themselves', escaping their normal, conscious state of mind, becoming wholly immersed in the idea that they wish to represent (Batteux, 1746, pp.51–7, esp. pp.54–5). Batteux makes an interesting distinction in his discussion between the notion of possession *by the music* and possession *by the musical ideas themselves*, which, having once seized the composer's imagination, cause him, involuntarily, to apply his powers of genius to form a work of art.[30] This is perhaps a partial concession to the abiding Aristotelian position within which the very notion of supernatural influence, as opposed to rational explanation, was highly suspect. According to such a critique, within the mind of the creative artist the ideas (the stuff of inspiration) were given shape by applying the various technical processes of his art.

Such neo-Platonic vocabulary is also encountered in contemporary or remembered descriptions of Mozart's playing and composing. On 29 September 1769, Dr Daines Barrington reported as follows to the Secretary of the Royal Society, London, on Mozart's capacity for invention as a small boy:

> Having been informed, however, that [Mozart] was often visited with musical ideas, to which, even in the midst of the night, he would give utterance on his harpsichord; I told his father that I should be glad to hear some of his extemporary compositions ... The father shook his head at this, saying, that it depended entirely upon his being, as it were, musically inspired, but that I might ask him whether he was in humour for such a composition ... I said to the boy, that I should be glad to hear an extemporary Love Song ... The boy ... looked back with much archness, and immediately began five or six lines of a jargon recitative proper to introduce a love song ... Finding that he was in humour, and as it were inspired, I then desired of him to compose a Song of Rage ... The boy again looked back with much archness and began five or six lines of a jargon recitative proper to introduce a Song of Anger ... This lasted about the same time as the Song of Love; and in the middle of it, he had worked himself up to such a pitch, that he beat his harpsichord like a person possessed, rising sometimes in his chair (Deutsch, 1965, pp.97–8).

Legends surrounding these incredible feats of memory and creativity were supported by Constanze Mozart, and her sister, Sophie Haibel, after Mozart's death. In conversation with Vincent and Mary Novello in Salzburg on 14 July 1829, for example, Constanze claimed that Mozart only resorted to pen and ink at a late stage of the compositional process:

> *Question* In composing, whether he sat at the [keyboard] and tried over different passages as they occurred to him, or whether he deferred writing down any piece until he had completely constructed and finished it in his own mind, and then *scored* it at once ... ?
> *Vincent*['s note of Constanze's reply]. He seldom went to any instrument when he composed ... In composing, he would get up and walk about the Room quite abstracted from everything that was going on about him.
> *Mary*['s note of Constanze's reply]. When some grand conception was working in his brain he was purely abstracted, walking about the apartment and knew not what was passing around, but when once arranged in his mind, he needed no Piano Forte ... He could never entirely abstract himself from his musical thoughts. Billiards he was very fond of, but he composed whilst he played, [and] if he conversed with his friends, he was always at work in his mind (Hughes, 1955, pp.77–8).[31]

The phrasing of the question suggests the kind of answer the Novellos had anticipated, implying that anecdotes about Mozart's astonishing memory for detail were already quite commonplace. One such account appears in Jean-Baptiste-Antoine Suard's 'Anecdotes sur Mozart' of 1804:

> When he was seized by an idea, he could not be dragged away from his composition. He composed in the midst of friends; he passed whole nights in work. At other times he was sometimes only able to finish a work at the

very moment when he had to perform it. It even came about one day that, having to do a piece for a court concert, he had no time to write out the part that he was to play. The Emperor Joseph, happening to glance at the music paper which Mozart appeared to be following, was astonished to see on it nothing but staves without any notes, and [he] said to him: 'Where is your part?' – 'There', said Mozart, putting his hand to his forehead (Deutsch, 1965, pp.497–501).

According to such emergent aesthetic doctrines, themes such as that which opens the slow movement of K.488, or the curious harmonic successions at the beginning of K.595's first movement development (shifting into the flattened supertonic) occurred to Mozart while 'possessed and out of his mind',[32] 'the performance of the inspired madman' who is 'roused to inspired expression'. No amount of technique could give rise to the initial melodic inspiration that he experienced.

Such emerging conceptions of genius in late-eighteenth-century aesthetics appear to sit uncomfortably with the notion of formal rhetoric. Nevertheless, a point of mediation between the two worlds did exist, namely, topics. Topics were a branch of the discipline of rhetoric, 'sources of argumentation' held in common by both the orator and his audience, and from which he might develop his case. Topics might be compared to stereotypes, not pejoratively, as carica- tures, but rather as clarifying strategies, or lines of argument. Applied to classic period music, topics functioned as recognisable 'codes' according to which pieces were composed and understood, providing a channel of commu- nication connecting composer, performer and listener. Musically, topics include dance metres, such as the minuet; textural types, such as 'learned coun- terpoint', 'brilliant' or 'virtuoso' style; affective categories, such as *Sturm und Drang* and *Empfindsamkeit*. Their application in music is by now well known, especially through the work of Leonard Ratner (Ratner, 1980; Ratner, 1991), Kofi Agawu (Agawu, 1991) and Wye Allanbrook (Allanbrook, 1983; Allan- brook, 1996a; Allanbrook, 1996b). Topics embraced various musical typolo- gies: certain dance metres, such as the contredanse or minuet, for instance, but also features such as counterpoint and dramatic recourse to minor keys (both of which symbolised a more 'serious' intent). All these were familiar to audi- ences by association with opera (both *seria* and *buffa*) in which characters on the stage could be plausibly represented by appropriate music. Examples of well-known topics occurring in Mozart's piano concertos include the graceful 'singing Allegro' (the opening of K.414); *Sturm und Drang* (the first move- ment of K.466); march or quasi-military (the first movement of K.451, scored for trumpets and timpani; or the openings of K.459, 467); 'hunt' topics (the 6/ 8 finales of K.450 and K.456); 'brilliant' style, focusing on virtuosic runs of semiquavers (the finale of K.503); 'singing-cantabile' style (slow movement of K.467); 'passionate style' (the slow movements of K.453 and K.488); '*opera buffa*' (the concluding variation from the finale of K.453, starting with horns; the jaunty 'new' theme in middle of K.466's finale, beginning at bar 139 in the wind and reprised toward the end of the movement); and 'learned counterpoint', by means of which associations of 'serious' music for the liturgy might be evoked. The sheer mobility of topics in these works offered something for everyone. Within a short space of time the opening of the C major concerto, K.467, migrates through march, cantabile style, and counterpoint. As mentioned previously, the finale of the F major concerto, K.459, includes a prominent digression in the middle to a closely knit contrapuntal episode, amounting to the embedding of one topic ('learned counterpoint') within another (specifically, the contredanse). On a more general level, these works are full of solo–tutti interplay (K.453; K.459), so that their appeal is very broadly based from the point of view of texture as well as topic.

On the one hand, topics, although they could be committed to memory, inhabit a domain remote from the orator's (or creative artist's) person: they exist as abstractions which are given life only by their application within a particular situation. Thus, a 'genius' turns to such a fund of ideas for 'inspiration'.[33] On the other hand, topics were a key resource in the art of rhetoric. Many are described in the rhetorical treatises. Indeed, so essential were they that in the writings of Aristotle, topics were even the subject of a separate study (Tredennick and Forster, 1989). Especially useful to orators were topics of 'digression', which enabled the speaker's discourse to flow in a varied and interesting manner, retaining the attention of his listeners, while simultaneously amplifying the main point(s) at issue. Skilful presentation of the same point from contrasting angles was likely to impress that point on the audience in a convincing way.

Topics of 'digression' call upon several techniques, described in detail in rhetorical treatises. Quintilian, quoting Cicero's remarks in *De Oratore*, notes that 'great effect may be produced by dwelling on a single point, and amplifying the facts in course of statement, with a view to making our audience regard the point which we amplify as being as important as speech can make it ... we may employ digressions and then ... make a neat and elegant return to our main theme' (Butler, 1989, IX.i.26–8). Yet another rhetorical device employed by orators for digressive effect is that known as the *trope*, discussed by the author of *Ad Herrenium* and, in greater detail, by Quintilian, who describes it as 'the artistic alteration of a word or phrase from its proper meaning to another ... some tropes are employed to help out our meaning and others to adorn our style ... the changes involved concern not merely individual words, but also our thoughts and the structure of our sentences' (Butler, 1989, VIII.vi.1–3).

Both orators and composers need a store of techniques for making their raw materials work. Both have recourse to topics, which serve them as vehicles for the presentation of their ideas. In particular, an ability to 'improvise' upon topics demands an ability to apply techniques of *variation*, either in relation to the material itself or its setting, and it is this aspect of topicality in Mozart's piano concertos that will be pursued in the final section of this chapter, taking as a starting-point two recent thought-provoking essays by Kofi Agawu, who has argued for an approach to Mozart's music that takes account of his gift for 'variation', not understood in a limited genre-specific way, but as a mode of discourse that may be imported into any formal musical situation, regardless of genre (Agawu, 1996a; 1996b). What is highlighted in the 'variation model', proposed by Agawu is Mozart's gift for adapting his musical materials to novel situations, in ever new ways; what strikes us mainly is his inventive use of language:

> It is well known that Mozart had a gift for what might be described somewhat loosely as turning things around … A key compositional device, then, is variation, not only as a feature of formal variation sets but as a more general principle found in diverse forms and genres. Accordingly, a productive line of enquiry in to Mozart's music might take the variation technique as a point of departure … What remains to be investigated is … ways in which the strategy of 'turning things around' is used in non-variation movements (Agawu, 1996b, pp.128–9).

The flexibility found in topics of digression, crossing the boundary between local 'embellishment' and structural 'purpose', are also characteristic of Mozart's variation practice discussed by Agawu.

Elsewhere Agawu attempts a preliminary study of the first movement of K.503 from the variation perspective. His concern is not to discover a deep underlying unity within this movement, but instead to empower the music's mobile surface: pointing, to be sure, to connections between contrasting situations in which Mozart has 'turned things around', but not valorising these uniquely insofar as they point to any supposedly more 'meaningful' level of structure.[34] His most telling observations relate to the role of variation technique within localised continuity, such as bars 152–6, in which a dynamically evolving phrase is achieved by grafting successive layers of embellishment to its opening melodic pattern while the harmonic support remains essentially fixed. An illustration of this same procedure on a broader scale is the close of the tutti exposition and the first solo entry (bars 82–99): 'a single harmonic progression, V^7-I (or variant thereof), is heard several times in succession, while the figuration, durational pattern, and melodic profile are altered … there is in fact an unbroken chain of fifteen such occurrences between measures 82 and 99' (Agawu, 1996a, p.306).[35] The first solo entry, leading up to the return of the main theme at bar 112, continues with this context of V^7-I gestures, gradually supplanting them with interrupted cadences. An element not considered by Agawu here is the irony (another rhetorical figure – actually a *trope*) of beginning the solo piano part within a prominent context of closure. The migration within the passage as a whole from perfect to interrupted gestures is itself a species of variation, namely an adaptation of cadential function from 'ironic closure' at its inception to 'postponement', during its course, creating, by this application of 'codes', the expectation of ultimate resolution back to the tonic (fulfilled at bar 112).

While it provides a number of telling instances of Agawu's concept of Mozart's variation practice, the first movement of K.503 is by no means the only piece in which it operates. The illustration offered below comes from the finale of K.467, concentrating exclusively on the role of variation in the bar-to-bar continuity of the central episode (bars 239–313).

At bar 239, Mozart begins an episode in A major – an unusual key in the tonal context of this movement – which concentrates substantially on the main theme of the finale. In the course of this episode he is, in effect, 'varying' this theme, by means of internal changes to its length, intervallic shape and articulation profile, but also by means of changes to the environment in which it appears (including features such as tonality, harmonic profile, phraseology, texture and register). On one level, he is indulging in 'play', asking himself the question, 'What can I do with this theme?' This section might therefore be regarded as a performative act, rather than simply a 'text' requiring analysis. Approaching it not from a preconceived philosophical position such as 'greatness is unity', and valorising this section only insofar as its surface variety is reducible to a singularity (that is, the theme, or some yet more deeply embedded *Urlinie* of which it is in itself only a sign), but instead, as a celebration of the very act of play, we perhaps come closer to understanding it. Obviously, this episode has a 'purpose' within the design of the whole movement (for instance, as a point of tonal opposition, from which the aesthetic effect of the inevitable return of the tonic, C major, is to be measured). But seen as a 'moment', isolated from such considerations, its live improvisational quality takes centre stage. This episode is a personification of Mozart the improviser, speaking directly, rather than in the 'third person'. The technical means through which he gives life to this element of 'play' is variation.

In the first part of the episode (bars 233–8), Mozart works with the principal theme, as follows:

- the theme is fragmented (shortened to six notes)
- its intervals are adapted (ascending tone–semitone–semitone–minor third–falling tone)
- its harmonic context is redefined (a threefold succession of alternating local V–I chords over a V pedal, leading to A major)
- the revised harmonic context is allied to changes in the texture and register, *viz.*:
    - antiphonal migration through the ensemble (strings and finally solo piano) replaces original 'theme and accompaniment' status
    - descent through three successive octaves replaces exclusive treble register
    - ¨shift from staccato to legato articulation

The continuation (bars 239–77) throws attention on to the hitherto ambiguous scansion of the main theme. At the opening of the movement, its first bar is unharmonised, the tonic C major chordal support entering only in bar 2. Does the theme 'begin' in bar 1, or is this merely an upbeat preparation for the strong melodic appoggiatura (quavers a′–g′), timed to arrive with the first chord? The latter interpretation seems the likeliest, since, harmonically, it places the tonic and dominant supporting chords, respectively, on strong and weak positions within the phrase. At bar 239, Mozart experiments with this supporting framework. Coinciding with the resolution into A major (that is, a structural 'downbeat') is a single bar of left-hand accompaniment, which temporarily alters the effect of the theme's ascending chromatic quaver pattern in the next bar. No longer does it seem so pregnant with anticipation; rather its status has become consequential, no longer 'leading towards', but 'following on' (from the single bar of tonic Alberti bass texture). A similarly relaxed feeling is subsequently imparted to the wind entry with the main theme, this time following on from a half-cadence on the dominant, E. From this point, the focus is shifted from phrase beginnings to phrase endings, for Mozart now switches his attention to the theme's cadential suffix. Starting with the solo entry in bars 252–3, he separates just this element of the theme, the piano echoing the woodwind's phrase ending, and then repeating it sequentially a third higher (bars 254–5) before continuing to a cadence in A. A major is then confirmed by four extra bars in which the theme – now appearing as an integral unit, rather than in fragments – is treated not as a beginning, but as a terminating cadence (further extended by repetition in the woodwind to bar 265). At each stage throughout this passage the stability of the theme is tested, either by breaking it up into smaller units, or by shifting it laterally across the expected pattern of strong and weak accent patterns.

Following the woodwind cadence in bar 265, Mozart 'turns around' the theme in yet another direction. From its fragmented cadential suffix he generates a rising scale that swings the music into F (at bar 277). From this point, he returns to the theme's prefix (only), restoring its chromatic profile and treating it in dialogue between the piano left hand and the woodwind in alternating two-bar patterns, winding all the time around a circle of fifths (touching on F–C–G–D–A–E–B, supported skeletally by a suspension chain in the right-hand Alberti figuration). From bar 289 the prefix pattern is fragmented further (to just four quavers) and the solo–woodwind antiphony is increased to double speed. The episode ends with a transposed repetition of bars 239–44 into the tonic, C major, satisfyingly 'framing' the whole, though leaving as an open question the true scansion of the theme, which slips in casually at bar 314, its original 'fidgety' character irredeemably compromised following a single bar of Alberti accompaniment in the violins.

Within this episode, Mozart demonstrates to the full his genius for 'turning around' the content of his opening theme. It evolves by a process of almost continual transformation, reminding us that some of Mozart's contemporaries who criticised his compositions for indulging in excessive variety were perhaps not wide of the mark.[36] No sooner have we grasped one feature of the process than its premises are altered again. Nevertheless, as an exhilarating demonstration of his lively mind, this passage can hardly be equalled – except, of course, for almost every other bar of his piano concertos.

Notes

1. ' ... nun fehlen noch 2 Concerten zu den Subscriptions-Concerten. Die Concerten sind eben das Mittelding zwischen zu schwer und zu leicht – sind sehr Brilliant – angenehm in die ohren – natürlich, ohne in das leere zu fallen – hie[r] und da – können auch *kenner allein* satisfaction erhalten – doch so – daß die nichtkenner damit zufrieden seyn müssen, ohne zu wissen warum.'

2. On conventional understandings of eighteenth-century music and their socio-cultural contexts, see Gjerdingen, 1996.

3. Heinichen, 1728; Fux, 1725; Mattheson, 1737; Mattheson, 1739; Riepel, 1752; Riepel, 1755; Kirnberger, 1771–79; Daube, 1773; Forkel, 1788; Koch, 1782–93. This is but a small selection of texts relevant to the Austro-German picture; for an in-depth treatment of eighteenth-century musical theory (not restricted to Germany) see Lester, 1992.

4. Eighteenth-century treatises dealing with melody include: Riepel, 1752; Nichel-mann, 1755; Koch, 1782–93; Portmann, 1789; Daube, 1797–98. Key extracts from several of these writers are available in Allanbrook, 1998.

5. For a detailed discussion of Koch's melodic analyses see Baker, 1976.

6. Riepel's theories, while praised by Koch and in reviews by Marpurg, 1755–57 (i (1755), pp.340–3; ii (1756), pp.514–21; iii (1757), p 396), seem not to have been all that widely available, since in the 1757 issue Marpurg notes that some of his readers had apparently been unable to obtain copies of Riepel's text. As noted previously, Leopold Mozart owned a copy of one of Riepel's texts.

7. The juxtaposition of relatively energetic and placid elements at the opening of a piece is by no means unusual in Mozart. More famous later examples than K.242 include the openings of the concerto in E flat, K.482, the piano sonata in C, K.309, and the 'Jupiter' symphony, K.551.

8. The main melody is carried by the first violin part. In K.238 the likeness to Koch's theoretical models is fairly close. Mozart's later concertos tend to divide the principal melodic lines between different instruments within the ensemble to a far greater extent. The purpose of this demonstration is not to initiate a system-atic correlation of Mozart's melodic style and Koch's theoretical templates, but to illustrate how a particular melody's organisation relates to contemporary theoret-ical understanding.

9. Reports on individual pieces are given in Part Two.

10. A similar overall picture may be seen in the first movement of K.451 in D (also considered in Mozart's letter of 26 May 1784). At the beginning of the 'solo' exposition, the piano part outlines the tutti's main material, but in a profusely decorated style, heavy with scales and broken chords, setting the scene for what follows. Mozart's father considered both the D minor and C major concertos, K.466 and 467, which he received in a package from Wolfgang in Salzburg on 2

December 1785, along with the six quartets dedicated to Joseph Haydn (K.387, 421, 428, 458, 464 and 465), and the G minor piano quartet, K.478, as being especially challenging from the technical point of view, describing K.467 as 'astonishingly difficult' (see his letters of 14 January and 23 March 1786, and the entries for these works in Part Two.).

11. For further details, see the entry for K.491 in Part Two.

12. Further on this, see Chapter Seven, pp.143–4.

13. He added a flute to the ensemble in the alternative finale for K.175, the Rondo in D, K.382 (1782).

14. The revised scoring coincided with a second phase of compositional activity begun in spring 1786; see the entry for K.488 in Part Two.

15. For detailed investigation of this area of late-eighteenth-century German aesthetics, see Hosler, 1981 and Morrow, 1997. For a partial translation of and commentary upon Sulzer, see Baker and Christensen, 1996.

16. Leopold Mozart's education is described in Layer, 1975. The study of rhetoric was preceded by grammar. The principal classical texts were by Aristotle (see Freese, 1991; Heath, 1996; Tredennick and Forster, 1989), Cicero (see Hubbell, 1976; Sutton and Rackham, 1988; Caplan, 1989) and Quintilian (see Butler, 1989). *Ad Herrenium* (now generally agreed not to be the work of Cicero, though it shares some similarities with his *De Inventione*), Cicero's *De Oratore*, Quintilian's *Institutio* and Aristotle's *The 'Art' of Rhetoric* were all published for the first time in Italy during the later fifteenth century, and remained essential (and oft-reprinted) educational aids in Europe until the first half of the nineteenth century.

17. Bauer, Deutsch and Eibl, 1962–75, i, nos.2 and 8. See also vol.v (Kommentar) to these letters. Gottsched's works were enormously important in mid-eighteenth-century German letters and were widely reprinted. Leopold owned Gottsched, 1736 and Gottsched, 1748.

18. For a recent attempt to view the piano sonatas within such a theoretical framework see Irving, 1997, pp.104foll.; also Bonds, 1991.

19. Sulzer does not present these categories in a connected sequence in the *Allgemeine Theorie*, of course, since that is an alphabetically organised treatise. They appear as follows: *Erfindung*, vol.ii, pp.86–94; *Entwurf*, vol.ii, pp.78–80; *Anlage*, vol.i, pp.148–9; *Form*, vol.ii, pp.250–2; *Plan*, vol.iii, pp.696–700; *Anordnung*, vol.i, pp.51–3; *Ausarbeitung*, vol.i, pp.246–50. Although Sulzer mentions a category of *Ausführung* ('realisation'), no article of that title appears in his treatise. All appear continuously in translation in Baker and Christensen, 1996, pp.55–80.

20. Translation from Baker and Christensen, 1996, pp.160–161. Note that Koch subsumes Sulzer's categories of *Anlage* (layout), *Form* (form) and *Plan* (plan) under the single heading of Anlage (here translated as 'plan').

21. Koch is inconsistent regarding the status of the *Anlage*. By 'present themselves to the composer as a complete whole', he presumably intended to convey that the Anlage resided 'in the mind' rather than as a notated sketch (*Entwurf*), further confirmation that the *Anlage* lay close to the initial level of inspiration (*Erfindung*). Elsewhere he explicitly states that the *Anlage* 'visibly presented or written in notes is called the sketch [*Entwurf*]' (Baker and Christensen, 1996, pp.187–8). Yet *Entwurf* precedes *Anlage* in Koch's introductory listing of 'ways in which the fine arts are created' (Baker and Christensen, 1996, p.160) and he describes his own 'sketch' of Graun's aria as the *Anlage*. The former is suggestive of a degree of confusion over terms and their meanings; possibly the latter was a pedagogical necessity, for how else could a mental picture be represented in a

book other than in notated form? Further on Koch's systematic understanding of
the creative process, which lies beyond the scope of this discussion, see Nancy
Baker's 'Introduction' in Baker and Christensen, 1996, pp.119–30.

22.   As previously mentioned, Koch's notion of the *Anlage* as something residing in
      the mind, evidently preceding the conscious and notated work of realisation and
      elaboration, places that stage at the beginning of the rhetorical hierarchy in close
      juxtaposition to *Erfindung*.

23.   Probably, though not certainly, meaning *Ausführung*, rather than *Anordnung*,
      within Koch's terminology. Once again, Koch's application of rhetorical terms
      risks confusion. In his §52 (Koch, 1782–93, ii; Baker and Christensen, 1996,
      p.160) he places *Anordnung* (disposition) after the *Anlage*, suggesting a subse-
      quent rhetorical stage adjacent to the *Ausführung*; in his §55–6, however (Baker
      and Christensen, 1996, p.162) he treats the *Anordnung* as a prior stage to *Anlage*
      should the composer not be possessed of 'genius'.

24.   These precise colour shades are more difficult to determine in the black and white
      reproduction found in Mozart, 1991.

25.   Further on *elocutio* and its musical applications within the eighteenth century, see
      Irving, 1997, Chapter Twelve.

26.   This is discussed further in Chapter Seven in relation to extemporised embellish-
      ments in performance.

27.   He quoted from some, and acknowledges others, in the 'Short History of Music'
      prefaced to Mozart, 1756; Knocker, 1951, p.22.

28.   Some of the principal musical *figurae* are explained in Ratner, 1980, pp.83–91.

29.   It is worth noting that Batteux's treatise, which focuses on the principle of
      mimesis in the arts, was translated into German at quite an early stage in its
      history by the lexicographer Gottsched (Gottsched, 1754) and therefore had an
      impact beyond French-speaking culture.

30.   Batteux, 1746, p.56: 'the Muse [Batteux here uses the word 'Dieu'] does not
      arouse the man whom he influences, says Plutarch, he only gives him those vital
      ideas which [themselves] impart the sentiments to which he then responds'
      (author's translation). Plutarch's *Life of Coriolanus* (Batteux's source) is avail-
      able in Perrin, 1916. In the fuller context of the passage quoted by Batteux (on
      Homer), Plutarch notes '[Homer] does not represent the god [Muse] as taking
      away, but as prompting, a man's course of action; nor yet as creating impulses in
      a man, but rather conceptions which lead to impulses, and by these his creation is
      not made involuntary, but his will is set in motion ... [the gods] do not mould our
      bodies by their direct agency, by certain motives, conceptions and purposes, they
      rouse the active and elective powers of our spirits' (Perrin, 1916, pp.198–9, refer-
      ring to Homer's *Odyssey*, ix.299 and *Iliad*, i.188; vi.161).

31.   Hughes, 1955, pp.77–8, recording the Novellos' visit to Constanze Nissen in
      Salzburg in July 1829. See also Deutsch, 1965, p.538. See also Sophie Haibel's
      account of Mozart's demeanour: 'even at his most good-humoured he was very
      pensive ... he seemed the while to be working away deep in thought at some thing
      quite different'; quoted in Deutsch, 1965, p.537.

32.   The late-eighteenth-century notion of 'genius' was occasionally associated with a
      tendency towards surprising modulation schemes. See some of the reviews cited
      in Morrow, 1997, Chapter Six.

33.   'Searching for inspiration' is itself a much-rehearsed topic, visually captured in
      the often-reproduced portrait of Gluck in the Kunst-Historisches Museum,
      Vienna. Seated at the keyboard, hands poised, eyes turned aloft, the composer
      beckons the Muse from on high. The composition and the lighting of this portrait

combine to symbolise artistic detachment: Gluck is no mere 'mechanic', working with his notes according to rule; he is a 'genius', possessed by the Muse whose powers lie beyond the portrait's frame.

34. In this respect, Agawu's observations on the first movement of K.503 are in contrast to those expressed in Keller, 1956a. Agawu's account does, nevertheless, propose something approaching a hierarchy of variational levels operating within the Allegro maestoso, capable of sustaining meaningful structural connections across the broad span of the movement. For an application of these principles within a different genre, see Irving, 2001.

35. Mozart sketched the bulk of the solo passage several times before settling on the version considered by Agawu; this is considered in Part Two, pp.240–42.

36. For instance, Carl Dittersdorf, writing in 1787: '[Mozart's] overwhelming and unrelenting artfulness are not to everyone's taste' (Eisen, 1991a, no.54); and Johann Baptist Cramer, writing in the *Magasin der Musik* (23 April 1787): 'he aims too high in his artful and truly beautiful compositions ... his new Quartets ... dedicated to Haydn, may well be called too highly seasoned – and whose palate can endure this for long?' (quoted in Deutsch, 1965, p.290).

CHAPTER SEVEN

Performance Considerations

Keyboard instruments

Happily, there is today no shortage of excellent performances of Mozart's piano concertos played on fortepianos. The discovery of this new and exciting sound-world has been one of the most important – perhaps *the* most important – change in our understanding of this and other classical repertoires during the past generation.[1] Some, notably Richard Taruskin, are critical of the whole 'Early Music' enterprise, regarding performers' attempts to recapture the 'authentic' Mozart (or Josquin, or Monteverdi or Bach) more as an outcome of twentieth-century taste than as a truly re-creative activity (Taruskin, 1982; 1988; 1992).

While it is possible to perform Mozart's concertos very beautifully on a modern concert grand piano (indeed, it is desirable that this practice should continue unthreatened by 'authentic purists'), a fortepiano commensurate with the types of instruments familiar to Mozart will come closer to recapturing his own expectations of sonority in the concertos. The kind that he liked best was evidently that which has become known as the 'Viennese' fortepiano, with a peculiarly light key-action and neat escapement mechanism, its stringing and hammering producing, in consort with this action, a mellow, silvery tone underpinned by a delicate attack of remarkable clarity, allowing semiquaver passagework to penetrate with ease across the whole register of the keyboard, and at the same time affording a degree of balance between registers (in textures involving theme and chordal, or broken-chorded accompaniment, for example) to be achieved almost effortlessly, and with far greater clarity than is normally attainable on a modern concert grand, an instrument developed for a nineteenth-century repertoire entirely different in its sonorous demands. So great have been the benefits of the fortepiano in relation to Mozart's concertos in recent years that we are apt to assume that he had this instrument exclusively in mind. Yet this may not necessarily have been the case. What does the surviving documentary evidence tell us about the appropriate choice of keyboard instrument for Mozart's concertos?

On 4 December 1780, Leopold Mozart wrote to Wolfgang, then in Munich preparing for the forthcoming production of *Idomeneo*,[2] explaining that 'about half past eleven, Herr von Edelbach and three strangers came into the room ... Your sister had to play them a short piece on the fortepiano.' This seemingly innocuous remark is actually quite significant, for it is the earliest documented reference to the presence of a fortepiano (as opposed to a harpsichord) at the Mozart family home in Salzburg. In a famous painting of the Mozart family by

Johann Nepomuk della Croce dating from about this time[3] Mozart and his sister are seated at a single manual keyboard – evidently a fortepiano, not a harpsichord – in the family home; this may well be the instrument Leopold mentions in his letter.[4] Possibly he had bought the fortepiano in late 1780 and the visitors accompanying von Edelbach were curious to hear what this instrument could do. It may well have been the first of its kind in Salzburg.[5] Besides a square piano referred to in an 1805 inventory of instruments formerly owned by the Archbishop, Hieronymous Colloredo,[6] no other examples of fortepianos are documented in Salzburg before the reference to Leopold's instrument on 4 December 1780.[7] For evidence of Mozart's encounters with the fortepiano, we have to look outside Salzburg.

According to an anonymous report in Schubart's *Deutsche Chronik* of 27 April 1775, Mozart had fairly recently engaged in a fortepiano 'contest' with the composer Ignaz von Beecke:

> In Munich last winter [1774–5] I heard two of the greatest clavier players, Herr *Mozart* and Captain *von Beecke*; my host, Herr Albert ... has an excellent fortepiano in his house. It was there that I heard these two giants in contest on the clavier. Mozart's playing had great weight ... But no more than that; Beecke surpassed him by a long way. Winged agility, grace [and] melting sweetness [characterised Beecke's playing] (Deutsch, 1965, p.153).[8]

This was probably Mozart's first significant encounter with a fortepiano. His unfamiliarity with the possibilities of a touch-sensitive keyboard seems to be established by the qualities Beecke displayed and Mozart evidently lacked at this time ('agility, grace [and] melting sweetness').[9] By late 1777, however, Mozart's experience of the instrument had grown considerably. In a concert given in Augsburg on 22 October at Count Fugger's concert hall, Mozart performed K.242 in the version for three pianos. One Augsburg critic remarked on Mozart's playing in a review of this concert, in which Mozart also played some solo items (including the D major sonata, K.284 and some fugal improvisations): 'the rendering on the fortepiano [was] so neat, so clean, so full of expression, and yet at the same time so extraordinarily rapid, so that one hardly knew what to give attention to first, and all the hearers were enraptured'.[10] Almost contemporary with this is the testimony of Mozart's mother in a letter to her husband of 28 December 1777 to the effect that:

> he plays quite differently [here in Mannheim] from what he used to do in Salzburg – *for there are fortepianos here* [emphasis added – this aside is a further hint that fortepianos were apparently unknown in Salzburg at this date] on which he plays so extraordinarily well that people say they have never heard the like ... Although Beecke has been performing here, and Schubart[11] too, yet everyone says that Wolfgang far surpasses them in beauty of tone, quality and execution.

In Augsburg in 1777, Mozart discovered the fortepianos of Johann Andreas Stein. In a famous letter to his father, which might be construed as a thinly veiled plea to his father to purchase one of Stein's fortepianos, Mozart notes that:

> I shall begin at once with Stein's pianofortes. Before I had seen any of his make, Späth's claviers had always been my favourites.[12] But now I much prefer Stein's, for they damp ever so much better than the Regensburg instruments. When I strike hard, I can keep my finger on the note [key] or raise it, but the sound ceases the moment I have produced it. In whatever way I touch the keys, the tone is always even. It never jars, it is never stronger or weaker or entirely absent; in a word, it is always even. It is true that he does not sell a pianoforte of this kind for less than 300 gulden, but the trouble and labour which Stein puts into the making of it cannot be paid for. His instruments have this special advantage over others that they are made with escapement action ... When you touch the keys, the hammers fall back again the moment after they have struck the strings, whether you hold down the keys or release them.

Leopold's reply (23 October 1777) notes that 'I am glad Herr Stein's piano-fortes are so good, but indeed they are expensive.' At this time, Leopold owned a Stein clavichord, purchased in 1762,[13] another, probably by Christian Friederici (1709–80), which was ultimately given to Nannerl, and a two-manual harpsichord certainly the work of Friederici and which was bought probably during the early 1760s. Other harpsichords owned by Salzburg residents are sometimes referred to in the Mozart family correspondence. Countess Lützow, dedicatee of K.246, owned a harpsichord that was played by Mozart during a visit by the Archduke Maximilian of Austria in April 1775. Countess Lodron, for whom K.242 was composed, possessed several harpsichords. On 12 April 1778, Leopold reported to Mozart in Paris that Nannerl had been due to play a concerto on Countess Lodron's 'good harpsi-chord', but that this was cancelled since the Countess would only allow a different harpsichord (presumably of inferior quality) by the local maker, Egedacher, to be used.

Subsequently in Vienna, Mozart had much freer access to fortepianos. On 3 April 1781, Countess Thun lent Mozart her Stein fortepiano for a benefit concert at the Kärtnnerthortheater; he played on this same instrument in a contest with Clementi on 24 December 1781. The fact that he had to borrow instruments up to the end of the year may indicate that his own five-octave (F'–f''') fortepiano, by the Viennese maker, Anton Walter,[14] was not purchased before 1782. By late 1783, however, Mozart and his wife were fairly affluent, and had moved into relatively expensive accommodation at the Trattnerhof; possibly the Walter fortepiano was bought around the same time. At any rate, Mozart certainly had it in his lodgings early in 1785 when he was visited by Leopold. A special pedal attachment had been made for it, as noted by Leopold in a letter of 12 March 1785. This no longer survives, although Mozart is known to have used it at two concerts in which the concertos K.466 and K.467 were played.[15]

From all of this, it may be inferred that, before the end of 1780, Mozart may have had no opportunity to perform concertos on fortepianos in Salzburg. The early Salzburg concertos, K.175 (1773), K.238 (1776), K.242 (1776), K.246 (1776), K.271 (1777) and K.365 (1779) would therefore seem to have been written at the harpsichord, and, so far as local performances were concerned, played on that instrument. Nevertheless, Mozart perhaps had the sound-world of the fortepiano in mind in K.238, K.242, K.246 and K.271 since by January 1776 (the date of K.238) he may already have engaged in the fortepiano contest with von Beecke, added to which, there is documentary evidence for the performance of all these concertos on fortepianos during Mozart's stay in Augsburg in 1777.[16] So far as harpsichord performances of these works are concerned, the only serious problems lie in K.271 and K.365, both of which include finely graded dynamic indications or *fp* accentuations that appear to be beyond the capacity of the harpsichord to realise (at least convincingly).[17] Alternations of *forte* and *piano* of the type found at bars 127–30 in the slow movement of K.271 could, technically, be executed on a two-manual harpsichord (on which each manual was set to contrast the other), but K.271 frequently relies for its effect on juxtapositions within a phrase or bar that could only be rendered clumsily on the harpsichord. Examples include the following:

i   bars 82–3; 86; 92; 96; 100; 108–10; 115–17; 192–3; 211–15; 220; 225–
      30; 237–9; 258–9; cadenza (both sets 'A' and 'B' in NMA)
ii   bars 43–4; 74–5; 104–5; cadenza set 'A' (including a crescendo)
iii   bars 204–8; 269; 286; 290; 297–9 (another crescendo); 300; 324–8; 332–
      40; 459–66 (a gradual decrescendo)

The character of the springing phrase first sounded by the piano at bars 204–8 of the finale depends significantly upon the dynamic tapering. This cannot be effectively conveyed on a harpsichord, and it was perhaps conceived with foreknowledge of a touch-sensitive keyboard, whether or not one was immediately available in Salzburg. Arguably, the effect of a decrescendo could have been conveyed by the accompanying winds, but this does not solve the allied problem of articulation. On a harpsichord, the uniformity of attack produced by the plucked strings virtually neutralises the subtle conjoining of slurs and staccatos that lie at the heart of this phrase. Dynamic juxtaposition is scarcely evident within solo sections of K.365, which includes very few dynamics; accentuation is rather more problematic (potentially awkward corners here include bars 64, 74, 133, 137, 220, 256 and 262 of the first movement). A more fundamental issue in harpsichord performances of this concerto is articulation: Mozart's notation of bars 103–11 and 177–80 in the first movement, and the main theme in the rondo finale (sequentially developed by each piano in turn from bars 333–57), absolutely requires the variety of attack so characteristic of a fortepiano and precisely the quality lacking in a harpsichord.[18]

Orchestral size

How large an orchestra did Mozart envisage for performances of his piano concertos? This question is a crucial starting point in relation to historically informed performances of these pieces. But it is also central to our appreciation of the concerto genre as practised by Mozart. If the orchestra is relatively large, then the genre is strongly characterised by the sense of a 'competition' between a single voice and a multitude. This conception lies at the heart of Tovey's understanding of Mozart's concertos, discussed in Chapter Three ('Nothing in human life or history is much more thrilling ... than the antithesis of the individual and the crowd'). If, on the other hand, the orchestra is relatively small, then our impressions of the genre are radically shifted. Instead of competition, we sense co-operation; the opposition of single and multiple voices disintegrates somewhat, revealing different, quasi-chamber music features. In one sense, the concertos are what our listening responses make them; and those responses are profoundly affected by weight of numbers. These pieces are arguably misrepresented by a setting in which the concert grand piano is placed sideways-on in the centre of a stage, governed by a conductor elevated on a podium, physically wielding his (or her) authority over a symphony orchestra of perhaps 50 or more players.

Of course, such a setting is (at least nowadays) a fiction. There is no shortage of wonderful performances and recordings of Mozart's piano concertos played on modern keyboard instruments accompanied by an orchestra (either conducted or directed from the keyboard) whose string section has been pared down to chamber proportions, allowing both for the careful balancing of 'oppositional' effects, such as the first-movement recapitulation of K.503 and the delicate interplay between piano and woodwind at bars 261–75 in the first movement of K.488. Such performances offer a compromise reflecting the awareness that the exciting effects of volume and texture so central to the 'virtuosic–heroic' concerto as practised during the course of the nineteenth and early twentieth centuries in the works of Brahms, Tchaikowsky and Rachmaninov are peripheral to the expressive world of Mozart's pieces. Fortunately, too, they display a recognition that Mozart's piano concertos are not part of the 'orchestral' repertory in the same sense as are Brahms's or Tchaikowsky's or Rachmaninov's. Such a setting was the inevitable product of nineteenth-century concert life, in which the public production of music served a social purpose and had to be manifested in a suitably civic environment. That Mozart was posthumously caught up in this project had both positive and negative aspects. On the positive side, Mozart's concertos acquired a geographically widespread audience (ultimately on both sides of the Atlantic), cementing their artistic value to no small extent. Had they remained outside of the nineteenth-century concert sphere, they might forever have been overshadowed by competing repertoire. On the negative side, this 'civic' means of production constructed Mozart's piano concertos within the same generic environment as the 'virtuosic-heroic' repertoire, but as 'slighter' works in the same mould. By the end of the nineteenth century the public concert had become a major institution, alongside opera, giving credence to a 'canonic' list of masterpieces. Understanding of the concerto genre and its formal manoeuvres depended heavily upon its presentation within such a frame. It was inevitable, then, that Mozart's piano concertos should be measured against the standard procedures of nineteenth-century virtuoso exemplars, seeming slight in relation to the concertos of, say, Brahms or Tchaikowsky.

Fortunately, it is no longer necessary to indulge in the kind of historical 'rehabilitation' that regards Mozart's concertos as a lightweight, sub-Beethovenian species standing at the beginning of a progression leading ultimately to the herculean striving of Brahms or Tchaikowsky. We now recognise that we must 'abandon the notion of the concerto as an inherently competitive genre ... But the idea that the concerto is based on contrast can be retained, although with a subtle shift in emphasis ... between soloistic texture and ensemble texture ... between three groups, namely the soloist, the string band, and the wind band' (Edge, 1996a, p.446). Achieving this implicit balance in performance rests importantly upon the distinctive colours of period instruments, of course, and in particular upon the tonal characteristics of eighteenth-century wind instruments, both soloistically and collectively. Our impression of the sound-world of Mozart's piano concertos has been deeply affected by recent recordings in which the blending of a fortepiano, classical flutes, oboes, clarinets, bassoons, horns, trumpets, timpani and strings have revealed dimensions of colour, balance, register, texture and articulation that would have been commonplace in contemporary appreciation of these works, but which are obscured by the stridently 'metallic' sound of their modern counterparts. This new and exciting sound-world depends both on playing techniques as well as on instrumental design and usage. It is beyond the scope of this study to consider these technical and organological aspects.[19] Instead, the following section will investigate the issue of orchestral size, and especially the size and usage of the string group in eighteenth-century performances of Mozart's piano concertos. Determining how large Mozart's string ensemble may have been is highly problematic. Several methodologies may be brought to bear on the issue, including the interpretation of clues within the scores themselves; iconographical evidence; documentary evidence (personnel lists, reports and letters); and surviving performance materials. None of these provides conclusive answers, however.

Dynamics, articulations and scorings

It is a curious fact that, in solo entries, the accompanying strings (and, for that matter, woodwind) are consistently marked *piano* in the authentic sources.

This level continues almost without exception throughout the entire duration of a solo, irrespective of tempo and character. Illustrations may easily be found in movements in different tempos, exhibiting different topical characteristics and drawn from across the entire chronological spread of Mozart's concertos:

K.238, finale (gavotte topic): the opening statement and all reprises of the main theme are *piano*; in bars 34–5 and 81–5 there are *fp* or alternate *forte* and *piano* indications, reinforcing the solo.

K.414, first movement ('singing allegro', cantabile topic): string accompaniments consistently *piano*; at bars 169–70 and bar 180 foll., there are *mezzo forte* and *sfp* indications (within the prevailing *piano* dynamic), marking the syncopation.

K.467, first movement (march topic): at bar 162 *forte* is indicated, but here the additional volume is evidently intended as a reinforcement of the structure, rounding-off the end of the solo (otherwise, the accompaniment is consistently *piano*)

K.482, finale ('hunt' topic): at bar 73, exceptionally, the dynamic is *pianissimo* (unchanged throughout the remainder of the solo, until bar 189); nevertheless, the uniformity of dynamic throughout this extended passage, despite some significant shifts of character, register and texture, is remarkable.

By contrast, within the conjoining tutti sections, there is a much more flexible dynamic range, typically *forte*, but by no means confined to that level, as illustrated, for example, by the Larghetto of K.595. What are we to make of this state of affairs? Might the *piano* indications for these string accompaniments be evidence that, because the string section was typically quite large, it needed to play with restraint if the fragile sound of the solo fortepiano was not to be overwhelmed? Such an interpretation is problematic. First, the uniform *piano* dynamic is typically applicable to the wind also (for example, throughout the development sections of K.453, K.488 and K.595, in which the piano's role is accompanimental to prominent wind solos). Secondly, sheer numbers are not all that are required for the string section to overpower a solo fortepiano: because of the quality of attack, a single violin is perfectly capable of producing a volume equal if not superior to a fortepiano's limited sustaining power, so a *piano* dynamic would be just as necessary in certain situations if, say, the first violin part were played by one player or several. Thirdly, there is the question of the uniformity with which the *piano* marking is applied. It frequently lies uncontradicted for extended periods (during the development sections just mentioned, for instance), irrespective of quite profound changes of musical character.

Given that Mozart's polyphony is so characteristically animated by subtlety of articulation, such 'blanket' application of dynamic levels seems unusually arbitrary. Indeed, the very subtlety of those articulations suggests few rather than relatively many players on each part if they are to retain their crispness of effect. It is difficult to imagine a phrase such as the secondary theme stated by the first violins at bars 30–8 in the first movement of K.488 – which could easily come from a passage in a chamber work with just a single player per part – being produced with its implicit 'cleanness' by a more than a very few players. Mozart's very precise notation of articulations, which underpin so many dialogues between the soloist and strings (or winds) in these pieces, argue in the direction of relatively small performing forces. Throughout the opening tutti at the beginning of the G major concerto, K.453, the first violin part is articulated with great precision, principally involving staccatos and slurs. In particular, the rhythmic profile is brought into much sharper focus with relatively small numbers. Their combination with the flute and first bassoon at bars 94–100 is notoriously difficult to bring off with the requisite clarity and balance with more than just a handful of players.[20] The inference seems to be that in order to achieve the right quality of articulate utterance in such passages, only a very small string group will do.

A related issue is scoring. The opening solo entry in this movement introduces the element of dialogue between the piano's right hand and the woodwind that is to become so important a factor in the character of this movement. The interjections played by the winds in bars 78–9 and 82–3 depend crucially on the utmost clarity in rhythmic articulation and would suffer significant deterioration if set for first and second violins, unless only a single player (or perhaps three)[21] were envisaged on each part. The same is true of bars 255–9 and 284–90 later in the movement, in both of which locations the material is shared antiphonally between the piano and wind. Possibly Mozart scored these phrases for winds rather than strings not only because he wished to exploit the inherent colour contrasts and crisp 'focus', but because he expected relatively large numbers of strings in public 'academy' performances in Vienna (not to mention the varying acoustic locations in which his concertos might be played) and consequently did not risk scoring such penetrating lines for the multiple violins.[22]

These contrasting interpretations of possible meanings of dynamics, articulations and scorings in the string parts need to be weighed alongside the apparently authentic practice of ripieno performance in Mozart's piano concertos. It seems to have been the case that, in certain performance traditions, at least, the solo passages would have been accompanied by a reduced string ensemble, probably one player (or one desk) to a part, whereas the tuttis would have been performed by the whole string group. This practice lends a 'built-in' light and shade to the texture of a movement, and coincidentally marks out its main structural divisions. Many editions, including some volumes of NMA, are silent on this important issue. In Mozart's autograph scores, the 'tutti' and 'solo' sections are usually marked as such within the string staves. While these indications do indeed designate the main structural divisions within a concerto first-movement form, or in an episodic form, they serve also a practical purpose. Mozart himself, of course, knew perfectly well where these points of structural division occurred in his own compositions, and needed no prompting. But a copyist producing playing parts from the autograph would normally need guidance so that he could (i) include these prompts in the parts that played throughout a movement; and (ii) easily recognise those passages that would be omitted from the ripieno parts, which contain only the tutti passages (the solos being indicated by rests).

How widespread this ripieno performance practice was is difficult to determine. It is typically indicated in sets of parts copied either in or for Salzburg, and in some others produced in Vienna which may have been copied from the autograph, for example in the case of playing parts for K.459 now at Brno.[23] Examples of Mozart's own 'tutti' and 'solo' markings are clearly visible in the autograph scores of K.491 and K.537 available in facsimile.[24] Not all of the autograph scores contain 'tutti' and 'solo' indications, though. One such case is K.466, for which there also exists a complete set of performance materials copied under Leopold Mozart's supervision during winter 1785–86, and subsequently used in a performance at Salzburg by Heinrich Wilhelm Marchand (1769–c.1812) in March 1786. These playing parts were copied directly from the autograph,[25] and yet they contain specific ripieno parts, 'Violino primo [Secondo] Rip:no' which play only at the following points:

1st mvt bars 78–111; 115–73; 193–253; 288–355
2nd mvt bars 40–75; 84, beat 1; 92, beat 1; 108–34; 143–62
3rd mvt bars 63–166; 196–336; 389–411

The fact that a set of parts produced in Salzburg for a specific performance there was adapted to ripieno practice despite the lack of such indications in the autograph exemplar perhaps means that ripieno performance of piano concertos was a distinctive local tendency, one to which Mozart himself evidently subscribed in concertos written and performed in Salzburg up to 1781. What is unclear is whether or not he continued to perform his concertos this way after his removal to Vienna. The evidence of K.466 (and also K.467, whose autograph Mozart sent to Salzburg for copying in November 1785 along with K.466 and which likewise contains no tutti/solo designations)[26] is inconclusive. The lack of indications in the autographs showing ripieno–tutti contrast may suggest that his Viennese performances did not habitually reduce the numbers of strings playing in solo sections; alternatively, it could be argued that it would not be especially difficult for a copyist to determine from the score where the ripieno strings were to enter.

The former supposition (no ripieno–tutti contrast) is strengthened by some concrete evidence connecting Mozart with ripieno practice after 1781, but in Salzburg, not Vienna. The surviving orchestral parts for K.415 now at St

Peter's, Salzburg,[27] were evidently copied in Vienna (and not, as formerly thought, in Salzburg),[28] and yet these string parts include precise 'tutti' and 'solo' indications. But these markings were added afterwards by Mozart himself, *not* by the Viennese copyist.[29] Evidently, they relate to Mozart's performance of K.415 in Salzburg on 1 October 1783, reinforcing the impression that ripieno performances reflect a distinctive local tradition, rather than a widespread national one.[30] Mozart's tutti/solo indications in the parts for K.415 indicate ripieno strings as follows:

I   bars 60–147; 160–5; 169–287
II   bars 17–58; 63–85
III   bars 50–68; 73–130; 143–210; 217–55 (viola; bass)/259 (violins)

In summary, it seems clear that reduced string forces were expected throughout the solo sections in contemporary performances of Mozart's piano concertos, at least when they were played in 'family' circumstances at Salzburg.[31] Possibly this was the case in Viennese contexts too, though solid documentary proof is lacking in the absence of any playing parts besides autograph cadenzas that may be conclusively associated with Mozart's own Viennese performances.

Before leaving the ripieno issue, one further piece of evidence should be mentioned, this time from a theoretical, rather than a practical, source. Georg Friedrich Wolf's *Allgemeines musikalisches Lexicon* (Halle, 1787)[32] seems to be equating *solo* with *piano* in certain contexts: 'In polyphonic works in which each part is to be played by more than one performer [wo jede Stimme mehr als einfach besetzt ist] one employs [that is, 'notates'] *solo* rather than *piano* ... from that point only one player per part continues until the word *Tutti* indicates that the rest should enter again.' Wolf's comments appear in his definition of 'solo', not in a specific discussion of the concerto genre (indeed, his remarks apply equally to vocal and instrumental performances). He apparently means that whereas in a one-to-a-part performance, 'solo' sections were marked *piano* in the accompanying parts, in performances given by larger ensembles, these same sections would need to be specifically indicated by the word *solo*, so that the 'rank and file' players knew when to stop and when to start again. This could be taken to imply that the lack of specific 'tutti/solo' indications in Mozart's concerto autographs (such as K.466 and K.467, in which *piano* indications are found in the solo sections instead) signals one-to-a-part strings, ruling out ripieno performance in Viennese contexts. This would also hold true for the 'Salzburg' parts of K.415, discussed above. Here, the Viennese copyist's original *forte* and *piano* indications were supplemented by Mozart's addition of 'tutti' and 'solo' markings, suggesting that his adaptation of the Viennese material was necessary in order to allow the concerto to be performed in Salzburg by a rather larger ensemble than that envisaged in

Vienna. Whether it is safe to draw such an inference from Wolf's *Lexicon*, which possibly reflects north-German practice, and which was only printed in Vienna a decade after Mozart's death, is questionable. Nevertheless, his comments seem to point to an assumption that both instrumental and vocal genres – including, presumably, concertos – would be produced by both relatively small and relatively large forces ('wo jede Stimme mehr als einfach besetzt ist'), and that for the latter, specific guidance regarding tutti and solo participation was needed because the notation was not interchangeable without confusion.

Iconographical evidence

Contemporary representations of performances in paintings, engravings, almanacs and the like are an important tool for the student of performance practice. Such evidence offers a valuable range of information on the location of a performance (a large hall, a theatre, a chamber in a private home); on the participants (how many players are involved, and their relative placement); on what kinds of instruments are involved (and their design); and on playing techniques (how a violin or bow is held; the attitude of a keyboard player's hand towards the instrument and so on). But this kind of evidence must be handled with the greatest caution. While potentially informative in all these areas, such representations were first and foremost just that: artistic representations rather than draughtsmanship, in which technical aspects such as how many fingerholes or keys a woodwind instrument had, or the angle at which a violin or bow was held, take second place to such considerations as the overall visual composition of the picture. Literal interpretation of such pictures is a dangerous game for the musicologist. An apparently 'authentic' seating plan for a chamber ensemble may be nothing of the kind, but simply an arrangement which the artist (or whoever commissioned him) found spatially satisfying.

Very few representations of performances involving a harpsichord or fortepiano with an accompanying ensemble dating from the second half of the eighteenth century can be safely associated with concertos; for example, drawings or engravings of public instrumental concerts in halls and theatres represent the orchestral size and layout associated with opera or symphony performances, rather than concertos. How trustworthy the numbers and seating arrangements may be in such large assemblies is debatable. Representations of *Hausmusik* are arguably more exact (or, at least, less inexact). In fact, only one depiction from this period is specifically linked to a performance of a concerto. Entitled 'Concerto a Cembalo obligato Con Stromenti', this is an engraving by Johann Rudolf Holzhalb (Zurich, 1777) showing, in addition to the solo keyboard, two violins, a cello, two transverse flutes and two horns as accompanying instruments (Figure 7.1). Another picture, attributed to Johann Joseph

Figure 7.1 J. R. Holzhalb, 'Concerto a Cembalo obligato Con Stromenti (1777)'.
Zentralbibliothek Zürich, Neujahrstück ab dem Musiksaal 1777, AMG Q
333. Reproduced by kind permission of the Zentralbibliothek, Zurich

Zoffany,[33] shows a rather larger string group consisting of eleven violins and
violas (the numbers of each are unclear), three cellos, one violone or double
bass and a wind group comprising flute and pairs of oboes, bassoons and horns
in addition to the keyboard. The musicians are arranged in a semicircle around
the keyboard, which might, however, be playing a continuo, rather than a solo

part in a concerto. Neither of these two representations can be trusted as an authentic reflection of Mozart's preferred orchestral size – still less of seating. Holzhalb's engraving depicts a domestic performance in which a group of players standing or sitting around the walls of a small room whose only source of light (to judge from the uniform direction of shadow) is situated at the opposite side to the players, a circumstance in which the parts on their stands would be virtually invisible.[34] Moreover, the cellist and horn players are reading from a single stand, while the two flautists (and possibly also the two violinists) are reading from the same part. As regards the composition, Holzhalb skilfully directs our eye from bottom left around to right middle by means of line and by light and shade, a progression in which the main focal point is the brilliantly lit lady at the keyboard, conceivably a deliberate visual portrayal of her musical centrality in a concerto. Nevertheless, the weight of evidence for string numbers in such representations of *Hausmusik* appears to be that one or two players to a part was the norm.

Documentary evidence

The *Hausmusik* situation is one that was frequently encountered in the Mozart household in Salzburg. In a letter of 15 May 1784, referring to K.449, K.450, K.451 and K.453, Mozart notes that 'the music would not be of much use to you, because except for the E flat concerto [K.449], which can be performed *a quattro* without wind-instruments, the other three concertos [K.450, 451 and 453] all have wind-instrument accompaniments; and you very rarely have wind-instrument players at your house'. K.413–15 are similarly described by the composer as being performable 'à quattro' in his advertisements placed in the Viennese press early in 1783, offering '3 concertos, which may be performed either with a large orchestra with wind instruments or merely *a quattro*, viz. with 2 violins, 1 viola and violoncello, [; these] will not appear until the beginning of April this year, and will be issued (finely copied and supervised by himself) only to those who have subscribed thereto'.[35] The meaning of Mozart's phrase is open to two contrasting interpretations. 'À quattro' may mean literally 'with four accompanying players' (that is, string quartet); alternatively, it may mean 'in four polyphonic parts' (that is, strings only, with no winds – an interpretation that would accord with the sense of Mozart's letter regarding K.449). If these works were performed one-to-a-part, then the implication of tutti–solo alternations in the surviving performance materials is called into question, since there could be no reduction in numbers for the solos. If performed in a small chamber, 'à quattro', then the distinction between quasi-tutti and quasi-solo could still be effected by judicious application of dynamics: *forte* in the tuttis, *piano* in the solos, somewhat along the lines of the comments in Wolf's *Lexicon*, quoted above.

Specific references to 'public' or 'semi-public' performances of concertos in Salzburg are few and far between. The only information directly relevant to performances of Mozart's concertos is contained in a letter from Leopold Mozart to Wolfgang (then on tour in Paris) dated 12 April 1778. Leopold is describing a Sunday afternoon performance by an amateur orchestra directed by Count Czernin the previous Sunday in which Leopold himself played second violin, and at which, as mentioned above, Nannerl 'was to have played a concerto, but because the Countess [Lodron] would not make her fine harpsichord available ... she did not play after all' (author's translation). The names of the participants are given in Leopold's account, according to which there were eight first violins, six second violins, two violas, five or six cellos, two or three double-basses (one player evidently switched between cello and bass as required), two oboes, and two horns in addition to the various instrumental and vocal soloists.

Documentary reports of Viennese public concerts that make specific mention of the size of the ensemble invariably refer to symphonies or operas rather than concertos. One such account, that has sometimes been taken as justification for employing a relatively large ensemble in performances of Mozart's piano concertos, is his letter of 11 April 1781, relating to a concert at the Kärntnertortheater on 3 April that had been organised by the then newly constituted Tonkünstler-Sozietät: 'There were forty violins, the wind-instruments were all doubled, there were ten violas, ten double-basses, eight violoncellos and six bassoons.' A Mozart symphony (possibly K.297) was certainly performed by these forces, and the composer was clearly impressed with the way it came off ('the symphony went magnificently and had the greatest success'). However, no mention is made of a piano concerto, either in Mozart's letter or in the poster advertising this concert (Deutsch, 1965, p.195). It is not therefore entirely safe to assume that such a large string ensemble (the equivalent in modern terms of ten desks each of first and second violins; five desks of violas; four desks of cellos; and five desks of double-basses) would have been his normal expectation in a concerto performance. Indeed, the fact that Mozart lists in his letter the precise numbers of players involved in this concert may suggest that his intent was to impress a rather extraordinary and successful event on his father. While this may have been an unusually large string group, it was not unique in Viennese experience. Similar numbers of string players were assembled for two performances of Dittersdorf's oratorio, Esther, arranged by the Tonkünstler-Sozietät on 22 and 23 December 1785, in the interval of which Mozart played a new piano concerto (probably K.482).[36] According to a personnel list for these performances (likewise consisting of members of the Tonkünstler-Sozietät)[37] there were 19 first violins, 19 second violins, six violas, seven cellos, seven double-basses, two flutes, six oboes, four bassoons, four horns, two trumpets, two trombones and timpani. This gives a string section approximately equal in size to that of the 3 April 1781 concert at the Kärntnertortheater. But the size of orchestra required for an oratorio (in which, according to the personnel list, there were three altos, 16 tenors and 13 basses, in addition to the soloists and an unspecified number of, presumably, boy trebles and altos drafted in for the occasion) would need to be relatively large, and there is no convincing reason to suppose that all of the available personnel also played in Mozart's concerto during the Entr'act. As with the 1781 concert at the Kärntnertortheater, the simple documentary provision of orchestral numbers does not 'prove' anything about the typical size of a string ensemble in Mozart's Viennese productions of his piano concertos.[38]

The only safe inference to be drawn from such documentary reports seems to be that the numbers of string players expected in a 'public' production of a concerto may have been greater (sometimes considerably greater) than in a *Hausmusik* performance and perhaps bore some relationship to the particular performing space (hall, theatre, chamber). This may be inferred from an entry in the diary of Duke Ludwig von Bentheim-Steinfurt describing Mozart's performance of K.459 and K.537 in the Nationaltheater, Frankfurt-am-Main, on 15 October 1790, in which he specifically bemoans the fact that 'the orchestra was no more than rather weak with five or six violins but apart from that very accurate' (Deutsch, 1965, p.375). Given the duke's closing remark, his impression that the ensemble seemed too weak for such a situation may have had something to do with the relation of instrumental forces to the size of the theatre (especially as, Steinfurt notes, 'there were not many people [in attendance]'). That such 'public' performances – particularly of concertos with trumpet and timpani parts – were most effective with large forces seems to be the implication of the following remark found in a review of an edition of K.451 dating from 1792: 'It is only to be regretted that this masterly concerto, because of its scoring and obligato writing, is impractical for smaller musical circles [that is, *Hausmusik* of the à quattro kind that Mozart envisaged for K.413–15 and K.449] and can only be performed by large, fully-manned orchestras.'[39]

The evidence of orchestral parts

Extensive archival research by Dexter Edge (Edge, 1996a) has shown that late-eighteenth-century performing parts for the vast majority of Viennese concertos of all kinds (including Mozart's) survive in just single copies.[40] Even the small minority of concertos for which orchestral sets exist in duplicate or triplicate can normally be shown to result from later amalgamation of originally discrete 'single' sets, exhibiting different watermarks, with different stave-rulings, by different copyists. Although a small percentage of these sets may have been 'presentation copies' (that is, single sets, intended for the library of a private patron, from which duplicates might perhaps be copied if and when the need arose, and discarded afterwards), most do demonstrate some evidence of usage in performance. It seems unreasonable to suppose that all duplicate parts for such a large repertoire have been accidentally lost or destroyed, or else systematically discarded since.[41]

Edge's painstaking work suggests that the average number of first and second violin parts for a 'public' presentation of a Viennese instrumental work is approximately six each, although these figures are derived from standard copying charges per sheet paid by the Tonkünstler-Sozietät during the 1770s, 1780s and 1790s for instrumental pieces of all kinds (including, for instance, oratorios) that were presented by the society. Assuming this average figure to be acceptable, we next need to ask if these six parts were used by one or more players. Eighteenth-century violinists seem not to have played from music stands of the modern kind, but from 'benches' (similar to choirstalls). This is apparent from some of the contemporary iconographical evidence, including the 1777 Holzhalb engraving of a concerto performance referred to above (Figure 7.1). In this picture, the violinists (and the transverse flautists) are reading their respective parts from such a bench. Dittersdorf's autobiography also confirms this situation: 'I had long desks and benches made; for I introduced the Viennese method of playing while seated [to the Großwardein court, where Dittersdorf served as Kapellmeister] and arranged the orchestra in such a way that every player faced the audience' (Edge, 1996a, p.442). In such a seating plan, the maximum number of violinists able to read comfortably from a single part is two (this seems to be what is happening in the Holzhalb engraving, Figure 7.1). The inference is that an average number of violins in a 'public' performance would be either 12 or 24. To what extent this serves as a rule for 'public' performances of Mozart's piano concertos must remain an open question.

The weight of the various kinds of evidence discussed in the preceding sections seems to favour performance with a small string group. Clearly, the number of strings employed depended to some degree on the particular occasion and on the 'public' or 'private' location. Performance of Mozart's piano concertos accompanied by a string ensemble no larger than one to a part was probably quite commonplace, and certainly not restricted to 'à quattro' situations. Ripieno performance, alternating 'tutti' and 'solo' forces, appears to have been a personal preference of the Mozart family in Salzburg; its observation in Mozart's Viennese productions of his concertos is nowhere specifically indicated in, but is likewise not excluded by, the documentary evidence, which is all too absent in some respects, and in others, all too permissive of conflicting interpretations.

The bass line

Recent research by Cliff Eisen into the terminology and surviving performance materials relating to the 'basso' strand of Mozart's concertos has raised

the possibility that in the Salzburg concertos (or at least in Salzburg performances of those works) the cello may not have been employed (Eisen, 1996).
There are two overlapping issues here, the concept 'basso', meaning a
part-designation (the *bass part* in a polyphonic texture) and instrumental
nomenclature (a cello; a double-bass). In autograph scores written by Mozart
and his father, the polyphonic line that we recognise as the bass is consistently described to the left of the stave brace as 'basso'. To assume that this
automatically indicates cellos *and* double-basses playing the same strand is
perhaps mistaken. Authentic copies of playing parts, normally copied in
whole or in part by the Mozarts or else by known copyists working under
their supervision in Salzburg and which derive from these same autograph
manuscripts, distinguish equally consistently between cello and violone or
contrabasso (our modern double-bass) as distinct instruments with distinct
roles. Complete performing materials survive for K.175, K.238, K.242,
K.246, K.271 and K.365, for none of which there is a cello part and for each
of which there is, on the other hand, a violone part. Possibly, then, in Salzburg
performances at least, no cellos were envisaged. This may at first glance
appear detrimental to the focus of the ensemble, the violone/contrabasso
playing its notes an octave lower than notated, leaving an awkward textural
'gap' beneath the violas. But if this line was generally reinforced by the
pianist's left hand at the notated pitch – assuming that he or she fulfilled the
expected 'continuo' role discussed in the next section – and allowing for the
lighter voicing of eighteenth-century instruments, then this apparently unsat-
isfactory situation is mitigated somewhat.[42] Mozart is known to have
performed all of these concertos outside Salzburg and on these occasions
cellos may have been included:[43] his normal Viennese practice after 1781 was
certainly to include a cello part, sometimes, as in the slow movement of
K.482, strikingly independent of the double-bass.

Also to be considered in this regard is the status of the bassoon as a
component of the 'basso'. No bassoon parts are transmitted in any of the
authentic copies of K.175, K.238, K.242, K.246 or K.271. However, in both
authentic sets of playing parts for K.365, preserved at St Peter's, Salzburg
(1779–80) and Kroměříž (1781),[44] there are parts for bassoons 1 and 2. In
the former set, the copyist was Joseph Estlinger, a regular copyist for the
Mozarts; in the latter, the copyist is unidentified. Mozart himself annotated
the Estlinger copy, securing its authenticity.[45] Since the autograph score
does not include staves for the bassoons, these must be reckoned among
those instruments grouped generically under the term 'basso'. Possibly,
therefore, performances of Mozart's Salzburg concertos might on occasion
have included a pair of bassoons, even though they are not specifically
called for in his autographs. If so, they might have contributed to the 'definition' of the ensemble if no cellos were used.

Figured bass and 'col basso'

In most 'modern instrument' recordings and performances of Mozart's piano concertos (that is, played on a Steinway concert grand or equivalent, with an orchestra of modern strings, winds and brass, possibly regulated by a conductor) the soloist does not normally play during the tuttis. This familiar situation only emerged during the nineteenth century, and then, only slowly. In 1850, Czerny noted that 'the fortepiano ... has the principal part ... and the orchestra comes to the fore as a unified force only in the tutti (where the soloist rests)'.[46] Only a few years earlier, Czerny had recommended that 'During the Tutti (of a concerto &c.) the Player should at most, only touch the instrument softly along with the orchestra at the Fortissimo passages [that is, the tuttis]; or what is still better, he should abstain from playing at all.'[47] Contemporary with these remarks are those of Adolph Bernhard Marx, who advised that a solo part in a piano concerto should be notated so as to include detailed cues for the orchestral parts throughout the tutti so that, should occasion or preference demand, the soloist could intervene as director ('auch nöthigenfalls das Orchester in Ordnung halten kann').[48] The strong implication of all this commentary is that the participation of the concerto soloist in the tuttis had been a normal expectation in Mozart's day and for some time thereafter, and that only within the environment of a public concert life developed in central Europe in the generation following Beethoven's death did the 'dramatic' opposition of soloist and orchestra in concerto performances become reinforced by the pianist's conspicuous *silence* outside of the solo contributions. This method of performance arose in a context in which the soloist had begun to assume a more theatrical role of a lone voice against a crowd (as Tovey would have it), rather than as a participant in a genre that was still, to some degree, recognisable as chamber music, and in which the soloist still exercised considerable influence as director (or co-director) of the ensemble.

Reinforcing the implications of the theoretical literature is the documentary evidence of eighteenth-century performance materials. These leave no doubt that, in a performance in Mozart's day, the soloist would normally have played throughout the tutti, realising a figured bass. In the autograph scores of the concertos up to and including K.449, the orchestral bass line (written directly beneath the left-hand piano stave at the bottom of the page) was painstakingly figured. Moreover, in tutti passages, the piano staves in the autograph scores are habitually marked 'col basso', an instruction to a copyist that the bass line (notated directly beneath the left-hand piano stave in Mozart's scores) for tutti sections must be copied into the solo part. Figured bass notations are found in solo parts for all of the surviving 'Salzburg' performance materials for these concertos, copies made under the supervision of Leopold Mozart, and in which he sometimes entered the figuring himself once the keyboard part had been copied.[49] The inescapable conclusion is that the Mozarts envisaged perform-ances of piano concertos in which the soloist also assumed a 'continuo' role outside of the solo sections.

What of the style of the keyboard realisation itself? Only one example from Mozart's pen survives. In a manuscript copy of the solo part of the early C major concerto, K.246, prepared at Salzburg, Mozart added detailed realisa-tions of the figures, perhaps for the benefit of an inexperienced pupil.[50] The approach is fundamentally chordal, set out in three- or four-part harmony in simple, unobtrusive close position. Elsewhere Mozart's realisation is in bare octaves, sometimes *tasto solo*, leaving the right hand empty, and doubling the bass line at cello pitch. Overtly thematic contributions are restricted to occa-sional doubling of the leading orchestral melody; nowhere is there any attempt at an independent 'ornamental' right-hand part. At one point (bars 9–12 of the Andante) the realisation exactly doubles the wind chording. Significantly, this is the only point in the entire work where the winds have an unsupported 'solo' role (set antiphonally against the strings) and the keyboard realisation here may have been formulated so that the keyboard could act as a replacement for the winds if circumstances required.[51] The overall result, though simple, is a sophisticated amalgam of accompanying textures in the ritornellos, aptly setting off the intervening solo contributions. An important question, though, is whether such a realisation as Mozart provided in the case of K.246 is to be regarded as reflective of his usual practice in piano concertos, or whether it is deliberately and uncharacteristically simple.[52] While the style of realisation is well suited to the relatively formulaic K.246, it does not necessarily transfer well to other concertos, including the varied and extrovert textures and charac-ters of K.271. It would be dangerous to infer too much from this isolated case. Nevertheless, Daniel Gottlob Türk provides roughly contemporary guidance on continuo practice which accords quite closely with Mozart's annotations to the solo part of K.246 (Türk, 1800). Türk's examples are exclusively chordal, in three or four parts, enlivened by thicker chording in *forte* or *fortissimo* and occasional octave doubling of the bass line at cadence approaches. Like those given in Bach, 1753, all are pedagogical models, none of them extracted from 'real' compositions.[53] Very infrequently, passing notes are to be found. Türk's guidance on the range of continuo realisations also reflects Mozart's practice in K.246. He states that, in general, the soprano voice of a realisation should go no higher than e″ or f″ (and, even then, only when the underlying bass is rela-tively high in pitch), and that the keyboard part should not be pitched above the leading melody in the tutti part, as that would undermine the clarity of the texture (Türk, 1800, p.113). Conversely – and for similar reasons – the soprano part of the keyboard realisation should not drop below e′.[54]

Some commentators, notably Charles Rosen, have argued against the soloist's apparent continuo function (Rosen, 1971, pp.192 foll.). It is true that the picture presented by the surviving sources is not unambiguous. Mozart's scores of concertos from K.450 onwards do not regularly incorporate figuring of the bass line. This circumstance may be variously interpreted. The greater musical complexity of Mozart's Viennese concertos relative to those written in Salzburg, and in particular their progression through a varied succession of textures, arguably required more positive direction from the soloist-cum-director than the rhythmic punctuation of a continuo keyboard part could supply. In such pieces, at least the player's right hand had to be free to conduct the ensemble – possibly in collaboration with the *Konzertmeister* – rather than simply realise figured bass chords. Conversely, the lack of figuring in these scores may indicate that the generally larger orchestra employed in the later concertos was 'self-sufficient', needing less in the way of 'continuo' support from the keyboard than the more fragile textures of earlier works. Quite possibly, the presence of figuring in concertos composed for Salzburg and the general lack of figuring in the concertos postdating K.413–15 and K.449 (normally aimed at the Viennese public concert environment and in which performance 'à quattro' was no longer a stated option), may be a clue that, in the 'Salzburg' concertos, Mozart had to allow for the possibility of perform-ance with harpsichord (usefully doubling as continuo in tutti sections), whereas in Vienna, he could rely on the availability of a fortepiano, which, while more penetrating in 'solo' contexts, did not blend so well with the surrounding ensemble in a 'continuo' role. Whatever the truth of the matter, the continued presence of 'col basso' indications in Mozart's autographs of the Viennese works clearly presupposes the continuation of the soloist within tutti sections in some respect, reinforcing the texture here and there, or adding occa-sional weight or definition to the bass line, for instance.[55]

Embellishment and adaptation of the solo part

It is quite clear that in his own performances of his piano concertos, Mozart would have introduced improvised embellishments at certain points. Such embellishments were a normal expectation in the eighteenth century, as is evident from the detailed examination of this topic in treatises by C. P. E. Bach (Bach, 1753; Mitchell, 1949), Leopold Mozart (Mozart, 1756; Knocker, 1951) and Daniel Gottlob Türk (Türk, 1789; Haggh, 1982). All three authors actually caution against adding too many notes in their embellishments. Thus C. P. E. Bach:

> The concept [of improvised embellishment] is excellent but much abused ... Not everything should be varied, for if it is the reprise will become a new piece. Many things, particularly affettuoso or declamatory passages, cannot be readily varied. Also, galant notation is so replete with new expressions and twists that it is seldom possible even to comprehend it immediately [that is, to distinguish correctly its harmonic basis and thus

extemporise a suitable melodic variant over that pattern]. All variations must relate to the piece's affect, and they must be at least as good as, if not better than, the original (Mitchell, 1949, p.165).

Furthermore, in the Preface to his *Sechs Sonaten fürs Clavier mit veränderten Reprisen* (Bach, 1760), works written precisely in order to demonstrate the appropriate degree and type of embellishment that should be supplied in keyboard music, Bach recommends that players who are not already skilled in the art of embellishment, or else who are not at present in an appropriate mood to capture the correct *Affekt* underpinning a movement, should not extemporise additions, but rely on previously composed substitutes, such as those illustrated in the edition:

> Usually the embellishments [supplied by players] are misguided, and contradict the spirit of the composition, its emotional content, and its succession of ideas; nothing could annoy the composer more. Even when the piece is played by someone capable of correctly varying it, will it necessarily follow that he will always be in a suitable frame of mind to do so? ... [In these sonatas] I have borne in mind beginners and amateurs who, because of their age or occupation, have neither time nor resolve to face these difficulties ... [and] I have notated everything required to make these pieces most effective in performance, so that both beginners and amateurs might play them freely, even when they are not suitably disposed (author's translation).

The strong implication of these remarks is that the spontaneous addition of embellishments to a notated text was a practice likely to spiral out of control, and which required careful regulation if taste was not to be offended. By contrast, very few present-day performers are willing to risk such spontaneous embellishment – in performance, at least.[56] Possibly, their reluctance stems from an institutionally ingrained respect for the composer's intentions as conveyed in the notated text.[57] Possibly, too, that respect is overdone, or directed too much towards the faithful replication of every dot and dash of 'expression' at the expense of a living engagement with the music's *process*. The state of the autograph of K.491 (examined in some detail in Part Two) should give the lie to this anachronism. Here, Mozart altered the precise shape of the passagework several times, generally erasing previous versions, but not always, so that, in places, there is no such thing as a 'definitive' text for this most popular piece. Definitive texts are hard to come by in other Mozart keyboard works, too. Several of his solo piano sonatas, when published, sprouted written-out embellishments that appear nowhere in the autographs. Indeed, Mozart sometimes writes simply 'Da Capo' in his manuscript – not, evidently, an indication that the relevant passage was simply to be repeated note-for-note in performance, but a time and labour-saving shorthand (possibly for the benefit of authorised copyists) that, if taken literally, seriously misrepresents the 'living' surface of the music. In the autograph of the F major

Sonata, K.332, reprises of the slow-movement theme are unembellished; in the first edition, published in 1784, the reprise is remarkably ornate.[58] There are many places, especially in slow movements, where the piano concertos seem to require similar treatment. This can only be done effectively after much study of Mozart's own practices, allied to a thorough knowledge of the harmonic and tonal dimensions underlying classical melody.[59] While the purpose of extemporised embellishment in performance is precisely to open up a space in which the individuality of the player may be asserted, tasteful embellishment of Mozart's concertos ultimately rests on an ability to recognise stylistic boundaries beyond which it is unwise to interfere. All eighteenth-century writers are clear that it is a great fault to add embellishments where they are not required (for instance, where a right-hand passage already incorporates a good deal of elaboration, as in bars 17–39 in the finale of K.595). Leopold Mozart expressly states that some players 'following their own ideas ... ornament and contort a piece in truly idiotic fashion ... the embellishments are applied in the wrong places, too thickly crowded and for the most part confused' (Allanbrook, 1998, pp.123–24). It is therefore important to identify correctly those places in Mozart's concertos where tasteful embellishment might be added by a performer. Robert Levin has identified several such locations[60] which are summarised under the four headings below.

1) *Reprises of principal themes in ternary-form slow movements and rondo (or sonata-rondo) finales*
    Examples: K.466/ii; K.537/ii. In both cases, the reprises of the main theme should surely be decorated. Probably the decorations should serve a structural purpose, becoming progressively more elaborate during the course of the movement. As the themes themselves involve internal repetition, care needs to be exercised in order that the melodic texture does not become too active too soon. Levin has noted in the case of K.466 that in the reprise starting at bar 131 the literal repeat of the opening notated in the piano part would be followed (illogically) by a written-out elaboration in the tutti (bar 139 foll.), strongly implying that some degree of embellishment is required from the soloist at this point if an uncomfortable 'gear change' is not to disrupt the flow (Levin, 1990, p. 276). An example of a notated embellishment of a thematic reprise may be seen in the Larghetto of K.413, bar 35 foll. The character of the theme dictates the degree of embellishment that is appropriate. While the simple triadic outline of K.537's [Larghetto][61] will easily support progressive elaboration, the melodic profile of the Adagio theme of K.488 is possibly too sophisticated to bear further embellishment upon repetition at bar 53. Practical concerns play a part too: the thematic reprises in the Larghetto of K.595 pose no problems at bars 25 and 82, but that at bar 103 foll. is doubled by the flute and first violin and should perhaps be played as written, unless it be

considered that Mozart's odd scoring here is precisely designed to reinforce the main line sufficiently for the soloist to indulge in heterophonic
ornamentation.[62]

2) *Sequential extensions of themes*

Examples: K.491/ii, bars 9–12 (67–70); K.503/ii, bars 59–63. Both
passages invite elaboration from the second stage of the sequence,
injecting an element of momentum through the phrase not revealed in a
literal rendition. A sequence for whose second stage Mozart actually
notated an embellishment may be seen in K.271/ii, bars 28–9. Not every
sequence lends itself to embellishment, though: bars 70–74 in the second
movement of K.459 (already fully notated, including supplementary turn
symbols), and bars 105–9 in the Andante of K.453 (doubled by the wind),
for instance.

3) *Secondary cantabile themes in slow movements*

Examples: K.451/ii, bars 56–62;[63] K.537/ii, bars 44–53; K.595/ii, bars 14–
24, 49–58. The thematic structure typically involves a balancing ante-
cedent–consequent structure, repeated over identical harmonies, either
with or without modulation. The consequent portion often provides an
opportunity for melodic variation. Illustrations of a notated elaboration of
a consequent repeat may be seen in K.414/ii, bars 37–40 and K.488/ii, bars
20–24.

4) *Passagework whose shape is indicated at the outset but for which the
continuation is only sketched in outline*

Examples: K.482/iii, bars 346–7, 353–6; K.491/i, bars 261–2, 467–70. In
these cases literal performance of the phrase-extension in simple outline
destroys the continuity and renders the accompanying orchestral parts
more active than the solo; expansion of Mozart's incomplete notation is
evidently required. At bars 353–6 of K.482's finale, the intended effect is
probably of broken semiquaver octaves (certainly some contiguity with
the pattern of bar 352 is implied);[64] at bar 467 of the first movement of
K.491 the arpeggio pattern already under way in the previous phrase must
be extended as far as the cadential trill.

Eighteenth-century techniques for melodic embellishment may have been
related to the rhetorically inspired models for composition discussed in
Chapter Six. A relatively plain melodic line equates to the *Anlage* which the
composer subsequently rationalised, worked out and polished (at the rhetorical
levels of *Ausführung* and *Ausarbeitung*). Such hierarchical distinctions, understood as 'simple' and 'figured' melody, were commonplace in the compositional pedagogy of Mozart's time (indeed, Koch's hypothetical *Anlage* of
Graun's aria, mentioned in Chapter Six is one such illustration). Figured
melody builds upon simple melody, resulting in melodic 'decoration' of a
'plain' underlying pattern, a concept that may legitimately be traced back to

the species counterpoint demonstrations in Fux, 1725, each successively 'figured' species increasing in melodic complexity, while retaining the precise relation of consonance–dissonance inherent in the 'simple' *cantus firmus* model. The concept is incorporated in a number of eighteenth-century treatises to varying degrees, the most advanced demonstration being that in Koch, 1782–93, vol.iii, in which a simple eight-bar melody (the *Anlage*) is extended into an entire movement of 32 bars (the *Ausarbeitung*) entirely by techniques of melodic decoration and repetition (the *Ausarbeitung*) (Baker, 1983, pp.163–4).[65] Mozart's provision of embellishments for bars 56–62 in the Andante of K.451 sits well within such a theoretical framework, and there is evidence that he applied the concept of simple and figured melody in his own teaching.[66]

Against the foregoing discussion must be set an aesthetic objection held by some to the needless (as they see it) 'complication' of Mozart's melodies, whose essence might justifiably be felt to stem from their very fragility of utterance. It could plausibly be argued that the charming simplicity of bars 9–12 of the [Larghetto][67] of K.491 is compromised by any interference with its notated values: by embellishing the sequential continuation the player destroys its spirit rather than enhances it, ruinously undermining Mozart's carefully honed perfection of line. Whereas in the outer movements of Mozart's autograph of K.491 the right-hand part was at first only sketched in bare outline (numerous passages being 'realised' in detail later on),[68] no attempt was made to 'realise' this passage in the slow movement. It could be inferred from this state of affairs that Mozart's sparse notation of bars 9–12, being apparently no sketch, must instead exactly represent his finished intention and should be performed as such. A similar case could be made for non-interference in the slow movement of K.488. Towards the end (bars 84–92) is a phrase whose relatively long note values and wide register spread are not to be taken literally, but merely indicate in 'sketch' the outline of some pattern (possibly arpeggiaic in nature) that is to be extemporised by the player. On the other hand, this bareness could be interpreted as a deliberate paring-down of activity – reinforced by the string *pizzicato* – representing musically a withdrawal into an introverted realm of expression at the close of a uniquely pathetic Adagio. Such a psychological reading of this movement, 'personifying' the soloist as a channel for the representation of something beyond immediate experience, seems to have less to do with the documented concerns of Mozart's time than with traditions of interpretation originating in the emergent romantic aesthetics of the early nineteenth century.[69] Certainly, the survival of a contemporary source for K.488's Adagio containing written-out embellishments (possibly by Mozart's pupil, Barbara Ployer)[70] suggests that at least one early account of this concerto conformed to the expectation of creative intervention by the performer. Given that the weight of eighteenth-century evidence seems to be in favour of tasteful embellishment of appropriate points in a musical structure, the onus must rest on detractors to prove their case according to the aesthetic criteria of Mozart's time, and not by subjective whim.

An issue related to embellishment of the notated part is that of adaptation, especially adaptation of the solo part in 'à quattro' performances of K.413–15 and K.449. Occasionally, there are important wind lines that must presumably be supplied by the soloist in order to fill out occasional awkward gaps in the texture, such as result at bars 2 and 3 in the Larghetto of K.413 and bars 173–80 in the finale of K.414. The surviving performance materials at St Peter's, Salzburg, give no clues as to how such moments may have been realised, suggesting either that such Salzburg performances as were undertaken from these parts by Mozart or his sister were not 'à quattro', or else that occasional *lacunae* were tolerated (or resolved by verbal agreement among the players in rehearsal). Elsewhere, there are 'essential' wind lines that seem impossible to omit and likewise impossible for the soloist to supply: K.415, first movement, bars 177–82 and finale, bars 59–60, 226–7; K.449, finale, bars 238–42 (although the pedal B flat is covered to some extent by the piano's left hand).

Cadenzas and *Eingänge*

The cadenza in the classical concerto served a dual function. On the one hand, it was a vehicle for the demonstration of the soloist's digital virtuosity. On the other, it was a special opportunity for the player to display his or her command of the art of musical improvisation, ideally combining virtuosic scale and arpeggio figuration with selected thematic strands from the main body of the movement, teasing the whole into a coherent statement displaying something of the player's personality and skill. Tonal function was as important as appropriate use of previous themes in the cadenza, for this section of the concerto movement stood as a harmonic interruption between a 6/4 chord rounding off the previous tutti and the trill-and-perfect-cadence formula with which the cadenza itself led into the concluding tutti. A secure sense of tonal architecture was therefore a prerequisite of any convincing cadenza if the appropriate sense of closure was to emerge.[71]

Evidently, Mozart's normal practice was to improvise cadenzas in his own performances of his piano concertos. In a letter to his father of 22 January 1783, regarding K.175 and its new finale, the Rondo, K.382, he notes that 'I shall send the cadenzas and *Eingänge* to my dear sister at the first opportunity ... whenever I play this concerto, I always play whatever occurs to me at the moment.'[72] Nevertheless, he subsequently supplied many written examples of cadenzas, presumably for the use of his sister or for others in Salzburg who might have played these works (or else for study purposes). As Christoph Wolff has observed (Wolff, 1978–79; Wolff, 1991), Mozart's notated cadenzas tend always to be preserved in sources closely associated with the Mozart family. A significant number survive in copies evidently made directly from the autographs by either Leopold or Nannerl Mozart, most of which are preserved among the performance materials for the piano concertos in the collection of St Peter's, Salzburg.[73] Given that both Artaria and André published collections of Mozart's authentic cadenzas in the early years of the nineteenth century, it would seem likely that the cadenza autographs were preserved together as artefacts during Mozart's lifetime, and were loaned (or sold) by Constanze to the publishers after his death (Artaria, 1801; André, 1804).[74] These cadenzas have sometimes been reproduced in published texts of Mozart's concertos.[75] For a listing of the cadenzas and *Eingänge* according to several systems of numbering, see Table 7.1

The status of these cadenzas remains ambiguous. Excepting K.242 (in which a co-ordinated cadenza had to be written out for the three players) and K.488, Mozart did not write his cadenzas into the main body of the autograph score, but onto separate sheets whose watermarks show that he sometimes used up 'old' paper for this task.[76] In some cases these exemplars were probably intended to serve as models for the use of his students or patrons, showing the kind of thing he improvised in his own performances, hinting at the selection of suitable motives, the kind of treatment they might be given, and the balance of virtuosic display and tonal structure. Such hints would have been beneficial to performers not sufficiently skilled to improvise their own cadenzas.[77] For instance, the first two (of three) cadenzas to the early C major concerto, K.246, written for the Countess Lützow, perhaps reflect her limited technical ability.[78] The first is very short, for right hand only; the second is longer, built around similar scalic figures (unrelated to the substance of the main movement) and includes a rudimentary left-hand part articulating the principal harmonic outlines. Either would have proved suitable for a local, domestic performance given by the Countess herself. Mozart, who performed this work in Augsburg in the autumn of 1777, would clearly have attempted something more challenging. So far as Mozart himself was concerned, these written-out cadenzas almost certainly relate only obliquely to his own performances and are not necessarily to be regarded as literal records of what he himself played. Robert Levin (in Robbins, 1992, pp.186–7) has argued convincingly that Mozart improvised cadenzas, noting that contemporary reports of his concerto performances make particular reference to the splendid improvisations. Instead, they may have served as *aides-mémoires* upon which he improvised more elaborate 'live' renditions. Alternatively, where more than one version of a cadenza survives (K.271, K.414, K.456, for example), the notated texts may be interpreted as recording his successive layers of elaboration, each one pertaining to different performances of the work in question.

In the surviving cadenzas for the Salzburg concertos, Mozart tends towards the declamatory manner of the mid-eighteenth-century free fantasia, mingling together a variety of scalic and arpeggiaic figurations founded on one or other commonplace chord-progression and featuring conspicuous adjustments of tempo and time-signature. In the cadenzas for the Viennese works, by contrast,

Table 7.1 Mozart's cadenzas and *Eingänge*

This table lists Mozart's cadenzas and *Eingänge* according to the several systems of numbering drawn from K^6 and earlier editions and the published sets of Artaria and André; the watermark number for Mozart's autograph cadenzas (and a date for the paper) are also given, along with the current locations of autographs (and authentic copies).

Key

K^{6}626a, Teil i	numerical listing from K^6, pp.732-4 (**boldface** indicates an autograph)
K^{6}626a, Teil ii	numerical listing from K^6, pp.734-6
K.624	former numerical listing from K$^{3-5}$
NMAWz	Alan Tyson (ed.), *Wolfgang Amadeus Mozarts Werke: Wasserzeichen Katalog*, 2 vols. (Salzburg, 1996) [NMA supplementary volumes X/33/2]
Siglum	library (or other) location and call mark
Artaria	*Cadances Originales se rapportant à ses Concerto[s] pour le Clavecin ou Pianoforte, dédiées à Mr. l'Abbé Gelinek* (Artaria; Vienna, 1801)
André	*Trente-cinq Cadences ou points d'orgue pour pianoforte* (André; Offenbach-am-Main, 1804)
i [ii, iii]	first [second, third] movement
deest	work not included in the Köchel catalogue

K^{6}626a, Teil i	K.624	NMAWz	Siglum	Artaria	André
K.175					
i	1	1		I	12
i	**2**	1a	65	A-Ssp, Moz.285.1	
ii	3	2		II	13
ii	**4**	2a	65	A-Ssp, Moz.285.1	
K.238					
i	5		⎫		
ii	6		⎬ A-Ssp, Moz.290.1		
iii[1]	7		⎭		

---

[1] 'Cadenza per Rondeau: 3ter Eingang'.

K⁶626a, K.624 Teil i		NMAWz	Siglum	Artaria	André
K.246					
i	**8**	2b	28	A-Ssp, Moz.235.1	
i	**9**	2d	40	GB-Lbl, Add.Ms.61905	
i	**10**		51	I-Mc, Z.115.14.5	
ii	**11**	2c	28	A-Ssp, Moz.235.1	
ii	**12**	2e	40	GB-Lbl, Add.Ms.61905	
ii²	**13**	2f	72	Historical Society of Philadelphia, Simon Graz collection, Case 13, Box 11	
ii	**14**		51	I-Mc, Z.115.14.5	
K.271					
i	**15**	3	72	D-B, Mus.ms.autogr. W. A. Mozart 624(1)	23
i	**16**	3a	40	A-Ssp, Moz.295.1	
ii	**17**	4	72	D-B,Mus.ms.autogr. W.A. Mozart 624(1)	24
ii	**18**	4a	40	A-Ssp, Moz.295.1	
iii³	**19**	5		} Max Reis (Zurich)	
iii⁴	**20**	5			
iii⁵	**21**	5a	65	} A-Ssp, Moz.285.1	
iii⁶	**22**	5a	65		
iii⁷	deest			} A-Ssp, Moz.240.1	
iii⁸	deest				
K.365					
i	**23**	5b	51	A-Ssp, Moz.300.1	
i⁹	**deest**		51	A-Ssp, Moz.300.2	
iii	**24**	5c	51	A-Ssp, Moz.300.1	
iii	**deest**			CZ-KRa, II G 65/ A3259	

---

[2] Actually a cadenza to the slow movement of K.415.

[3] *Eingang* for bar 149.

[4] *Eingang* for bar 303.

[5] *Eingang* for bar 149.

[6] *Eingang* for bar 303.

[7] *Eingang* for bar 149 (NMA V/15/2, 'Fassung A').

[8] *Eingang* for bar 303 (NMA V/15/2, 'Fassung A').

[9] Autograph exemplar for A-Ssp, Moz.300. 1.

$K^6$626a Teil i	K.624	NMAWz	Siglum	Artaria	André
K.382/175iii					
25	6			III	14
26	6a	65	A-Ssp, Moz.285.1		
K.414					
i **27**	7	53			1
i **28**	8	66			2
ii **29**	11	74	D-B, Mus.ms.autogr.		5
ii **30**		66	W. A. Mozart 624(2)		
ii **31**	9	66			3
ii **32**	10a	74			4
ii **33**	10	53			
iii **34**	12	74			6
iii **35**	13				7
iii **36**	14		RO-Ba		8
K.413					
i **37**	6b	42	A-Ssp, Moz.305.1		
ii **38**	6c	42			
K.415					
i 39	15			IV	9
ii 40	16		A-Ssp, Moz.310.1	V	10
iii 41	17			VI	11
K.449					
i **42**	18	53	D-B, Mus.ms. autogr. W.A. Mozart 624(3)		22
K.450					
i **43**	19	56	F-Pn (Roman Rolland collection)		29
iii[10] **44**	21	62	(private collection)		31
iii **45**	20	62			30

---

[10] *Eingang* for bar 112.

K⁶626a Teil i	K.624	NMAWz	Siglum		Artaria	André

K.451

| i | **46** | 21a[32] | 66 | ⎫ A-Assp. Moz.320.1 | XIV | 27 |
| iii | **47** | 21b[33] | 66 | ⎬ | XV | 28 |

K.453

i	**48**	22	71	D-B, Mus.ms. autogr. W.A. Mozart 624(48)		15
i	49	23			IX	16
ii	50	24		I-Mc, 1181/7879		17
ii	51	25			X	18

K.456

i	52			RUS-Mcm		
i	53	26			XI	19
i	54	27			VII	20
iii	55			⎫ RUS-Mcm		
iii	56			⎬		
iii	57	28			VIII	21

K.459

i	**58**	29	58	⎫ H. Federhofer (Graz)	XIII	25
iii[11]	**59**		58	⎬		
iii	**60**	30	58	⎭	XII	26

K.488

| i | **61** | 31 | 80 | F-Pn, Malherbe 226 | | 35 |

K.595

i	**62**	34		⎫ Estnisches Historisches Museum, Tallinn (Estonia)	XVI	32
iii[12]	**63**	35		⎬	XVII	33
iii[13]	**64**	36		⎭	XVIII	34

---

[11] *Eingang* for bar 254.

[12] *Eingang* for bar 130.

[13] *Eingang* for bar 181.

K^{6}626a Teil ii	K.624	NMAWz	Siglum

K.40[14]

i	**C**	34		GB-Lbl, Add.Ms.47861
i[15]	**deest**			Max Reis (Zurich)

K.107[16]

i	**A**	40	⎫	PL-Kj
ii	**B**	40	⎭	
i	deest		⎫	US-Wc
ii	deest		⎭	

Date-ranges for watermarks (NMAWz):

28	1771–74
40	1776–77
42	1777–79
51	1779–80
53	1781; 1784–85; 1787
56	1781; the usage in K.450 is uniquely late (1784)
58	1781–84
62	1785
65	1783 (restricted only to cadenzas and *Eingänge* in K.175/382 and K.271)
66	1783 (for K.414); 1784 (for K.451)
71	1784
74	1784–86

---

[14] Based on L. Honauer, Sonata op.2, no.1/i.

[15] Copy by Leopold Mozart.

[16] Based on J. C. Bach, Sonata op.5. no.2/i.

his approach is more tightly structured, resorting not so much to conventional patterns of fantasy, but integrating in a developmental way thematic and harmonic material from the main body of the movement at hand.[79] This contrasting approach is highlighted by the last of three cadenzas that Mozart composed to the opening Allegro of K.246. In contrast to the rather rudimentary examples written for Countess Lützow, mentioned above, the third[80] is rather more extensive and refers at several points to thematic material heard earlier in the movement. Its opening relates to bar 61 of the main movement; at bar [5] it harks back to bar 64 foll.; bar [15] is derived from bar 73; finally, bar [23] is derived from bar 81 foll. The ideas taken up in the cadenza appear in the same order in which they originally appeared in the Allegro itself. The fact that, unlike its two predecessors, this cadenza is in Mozart's later idiom, thematically dependent on the movement to which it belongs, may suggest that it was composed after Mozart's removal to Vienna, though it evidently found its way to Salzburg for some purpose, since in a letter of 10 April 1782 Mozart asked his father to return the piece to him (possibly for the use of his Viennese students). The paper on which the cadenza is written bears a watermark also found in the compositions of the early Vienna years (Tyson, 1996, no.51).

The degree to which definite thematic references to the parent movement influence the structure of Mozart's later cadenzas varies from case to case. In the first-movement cadenza to K.451, an opening reference to the dotted bass descent of bar 10 foll. of the Allegro soon gives way to a series of brilliant triplet quaver arpeggios, covering a wide range of the keyboard. In the second of the cadenzas to the Allegro of K.414[81] the quotation of a decorated version of the main theme at bar [12] is quite casual, a connecting interlude between passages of bravura display. The same is true of the first of three known cadenzas for K.456's Allegro vivace; the second and third are rather longer and far more virtuosic, and introduce a passing reference to bars 54–5 of the Allegro vivace towards the end, in each case adapted to a chromatic chordal context. In both cadenzas supplied for the first movement of K.271[82] Mozart lays considerable stress on the figure first sounded at bar 14 foll. of the main movement, allowing it to dominate the first half of each cadenza. In the second cadenza Mozart additionally quotes the theme from bar 34. Much of the first half of Mozart's cadenza for the Allegro of K.450 derives from the substance of bar 119 foll. and bar 25 foll. of the Allegro, contrasting with the second half which returns to the brilliant virtuosity so characteristic of the movement as a whole. A similar approach is found in the first-movement cadenza of K.459.

Mozart's cadenzas to the first movements of K.453 and K.595 are among the most heavily dependent of any of his notated cadenzas on the material of their respective Allegros. In the former, Mozart introduces the main theme at the opening, immediately develops a new continuation, related in scansion and rhythm, over an Alberti-style bass, before building up a chordal texture featuring imitations of the theme over a pedal A. This texture dissolves into passagework leading to a quotation of the theme from bar 35 of the main movement, simulating by octave displacement the colouristic echo effects between wind and strings (or, indeed, piano and wind during the 'solo' exposition) and fragmenting the paired quaver idea. The cadenza to K.595 begins with a reference to the string figure from bar 39 of the main movement, developing this at some length before turning to the theme from bar 16, whose suffix is extended by repetition and embellishment (including augmentation of the semiquavers at bars [19–20] into quavers at bars [20–21]). Subsequently there are quotations of the dotted figure from bar 5 of the main movement and a variant of the opening theme in canon between the hands, leading to the culminating dominant-7th chord. In each of the concertos K.453 and K.595 the cadenzas indulge in actual development of thematic material, a feature which sets them somewhat apart from Mozart's other examples, contributing something vital to the movements in which they lie, extending the expressive range rather than serving as mere appendages.[83]

One of Mozart's best-known later cadenzas, that to the first movement of K.488, stands outside this trend, deriving none of its material from the foregoing Allegro.[84] Beginning with ascending scale flourishes, it briefly settles on a dominant pedal before dissolving in a diminished–7th arpeggio (bar [6]). This is founded on the pitch D sharp, from which the bass line falls two further steps, to D natural and C sharp (bars [7–10]). Such descending bass lines, supporting 'free' harmonic progressions elaborating rapid passagework, are quite typical of Mozart's notated cadenzas, though in the majority of cases they appear within a tightly controlled succession of motivic references; in K.488 the situation is different owing to the lack of any obvious relationship to the main material of the movement.[85] At bar [15] Mozart continues with a further descending bass pattern (F 5/3–E 6/4–D sharp diminished–7th) preparing the dominant pitch, E, at bar [21], an important point of structural articulation following which the passagework transfers to the left hand in chromatic scales followed by a final flourish and trill in the right hand, heralding the return of the tutti. Intervening between the two 'free' harmonic patterns in this cadenza is a brief, sequentially inspired motivic phrase, bars [11–14], suspending the predominantly virtuosic texture and separating the cadenza into three clearly defined and contrasted periods. Though somewhat 'loose' in its succession of ideas its harmonic focus is strongly directed towards the 'gravitational pull' of the dominant degree and its important role in co-ordinating tonal tension and release within a cadenza which takes on a dramatic function as a solo interruption of the closing tutti portion of the movement.[86]

Eva and Paul Badura-Skoda have convincingly demonstrated that Mozart's cadenzas typically subdivide into three regions, broadly following a 'beginning–middle–end' strategy.[87] The beginning may be either 'virtuosic' or 'thematic' in substance. Virtuosic cadenza openings include the longer of the two written for the first movement of K.414,[88] K.459 and K.488. Typically, following a virtuosic opening, Mozart will quote a theme (frequently the main theme) in the tonic: for example, in the first cadenza for the first movement of K.456, following a virtuosic opening, Mozart introduces the main theme in alternation with figurative punctuation from the right hand. Though thematic cadenza openings tend to quote the main theme, as in the first movements of K.365 and K.453, this is not exclusively the case. In the first movement of K.271, both cadenzas that Mozart provided start out by referring to material from bar 14 foll.; in K.414, the first of two cadenzas supplied by Mozart opens with material from the middle of the movement (bar 50 foll.); that for the finale of K.459 takes off with the fugato theme from bar 32 foll.; in the Allegro of K.595, the opening of the cadenza derives from the orchestral material of bars 39 foll.; in K. 415, K.449, K.450 and K.456, the first-movement cadenzas begin with reference to the closing tutti material immediately before the 6/4 pause chord. Thematic openings (which evolve from the initial 6/4 chord) invariably dissolve in passagework of some kind, sometimes relating to figurations from earlier in the movement (K.450), more often continuing freely (K.453). A recurrent fingerprint in the first section of Mozart's cadenzas is a falling chromatic bass line (K.271, K.449, first movements; K.414, slow movement). Pedal points are also found (K.413, K.459, first movements).

Middle sections of cadenzas also tend to quote from the main body of the movement, but here secondary material is preferred. Examples include the first movements of K.271, K.415, K.450, K.453, K.456, K.459 and K.595. Alternative strategies are pursued in, for example, the finale of K.595, whose cadenza eschews secondary material, treating instead just the main material, fragmented into two components, the consequent portion of the main theme (bars 5–8) being reserved for the middle section. Middle sections of cadenzas tend towards a 'developmental' function. The most familiar technique employed here is sequential repetition of a secondary thematic fragment, as in the first-movement cadenzas of K.271 (bars [17–29]), K.449 (bars [15–25]) and K.453 (bars [19–26]). Tonally this section may rove quite substantially away from the 'home' tonic (as in K.453), but will always eventually alight on the dominant, or dominant of the dominant, in preparation for a return to the tonic, announced by a 6/4 chord (connecting, retrospectively, to the tutti pause chord with which the cadenza was begun) that leads to the normally virtuosic final section which highlights passagework above all, but sometimes, as in the first-movement cadenzas of K.453 and K.595, recalls subsidiary thematic material from the movement, before leading into the final trill.

Texturally, the cadenzas are, in the main, homophonic rather than contrapuntal. Polyphony does, however, occur, either at the beginning (K.365, K.451, first movement), middle (K.451, finale) or end (K.595, first movement), often shedding new light on its material whose contrapuntal possibilities had not been exploited during the main course of the movement.

No original cadenzas are known to the first movements of K.466, K.467, K.482, K.491, K.503 and K.537. In the case of K.503 a cadenza by Mozart's son, Wolfgang junior, dating from the early nineteenth century, survives in the Conservatorio di Musica Giuseppe Verdi, Milan (Fonds Noseda). Cadenzas to Mozart's concertos by other composers and performers survive. André published several (for K.467, K.482, K.488, K.491, K.503 and K.595) by Philipp Karl Hoffmann (1769–1842), one of Mozart's personal acquaintances (Hoffmann, 1801–03; King, 1959); Beethoven supplied cadenzas for the first movement and finale of K.466, which he evidently played between the acts of a production of *La Clemenza di Tito* on 31 March 1795.[89] Others for that work were written by Mendelssohn (unfortunately lost) and Clara Schumann.[90] All these later cadenzas tend towards fuller virtuoso display than Mozart's own – a reflection of the growing fashion for such styles of performance in the generation following his death.

The *Eingang*

Shorter than the cadenza, and serving a different function within a movement, is the fermata 'lead-in', or *Eingang*. This is a short flourish of passagework to be played by the soloist, typically during the course of the second or third movement of a concerto at a pause chord (for example in K.467, bar 177). *Eingänge* generally occur as a punctuation on the dominant (normally dominant-7th) chord between sections of a rondo-type movement, effecting a smooth transition to a reprise of the main theme by the solo. Mozart provides written-out examples of *Eingänge* in some concertos (K.271, K.450, K.414, K.595, for example); in other pieces (including K.467) they must be improvised by the player.

Typically the notated *Eingänge* incorporate scalic and arpeggiaic passagework of a fairly 'neutral' quality and – unlike Mozart's cadenzas – do not derive their material from that of the movement itself (K.415 and K.450 are exceptions). One pattern is to extend a single chord, as in the finales of K.271, bar 232, K.450, bar 112 (leading atypically to a quotation of the main theme) and K.459, bar 254 (which maps out a phrase-pattern of three-bar units punctuated by left-hand entries). An alternative to this is the more developed *Eingang* such as that located in the finale of K.271, bar 149. Mozart provided no fewer than three *Eingänge* at this point.[91] The first and longest contains several harmonic digressions away from the dominant-7th pause chord, supported by alternations of tempo. In the first of two *Eingänge* which Mozart provided for the Andante of K.414, bar 72, there is a chromatic succession through V–$V^{[7\#/6/4/2]}$ – V^7–I. The first of the two *Eingänge* required in the finale of K.595 casts an interesting perspective on the limits of harmonic style tolerated by Mozart. No *Eingänge* were written into Mozart's autograph, though an example appropriate to bar 130 appeared as no.xvii in Artaria's *Cadances Originales* (1801).[92] It was considered to be of dubious authenticity by the editors of NMA on the grounds of its 'disorganised and purposeless modulation scheme' (deriving so they thought from a corrupt copy), and was consequently omitted in that edition.[93] In fact, it turned out to be authentic, as proved by the rediscovery of an autograph (Rehm, 1986).[94]

The desirability of attaching cadenzas and *Eingänge* in a nineteenth-century (or later) idiom to Mozart's concertos raises a broader point worthy of some discussion. For the performer of a Mozart piano concerto, whether that be Beethoven, Mendelssohn, Clara Schumann or a present-day artist, a cadenza or *Eingang* offers the opportunity for creative commentary upon the movement concerned, utilising its material afresh and leaving, hopefully, something of a personal stamp upon the performance. Mozart may or may not have regarded his concertos as works that would outlive him; the fact that he strove to have some of them published during his lifetime may suggest that he did think of them as artefacts not restricted to a particular time and place; or, alternatively, it may indicate that he was interested only in the immediate financial return that a sale to a publisher would realise. Whatever the truth of this, Mozart could not legislate for (or against) the treatment that his works might receive at some point in the future once they had been released into the public domain of concert representation. He may have regarded his concertos as fair game for later generations of performers to do with as they wished, adapting them, as did Cramer and Hummel, to the style of their own times. Or he may have disputed their right to adapt his texts, preferring that they be respected absolutely. (The state of the autograph of K.491, however,[95] strongly implied that Mozart took a flexible view of his own texts.) There can be nothing other than a speculative resolution of this quandary. But it points up two important issues of identity.

The first takes as its starting-point the unassailable authority of the text. According to some people, Mozart's piano concertos are textual artefacts not to be meddled with. The particular configuration of the notes, rhythms, harmonies, phrases and so on recoverable from an autograph text positions a Mozart piano concerto as something concrete, deliberate, something intended by the composer. Moreover, it is something that we understand as a work of the classical period. Its style is that of late-eighteenth-century classicism; moreover, it is consistently so, holding to the one style throughout, not deviating between different styles. Its consistency is an important element of its essence, something that marks out its identity. To add a cadenza in a different style, especially something radically different (conceived for an audience that had become familiar with a much more chromatic harmonic norm than obtained in Mozart's day, for instance), is a falsification of its identity. It makes of Mozart's concerto a work whose identity no longer resides within a single style (represented by the notated text), but which instead depends upon juxtaposition against a different style. Mozart's concerto and the foreign cadenza that has been appended to it are at different points along a historical trajectory, and it is within this imported dimension that Mozart's concerto is now forced to parade reclothed and ridiculed. Its integrity has been corrupted. Far better to take Mozart's own notated cadenzas as models of the kind of procedures he envisaged, all of them emanating from within the classical style, assuring the sanctity of utterance.

Such a view invests a great deal in the textual identity of a work, regarding a Mozart piano concerto as a phenomenon that possesses a fixed objective status represented by its text. Tamper with the text, and you tamper with the identity of the work. Set against this text-based authority is a different approach that privileges the audience, that is a reception-based authority investigated in recent critical traditions stemming from Hans-Robert Jauss (Jauss, 1974) and Roland Barthes (Barthes, 1977). The identity of the work, according to this tradition, resides not in the notated text ('standing for' the work in essence), but in the sum total of the experiences and associations brought to that notated text by the reader. The reader's situation is a crucial element in a communicative process; the reader is part of the making of the work, which therefore becomes something that extends beyond its notated text, something which may (and probably will) be different on each separate occasion, according to the particular viewpoint from which it is approached, something which is 'constructed' anew by each reading of it. Within such a critical framework, the objections to the opposing of internal and external styles that threaten to corrupt Mozart's music dissolve. Integrity of utterance, stylistic purity, guarantees of identity are all chimeras. The addition of cadenzas in a foreign style are a natural part of the continuing life of the work, since the work is something that is conjured by the reader in relation to the text left by the author: a document encoding his thought, yes, but not the work itself, which is instead something additive, situated in the mind of the reader, stimulated by the act of reading (or listening), exhibiting not fixity but movement. And this is not restricted to cadenzas and *Eingänge*, but to each and every aspect of Mozart's piano concertos in performance. Preserve the text, and you risk diminishing the life; relive the text and you risk destroying it. That is the challenge posed by Mozart's piano concertos.

Notes

1.   This is not the place to enter into a history of the fortepiano, which developed rapidly in sophistication from very humble beginnings during the eighteenth century, its manufacture spreading eventually across most of Europe. Extensive references to further specialised literature is given in the following studies which have, collectively, informed the following introductory discussion: Badura-Skoda, 1962; Maunder, 1992; Komlós, 1995; DeVal, 1996; Maunder and Rowland, 1995; Rowland, 1998.

2   *Idomeneo* received its première at the Residenztheater, Munich, on 29 January 1781.

3. Original in A-Sm; the painting is much reproduced in the Mozart literature.

4. Leopold is standing behind the instrument, holding a violin; his recently deceased wife is represented by a portrait on the wall behind the family group.

5. Richard Maunder speculates that Leopold's fortepiano may have been given to Nannerl, in which case it may have been the instrument by the Salzburg organ-builder, Egedacher, that is mentioned in correspondence between Nannerl and Leopold in 1784; see Maunder, 1992, p.215.

6. This piano ('Zweybrucken, 1775') is at present in the Museum Carolino Augusteum, Salzburg. No connection with Mozart is established and, given the state of relations between Mozart and Colloredo, it seems unlikely that the Archbishop would have allowed Mozart to use it.

7. Probably Mozart played K.415 on this instrument when he next visited Salzburg in autumn 1783. For this performance, see the entry for K.415 in Part Two.

8. Ignaz von Beecke (1733–1803) was in the employ of Count Oettigen-Wallerstein; see Clive, 1993.

9. For all the ambiguity of terminology here ('clavier'; 'fortepiano'), it is apparent that the instrument involved was a fortepiano.

10. *Augsburgische Staats- und Gelehrten-Zeitung*, 28 October 1777; quoted in Deutsch, 1965, pp.167–8.

11. Christian Friedrich Daniel Schubart (1739–91), organist at Ludwigsburg, 1769–73, and founder, in Augsburg, of the journal, *Deutsche Chronik*, from which the review of Mozart's concert at Count Fugger's quoted above is taken.

12. Fritz Jakob Späth (1714–98) was a Regensburg instrument-maker with whom Stein had studied in 1749–50. There is no evidence that Mozart ever owned a Späth fortepiano.

13. A photograph of this instrument (currently in the Magyar Nemzeti Museum, Budapest) is reproduced as illus.2 in Maunder, 1992.

14. A-Sm; currently in the Mozart Geburtshaus, Getreidegasse 9. For a photographic reproduction, see Maunder, 1992, illus.3.

15. For details, see the entries for these works in Part Two.

16. For details of these performances, see the entries for these works in Part Two. All the concertos written after his removal to Vienna were clearly conceived for fortepiano, sometimes (K.466, K.467) with the additional pedal attachment.

17. While Mozart's autographs of K.271 and K.365 were not available to the editor of NMA V/15/2, the notation of dynamics and articulation printed there is indeed present in the now rediscovered autographs and is clearly authentic.

18. Even if the hands were playing on separate manuals (and therefore distinguished in colour), the underlying triplet quaver accompaniment to bars 333–57 in the finale would produce so many attacks that even the illusion of slurring that can be conveyed by a skilled harpsichordist would be largely obscured.

19. For authoritative introductions to both aspects and recommendations for further reading, see Badura-Skoda, 1962; Brown and Sadie, 1990; Neumann, 1986; Rowland, 1998; Maunder and Rowland, 1995; Stowell, 1992; Lawson, 1995; Lawson, 1996; Herbert and Wallace, 1997.

20. In addition to questions of clarity and balance of strings and wind in combination, there is the equally important issue of continuity, represented, for instance, by bars 47–51 from the first movement of the B flat concerto, K.456. Here the neatness of rhythm and articulation in bar 51 could suffer markedly by comparison with bars 47–50, if the sharply focused single wind lines were followed by a

broader sound involving many players to each string part, even allowing for the *forte* dynamic.

21. Two players per part – that is, one desk – create additional practical problems of timing and tuning; either one player or three players gives a better result.

22. A passage of a similar nature is that at bars 102–6 and 243–5 in the finale of K.595, alternating piano right hand and flute/oboe: a single violin could do this just as well; several desks could not.

23. See the entry for that concerto in Part Two.

24. For publication details of these, see Bibliography, Section A$_j$, p.254.

25. A-Ssp, Moz.275.1.

26. Parts are known to have been copied in Salzburg from this autograph; regrettably they do not survive, although, to judge from the playing parts for K.466, they would also have been adapted to ripieno practice. See also the entry for K.467 in Part Two.

27. Moz.260.1.

28. For details, see Edge, 1996c, the three concertos K.413, 414 and 415 are A-Ssp, Moz.250.1, 255.1 and 260.1 respectively.

29. A facsimile of the violin 1 part, showing Mozart's annotations, is in NMA V/15/ 3, p.xix.

30. Nevertheless, these indications subsequently appeared in the edition of K.415 published by Artaria as 'Op.IV' (Mozart, 1785b).

31. It may be noted that ripieno performance is clearly understood in the surviving 'Salzburg' performance materials for the much later concerto, K.595 (A-Ssp, Moz.280.1), which were copied in Vienna and which stem from the collection of Nannerl Mozart. These parts are the work of a Viennese copyist, possibly Joseph Arthofer; see Schmid, 1970. Dexter Edge's painstaking examination of literally hundreds of surviving sets of performance materials relating to Viennese concertos supports ripieno practice in only a tiny minority of cases; see Edge, 1996a.

32. This source is advanced by Dexter Edge (Edge, 1996a, p.440), but in a different context; the translation here, though, is my own.

33. Reproduced in *Early Music*, **19** (1991), p.501.

34. It is true that a large mirror depicted on the wall behind the keyboard player might reflect some of that light, but it is hung too high to be of any benefit to the players.

35. For details on the publication history of K.413–15, see the entries for those works in Part Two.

36. For further discussion, see the entry for K.482 in Part Two.

37. Vienna, Stadt- und Landesarchiv, Haydn-Verein, A1-3b, reproduced in Edge, 1996a, pp.[432–3].

38. Dexter Edge's extensive study of personnel lists of Viennese orchestras – both 'societal' and *ad hoc* – during the second half of the eighteenth century seems to show that the number of first and second violins combined could range between about sixteen at the lower end of the spectrum to about forty (exceptionally) at the upper end; between four and six each of violas and cellos and four double-basses. These figures are amalgamated from a survey of different types of 'public' orchestra, including opera orchestras and, as Edge notes, require careful interpretation regarding their usefulness in respect of the concerto repertoire. See Edge, 1996a.

39. *Musikalische Korrespondenz der teutschen Filarmonischen Gesellschaft*, 16 May 1792; Eisen, 1991a, no.180. The same inference, drawn in the opposite direction, may be made from Mozart's letter of 15 May 1784 regarding K.449, K.450, K.451 and K.453, mentioned above.

40. Edge examined over 400 surviving sets of parts for Viennese concertos, or copies of Viennese concertos.

41. In fact, separate ripieno parts, such as those for K.466 at A-Ssp, Moz.275.1, are, in a sense, 'duplicates'. Other Mozart concertos for which ripieno duplicates survive include K.175, K.365, K.453, K.503 and K.595; see the entries for these pieces in Part Two.

42. A so-called 'eight-foot' violone (sounding at notated pitch), as was apparently envisaged by J. S. Bach in performances of some of the Brandenburg concertos (see the essay by Christopher Hogwood in the booklet accompanying his 1985 recording with the Academy of Ancient Music, Decca: L'Oiseau-Lyre 414 187–2), seems not to have been employed in Salzburg. Leopold Mozart (Knocker, 1951, p.3) notes that the violone sounds a whole octave lower than notated, indicating that he had the '16-foot' variety in mind.

43. See the respective entries in Part Two for details.

44. For details of these sources, see the entry for K.365 in Part Two.

45. These annotations can be seen in the facsimile in NMA V/15/2, p.xx.

46. Czerny, 1850, i, p.124 (written c.1839); translation from Ferguson, 1984, to which the following paragraph is indebted.

47. Czerny, 1839, iii, p.87; translation from Ferguson, 1984. Occasionally one finds eighteenth-century performance materials conforming to this scheme. The solo part in the set of orchestral materials for K.467 in CZ-KRa, II G 77 contains extensive cueing of the principal orchestral lines throughout the tuttis, quite sufficient to allow direction from the keyboard.

48. Marx's comments appear in his article, 'Koncertstimme', in Schilling, 1835, iv, p.198.

49. For details of these materials now in the library of St Peter's, Salzburg, see the entries for individual works in Part Two. For K.415, two sets of figuring survive, one (the most accurate) added by Leopold Mozart into the 'Salzburg' copy of the keyboard parts, the other (containing numerous errors) in Artaria's first edition of 1785, presumably prepared by the publisher. A page of the 'Salzburg' piano part, showing Leopold's figuring, is reproduced in NMA V/15/3, p.xviii. Nannerl Mozart's figuring for the solo part of K.449 is reproduced in NMA V/15/4, p.xv. From K.450 onwards, 'Salzburg' performance materials survive only intermittently but where they do (for example K.466 and 595) the solo parts contain figuring.

50. Mozart's realisations are printed in NMA V/15/2 and in Paul Badura-Skoda's Eulenburg edition of K.246 of 1968 (no.1269). For source details, see the entry for K.246 in Part Two.

51. A point made in Grayson, 1999, p.106. At two points later in the movement (bars 43–6 and 105–8) this antiphonal pattern recurs, piano answering the strings. Conceivably, Mozart's chordal realisation at bars 9–12 of K.246's Andante may be taken to imply that keyboard continuo in the piano concertos was only essential in performances without winds.

52. Some scholars have taken Mozart's realisation of the figures in K.246 as representative of his normal practice. See, for instance, Badura-Skoda, 1962, pp.198 and 207–8; Neumann, 1986, pp.254–5.

53. As found, for instance, in Mozart's realisation of the figures at bars 35–6 in the first movement of K.246.

54. For a discussion of eighteenth century realisations of figured basses in K.238, see Derr, 1996a.

55. Tutti sections in published sets of performance materials issued by Artaria and André during the decade after Mozart's death frequently supply realisations of

(normally unfigured) basses – generally of a chordal nature, and offering ample opportunities for the kind of rhythmic 'punctuation' necessary in directing a performance – in the right-hand stave of the solo part. At times, these printed realisations include cues (generally printed in smaller type) showing the most important orchestral lines and entries which might have been relevant in a performance directed from the keyboard. Some illustrations taken from prints of K.450, K.456, K.459 and K.482 are given in Ferguson, 1984.

56. The most honourable exceptions are Robert Levin and Malcolm Bilson, both in their live performances of these works, and in recordings.

57. Reinforced, it must be said, by the attitude implicit in C. P. E. Bach's comments above, which assume an intention on the part of the composer that could be transgressed by inappropriate embellishment: 'contradict[ing] the spirit of the composition ... nothing could annoy the composer more'.

58. Autograph: Princeton University Library, William H. Scheide collection; print: Mozart, 1784. Conversely, embellished reprises that appear in no published edition of K.457's slow movement survive on separate sheets in the recently rediscovered autograph (Internationale Stiftung Mozarteum, Salzburg). For details, see Irving, 1997, pp.73–82.

59. Players of the generation after Mozart did not shy away from adding embellishments to his works. The published arrangements, Hummel, 1828–42, Cramer, 1825–37 and Hoffmann, 1801–3, for instance, unashamedly adapt Mozart's melodic idiom to the emerging virtuosity of early-nineteenth-century concert pianism. For some brief extracts of the style of each of these embellishers, see NMA v/15/6, pp.xii–xiii. For a detailed investigation of the Hummel and Cramer examples see Grayson, 1996.

60. See Levin, 1990; Levin, 1992, to which the following discussion is indebted. Further on this topic, see Badura-Skoda, 1962, pp.178 foll.; Badura-Skoda, 1996; Neumann, 1986, pp.247 foll.

61. The tempo marking for this movement is editorial, occurring only in the first and subsequent editions, rather than in the autograph.

62. Note that the rhythm in the right hand of the piano part needs adaptation to fit that of the accompanying instruments (ending with a pair of demisemiquavers).

63. An embellishment evidently stemming from Mozart – and surprisingly restrained, in keeping with the advice of contemporary treatises, including his father's – is printed in NMA V/15/4. It is written into the solo part of the Salzburg performance materials for this work (for details, see the entry for K.451 in Part Two) and is presumably related to Mozart's letter of 9–12 June 1784, noting that Nannerl Mozart 'is quite right in saying that there is something missing in the solo passage in C in the Andante of the concerto in D.' Evidently, Nannerl had been suspicious of the rather bare notation of this passage in the autograph. Mozart promised to 'supply the deficiency' as soon as possible; almost certainly, this is the textual elaboration notated in the Salzburg piano part.

64. An editorial realisation is provided in NMA V/15/6.

65. Koch may have been influenced by a similar model of melodic extension in Riepel, 1755, pp.64–5 and 69–70. Further on this topic, see Ratner, 1980, pp.83–98; Sisman, 1982.

66. For instance in the composition exercises of Thomas Attwood, discussed in Irving, 1997, pp.75–9. The notion of 'simple' and 'figured' melody also has application in relation to sets of variations. Beyond the initial statement of a theme, subsequent variations may be interpreted as 'figured' versions of the 'simple' original.

67. Again, the tempo marking is editorial.

68. See the discussion of this in the entry for K.491 in Part Two.

69. For instance in the writings of F. W. Schlegel, published in *Das Athenäum* (from 1798); in Jean-Paul Richter's *Vorschule der Ästhetik* (1804); E. T. A. Hoffmann's article, 'Beethoven's Instrumental Music' (1813); and culminating in the philosophy of Arthur Schopenhauer's *Die Welt als Wille und Vorstellung* (1818; vol.ii, 1844), in which music was revealed as that art in which the *noumenal* (as opposed to the *phenomenal*) was directly represented. See Samson, 2001; Bowie, 2002.

70. See the entry for K.488 in Part Two. These embellishments have been frequently criticised for their crude recourse to extended chromatic scale-runs which perhaps sit uncomfortably with the finely etched lines of this siciliana (Mozart's only instrumental movement in F sharp minor); see for instance, Frederick Neumann's caustic opinion (Neumann, 1986, p.252).

71. It is worth recording that Koch believed the title 'cadenza' to be a misnomer. He describes it as 'either a free fantasy or a capriccio, which is mistakenly called a cadenza because it is made at the close of the composition' (Baker, 1983, p.211).

72. On Mozart as improviser, see Komlós, 1991.

73. For details of watermarks in the cadenza sheets, see the entries for individual concertos in Part Two.

74. There is no mention of a folder of cadenzas in the contract of November 1799, in which the bulk of the autographs in Constanze Mozart's possession was sold to André.

75. The cadenzas are all incorporated in the main movement texts in the NMA. Alternatives are sometimes given in appendices. Those of doubtful authenticity tend not to be printed with the relevant concerto texts, but appear in Serie X.

76. For instance, the cadenzas to the outer movements of K.365, K^{6}626a/K.624, Teil i, 23, 24, are written on a 1775 paper (Tyson, 1996, no.35), although the concerto was not apparently composed until 1779.

77. Some discussion of this situation is given by Hermann Beck in his Vorwort to NMA V/15/vii, p.ix.

78. K^{6}626a/K.624, Teil i, 8, 9. The first is written into the solo part, which also contains Mozart's own specimen realisations of the figured bass. As mentioned previously, this source clearly betrays evidence of pedagogic function, and is therefore perhaps not to be regarded as a typical exemplar of Mozart's normal practice.

79. Discussed further in Badura-Skoda, 1962, pp.214–41 and in Wolff, 1978–79.

80. K^{6}626a/K.624, Teil i, 10.

81. That is, Cadenza B as printed in NMA V/15/3; K^{6}626a/K.624, Teil i, 27.

82. K^{6}626a/K.624, Teil i, 15, 16.

83. On Mozart's cadenzas as 'secondary developments', in which he rearranges and reinterprets material from t he main body of the movement in surprising ways, see Robert Levin's remarks in (Robbins, 1992, pp.186–7). For a detailed analysis of the cadenzas to K.453, see Levin, 1990, pp.281–2.

84. K^{6}626a/K.624, Teil i, no. 61.

85. A passing resemblance to the material of bars 158–9 is noted in Badura-Skoda, 1962, p.260; see also Faye Ferguson's contribution to the discussion of Robbins, 1992 (at p.187), noting that the reference to motives from the development section of the movement (but from no other location) may have been deliberately intended to enhance the profile of the development section and retrospectively realign the overall proportions of the movement (presumably so that the freely episodic development did not appear marginalised by comparison with other sections).

86. Philip Whitmore has offered the intriguing speculation that this cadenza's 'neutral' quality was a deliberate ploy designed to preserve an important dimension of authorial originality in a work that Mozart may have intended to publish (though no edition was actually forthcoming in the composer's lifetime). By providing a cadenza largely founded on routine scale and arpeggio patterns, Mozart could assist amateur purchasers incapable of designing their own cadenzas, while at the same time letting slip no clues about his own unique improvisatory gift in a genre that he seems to have wished to contain within his immediate family circle as much as possible. See Whitmore, 1991, pp.140–142.

87. Such a structure is followed in Badura-Skoda's own cadenzas, printed in Badura-Skoda, 1967.

88. That is, Cadenza B as printed in NMA V/15/3; K^{6}626a/K.624, Teil i, 27.

89. WoO (Werk ohne Opuszahl) 58,1 and WoO 58,2; see Beethoven, 1967, pp.44 and 46 respectively.

90. Further on Mendelssohn's performances, see the entry to K.466 in Part Two; *Clara Schumann: Fünf Kadenzen für Klavier zu 2 Händen*, Leipzig: Peters (n.d.).

91. All are given in NMA V/15/2.

92. K^{6}626a/K.624, Teil i, 63; printed in NMA Serie X/29 and *Kritische Berichte* to NMA V/15/8, p.H/102 (see also pp.H/43–4). An *Eingang* must also be improvised at bar 181.

93. NMA V/15/8, p.xxvi.

94. For further details, see the entry for K.595 in Part Two.

95. See the entry for this piece in Part Two.

PART TWO
Mozart's Piano Concertos: A Register

Piano concerto in D major, K.175

i. Allegro, $\frac{4}{4}$, 238 bars; ii. Andante ma un poco adagio, $\frac{3}{4}$, 119 bars; iii. Allegro, $\frac{2}{2}$, 281 bars; later replaced by Rondo, K.382, $\frac{2}{4}$, 237 bars.

Scoring: solo keyboard (harpsichord or fortepiano); violins 1 & 2; violas; bass [= cello, bass and bassoon *ad lib.*]; 2 oboes; 2 horns; 2 trumpets; timpani (with additional flute in K.382).

Composed in Salzburg in December 1773; new finale (K.382) added Vienna, March (?) 1782.

Regrettably, the autograph of this, Mozart's first 'original' piano concerto, is lost. It formed part of the collection of Mozart's autographs purchased by André, and remained in his family's possession until 1860. Thereafter it was in the Graßnick collection (Berlin) and was known to the editors of the first three Köchel catalogues. Its title-page apparently bore the legend 'Concerto per il clavicembalo del Sgr. Cavaliere Amadeo Wolfgango Mozart nel Decembre 1773'. K.175 was, in its day, one of Mozart's most popular and frequently performed concertos, for which the composer himself evidently had an enduring high regard. In 1782 he composed a new finale (the 'Rondo', K.382 – actually a set of variations) for use in Viennese performances (see below).[1] K.175 (with the K.382 finale) was apparently published for the first time as 'op.vii' in the *Journal des pièces de claveçin* by Boyer in Paris (1785), according to the title-page of a separate edition issued by the same publisher that year (Mozart, 1785a; Haberkamp, 1986 [K.175]).[2] It was subsequently published by Johann Anton André (Mozart, 1802a); this is the only contemporary source known today that carries the solo part of the original finale. Eighteenth-century manuscript parts survive at Salzburg (St Peter's), Melk and Kroměříž – the latter two incorporating K.382 as finale.[3] The Salzburg parts comprise: 1) the complete orchestral materials to K.175 with its original finale; 2) the solo part, with K.382 as finale; and 3) full orchestral parts for K.382. Judging from the appearance of just a single watermark in all but one leaf of the paper (found elsewhere among Salzburg sources only in works from 1782– 84), it would seem that all of this material originated at one and the same time, namely about a decade after K.175 was composed, and after the substitute finale had been added. Presumably, the Salzburg copies of this concerto were made shortly after Mozart sent the Rondo to Leopold on 23 March 1782 (see below). Evidently, no playing parts contemporary with the composition of K.175 in 1773 survive. Autograph cadenzas by Mozart to the first two movements of K.175, and to the associated Rondo, K.382, exist.[4]

Precisely what was meant by 'clavicembalo' on the title-page of K.175 is difficult to clarify. The keyboard range required is relatively narrow (A′–d‴), suggesting that it may have been conceived in 1773 for an instrument of limited compass. (Mozart's other early piano concertos, beginning with K.238 in B flat (January 1776), use a significantly wider range, F'–f'''.) Close comparison of bars 84–6 and bars 200–202 in the first movement implies that Mozart had to adapt the precise shape of his right-hand passagework in order to make it fit the restricted compass of the 'clavicembalo'. Bars 200–202 pose no problem, since their right-hand pitches lie relatively low (a'–d''–f sharp''–d''–a''–f sharp''–g'' and so on). However, at bars 84 and 86, where Mozart had modulated to the generally higher tessitura of the dominant key, his text (as given in the first edition, and subsequent editions based on the still-available autograph) avoids the high e''' which would result by straightforward analogy.[5]

Mozart played this piece often, to judge from Wolfgang's and Leopold's correspondence. Leopold noted in a letter of 21 December 1774 that it was one of the pieces that Wolfgang took on the journey to Munich. Little more than three years later, Mozart played 'mein altes Concert ex D' in Mannheim, where it apparently made a hugely favourable impression (letter of 14 February 1778). It was in Vienna, however, that this concerto was to enjoy its most striking success, especially during Lenten 'academies' (concerts), organised either by Mozart himself, or by others. For instance, it was performed by Mozart on 3 March 1782 (letter of 23 March), 11 March 1783 (letter of 12 March), 23 March 1783 (letter of 29 March, describing the work as 'a great favourite here') and again on 30 March (letter of 12 April). K.175's extraordinary popularity was due in large part to its new finale, the Rondo, K.382, which Mozart presumably composed for the first of these performances in March 1782. He soon sent a copy of the Rondo home to Salzburg, noting in his accompanying letter of 23 March that year that it had caused quite a stir ('welches hier so großen lärm macht'), and cautioning Leopold and Nannerl to guard it like a jewel, as it was intended only for himself and his sister to play.

The Rondo replaces a rather intellectual, contrapuntally conceived sonata-form finale with an overtly tuneful variation set, ending with a brisk $\frac{3}{8}$ 'finale'. Evidently Mozart reckoned that the earlier version would not sufficiently capture the attention of his Viennese audience and so set to work on something in a lighter idiom that would perfectly match their taste and gain their approval. It is scored for a slightly different orchestra, now including a single flute at the top of the woodwind chorus. This development poses interesting questions for the scoring of K.175. The surviving sets of orchestral materials preserve two alternative versions of the oboe and horn parts. In the parts at St Peter's, Salzburg (Hortschansky, 1989–90, pp.37–54), the two oboe parts and the first horn part are of a consistently higher tessitura compared to those preserved in Melk and Kroměříž. A tempting assumption following from this is that at some stage (presumably March 1782) the oboe and horn lines of the existing text of K.175 were altered (by Mozart?) in order that a flute part could be incorporated at the top of an expanded wind texture throughout, corresponding to the scoring of the new Rondo finale, K.382.[6] However, there are unresolved problems with this hypothesis. First, no flute part for the original text of K.175 exists in any of these surviving orchestral sets. Secondly, why was it necessary to apply the revised oboe and horn setting to the original finale as well, if this was superseded by K.382? Possibly the more colourful scoring occurred to Mozart before the composition of K.382, in which case the scoring of that replacement finale simply continued an already decided plan. At any rate, the new finale was a conspicuous success. Copies were advertised for 30 Kroner by Lorenz Lausch in the *Wiener Zeitung* in April 1785 (that is, just the Rondo, as a separate work).

Notes

1.   Both the original and revised finales are given in NMA V/15/1; earlier editions typically give only the revised finale, K.382.
2.   Only the keyboard part of Boyer's print survives.
3.   A-Ssp, Moz.340.1–3 (Tyson, 1996, nos.43 and 46), copied by Joseph Estlinger, Felix Hoffstätter and three other unidentified Salzburg copyists (see Eisen, 1991b, pp.253–[307], at pp.286–7; Schmid, 1993; Halliwell, 1998, pp.430–43); A–M, IV 294, c.1800(?), including ripieno string parts; CZ-KRa, II G 69/A3263 (of which the keyboard part was probably copied by Johann Radnitzky, a Viennese copyist active during the 1780s).
4.   K[6]626a/K.624, Teil i, 2, 4 and 26; A-Ssp, Moz.285.1; Tyson, 1996, no.65. For a facsimile, see NMA V/15/1, p.xi. A slightly different version of these cadenzas is preserved in the Artaria and André editions: K[6]626a/K.624, Teil i, 1, 3 and 25.
5.   In NMA the editor opted for an exact analogy with bars 200–202, assuming the availability of a broader range on a modern instrument.
6.   A sketch for the oboe parts of the slow movement survives in the Verlagsarchiv André (Offenbach-am-Main): NMA X/30/3,18 (Skb1778b).

Piano concerto in B flat major, K.238

i. Allegro aperto, $\frac{4}{4}$, 202 bars; ii. Andante un poco adagio, $\frac{3}{4}$, 85 bars; iii. Rondeau. Allegro, $\frac{2}{2}$, 291 bars.

Scoring: solo keyboard (harpsichord or fortepiano); violins 1 & 2; violas; bass [= cello, bass and bassoon *ad lib.*]; 2 flutes (in the Andante); 2 oboes; 2 horns.

Composed in Salzburg in January 1776.

The autograph of K.238 is today in the Library of Congress, Washington D.C.[1] At one stage in its history it was bound together with the autograph of K.175 (now lost). This, at least, is the state of affairs as reported in the original edition of Köchel (1862), at which point the composite autograph was still in the possession of the André family. It is written on a type of paper favoured by Mozart in the mid-1770s known as 'Klein-Querformat', ruled with ten staves and measuring c.170 x 225 mm.[2] Above the top stave on the first music page is written 'Concerto di cembalo. Del Sgr. Cav: Amadeo Wolfg: Mozart mp. [*manu propria* – in his own hand] Nel gianaro 1776. à Salisburgo'. Manuscript orchestral sets survive, at St Peter's, Salzburg, and at Kroměříž (Hudební-Archiv).[3] The first edition of K.238 appeared in 1793 (Mozart, 1793). Cadenzas to all three movements are known from copies in Leopold's hand.[4]

This concerto seems, like its predecessor, K.175, to have been intended primarily for Mozart's own use in concert tours (also, perhaps, for the use of his sister). On 4 October 1777, for instance, Mozart gave a private performance of some of his recent compositions (Deutsch, 1965, p.165),[5] including K.238 (also K.246 and K.271) for his host, Franz Joseph Albert, an innkeeper on the Kaufingerstrasse, Munich and the owner of an 'excellent fortepiano'.[6] Later the same month (22 October) it was performed at a public concert in Augsburg, along with the three-piano concerto, K.242, two recent symphonies and some solo keyboard works, possibly including the D major sonata, K.284 (Deutsch, 1965, pp.165–8, *passim*).[7] It was included (along with K.175 and some arias from *Lucio Silla*) in a concert on 13 February 1778 at the home of Christian Cannabich, the Konzertmeister of the orchestra of the Elector Palatine, Karl Theodore, in Mannheim. This time, however, the solo part was played by Cannabich's daughter, Rosa, who was Mozart's pupil at about this time. One further possible performance of K.238 is that given for the Wiener Tonkünstler-Sozietät on 3 April 1781, although the concerto played on that occasion might have been K.271 in E flat (Deutsch, 1961, p.173).[8]

This concerto is especially noteworthy for its delicate scoring. In the slow movement, Mozart replaces the pair of oboes with a pair of flutes, and marks the strings variously *pizzicato* and *coll' arco*. The tonal distinction between a flute and an oboe in Mozart's day was less sharp than is the case with their modern equivalents, but nevertheless, the flutes add significantly to the curious luminescence of this Andante. A passage of particularly striking effect is that at bars 36–7 (cf. bars 73–4), in which the treble register is brought into focus by Mozart's finely judged scoring of flute octaves, string *pizzicatos* and the piano's staccato accompaniment of chromatic sextuplets – a moment prefiguring the magical effects found at bars 103–10 in the Larghetto of K.595 (also in E flat and also featuring flute, strings – just the first violins – and piano solo). While there are no dynamic markings in the solo part, it calls for quite subtle shadings, for instance in the balancing of melody and accompaniment at bars 9–16 and throughout the chromatically enhanced continuation (bars 18–33; cf. bars 55–70). Precise distinctions of legato and staccato at bars 34–7 (cf. bars 71–4) add to the fragility of this movement.

On 11 September 1778 Mozart had noted in a letter to Leopold the possibility of publishing K.238 as part of a set of three concertos (along with K.246 and K.271) in Paris: 'As for my three concertos, the one written for Mlle Jeunehomme [K.271], the one for Countess Lützow [K. 246] and the one in B flat [K.238], I shall sell them to the man who engraved my sonatas [for piano and violin, K.301–6], provided he pays cash for them. And, if I can, I shall do the same with my six difficult sonatas [K.279–84]'. The intended publisher was Sieber; nothing came of either proposal.

Notes

1. US-Wc, Gertrude Clarke Whittall collection, ML 30.8b.M8 K.238 Case.
2. For a description see Tyson, 1987, pp.165–6, 171. K.238 is written on 'Type II' according to Tyson's classification (Tyson, 1996, no.35).
3. A-Ssp, Moz.230.1, copied by Joseph Estlinger (Eisen, 1991b, Table II), and including, in the Andante, some annotations by Mozart himself (tempo markings and *coll'arco* and *pizzicato* indications); for a facsimile, see NMA V/15/1, p.xiii; CZ-KRa, II G 66/A3260 (a second set of playing parts copied in the late eighteenth century survives in CZ-KRa II G 66/A4800, in which the solo part has inauthentic cadenzas for all three movements). See Derr, 1996a.
4. K^{6}626a/K.624, Teil i, 5, 6 and 7; A-Ssp, Moz.290.1 ('Cadenza per Rondeau: 3ter Eingang').
5. Also referred to in Mozart's letter of 6 October 1777.
6. According to Daniel Schubart's *Deutsche Chronik*, Augsburg, 27 April 1775, quoted in Deutsch, 1965, p.153.
7. Also mentioned in Mozart's letter of 23–4 October 1777.
8. K.175 in D was not performed in the capital until 3 March 1782 (with its replacement finale, the Rondo, K.382), while playing parts for K.246 in C were requested in a letter to his father dating from 10 April 1782.

Concerto for three (or two) pianos in F major, K.242

i. Allegro, $\frac{4}{4}$, 265 bars; ii. Adagio, $\frac{4}{4}$, 65 bars; iii. Rondeau. Tempo di menu-etto, $\frac{3}{4}$, 212 bars.

Scoring: three (or two) solo keyboards (harpsichords or fortepianos); violins 1 & 2; violas; bass [= cello, bass and bassoon *ad lib*.]; 2 oboes; 2 horns.

Composed in Salzburg in February 1776.

The autograph of K.242 was formerly in the Berlin Staatsbibliothek, Preussischer Kulturbesitz, from which it was removed during the Second World War. It is currently in the Jagiellonian University Library, Kraków.[1] K.242 was written on ten-stave Salzburg 'Querformat' paper – and not 'Klein-Querformat', which was Mozart's preferred paper-type during this period – to which, however, two additional staves had to be added by hand with a rastrum, one above and one below the main printed span, in order to fit the three piano parts into six staves and the orchestral parts (strings, oboes and horns) into a further six.[2] The autograph bears the designation 'Originale del Concerto à 3 Cembali di Amadeo Wolfgango Mozart nel Febraro 1776' at the top of the first music-page. Four autograph sheets containing Mozart's arrangement of the solo parts for two pianos are appended to the autograph of the original version, bearing the description 'I soli del Concerto a tre Cembali, accomodati a due'. Mozart supplied cadenzas for K.242 in the autograph score; in such a multi-instrument concerto, there is, naturally, no possibility of improvised cadenzas. The first edition, published by André (Mozart, 1802b), presents the version for two pianos that Mozart had himself arranged, probably during 1779 (the date of the E flat concerto for two pianos, K.365); André's edition describes K.242 as '2ème Concerto pour 2 Claviers'.

There are two surviving sets of orchestral parts for K.242, in the Staatsbibliothek zu Berlin (Musikabteilung) and Stanford Memorial Library (USA).[3] Possibly these two sets are related. Certainly their textual readings are very close, suggesting that either one was copied from the other, or else that they were independently copied from a common source (now lost). They each contain full orchestral material and solo parts for each of the three pianos of the original version.[4] In addition, the Berlin set preserves a first piano part (only) for the revised two-piano version, while the Stanford set preserves a complementary second-piano part (only). One of the Stanford copies of the violin 1 and 'basso' parts, and also the third-piano part, contain some annotations and corrections in Mozart's hand[5] and there is testimony that the provenance of this source goes back to Mozart himself.[6]

K.242 was composed for the use of Countess Antonia Lodron and her two daughters, Aloisia and Josephina, in Salzburg. It occupies a rather special place in Mozart's concerto output, as the three solo parts, varying in difficulty, allow us to imagine something of the respective personalities of their intended executants (the third part is the easiest, reflecting Josephina's limited technique). Performances of the work were not restricted to Salzburg, however. Mozart himself took part in a public performance in Augsburg on 22 October 1777, a concert announced in the *Augsburgische Staats- und Gelehrten Zeitung* the previous day. The other parts were performed by Johann Michael Demmler, the Augsburg cathedral organist, and the forte-piano maker, Johann Andreas Stein. A review of this concert praises Mozart's composition as being

> thorough, fiery, manifold and simple; the harmony so full, so strong, so unexpected, so elevating; the melody so agreeable, so playful, and every-thing so new; the rendering on the fortepiano so neat, so clean, so full of expression, and yet at the same time extraordinarily rapid, so that one hardly knew what to give attention to first, and all the hearers were enraptured. One found here mastery in the thought, mastery in the performance, mastery in the instruments, all at the same time. One thing always gave relief to another, so that the numerous assembly was displeased with nothing but the fact that the pleasure was not prolonged still further.[7]

Mozart was described in this review as 'a virtuoso who may place himself side by side with the great masters of our nation'. K.242 was later performed in Mannheim on 12 March 1778 by Rosa Cannabich, Aloysia Weber and Thérèse Pierron (one of Mozart's pupils, then a talented 15-year-old), at a private musical gathering at the home of Christian Cannabich in Mannheim (Deutsch, 1965, p. 174). Mozart noted in a letter to his father of 24 March 1778 that, after three rehearsals, the performance had been a great success ('wir haben 3 Proben gemacht, und es ist recht gut gegangen').

Possibly because the third solo part would offer only limited challenges to players outside of the Lodron family circle, and in order to exploit wider performance opportunities, Mozart arranged the work for just two pianos, initially, perhaps, for performance by himself and his sister. Nannerl Mozart's diary for 3 September 1780 notes that they had played the work together at the archiepiscopal court in Salzburg (Bauer, Deutsch, Eibl, 1962–75, iii, p.9; Deutsch, 1965, p.188). Subsequently, in a letter of 27 June 1781 to his father, Mozart asked that copies of the 'two concertos for two pianos' be sent to him in Vienna, referring evidently to K.365 and to the revised text of the present work. Documented Viennese performances of K.242 as a double concerto are lacking, but attempts to circulate the work were apparently made. The impor-tant Viennese music dealer, Johann Traeg (1747–1805), who frequently offered manuscript copies of Mozart's work for sale during the 1780s, adver-tised manuscript copies of 'double concertos' (probably K.242 and K.365) in the *Wiener Zeitung* on 14 September 1785.

Notes

1. PL-Kj, Mus.ms.autogr. W. A. Mozart 242; Tyson, 1996, no. 39. It is bound together with the autograph of K.365, for two pianos. This source was not available to the editor of NMA V/15/1. For facsimiles, one from the first movement (containing bars 245–53, leading up to and following the cadenza) and a cancelled sketch of the second-movement cadenza, see Schiedermair, 1919, pl.20; and Schünemann, 1936, pl.40. The former page is also reproduced in NMA V/15/1, p.xiv.
2. It is clear that Mozart had difficulty obtaining music paper ruled with more than ten staves in Salzburg; see Tyson, 1987, Chapter Fourteen.
3. D-B, Mus.Ms.15468/3, the solo keyboard, violin parts copied by Felix Hofstätter (Eisen, 1991b, Table II), the remainder being apparently the work of unidentified Viennese copyists (see Eisen, 1996, Appendix); US-STu, Special Collection, MLM 766. The Stanford parts are on a Salzburg paper used in works from 1777–78 and are possibly to be associated with Mozart's performance of K.242 in Augsburg on 22 October 1777.
4. The Stanford set contains also a duplicate of all the orchestral parts.
5. One such is the addition of two bars' rest at the end of the second system of the facsimile reproduced in NMA V/15/1, p.xv.
6. Julius André and Heinrich Henkel stated that Mozart used this set of playing parts in his own performances (noted in K^6, p.251). Despite the presence of Mozart's autograph annotations, doubts have recently been raised about the Salzburg provenance of this source (Eisen, 1991b, p.281, n.55).
7. *Augsburgische Staats- und Gelehrten Zeitung*, 28 October 1777, cited in Deutsch, 1965, pp.165–8, *passim*; see also Mozart's letter of 23–25 October 1777, which refers to this concert. The B flat concerto, K.238, was also performed (by Mozart) on this occasion.

Piano concerto in C major, K.246

i. Allegro aperto, $\frac{4}{4}$, 203 bars; ii. Andante, $\frac{2}{4}$, 133 bars; iii. Rondo. Tempo di menuetto, $\frac{3}{4}$, 303 bars.

Scoring: solo keyboard (harpsichord or fortepiano); violins 1 & 2; violas; bass [= cello, bass and bassoon *ad lib.*]; 2 oboes; 2 horns.

Composed in Salzburg in April 1776.

This work was composed for Countess Antonia Lützow – wife of the Commandant of the Festung Hohensalzburg – who was evidently one of Leopold Mozart's pupils, and an influential personage in provincial Salzburg. The autograph score of K.246 is one of those removed at the end of the Second World War from the Berlin Staatsbibliothek, Preussischer Kulturbesitz. For many years it was thought lost (although it was known to the compilers of the first three editions of Köchel, and had formed the basis of the old Breitkopf & Härtel *Gesamtausgabe*); fortunately, it had been transferred, along with a number of other Mozart concerto autographs, to the Jagiellonian University Library in Kraków, where it at present remains.[1] Like the majority of Mozart's autographs from this period, it is written on ten-stave 'Klein-Querformat' paper. At the top of the first music page is the legend, 'di Amadeo Wolfgango Mozart mpr. nel Aprile 1776 in Salisburgo'. The first edition was published by André (Mozart, 1800a), described as 'Edition faite d'après la partition en manuscrit', that is, based on the autograph, which he had previously purchased from Constanze. Manuscript copies of playing parts exist at St Peter's, Salzburg (copied either directly, or else at one remove, from the autograph), and Kroměříž.[2] The St Peter's material was copied under the supervision of Leopold Mozart and includes annotations by Wolfgang in the solo piano part (Schmid, 1970).[3] Particularly important are his extensive continuo realisations (printed in small type in NMA).[4] It is likely that they were intended for a pupil inexperienced in the art of continuo realisation; conceivably, this pupil was Thérèse Pierron, the daughter of Mozart's landlord in Mannheim during autumn–spring 1777–78, to whom he taught the piece (see below). In many ways, this concerto is an ideal teaching piece. Its technical demands are few and easily surmounted. Most of the passagework is restricted to the right hand and involves only the most straightforward changes of hand-position (frequently requiring only the 'white' keys of the piano); in the main, the left contributes simple accompaniments; it develops essential facets such as cantabile playing (in the Andante especially) and a secure rhythmic sense (for instance, in the middle episode of the Menuetto finale, bars 113–93, necessitating clean handling of dotted rhythms, syncopation and contrapuntal textures); above all, its design is conventional, in the sense that large portions within each movement are recapitulated fairly exactly, reducing the actual amount of note-learning required for performance.

We are especially fortunate that several autograph cadenzas survive for the first two movements of this concerto (in addition to the *Eingang* at bar 193 of the finale, which is recorded in the autograph score).[5] Mozart composed three sets of cadenzas for the Allegro aperto and for the Andante, their varying difficulty further strengthening the hypothesis that K.246 served as an 'instructional' piece for the use of Mozart's pupils.[6] All are recorded in the text of the NMA as 'A', 'B' and 'C' in each movement.[7] Probably Mozart's set 'B' cadenzas, notated on a single leaf of eight-stave 'Klein-Querformat' paper, contemporary with that of the autograph itself, are the earliest.[8] The set 'A' cadenzas were added on unused staves of the solo part in the St Peter's orchestral material,[9] and therefore probably at some point after the original copying of this source.[10] Mozart's set 'C' cadenzas were written on a single sheet of ten-stave 'Querformat' paper (c.225 x 305mm), a type that he did not use habitually before the beginning of 1779.[11]

While K.246 may have been intended primarily as a teaching-piece, Mozart did perform it himself in Munich on 4 October 1777, along with K.238 and K.271.[12] According to Mozart's letters of 17 January and 22 February 1778, his pupil, Thérèse Pierron, gave two public performances of the work in Mannheim, on 14 January 1778 and again on 23 February 1778. On the former occasion, as mentioned in Mozart's letter of 17 January, the Abbé Vogler[13] was present and sight-read the work rather badly (according to Mozart), playing everything much too quickly, and missing out many details in the process:

> Before dinner he had scrambled through my concerto [K.246] at sight (the one which the daughter of the house [Thérèse Pierron] plays – written for Countess Lützow). He took the first movement *prestissimo*, the Andante *allegro* and the Rondo, believe it or not, *prestissimo*. He generally played the bass differently from the way it was written, inventing now and then quite another harmony and even melody. Nothing else is possible at that pace, for the eyes cannot see the music nor the hands perform it ... it is much easier to play a thing quickly than slowly: in passagework you can leave out a few notes without anyone noticing it. But is that beautiful? ... [Good sight-reading consists of] playing the piece in the time in which it ought to be played, and playing all the notes, appoggiaturas and so forth, exactly as they are written and with the appropriate expression and taste, so that you might suppose that the performer composed it himself. Vogler's fingering too is wretched; ... he does all the treble runs downwards with the thumb and first finger of his right hand.

K.246 was also performed back home in Salzburg by Nannerl Mozart during her brother's prolonged absence in 1777–79;[14] she, in turn, coached her pupil, Mlle Villersi, for a performance of the piece. According to Leopold:

> We still have our amateur concerts in Lodron's hall every Sunday ... Well, Mlle Villersi was asked to perform. Countess von Lützow had had Wolfgang's concerto [K.246] copied for her some time ago[15] and Spitzeder had

taught it to her [Villersi]. Thinking that she could play it very well, she tried it in her own room with the violins. Bullinger was there too. They all told her, and she agreed, that she played it abominably. So she came out to our house in tears and begged us to coach her, postponing her performance by a fortnight and ending by learning it so proficiently that she really did herself great credit (Eisen, 1991a, no.1).[16]

Evidently, several copies of K.246 were in circulation at this time. In addition to the autograph, there was Countess Lützow's copy, from which a further copy (presumably of just the solo part) had been made for Villersi. Mozart had taken a different set of parts for K.246 with him on the Mannheim–Paris journey (from which the various performances by himself, Pierron and Vogler took place). Possibly these were left with Sieber in Paris for intended publication along with K.238 and K.271 (letter of 11 September 1778; cf. entry for K.238). Another set must have remained in the family library, since in a letter of 10 April 1782 Mozart urgently requested Leopold to send him a copy of 'mein Concert für die gräfin litsow', probably for the use of his Viennese piano students. Possibly the two cadenzas, set 'C', were composed at this time; admittedly, they were written on to ten-stave 'Querformat' paper datable to 1779, rather than on the 12-stave variety that Mozart normally used after he moved to Vienna, but Mozart habitually used up odd sheets of older paper stocks for cadenzas.[17]

Notes

1. PL-Kj, Mus.ms.autogr. W. A. Mozart 246/271; Tyson, 1996, no.35. It is bound together with the autograph of K.271 in E flat. This source was not available to the editor of NMA V/15/2.
2. A-Ssp, Moz.235.1; CZ-KRa, II G 68/A3262.
3. The copyists were Joseph Estlinger and another unidentified Salzburg copyist (no.27 in Schmid's catalogue, but there misattributed to copyist 32).
4. A facsimile of his continuo realisation towards the close of the Andante (bars 115–33) is reproduced in NMA V/15/2, p.xvi.
5. It is to be found also in the solo part of the St Peter's orchestral material (A-Ssp, Moz.235.1).
6. This may also explain the extensive provision of continuo realisations in the solo part, for which see Chapter Seven.
7. The set 'A' cadenzas are K^{6}626a/K.624, Teil i, 8, 11; Tyson, 1996, no.28. set 'B', K^{6}626a/K.624, Teil i, 9, 12; Tyson, 1996, no.40. set 'C', K^{6}626a/K.624, Teil i, 10, 14]; Tyson, 1996, no.51. In K^6, p.255, four cadenzas to the Andante are noted by *incipit*. The third of these actually belongs to the slow movement of K.415 (*q.v.*); the fourth ['Kadenza (d)'] is for K.246 (= NMA's 'Cadenza C').
8. London, British Library, C. B. Oldman collection, GB-Lbl, Add.Ms.61905. A copy of the set 'B' cadenzas in Leopold's hand also exists in a private collection.
9. As shown, for example, in the facsimile mentioned in note 5 (the first-movement cadenza 'A' in A-Ssp, Moz.235.1 was added to the page containing the end of the first movement and the beginning of the second). The copyist of the keyboard part

was Joseph Estlinger; the other parts are by an unidentified Salzburg copyist (Eisen, 1991b, Table II).

10. Possibly, indeed, for Thérèse Pierron in Mannheim during later 1777 or early 1778.

11. I-Mc, Z.115.14.5 (formerly 12259).

12. Letter of 6 October 1777. By this date, Mozart had probably begun to conceive of these three concertos as a conveniently varied group, demonstrating different aspects of his craft, although they were not originally composed in close succession (January 1776, April 1776, January 1777, respectively). In September 1778 he tried (unsuccessfully) to have them published as a set by Sieber in Paris.

13. For Vogler, see Chapter One, n.17. Mozart's comments incidentally give us some interesting insight into his own preferred methods of playing, if only in a negative way, in his criticism of Vogler's approach.

14. As noted by Leopold in a letter to Wolfgang of 29 January 1778.

15. Villersi's copy of K.246 was presumably made from a 'presentation' copy made for Countess Lützow shortly after the concerto's composition in 1776.

16. See also Leopold's letter to Wolfgang of 29 January 1778.

17. Mozart was still using up 'Klein-Querformat' paper as late as 15 February 1783; a sheet enclosed in Mozart's letter to Nannerl of that date contains cadenzas for the first two movements of K.175 and to its recently composed finale supplement, the Rondo, K.382, along with two *Eingänge* for the finale of K.271 (see Tyson, 1987, p.166 and n.13).

Piano concerto in E flat major, K.271

i. Allegro, $\frac{4}{4}$, 307 bars; ii. Andantino, $\frac{3}{4}$, 131 bars; iii. Rondeau. Presto, $\frac{2}{2}$, 467 bars.

Scoring: solo keyboard (harpsichord or fortepiano); violins 1 & 2; violas; bass [= cello, bass and bassoon *ad lib.*]; 2 oboes; 2 horns.

Composed in Salzburg in [December 1776?–] January 1777.

The autograph of the E flat concerto, K.271, is at present in the Jagiellonian University Library, Kraków,[1] whence it was removed from the Berlin Staatsbibliothek, Preussischer Kulturbesitz, at the end of the Second World War. It is on Mozart's favoured ten-stave Salzburg 'Klein-Querformat' paper and bears at the top of the first music-page the legend 'Concerto per il Clavicembalo del Sgr. Caval. Amadeo Wolfgango Mozart nel [erased: Decemb:] Gianaio 1777'.

It was written for the French virtuoso pianist, Mlle Jeunehomme (normally 'Jenomy' in the Mozarts' correspondence), who visited Salzburg on tour during December 1776. A set of performing parts, copied probably under the supervision of Leopold Mozart in Salzburg, and including his annotations, survive.[2] The first edition, published by André, dates from as early as 1792, that is, some seven years before he had the opportunity to purchase a large quantity of autographs from Mozart's widow (Mozart, 1792a).[3] André's source may possibly have been an earlier French edition, now lost. In September 1778, Mozart had endeavoured to have K.271, along with K.238 and K.246, published as a set by Sieber in Paris (letter of 11 September). Apparently nothing came of that proposal. However, in a catalogue of new compositions from the rival Parisian publishing-house of Heina, an unidentified concerto by Mozart ('Concerto/P.r le Clavecin ou F.e P.o /Mozard/4 livres, 10 sous') was advertised for sale in 1780 (Devriès & Lesure, 1979, vol.i (Catalogue), no.94). Possibly, this was K.271 (although no exemplar is known); if so, then, as was the case with several other works originally published by Heina,[4] André may simply have copied his 1792 edition from that source.

No fewer than ten authentic cadenzas and *Eingänge* for K.271 survive, six in autograph sources, the other four in copies made by Mozart's father and sister. The autograph items are as follows:

- cadenzas to the first and second movements, identified in NMA V/15/2 as 'Cadenzas B'[5]
- *Eingänge* for the finale, identified in NMA V/15/2 as 'Erster [/Zweiter] Eingang B'[6]
- *Eingänge* for the finale, identified in NMA V/15/2 as 'Erster [/Zweiter] Eingang C'[7]

The copies are as follows:

- Leopold Mozart: cadenzas for the first two movements, identified in NMA V/15/2 as 'Cadenzas A'[8]
- Nannerl Mozart: two *Eingänge* (NMA V/15/2, set 'A') copied from the autograph score into the solo part of an evidently composite set of orchestral materials for K.271[9]

Regrettably very little is known of the work's early performance history. For instance, Mlle Jeunehomme's own performances of it are completely undocumented, as are Mozart's opinion of and relations with her. Its thoroughly virtuosic character and prodigious technical demands (especially in the finale) suggest that Jeunehomme's talents were indeed considerable and her contemporary reputation well deserved. Conceivably, her playing was famed for its declamatory quality, amply exploited in Mozart's Andantino (which also exploits the half-tones of *sordino* strings). Possibly, too, the concerto's striking opening, in which the soloist is almost immediately present in opposition to the tutti, may have been specifically designed both to capture the attention of the original Salzburg audience and to flatter the executant, assuming that Mlle Jeunehomme performed the work during her visit there in winter 1776–77. All this, however, is speculative; the lack of solid evidence surrounding the work's genesis and reception is indeed frustrating. The earliest known performance of K.271 by Mozart himself is recorded in a letter of 6 October 1777, documenting a concert two days earlier that had also included K.238 and K.246.[10] It is possible that this concerto was the one that Mozart performed at a concert of the Wiener Tonkünstler-Sozietät on 3 April 1781 (Deutsch, 1961, p.173).[11]

Notes

1. PL-Kj, Mus.ms.autogr. W. A. Mozart 246/271; Tyson, 1996, no.35. It is bound together with the autograph of K.246 in C. This source was not available to the editor of NMA V/15/2.
2. A-Ssp, Moz.240.1. For a facsimile of one page from the keyboard part, including Leopold's figuring of the bass line, see NMA V/15/2, p.xviii. A copy of the keyboard part, in the hand of Aloys Emmanuel Förster, is in A-Wn, S.m.1252; see Edge, 1996c, pp.64–5 (n.34).
3. André also published K.449 (composed in 1784) in the same year. For Constanze's contract with André, see Deutsch, 1965, pp.490–2.
4. For example, K.179, K.180, K.254, K.354 and K.310; see Irving, 1997, pp.64–5.
5. K⁶626a/K.624, Teil i, 15, 17; D-B, Mus.ms.autogr. W. A. Mozart 624(1); Tyson, 1996, no.72, (1784); see also Tyson, 1987, p.232. Note that the designations of these cadenzas differ in NMA and in K⁶: Mozart's autograph cadenzas, printed in NMA as 'B' in each of the first and second movements, are Fassung (a) in K⁶.
6. K⁶626a/K.624, Teil i, 19–20; Max Reis collection, Zurich; [= K⁶ Fassung A].

7. K⁶626a/K.624, Teil i, 21–2; A-Ssp, Moz.285.1; Tyson, 1996, no.40 [= K⁶
    Fassung B]. This cadenza sheet also contains cadenzas for K.175 (first and
    second movements) and K.382, enclosed within a letter sent by Mozart to his
    sister and father in Salzburg on 15 February 1783 (Tyson, 1987, p.345, n.13).
8. K⁶626a/K.624, Teil i, 16, 18; A-Ssp, Moz.295.1 (= K⁶ 'Fassung B').
9. K⁶ deest; A-Ssp, Moz.240.1. These were presumably the earliest *Eingänge* to
    K.271's finale, and may be contemporary (or roughly so) with its composition.
    Nannerl wrote the solo part, on paper datable to c.1777; M. H. Schmid's 'Salz-
    burg copyist 9' wrote everything else on paper datable to 1784 (Schmid, 1980–
    83. See also Halliwell, 1998, pp. 430–4; Schmid, 1993. A second set of playing
    parts for K.271 survives in CZ-KRa, II G 67/A3261, including an incomplete
    keyboard part with cadenzas to the first two movements in the hand of Emmanuel
    Aloys Förster (a partial facsimile of Förster's first-movement cadenza is shown in
    Edge, 1996c, fig.5).
10. See also Deutsch, 1965, p.165. By this date, Mozart had probably begun to
    conceive of these three concertos as a conveniently varied group for use in his
    tours, each demonstrating different aspects of his craft, although they were not
    originally composed in close succession (January 1776, April 1776, January
    1777, respectively).
11. The only other concerto that could have been played on this occasion is that in B
    flat, K.238. K.175 in D was not performed in the capital until 3 March 1782 (with
    its replacement finale, the Rondo, K.382). Mozart evidently did not have the
    playing parts of K.246 in C available in Vienna until a year after the Tonküns-
    tler-Sozietät performance (he requested them in a letter to his father of 10 April
    1782).

Concerto for two pianos in E flat major, K.365.

i. Allegro, $\frac{4}{4}$, 303 bars; ii. Andante, $\frac{3}{4}$, 105 bars; iii. Rondeaux. Allegro, $\frac{2}{4}$, 504 bars.

Scoring: two solo fortepianos; violins 1 & 2; violas; bass [= cello, bass and bassoon *ad lib*.]; 2 oboes; 2 horns [2 clarinets, 2 trumpets, timpani (see text)].

Composed in Salzburg in early 1779.

The autograph of K.365 (bearing the legend 'Concerto à due Cembali' on the first music-page) was among those purchased from Constanze Mozart by André in 1799. It was removed – along with numerous other Mozart concerto scores – from the Berlin Staatsbibliothek, Preussischer Kulturbesitz at the end of the Second World War. It is currently in the Jagiellonian University Library, Kraków.[1] Although the autograph bears no specific date, the fact that it is written on ten-stave Querformat paper (a type that Mozart began to use habitually after his return to Salzburg following the extended Mannheim–Paris journey of 1777–79, and to which he certainly did not have access during that prolonged absence from home), argues strongly for a composition date during spring 1779. Almost certainly it was originally conceived as a piece for Mozart to perform with his sister. At about this time he had probably arranged the F major concerto, K.242 (originally for three pianos), for the same purpose; at any rate, Nannerl Mozart's diary for 3 September 1780 notes that they had played the work together (Bauer, Deutsch, Eibl, 1962–75, iii, p.9). Possibly, the opportunity for Mozart once again to partner his talented sister at the keyboard provided a stimulus for the revision of K.242 and the composition of K.365.

A significant amount of correspondence relating to this work survives. On 27 June 1781, Mozart wrote to his father from Vienna requesting that he send playing parts of K.365 for use in the capital with Josepha Auernhammer: 'Please have the sonata in B flat à quatre mains [K.358] and the two concertos for two claviers [K.242 in the two-piano arrangement and K.365] copied for me and send them to me as soon as possible.' These had still not arrived at the end of September, as Mozart notes somewhat caustically in a letter of 26 September 1781: 'Fräulein Auernhammer and I are longing to have the two double concertos. I hope we shall not wait as vainly as the Jews for their Messiah.' They had finally arrived by 13 October. By 3 November, Wolfgang had promised to send Leopold completed copies of the cadenzas that he was then busy writing into the second piano part. Mozart and Auernhammer performed K.365 publicly on two occasions, on 23 November 1781 and 26 May 1782. On 24 November 1781, Mozart reported to his father that the 'academy' given by Josepha Auernhammer and himself the previous day (a concert attended by Countess Thun, Baron van Swieten, Baron Godenus, Baron Wezler von Plankenstern, Count Firmian and Herr von Daubrawaick) had been a great success.[2] The following May, K.365 was given in a rather more public setting, at one of the Augarten concerts organised by Philipp Jakob Martin.[3] K.365 evidently remained popular beyond these early Viennese performances. Manuscript copies for sale at 4 fl. 22 kr. were advertised in the *Wiener Zeitung* on 18 August 1784 and again on 11 August 1792 through the music-dealer, Johann Traeg (Deutsch, 1965, pp.227, 464).

Fortunately, Mozart's cadenzas, mentioned in his letter of 3 November 1781, still survive.[4] They are written on two bifolia containing the cadenzas for the first and third movements, respectively, those for the first piano being in Leopold's hand, those for the second piano, in Wolfgang's.[5] Also at St. Peter's is a further autograph bifolium of the first-movement cadenza for the first piano that had probably served as a copytext for Leopold.[6] In the Kroměříž Schloß-archiv[7] is yet another autograph cadenza, this time an early version of the cadenza for the finale (first piano only). Playing parts for K.365 survive in St Peter's, Salzburg and Kroměříž, both substantially the work of the Salzburg copyists Felix Hofstätter and Joseph Estlinger who was probably working under Leopold's close supervision.[8] Autograph annotations by Wolfgang may be seen in the bassoon and horn parts of the Salzburg set.[9]

The exact nature of the intended orchestral accompaniment for K.365 is problematic. The surviving contemporary orchestral parts associated with the Mozart family[10] do not include parts for clarinets, trumpets and timpani, although these were included in the Breitkopf & Härtel *Gesamtausgabe* of 1881 (reprinted in 1891). Neither does the first edition, published by André in 1800 (Mozart, 1800b), nor the 1804 edition issued by Breitkopf (Mozart, 1804). A hint that at least the clarinet parts may be authentic is offered, first, by Nissen's annotation on the first music-page of the autograph 'mit den Stimmen der fagoti und Clarinetten' (Wolff, 1984, p.40) and secondly, by André's manuscript catalogue of 1833, which lists among the orchestral materials for this piece some 'specially adapted clarinet parts'. Otto Jahn hypothesised that these clarinet parts were written especially for a Viennese performance, possibly that of 26 May 1782, at which additional winds would have been necessary for the performance of a symphony by Baron van Swieten and another (possibly, K.297) by Mozart. No trace of any contemporary score containing clarinets (or trumpets or timpani) has been found, however, although it is possible that supplementary wind and brass parts for a special occasion would have been set out only on a separate score sheet (known to André but subsequently lost).[11]

Notes

1. PL-Kj, Mus.ms.autogr. W. A. Mozart 242/365; Tyson, 1996, nos.51, 52. It is bound together with the autograph of K.242 for three (two) pianos. This source was not available to the editor of NMA V/15/2.

2.   Mozart and Auernhammer played K.365 and also the D major sonata for two pianos, K.448, composed specially for this occasion.
3.   According to Mozart's letter of 25 May 1782: 'Tomorrow our first concert takes place in the Augarten ... A symphony by van Swieten and one of mine [K.338] are being performed ... and Fräulein Auernhammer and I are playing my E flat concerto for two pianos.'
4.   A-Ssp, Moz.300. 1. The cadenzas are K⁶626a/K.624, Teil i, 23,24; Tyson, 1996, no.35.
5.   For a facsimile, see NMA V/15/2, p.xix.
6.   A-Ssp, Moz.300.2.
7.   CZ-KRa, II G 65/A3259. See also NMA V/15/2, Anhang. This work was frequently performed by Mendelssohn (with Hiller and Moescheles as partners) during the 1830s and 1840s, and parts of cadenzas to the outer movements composed by Mendelssohn survive; see Todd, 1991.
8.   A-Ssp, Moz.245.1; CZ-Kra, II G 45, respectively. Cliff Eisen has recently suggested, on the basis of watermark evidence, that the Kroměříž source was that sent by Leopold to Wolfgang in Vienna in October 1781 (Eisen, 1991b, p.281). A later set in A-M, IV 298, c.1800(?) includes ripieno string parts.
9.   For a facsimile, see NMA V/15/2, p.xx.
10. That is, both the St Peter's and Kroměříž copies.
11. These supplementary parts are printed in small type in NMA V/15/2.

Three concertos in A major, K.414, in F major, K.413 and in C major, K.415

The three concertos in A major, K.414, in F major, K.413 and in C major, K.415, were Mozart's first piano concertos written after his removal to Vienna. They are approached here as an integral set of three concertos, rather than as three independently conceived, isolated works. The autographs of K.413–15 (on 12-stave 'Querformat' paper – a type that was to serve Mozart for many of his Viennese instrumental compositions) are today in the Jagiellonian University Library, Kraków.[1] All three scores are notated in an uncharacteristically rushed, untidy script. In part, this may have been consequential upon the composer's strategy for marketing the works in Vienna early in 1783. On 28 December 1782, Mozart had written to his father famously listing the characteristics of all three of these 'subscription' concertos (that they tread a middle path between the too easy and the too difficult, and so on – see below), and noting specifically that only one of the three (probably K.414 in A) was already complete at the time of writing. Nevertheless, by 15 January 1783, Mozart had placed an announcement in the *Wiener Zeitung*, offering all three concertos for sale in finely produced manuscript copies, available on subscription:

> Herr Kapellmeister Mozart herewith apprizes the highly honoured public of the publication of three new, recently finished pianoforte concertos. These 3 concertos, which may be performed either with a large orchestra with wind instruments or merely *a quattro*, *viz*. with 2 violins, 1 viola and violoncello, will not appear until the beginning of April this year, and will be issued (finely copied and supervised by himself) only to those who have subscribed thereto. The present [announcement] serves to give the further news that subscription tickets may be had of him for four ducats (Deutsch, 1965, p.212).[2]

If this statement is to be believed, it would appear that the composition of the two remaining concertos was accomplished during the first fortnight of 1783. In any event, sufficient copies of all three would need to have been produced during the next two months to satisfy the anticipated demand for subscriptions, and Mozart may have had to complete his autographs in a hurry, so that the professional manuscript copies, 'finely copied and supervised by himself', could be made in advance, although in a letter of 22 January 1783 Mozart tells his father that 'they cannot be copied, as I shall not let them [presumably the autographs] out of my hands until I have secured a certain number of subscribers', a remark that implies that production of the subscription copies had not then commenced.[3]

More probably, the untidy appearance of the autographs reflects Mozart's compositional problems with K.413–15. These were, after all, the first piano concertos he had written in Vienna, works with which he could potentially make his name in the capital as composer and performer. Certainly, to judge from his letter to Leopold of 28 December 1782, he intended them to appeal to a broad range of musical sensibilities: 'These concertos are a happy medium between what is too easy and too difficult; they are very brilliant, pleasing to the ear and natural, without being vapid. There are passages here and there from which connoisseurs alone will derive satisfaction; but these passages are written in such a way that the less learned cannot fail to be pleased, though without knowing why.' Possibly, Mozart's striving for such a sophisticated mode of musical expression is reflected in the state of his manuscripts, which reveal layer upon layer of painstaking refinement. All three scores contain numerous revisions to the solo part (especially concerning details of passage-work).[4] Moreover, there are frequent significant erasures and revisions, even excisions of whole passages. For example, in the finale of K.414, Mozart originally drafted the opening of a central episode in B minor following bar 107 (including some solo figuration pre-empting rhythmically that at bars 132–5), but immediately deleted it. The first ten bars of the cancelled passage are on fol.[33v],[5] the remainder on the first leaf of a bifolium that he subsequently tore out of his manuscript.[6] He proceeded with the eventual reading of the ensuing passage (bar 108 foll.) on fol.[34r]. The conclusion of this movement is also rather messy in the autograph. Following the fermata at bar 180, the continuation on fols.[37v–38] is of bars 197 to the end of the movement; bars 182–97 are found later on fols.[38v] and [39v],[7] and were perhaps an afterthought, keyed into the autograph by means of a *siglum* on fol.[37v]. In the case of K.415, Mozart originally drafted 17 bars of a $\frac{3}{4}$ slow movement in C minor, but cancelled it on fols.19v–20r, immediately following the conclusion of the Allegro (on fol.19r);[8] the F major Andante that replaced it follows immediately afterwards in the autograph. Between bar 43 and bar 44 in the finale, Mozart originally continued with a four-bar chordal passage analogous to bars 46–9, but featuring augmented-6th enhancements of the dominant, G. This was cancelled on fol.28v, and replaced with bars 44–9 as they now stand.

There is good reason to suppose that Mozart worked simultaneously on all three of the concertos in this set. No fewer than five different paper-types are distributed among the autograph scores.[9] Assuming that he used up one stock of paper before moving on to another of a different type, it would appear that he was engaged simultaneously on the composition of the first two movements of K.414 and the first movement of K.413; the finale of K.414 and the slow movement of K.415; the slow movement of K.413 and the first movement of K.415; and the finales of K.413 and K.415. Such a detailed chronology may be expecting too much of paper analysis, however. The same papers are to be found in other works written rather earlier in 1782, and odd sheets were certainly left over at various stages of the work. Bars 182–97 in the finale of K.414, for instance, were evidently an afterthought, tacked on once the movement had been provisionally completed. The additions were made on a separate leaf (fol.39) tipped in at the end of the manuscript; this leaf is of the same paper-type as that used for the first portion of the finale, and for the slow movement of K.415, to which he returned having used up a different stock of paper for the bulk of K.414's finale. The picture is certainly very complicated, and perhaps impossible to recover with exactitude; what may be asserted confidently is that all three concertos originated in close proximity. So although Mozart told his father that only one concerto (K.414) had reached completion by 28 December 1782, the others could not have been far behind.

An attempt further to refine the chronology of these three concertos through close analysis of the ink-types found in the autograph has been made by John Arthur (Arthur, 1996, pp.35–4, specifically his Table 3.1). Arthur presents a detailed description of the several ink-types to be observed in Mozart's manuscript, from which he derives some sensitive and carefully qualified speculations, including the idea that K.414's finale may have been completed at a separate stage from the first two movements (as, indeed, is suggested by the paper-types). Arthur's thesis rests, like the paper-type analysis, on the assumption that Mozart was systematic (or relatively so) in his use of inks, typically using different inks for separate stages in the writing process: for instance, initial 'particella' (the leading melodic line in strings or piano, and the bass line); completion of inner string parts; completion of subsidiary wind parts. Reading the manuscript in this way, Arthur offers some interesting glimpses into the relative chronology of these three works. Although Arthur does not investigate the issue of Mozart's corrections to the piano parts of these concertos, it appears from his interpretation of the ink-types that those in the first movements of K.414 and K.415 were effected in the same ink as was used for the completion of the string parts (what Arthur terms 'non-particella parts') in the first two movements of K.414, but in a different ink from that used for the completion of the string parts in the first movement of K.415. A possible sequence is: (1) correction of the piano part within the existing 'particella' of K.414's first movement; (2) completion of the string and subsequently wind parts of this movement; (3) correction of the piano part within the existing 'particella' of K.415's first movement; (4) completion of the string parts of this movement; (5) completion of the wind parts of this movement. At any rate, Mozart's detailed alterations to the solo parts seem, on this evidence, to be firmly situated within the process of its composition, rather than retrospectively after the movements (including the wind parts, added subsequently in different inks) had been completed. Set against all this, however, must be the caution that the distinction between ink-shades to be observed in Mozart's autograph score could be merely an unavoidable corruption of the original appearance occasioned by changes to the chemistry of the ink and paper over two centuries. Whether the appearance of the manuscript now may safely reflect that original state, and consequently support detailed chronological interpretation, remains an open question.[10] Certainly, interpretation of ink-shades is potentially perilous, a fact borne out by the numerous caveats with which Arthur peppers his own essay.

All three works are preserved (in varying states of completeness) in authentic manuscript performance materials at St Peter's, Salzburg.[11] It is possible to associate at least some of these manuscript parts with a known performance of K.415 that Mozart gave in Salzburg on 1 October during an extended home visit, at which time the revisions to all three concertos may also have been made. 'Tutti' and 'solo' annotations to the string parts were made by Mozart, presumably for this performance.[12] Dexter Edge has shown that, contrary to traditional assumptions, the playing parts for K.415 now at St Peter's Library, though intended for Salzburg performances, did not actually originate in Salzburg, but were prepared in Vienna by Joseph Arthofer, a copyist who worked for Mozart during 1783 (Edge, 1996c, at pp.54–5).[13] Whether the Salzburg parts represent one of the professionally copied sets offered on subscription early in 1783 remains an open question; no other surviving exemplar definitely associated with the subscription copies is known. If the parts now in St Peter's are indeed the remains of a copy of the subscription set, then the revisions would presumably date from early 1783, prior to their public issue. On the other hand, it is possible that the 'Salzburg' parts, though copied in Vienna, have nothing specifically to do with the subscription set. Precisely when these copies arrived in Salzburg is uncertain. Possibly Mozart brought them with him to Salzburg in early summer 1783. It is known that his father had one of the 'official' subscription copies by 3 April 1784, since he sent one (at the advertised price of 4 Ducats) to the family friend, Sebastian Winter, at the Donaueschingen court on that date.[14]

Despite Mozart's professed appeal to a broad selection of tastes in these pieces, it is hard to know if the concertos truly made their mark on Viennese amateurs and connoisseurs. While the continued marketing of these concertos during 1783 may imply an enduring interest and demand, it is equally possible that Mozart had to keep reminding potential purchasers of their existence because they had not sold especially well at first. In a letter to Baroness Waldstätten of 15 February 1783, Mozart explains that he could not at that time repay a loan since sales of the concertos K.413–15 on subscription were proceeding only very slowly, and he had counted on getting a reasonable financial return in a short space of time. His letter of 26 April 1783 to the Parisian publisher, Sieber, offering these works for publication for the sum of 30 Louis d'or, might also be viewed in the context of immediate financial hardship; the wording of his letter stresses – as did contemporary Viennese advertisements – the flexibility of these concertos ('welche mit ganzen orchester als mit oboen und Horn – wie auch nur à quatro können Producirt werden'), probably in a bid to impress upon the publisher the appeal of these concertos to a wide range of performance situations (both 'public' and 'domestic') and the consequent likelihood of significant sales.[15] Whatever the true financial return on K.413–15, Mozart tried to present a glowing picture of his success in letters to his father at this time. He stresses only the positive side of his entrepreneurial activities as a concertiser and teacher.

The concertos were eventually published by Artaria (as Op.iv nos.1–3) early in 1785 (Mozart, 1785b), that is, some two years after Mozart had initially offered them on subscription. Once the works had appeared in print, they seem to have made a very favourable impression, at least so far as sales were concerned. On 12 January 1785 Artaria placed an advertisement for the orchestral parts of K.413–15 in the *Wiener Zeitung*; further announcements of this edition appeared in the *Provinzialnachrichten Wien* (5 March 1785: 'At the art establishment of Artaria Comp ... three Pianoforte Concertos by Herr Kapellmeister Mozart, in A maj., F maj., and C, have been engraved, and each is to be had at 2 fl. 30 kr') and in the *Wiener Realzeitung* for 29 March 1785 (Deutsch, 1965, pp.218, 226, 234, 238, 242). Issued as three separate 'livres', opp.IV nos.1, 2 and 3,[16] they shared a common title-page:

> Grand Concert/pour/Le Clavecin où Forte-Piano/avec l'accompagnement des deux Violons, Alto,/et Basse, deux Hautbois, et Deux Cors/composé par/W.A. Mozart/Oeuvre IV. Livre 1. [2; 3][17]/Publié a Vienne chez Artaria Comp.

The distribution as three separate items, rather than as an integral set of three, proved to be a highly successful marketing strategy. Sales were unusually brisk and a second impression had to be issued. Not counting sales through Artaria's foreign agents in London, Paris, Hamburg and Amsterdam, it has been calculated that over 500 copies must have been sold by 1801.[18] Certainly, the concertos continued to be widely advertised for several years after their first publication.[19]

Before turning to the individual pieces, it should be noted that their textures demonstrate a strong interest in counterpoint, a factor perhaps influenced by Mozart's recent involvement with Baron van Swieten. Swieten was especially fond of counterpoint and had assembled an impressive library of fugal works by baroque masters which he allowed Mozart to study.[20] This emerging fascination with contrapuntal textures is apparent in the finale of the G major string quartet, K.387 – a work contemporary with these three concertos.[21] In fact, the string writing in the concertos frequently comes close to the intimate interaction of chamber music (particularly with respect to the use of the viola). Examples could be cited from any of these pieces, but the opening tutti exposition of K.413 in F offers a particularly rich stock of illustrations. At bar 12 there is dialogue between the first violins and violas; this gives way at bar 17 to an integrated texture in which all four string parts contribute vitally and independently to the whole; bars 24–31 are rescored at bar 32 foll., the viola taking over that strand formerly presented by the second violins (again reminiscent of the fluidity characteristic of Mozart's string quartet writing as demonstrated in the 'Haydn' quartets); and the exposition ends with contrapuntal imitation into which the solo is absorbed at bar 56. In all of this the oboes and horns, while providing reinforcement, chordal punctuation, or a supportive 'halo' of sound, are not pro-active in the musical argument. One can well imagine how attractive such pieces may have been to potential purchasers of Mozart's concertos able to mount the minimal forces for a domestic 'chamber' performance.

Piano concerto in A major, K.414

i. Allegro, $\frac{4}{4}$, 298 bars; ii. Andante, $\frac{3}{4}$, 105 bars; iii. Rondeau. Allegretto, $\frac{2}{2}$, 212 bars.

Scoring: solo fortepiano; violins 1 & 2; violas; bass [= cello, bass and bassoon *ad lib*.]; 2 oboes; 2 horns.

Composed in Vienna in late 1782.

Besides the autograph (Jagiellonian University Library, Kraków), existing sources for K.414 comprise two sets of printed orchestral materials, the first issued by Artaria in 1785 (Mozart, 1785b) and the second published by André in 1802 (Mozart, 1802c), each comprising, in addition to the solo part,[22] a full complement of playing parts for the strings, 2 oboes and 2 horns. An early set of manuscript parts (St Peter's, Salzburg)[23] is regrettably incomplete; all that remains besides the solo part (whose readings incorporate significant revisions from the autograph score) are two autograph horn parts. Nevertheless, the fact that Salzburg copies exist at all for a work composed in Vienna is perhaps indicative of a performance for which parts had to be provided. Such a performance could, conceivably, have taken place in the summer of 1783, during Mozart's extended visit. Another (complete) set of playing parts survives at Kroměříž.[24] There are two sets of autograph cadenzas and *Eingänge* for K.414. Set 'A' in NMA V/15/3[25] is contemporary with the composition of the concerto in late 1782. Set 'B'[26] is rather later, and might have been connected to the appearance of Artaria's printed edition in 1785.

An extended sketch for part of the first movement of K.414 survives.[27] It all relates to the solo exposition, specifically to bars 85–93; bars 98–9; and bars 116–26. Bars [1–6] of the melodic sketch lie very close to the final text (the dotted rhythm of bar 6 being simplified to a minim–crotchet resolution in the right hand of bar 91); bars [7–8] cover the same implied harmonic ground as bars 92–3, but replace ascending and descending quaver scales of E major with a chromatic descent in crotchets from e''' to a''. The extension of a B major seventh chord through bars 98–9 is implied by the slightly different patterns in bars [13–14] of the sketch (in which the right-hand semiquavers are given a harmonic underpinning on an adjacent stave – the left hand of bars 98–9 clearly evolved from this). Finally, the solo entry at bar 116 is quite precisely worked out at bars [25–33] of the sketch, including the hand-crossing in bars

120–122 and some of the detailed rhythms and chromatics of bars 123–6, although bearing a slightly different melodic profile. The remainder of the sketch, which extends to the end of the first solo, was discarded, although perfectly acceptable in its own right.[28]

A work often cited in relation to K.414 is the Rondo in A, K.386 (dated 19 October 1782 on the first music-page of the now incomplete and very widely dispersed autograph).[29] Einstein believed that it was the finale of the A major concerto, either a replacement for the finale known today, or even, perhaps, its predecessor.[30] Such a link seems promising at first sight, given the key, scoring, the close proximity in date, and, interestingly, a coincidence of paper-types (K.386 is written on the same paper to which Mozart turned at bar 131 of K.414's finale). On further inspection, however, the connections begin to fail. While Mozart specifically noted in the advertisement for K.413–15 that they could be performed 'à quattro', K.386 could certainly not be played this way, principally because of its extraordinary *obbligato* cello part. A more telling factor is the physical location of the usual finale within the autograph of K.414: it begins on the reverse side of the same leaf on which Mozart had concluded the Andante, not on a new gathering of paper (not even on a new sheet). So the Rondo, K.386 cannot have been Mozart's original finale. Possibly, it was composed specially for Mozart's pupil, Barbara Ployer. In a letter of 31 May 1800, Constanze Mozart wrote to André (who had recently purchased the autograph of K.386 as part of Mozart's *Nachlaß*) explaining that, although the autograph of the 'Clavier Rondò mit begleitung des Orchesters' [presumably K.386] was incomplete (and therefore unusable as the basis for a projected edition), the piece would be in the possession of 'Fräulein Ployen'.

Piano concerto in F major, K.413

i. Allegro, $\frac{3}{4}$, 378 bars; ii. Larghetto, $\frac{4}{4}$, 68 bars; iii. Tempo di Menuetto, $\frac{3}{4}$, 231 bars.

Scoring: solo fortepiano; violins 1 & 2; violas; bass [= cello, bass and bassoon* *ad lib.*]; 2 oboes; 2 horns.
*Bassoon parts were retrospectively composed for the Larghetto.

Composed in Vienna in late 1782 (early 1783?).

Besides the autograph (Jagiellonian University Library, Kraków), existing sources for K.413 comprise two sets of printed orchestral materials, the first issued by Artaria in 1785 (Mozart, 1785b) and the second published by André in 1802 (Mozart, 1802c), each analogous to those for the associated K.414, except for the provision in André's print of two bassoon parts (*obbligato* in the

Larghetto). Both cadenzas (copies in Leopold's hand of, presumably, autograph originals) are included in a solo part at St Peter's, Salzburg,[31] evidently the only item remaining from a complete set of manuscript orchestral materials. Another (complete) early copy of playing parts is in Kroměříž.[32] As noted in connection with the playing parts for K.414, the existence of such a part in Salzburg may be indicative of an otherwise undocumented performance there (between July and November 1783?).

Piano concerto in C major, K.415

i. Allegro, $\frac{4}{4}$, 313 bars; ii. Andante, $\frac{3}{4}$, 88 bars; iii. Rondeau. Allegro, $\frac{6}{8}$, 262 bars.

Scoring: solo fortepiano; violins 1 & 2; violas; bass [= cello and bass]; 2 oboes; 2 horns; 2 bassoons; 2 trumpets; timpani.

Composed in Vienna in late 1782 (early 1783?).

Besides the autograph (Jagiellonian University Library, Kraków), existing sources for K.415 comprise two sets of printed orchestral materials, the first issued by Artaria in 1785 (Mozart, 1785b) and the second published by André in 1802 (Mozart, 1802c), each analogous to those for the associated K.414, except that they both include a single part for the two bassoons. The trumpet and timpani parts appeared in print for the first time only in André's 1802 edition, although it is conceivable that these parts had formerly been recorded with the autograph in a separate score (now lost). The first documented performance of K.415 was in the Mehlgrube, Vienna, at Mozart's academy on 23 March 1783. For this première, attended by Joseph II, Mozart probably wished to make a spectacular impression, and he may have invented the trumpet and timpani parts to achieve that aim; among the other works performed on that occasion were his 'Haffner' symphony, K.385, and the D major piano concerto, K.175, both of which required the same larger instrumentation.[33] K.415 was performed for the second time one week later (30 March) at an academy given by the singer, Thérèse Teyber.[34]

Excepting the trumpet and timpani parts, there is a full set of playing parts for K.415 at St Peter's, Salzburg,[35] copies that were perhaps made specifically for a performance by Mozart himself in Salzburg on 1 October 1783.[36] The continuo figuring of the solo part in this set is in the hand of Leopold Mozart.[37] A separate copy of the solo keyboard and violin parts (made by the same copyist, and just possibly relating to the advertised 'subscription' copies) survives.[38] Contemporary copies (doubtless prepared from Mozart's autographs) of the cadenzas to the first two movements and *Eingänge* for the Rondo finale survive among the Salzburg performance materials at St

Peter's.[39] For the *Eingang* in the slow movement there exists an autograph previously identified (by Einstein in Köchel, 1937 and also in Köchel, 1964) with the Andante of K.246.[40]

Notes

1. PL-Kj, Mus.ms.autogr. W. A. Mozart 382/414/413/415; Tyson, 1996, nos.56, 59, 60 (K.413); 56, 58, 60, 61 (K.414); 56, 58, 59 (K.415). These three concertos are bound together with the Rondo, K.382. The autographs were not available to the editor of NMA V/15/3.

2. By 22 January, Mozart was beginning to despair that, despite three newspaper announcements, subscriptions were still unforthcoming.

3. Further copies of these works were offered by Johann Traeg in the *Wiener Zeitung* on 27 September and again in the *Wienerblättchen* on 30 September that year ('new manuscript music is again to be had, *viz.* the 3 latest pianoforte concertos by Mozart at 10fl.': Deutsch, 1965, pp.218–19; Eisen, 1991a, no.53), and again on 4 November 1783 and 10 July 1784 (both times from Lorenz Lausch's copy shop: Eisen, 1991a, no.54; Deutsch, 1965, p.226; Edge, 1996c, p.64 (n.29)).

4. Some examples from first movements, involving amendments to piano figuration within an unaltered harmonic framework: K.414, bars 98–9/102–4 (originally a″–b″–g sharp″–a″–f sharp″, and so on in the right hand, followed by an ascending changing-note pattern); 111–12 (the earlier fuller left-hand chording in repeated quavers is replaced by a less cluttered texture); 137–40 (slightly broader spans of broken chords are eliminated); 224–9 (analogous to bars 98–9 foll., implying that these alterations were made once the movement had been completed, rather than during the process of composition); K.413, bars 102–4/106–8/197–8/201–3/281–3/285–7 (originally with a harmony note, rather than a semiquaver rest on the first beat in the left hand); 344–6 (the left hand originally doubling the right at the lower octave in semiquavers); K.415, bars 119–20 (the left hand originally doubled the viola line in quavers); 128–9 (the changing-note pattern adjusts the earlier placement of chromatic non-harmony notes in relation to the main beats); 142–5 (originally in arpeggios); 175 (the left hand was originally in semiquavers, outlining contrary-motion arpeggios against the right hand); 182–7 (elimination of some changing-note patterns). Full details are given in the *Kritische Berichte* to NMA V/15/3.

5. The autograph of K.414 is not foliated; instead, the successive gatherings (in eights) are numbered from 1 to 10; the cancellation occurs on the reverse of the leaf numbered 9.

6. Now in CZ-KRa, A4526; see Croll, 1966.

7. The piano part of bars 193–7 was sketched on the top two staves of fol.[38v]; bars 182–92 appear on staves 3–11.

8. A facsimile of its first eight bars is given in Tyson, 1987, pl.11.2. Something of its pathetic character (and even thematic material) found its way into the $\frac{2}{4}$ Adagio sections of the finale (bars 49–64 and 216–33).

9. For further details, see Tyson, 1987, p.276, from which this information is derived.

10. Further on this issue, see the entry for K.537 below.

11. A-Ssp, Moz.250.1 (K.413); 255.1 (K.414); 260.1 (K.415). These manuscripts

stem from the estate of Nannerl Mozart; see Wolff, 1986. Moz.260.1 (K.415) does not include trumpet or timpani parts.

12. On the possible significance of this for performance practice, see Chapter Seven, pp.136–7.

13. See also the entries for the individual concertos below.

14. On 22 April 1784, Leopold again wrote to Winter that the pieces had been dispatched to him almost three weeks previously, but had evidently been lost.

15. Possibly this is why mention of the necessity for trumpets and drums in K.415 is omitted: too big an orchestral complement might have discouraged potential purchasers. The relevant portion of Mozart's letter reads as follows: 'This is to inform you that I have three piano concertos ready, which can be performed with full orchestra, or with oboes and horns, or merely a quattro. Artaria wants to engrave them. But I give you, my old friend, the first refusal ... Since I wrote those piano concertos, I have been composing six quartets for two violins, viola and cello [the 'Haydn' string quartets, K.387, 421, 428, 458, 464 and 465]. If you would like to engrave these too, I will gladly let you have them. But I cannot allow these to go so cheaply; I mean, I cannot let you have these six quartets under fifty Louis d'or'.

16. Also with separate print numbers (41, 42 and 56).

17. The appropriate 'livre' number was added by hand in each case.

18. See NMA V/15/3, p.viii. Copies of imported prints of K.413–15 (as 'Morat['s] Gran Concerto, per im Cimbalo Op.1, 2 and 3', following the separate 'Livres' of Artaria's print) were advertised at six shillings each in London in *The Daily Universal Register* on 24 September 1785; Eisen, 1991a, no.212. Also, there was an advertisement in the *Staats- und gelehrte Zeitung des hamburgischen unpartheyischen Correspondenten* in late 1785 for Mozart's 'Grand Concert pour le Clavecin avec l'Accompagnement de deux violons, Alto & Basse, deux Hautbois & deux Cors, composé par W. A. Mozart, Oeuvre IV. Livre I [...II. III...] publié à Vienne chez Artaria & Compag ... All three are very well composed and contain much that is new, as well as various brilliant passages'; Eisen, 1991a, no.139.

19. In 1787 in the *Neuen litteratur und Völkerkunde*, Dessau, for instance; Deutsch, 1965, pp.291–2.

20. See further, Chapter 6, p. 97.

21. The autograph of K.387 is dated 31 December 1782.

22. Although in Artaria's edition the separate solo part is denoted by the neutral term 'cembalo', it is clear from the title-page that the fortepiano was an alternative. André's 1802 edition specifies the fortepiano: 'Grand Concerto/pour le/ Piano-Forte/avec accompagnement de/plusieurs instrumens/composé par/W. A. Mozart/Oeuvre 4eme L[ivre] 1. [2. 3.]/Edition faite d'après le manuscrit original/ del'auteur'.

23. A-Ssp, Moz.255.1. Dexter Edge has recently argued that these parts, though intended for Salzburg performances, were prepared in Vienna by Joseph Arthofer, a copyist who worked for Mozart during 1783; see Edge, 1996c, pp.54– 5. These performance materials (and those surviving for K.413 and K.415) evidently formed part of Nannerl Mozart's library; see Schmid, 1980–83. Leopold refers to these parts in his letter to Nannerl of 16 September 1785, noting that in these concertos the oboes and horns are inessential (Bauer, Deutsch and Eibl, 1962–75, p.880).

24. CZ-KRa, II G 70/A3264 (by the same copyist as the orchestral parts for K.413 in the same collection; see below).

25. Note that this set corresponds to Fassung B in K⁶. The set 'A' cadenzas are K⁶626a/K.624, Teil i, 28, 30, 31, 35, 36. D-B, Mus.ms.autogr. W. A. Mozart

624(2) (first and second movements); RO-Ba, no shelfmark (finale); Tyson, 1996, nos.66, 74.

26. K⁶626a/K.624, Teil i, nos.27. 29, 32–4. D-B, Mus.ms.autogr. W. A. Mozart 624(2), a bifolium also containing sketches to the first movement of K.488; Tyson, 1996, no.53. Cadenzas by Hummel survive in manuscript at CZ-K, Sig. Schwarzenburg K.27, no.776 ('Cadenze per sette Concerti di Mozart pe[r i]l Piano Forte ... Composte del Sigre. Giov: Nep: Hummel ... Opera 4ta ...').

27. See NMA V/15/3, Anhang. The sketchleaf is in A-Sm, Sig. KV385o; see NMA X/30/3, 32 (Skb 1782d). Preceding it is a leaf containing another sketch for a C major concerto Allegro (to K.415?); that leaf also contains sketches for *Die Entführung aus dem Serail*, K.384, possibly, therefore, suggestive of a date of summer/autumn 1782 for the concerto sketches. See Somfai, 1996. For information on the C major sketch (which might plausibly relate to K.467), see Plath, 1959 (including also a facsimile).

28. It continued from the E major cadence at bar 127 with a series of chromatically inflected ascending scales, supported by a chordal scheme passing through C sharp minor, F sharp minor and A major (one chord per bar), cadencing after a further bar in E. Thereafter, Mozart repeats this four-bar chord progression in invertible counterpoint, assimilating a suspension chain in the treble part. His eventual text (bars 127–45) hints at similar harmonic territory at first (C sharp minor and F sharp minor chords in bar 128) and also involves varied repetition of a phrase (bars 131–7; 137–45), though one founded on different material (possibly suggested by the arpeggios at bars [43–4] of the sketch?). See NMA V/ 15/3, p.201. A continuity draft of bars 193–7 of the finale also survives in the main body of the autograph; see NMA X/30/3. 42 (Skb 1782δ).

29. For a detailed investigation of this piece, and the ongoing process of recovery of the autograph, see Tyson, 1987, Chapter Seventeen. The Rondo is printed in NMA V/15/8, pp.173–87.

30. This is discussed both in K⁶ and in Einstein, 1946, p.299.

31. A-Ssp, Moz.250.1, copied in Vienna by Joseph Arthofer (see Edge, 1996c, pp.54–5); Leopold's copies of the cadenzas (notated on a separate sheet) are A-Ssp, Moz.305.1 (K⁶626a/K.624, Teil i, 37, 38); Tyson, 1996, no.42. Cadenzas by Hummel survive in manuscript at CZ-K, Sig. Schwarzenburg K.27, no.776 ('Cadenze per sette Concerti di Mozart pe[r i]l Piano Forte ... Composte del Sigre. Giov: Nep: Hummel ... Opera 4ta ...').

32. CZ-KRa, II G 71/A3265; the keyboard part with cadenzas to the first movement and finale is in the hand of Emmanuel Aloys Förster, whereas the orchestral parts are in a different hand (identical to that found in the surviving orchestral parts for K.414 at Kroměříž).

33. A notice in Cramer's *Magazin der Musik* for that date claims that Mozart's two 'new concertos' were very well received by the audience. However, Mozart's letter of 29 March makes it clear that the other concerto was K.175 (not exactly 'new' in spring 1783), and not one of the other 'subscription' concertos, K.413 or K.414.

34. Noted in Mozart's letter to Leopold of 12 April 1783.

35. A-Ssp, Moz.260.1. As mentioned above, these parts were evidently copied not in Salzburg, but in Vienna; see Edge, 1996c, pp.54–5.

36. On the circumstances of this performance, see Eibl, 1965, p.90.

37. Leopold's figuring for K.415 is substantially fuller that that given in the later Artaria print. Both his and the printed figuring are provided in NMA (Leopold's appearing above the piano's left-hand stave).

38.   A-Wgm, VII 25699/Q 16274. A further early copy of the solo keyboard part is at
      CZ-KRa, II G 63/A3257.
39.   A-Ssp, Moz.310.1. The tempo markings are in Leopold's hand. K⁶626a/K.624,
      Teil i, 39, 40, 41. These cadenzas and *Eingänge* were subsequently taken over for
      the Artaria and André prints. Cadenzas by Hummel survive in manuscript at
      CZ-K, Sig. Schwarzenburg K.27, no.776 ('Cadenze per sette Concerti di Mozart
      pe[r i]l Piano Forte ... Composte del Sigre. Giov: Nep: Hummel ... Opera 4ta ...').
40.   The correct identification was made by Robert Levin. Currently held by the
      Library of the Historical Society of Philadelphia/Pennsylvania, Simon Graz
      collection: Case 13, Box 11; (K⁶626a/K.624, Teil i, 13); Tyson, 1996, no.72. For
      this *Eingang*, the Artaria and André editions give only a decorated variant of
      Mozart's falling scale (shown in NMA). Its relation to the autograph is unclear,
      particularly given the replication in the printed texts of the St Peter's copies of all
      the remaining cadenzas and *Eingänge*. Possibly the autograph is a later expansion
      for an otherwise unknown performance of K.415.

Piano concerto in E flat major, K.449

i. Allegro vivace, $\frac{3}{4}$, 347 bars; ii. Andantino,* $\frac{2}{4}$, 124 bars; iii. Allegro ma non troppo, $\frac{2}{2}$, 322 bars.
[*beneath the 'Basso' stave: 'Andante']

Scoring: solo fortepiano; violins 1 & 2; violas; bass [= cello, bass and bassoon *ad lib*.]; 2 oboes; 2 horns *ad lib*.

Composed in Vienna; dated 9 February 1784 (autograph and *Verzeichnis*).

K.449 is the very first work that Mozart entered into his personal 'Verzeich-nüss aller meiner Werke'. It is described there as '*1784. den 9:ten Hornung. Ein Klavier Konzert. Begleitung. 2 Violini, Viola e Basso. –* (2 oboe, 2 corni ad libitum)'. The autograph (on 12-stave 'Querformat' paper), removed from the Berlin Staatsbibliothek, Preussischer Kulturbesitz at the end of World War Two, is today in the Jagiellonian University Library, Kraków.[1] It bears the legend 'Di Wolfgango Amadeo Mozart per la Sig^{ra} Barbara de Ployer Viena li 9 di Feb^{ro} 1784' on the first music-page.[2] Playing parts survive at Salzburg, copied from the autograph.[3] The solo part of this set is in the hand of Nannerl Mozart[4] and incorporates a separate leaf on which she wrote a variation of bars 188–203 of the first movement (possibly suggested by Mozart: they appear also in the autograph). Continuo figuring for this part was added by Leopold Mozart. Probably Nannerl played this piece in Salzburg.[5] Manuscript copies of six concertos by Mozart (among which was K.449) were advertised in the *Wiener Zeitung* on 10 July 1784.[6] The first edition was produced by André (Mozart, 1792b), that is, some seven years before he purchased the Mozart *Nachlaß* from Constanze.[7] An autograph cadenza for the first movement survives.[8]

The E flat concerto, K.449, is mentioned for the first time in Mozart's corre-spondence on 20 February 1784, when he promised to post the autograph to his father in Salzburg 'in a few days ... The concerto is ... the original score and this too you may have copied;[9] but have it done as quickly as possible and return it to me.' In fact, K.449 was not posted until 15 May; it had arrived, along with the autographs of K.450, K.451 and K.453, within a few days, since by 26 May Mozart refers to his father's previous acknowledgement of their safe receipt.[10] Mozart performed this work for the first time in Vienna on 17 March 1784.[11] His pupil, Barbara Ployer (the work's dedicatee), played it the following week, on 24 March. Although K.449 was completed in close prox-imity to the two grander concertos in B flat, K.450, and D, K.451, and a second for Barbara Ployer in G, K.453,[12] Mozart seems to have regarded it as belonging to an earlier tradition performable, like K.413–15, 'à quattro' (meaning piano and four-part strings – that is, violins, viola, bass – with only optional wind). In his letters of 15 and 26 May 1784, he compares the scoring and idiom of K.449 with his other most recent concertos, K.450, K.451 and K.453. On 15 May he notes:

> no one but myself possesses these new concertos in B flat [K.450] and D [K.451], and no one but *myself* and Fräulein von Ployer (for whom I composed them) those in E flat [K.449] and G [K.453] ... I formed the opinion ... that the music would not be much use to you, because except for the E flat concerto, which can be performed *a quattro* without wind-instruments,[13] the other three concertos [K.450, K.451 and K.453, which Mozart had posted to Salzburg that day, along with K.449] all have wind-instrument accompaniment; and you very rarely have wind-instrument players at your house.

Talking about the technical demands of K.450 and K.451, he notes on 26 May that the former was the more taxing, and wonders which of the other concertos, K.450, 451 and 453, will please Leopold and Nannerl the most. He continues: 'That in E flat [K.449] is not of the same kind. It is a concerto of a very special kind [*von ganz besonderer Art*], written more for a small orchestra than a large one.'

The fact that K.449 is closely related in manner and scoring to the three 'subscription' concertos, K.413–15, of late 1782/early 1783 calls into question the date of 9 February 1784 given for the work in Mozart's *Verzeichnis*. K.449's genesis is, in fact, rather complicated. An origin contemporary with K.413–15 is suggested by Alan Tyson's detailed investigations of the paper of all four concerto autographs (Tyson, 1987, pp.153–5).[14] His findings are that the first ten leaves of K.449 are on a paper identical in watermark and rastrology to that found in much of K.414's finale and in the Rondo in A, K.386 (dated 19 October 1782), whereas the remainder of the piece is on paper of a different type, datable to early 1784.[15] Furthermore, on the last two leaves of the earlier paper (fols. 9r–10v) there is an obvious 'break' in composition;[16] at the top of fol.10v (staves 1–4) is an unrelated sketch for a tenor aria,[17] followed beneath by bars 193–203 of K.449's first movement. Evidently, Mozart began K.449 simultaneously (or nearly so) with the three similarly scored 'à quattro' concertos, K.413–15, in late 1782 – early 1783. To judge from the ink and handwriting, he ceased the initial phase of work on the first movement of K.449 after bar 170 (at the end of fol.9r). Having left the concerto alone for a considerable period of time, perhaps a year, he returned to complete K.449 in early 1784. On reaching the top of fol.10v, however, he had to delete the tenor sketch and squash the concerto texture onto just the eight remaining blank staves, the oboes and horns being allocated to staves 8 and 9 respectively (and so designated to the left of the stave brace). The present-day appearance of stave 8 is a particularly confusing jumble: as well as the oboe parts for bars 193–4, 196–8 and 200–202, it contains Mozart's revisions to the right hand of the piano part for the whole of this passage. Evidently these alterations to the shape of the semiquaver arpeggio passagework[18] were made after the oboe line had been written and, having decided on revision, Mozart had no other alternative but to use staves 8 (oboes) and 9 (horns, not actually playing at this point in the movement).[19] From fol.11 (bar 204) onwards, Mozart continued on a new paper-type, finishing the work on 9 February and entering it in the *Verzeichnis*. K.449 apparently remained a 'torso' for most of 1783, being completed in time for a potentially lucrative series of concerts scheduled for spring 1784.[20]

Notes

1. PL-Kj, Mus.ms.autogr. W. A. Mozart 449; Tyson, 1996, nos.61, 70, 71. The autograph was not available to the editor of NMA V/15/4. Facsimile in Schiedermair, 1919, pl.43; also reproduced in NMA V/15/4, p.xiii. Mozart added the incipit of the movement to this leaf.
2. In a letter of 20 February 1784, Mozart told Leopold that Ployer had paid handsomely for the concerto.
3. Interestingly, fols.35–35v and 38r in the finale (bars 245–68 and 314 to the end, respectively) are not autograph, but in the hand of a Viennese copyist (as yet unidentified). These folios are each single sheets stuck into the main body of the finale and are differently ruled (the right-hand edge of stave 1 on fols. 35r–35v having a distinctive pattern in which the top two lines extend significantly into the right margin; on fol.38r the left-hand edge of stave 1 is characterised by leftwards extension of line 4). Why Mozart's autograph sheets were removed is unclear.
4. A-Ssp, Moz.265.1; facsimile in NMA v/15/4, p.xv.
5. There is mention of unspecified cadenzas which Leopold was having copied for Nannerl in a letter of 25–26 March 1785; Ruth Halliwell believes one of these to have been possibly for K.449 (Halliwell, 1998, p. 479, n.25). Furthermore, on 14 September, Leopold Mozart wrote to Nannerl, enclosing the keyboard parts of three 'new' concertos to go with one she already had. These works were K.449, K.450, K.451 and K.453, though precisely which one Nannerl already had by this date is difficult to establish with certainty; Halliwell makes a persuasive case for it to have been K.451 (Halliwell, 1998, p.465, n.19).
6. Deutsch, 1965, p.226.
7. André also published K.271 in the same year. Presumably, his text of K.449 derived from manuscript copies already in circulation.
8. K⁶626a/K.624, Teil i, 42; D-B, Mus.ms.autogr. W. A. Mozart 624(3); facsimile in NMA V/15/4, p.xiv; Tyson, 1996, no.53.
9. Mozart intended to send in the same post the autograph of the 'Linz' symphony, K.425.
10. The Salzburg playing parts, A-Ssp Moz.265.1, were presumably copied shortly afterwards.
11. Letter of 17 March 1784, noting that his 'new concerto was well received.' According to K⁶ the concerto played was possibly K.450 in B flat, completed on 15 March (and therefore 'new' on 17 March). Such an interpretation is problematic since K.450 includes a large wind section (2 oboes, 2 *obbligato* bassoons, 2 horns and an additional flute in the finale). Given this fact, and especially the extensive contribution of the winds throughout all three movements lasting 308, 113 and 315 bars respectively, it seems unlikely that playing parts could have

been prepared in such a short time for a performance (let alone rehearsals). Barbara von Ployer (1765–1811) studied with Mozart during 1784. She was an amateur pianist, of excellent ability. In Vienna, she lived with her father's cousin, Gottfried Ignaz von Ployer, a court official, who was a subscriber to Mozart's 'Trattnerhof' concerts that year. Her composition exercises with Mozart have been published in NMA X/30/2.

12. Completed on 15 March, 22 March and 12 April 1784, respectively.

13. The designation 'à quattro' may literally have meant single strings: it may be of significance that, in the *Verzeichnis* entry for K.449, Mozart describes the accompaniment as for '2 Violini, Viola [singular] e Basso ...' whereas for K.450, K.451 and all subsequent piano concertos his entries read '2 Violini, Viole [plural] e Basso ...' See NMAV/15/4, p.ix.

14. Before the late 1970s none of the autographs was available for study.

15. Tyson, 1996, no.61 (fols. 1–10), nos.70, 71 (remainder).

16. Visible in the facsimiles published in Tyson, 1987, pp.154–5.

17. 'Müsst' ich auch durch tausend Drachen', K.435. For further discussion of this sketch, see NMA X/30/3, 42 (Skb 1783α).

18. Shown in small type as *ossias* in the NMA text. The effect of the revision – which does not interfere with the original harmonies – is to transfer the semiquavers to the right hand (they were formerly spread between the hands in a different configuration).

19. Mozart began the revision to the piano passagework at the foot of fol.10 (bar 190).

20. In a letter of 3 March 1784, Mozart refers to these forthcoming concerts in which he would play 'new things' (including, it would seem, K.449).

Piano concerto in B flat major, K.450

i. Allegro, $\frac{4}{4}$, 308 bars; ii. [Andante], $\frac{3}{8}$, 113 bars; iii. Allegro, $\frac{6}{8}$, 316 bars.

Scoring: solo fortepiano; violins 1 & 2; violas; bass [= cello, bass]; flute (only in the finale); 2 oboes; 2 bassoons; 2 horns.

Composed in Vienna; dated 15 March 1784 (*Verzeichnis*).

The autograph of K.450 is in the Herzogin Anna Amalia Bibliothek (Thüring-ische Landesbibliothek), Weimar.[1] Unusually, there is no self-ascription on the first music-page; a precise date and a list of instrumentation are given in Mozart's *Verzeichnis*, however. An autograph sketch for the opening theme of the finale survives.[2] While no manuscript playing parts associated with Mozart's family are known, it is almost certain that some were produced. In a letter of 15 May 1784, Mozart tells his father that the same day he had mailed autograph scores of four recent piano concertos to Salzburg, including this one.[3] Suspicious of Salzburg copyists, who might have circulated additional copies of the works for their own profit, Mozart begs his father in this letter not to let these precious manuscripts out of his house. Authorised manuscript copies of six concertos by Mozart (among which was K.450) were advertised shortly afterwards in the *Wiener Zeitung* on 10 July 1784 (Deutsch, 1965, p.226). The first documented edition is that produced by Artaria in Vienna (Mozart, 1798a). However, the first violin and cello parts in this edition do not conform to Artaria's usual engraving procedures, and may have been taken over from plates produced by Hoffmeister around 1786; no exemplar of such an edition is known, though.[4] Autograph cadenzas survive to the first move-ment and finale; also an *Eingang* to the finale (bar 112).[5]

The autograph of K.450 contains a number of interesting revisions made during the course of composition, affording us a glimpse into Mozart's working methods. The original passagework in the solo part at bars 112–15 and bars 126–36 of the first movement are cancelled and replaced on the staves above. Especially noteworthy are his revisions to the theme of the Andante variations.[6] Bars 3–8 of the violin 1 theme on fol.20r of the autograph are cancelled and replaced with the familiar text which is thematically quite different (omitting an attractive sequence in bars 5–6, for example), but caden-tially and tonally similar to the version eventually preferred, modulating at the end of the eight-bar phrase to the dominant, B flat. The bass part for this phrase (bars 3–8) is also cancelled on the bottom stave of fol.20r and replaced with a different bass line on the stave above. Following the opening phrase, the piano enters with a decorated repeat (unaccompanied). At bars 11–16 its part is also cancelled and replaced on the staves above, to conform to the revision of the violin 1 and bass lines of bars 3–8. And so on, throughout much of this move-ment.[7] The interesting point to note about these revisions to the theme and its supporting bass is that the inner harmonies visible in the unaltered violin 2 and viola staves will only fit the revised melody and bass, meaning that, for much of the time, the score as Mozart was extending it in his original version consisted of only the outer strands of the texture, which he drafted forwards through pages at a time. The accompanimental 'filling' for the middle strings was added at a much later stage – a technique observable on detailed inspection of large numbers of Mozart's orchestral autographs – and in the case of this movement, only after Mozart had reflected upon and substantially reworked the shape of his variation theme.[8]

In a letter to his father and sister of 26 May 1784, Mozart describes the solo piano part of K.450 ('a piece to make the player sweat') as being more demanding than that of K.451, completed a week later. Perhaps he viewed both concertos as vehicles for his own virtuosity. In K^6 the possibility is raised that K.450 was performed for the first time at the Trattnerhof on 17 March 1784, that is, just two days after its completion. Almost certainly, though, the concerto performed on that occasion was K.449 in E flat.[9] K.450 was certainly performed at a similar academy on 24 March, the second concert of his successful subscription series held that spring. He probably repeated it at a concert on 1 April (postponed from 21 March); the surviving programme announces that 'Herr Mozart, Kapellmeister, will play an entirely new Concerto on the Fortepiano' (Deutsch, 1965, p.223).[10]

Notes

1. D-WRz, Mus.MV: 125. Viennese 12-stave 'Querformat' paper; Tyson, 1996, nos.58, 71, 72, 73.
2. US-NYp, Rare Books Division (Vollmer Collection, Astor, Lenox and Tilden Foundations). See NMA X/30/3, 58 (Skb1784a); also reproduced in facsimile and transcription in NMA V/15/4, Anhang. Sketches for the harmonies of bars 17–18 also survive on this leaf.
3. The others were K.449 (previously mentioned in a letter of 20 February), K.451 and K.453. On 14 September, Leopold Mozart wrote to Nannerl, enclosing the keyboard parts of three 'new' concertos to go with one she already had. These works were K.449, K.450, K.451 and K.453, though precisely which one Nannerl already had by this date is difficult to establish with certainty; Ruth Halliwell makes a persuasive case for it to have been K.451 (Halliwell, 1998, p.465, n.19).
4. On this matter, see the entry in K^6, p.484. Slightly later editions than Artaria's were produced by André (1799) and Breitkopf (1800).
5. $K^6$626a/K.624, Teil i, 43, 45, 44; Tyson, 1996, nos.56 (1st mvt.), 62 (finale). That to the first movement is in F-Pn (Roman Rolland collection, Ms. 21021) and appeared in a facsimile reproduction appended to a piano arrangement of *Die Zauberflöte*, published by August Schlesinger in Paris in 1822 (the *incipit* of the first movement, also in Mozart's hand, may be seen on this leaf); the *Eingang* and cadenza to the finale are in a private collection.
6. Reproduced in facsimile in NMA V/15/4, pp.xviii, xix. See also Moser, 1951.

7.   The NMA facsimile on p.xix shows the continuation through bars 20–28 (fol.20v of Mozart's autograph), demonstrating the same procedure of cancellation and replacement for bars 17–20 (strings, stating the second part of the binary-form theme) and bars 25–8 (the piano's varied repetition).

8.   That the inner parts were added as an 'afterthought' does not mean that they are insignificant or characterless, of course. In fact, the violin 2 and viola strands in bars 3–8 and 17–20 are calculated with great subtlety in terms of their rhythm, chromatic profile, articulation, register (note the overlapping in bars 19–20, for instance).

9.   See the remarks in the entry for K.449 above.

10. Alternatively, the 'entirely new' concerto may have been K.451 (*q.v.*), completed on 22 March 1784. Mozart refers to this concert in a letter of 10 April. Apologising to his father for a tardy response to a previous letter received by 20 March, Mozart explains that he has recently been very busy with his three subscription concerts (held on 17, 24 and 31 March) and with the concert of 1 April, held at the National-Theater.

Piano concerto in D major, K.451

i. Allegro assai, $\frac{4}{4}$, 325 bars; ii. Andante, $\frac{3}{2}$, 99 bars; iii. Allegro di molto, $\frac{2}{4}$, 394 bars.

Scoring: solo fortepiano; violins 1 & 2; violas; bass [= cello, bass]; flute; 2 oboes; 2 bassoons; 2 horns; 2 trumpets; timpani.

Composed in Vienna; dated 22 March 1784 (autograph and *Verzeichnis*).

The autograph of K.451 (on 12-stave 'Querformat' paper), removed from the Berlin Staatsbibliothek, Preussischer Kulturbesitz at the end of World War Two, is today in the Jagiellonian University Library, Kraków.[1] Playing parts (copied from the autograph) survive at Salzburg, the solo part of which is in the hand of Nannerl Mozart.[2] These were copied from the autograph score which Mozart sent to Leopold on 15 May 1784, along with three other concertos.[3] Continuo figuring for the solo part was added by Leopold Mozart. Manuscript copies of six concertos by Mozart (among which was K.451) were advertised in the *Wiener Zeitung* on 10 July 1784 (Deutsch, 1965, p.226). The first edition of K.451 has been a matter of some confusion. According to K[6], two versions had appeared in Paris in 1785. The first was included in Boyer's anthology of solo keyboard music, 'Pièces de claveçin', of which no copy is at present known; the second, quoted from the *Westfals Hamburger Lagerverzeichnis* (July 1785), had apparently been issued in parts with the following instrumentation: 'Clav. -Conc. a 10 con 2 Oboe e Flauto, 2 cor ad lib. D dur [no.14]'.[4] In fact, neither of these citations truly refers to K.451, but to K.175 in the same key, which Boyer had indeed issued that year, first as a solo keyboard arrangement in 'Pièces de Claveçin' and subsequently in separate orchestral parts.[5] The first edition of K.451 is actually that issued in Speyer by Bossler (Mozart, 1792c);[6] André also produced an edition later the same year.[7] No autograph cadenzas for K.451 survive among the Salzburg performance materials, although Nannerl's copies of cadenzas to the outer movements do.[8] On the back of the leaf containing Nannerl's copy of the finale cadenza is a decoration of bars 56–63 of the Andante. Both cadenzas and the embellishment to the Andante theme are certainly authentic. In his letter of 9–12 June 1784, Mozart had noted: '[Nannerl] is quite right in saying that there is something missing in the solo passage in C in the Andante of the concerto in D. I will supply the deficiency as soon as possible and send it with the cadenzas.'[9] Given her close involvement with the copying of playing parts for K.451, and her close attention to matters of embellishment, it is likely that Nannerl played the work in Salzburg (though no documented performances are known).[10] Mozart himself had performed it at the Trattnerhof on 31 March 1784, the third and final concert of his successful subscription series that spring.[11]

K.451 was discussed in Mozart's correspondence in relation to K.450, a work which had been completed just a week earlier on 15 March. Although he regarded K.451 as a difficult piece, he felt that K.450 was still more demanding technically ('a piece to make the player sweat', as he noted on 26 May 1784.) Probably Mozart intended K.451 as a companion piece to K.450, spectacular in its virtuosity and scoring, and designed to secure for him a favourable public impression both as composer and executant. In a letter of 8 August 1786 to Sebastian Winter at Donaueschingen, Mozart offered this concerto (along with the concertos K.453, 456, 459 and 488, some symphonies, a sonata and a terzetto) to Prince Josef Benedikt, Fürsten von Fürstenberg, for the use of his court orchestra, carefully notating incipits for these pieces.[12] The fact that he attempted to encourage interest in the work some two and a half years after its composition is perhaps to be understood in relation to a comment Mozart had made to his father on 26 May 1784 that, in the case of K.450, 451 and 453, 'Only today I could have got 24 ducats for one of them, but I think that it will be more profitable for me to hold on to them for a few years more and then have them engraved and published.' None of the works was actually published during his lifetime.

A review of the Bossler edition appeared in the *Musikalische Korrespondenz der teutschen Filarmonischen Gesellschaft* (Speyer) on 16 May 1792 (Eisen, 1991a, no.180). The anonymous reviewer described K.451 as

> a great treasure. [The recently-deceased Mozart's] original writing style ... the fullness of the harmony, the surprising turns of phrase, the skilful diffusion of shadow and light and many other excellent characteristics, which make Mozart a model for our time, make us feel very deeply his loss. This concerto ... is among the most beautiful and brilliant that we have from this master, with respect to both the ritornellos and the solos ... Unquestionably [the finale] has the greatest difficulties; but with respect to the modulation also very excellent beauties.

Notes

1. PL-Kj, Mus.ms.autogr. W. A. Mozart 451; Tyson, 1996, no. 73. The autograph was not available to the editor of NMA V/15/4.
2. A-Ssp, Moz.270.1 (parts); Moz.705.1 (solo); facsimile in NMA v/15/4, p.xv. The viola part for this set is also in Nannerl's hand.
3. K.449 (previously mentioned in a letter of 20 February), K.450 and K.453.
4. K[6], p.486.
5. Listed in K[6], p.197. For publication details, see the entry for K.175 above.
6. See also the entry for K.451 in Haberkamp, 1986. Bossler had previously produced an edition of Mozart's F major Rondo, K.494 in 1786.
7. Verlagsno.476.
8. K[6]626a/K.624, Teil i, 46, 47); A-Ssp, Moz.320.1; facsimile of first movement cadenza in NMA V/15/4, p.xiv. These cadenzas are reproduced in André's edition. Cadenzas by Hummel survive in manuscript at the CZ-K, Sig. Schwarzenburg K.27, no.776 ('Cadenze per sette Concerti di Mozart pe[r i]l

Piano Forte ... Composte del Sigre. Giov: Nep: Hummel ... Opera 4ta ...'); copied from Hummel, 1828–42.

9.   Reproduced in NMAV/15/4, p.208 and K^6, p.486.

10. On 14 September, Leopold Mozart had written to Nannerl, enclosing the keyboard parts of three 'new' concertos to go with one she already had. These works were K.449, K.450, K.451 and K.453, though precisely which one Nannerl already had by this date is difficult to establish with certainty; Ruth Halliwell makes a persuasive case for it to have been K.451 (Halliwell, 1998, p.465, n.19).

11. It is possible that he repeated it at a concert held in the National-Theater on 1 April (an event postponed from 21 March). The surviving programme refers to the performance of an 'entirely new' piano concerto (K.451 was completed on 22 March). It is more likely that the concerto performed at the rearranged concert on 1 April was K.450 (*q.v.* completed on 15 March); K.451 would not have been ready in time for the concert originally planned for 21 March, and it was in any case given in the third of Mozart's subscription series, the previous day (31 March).

12. Eventually, Mozart sent three concertos, including that in A major, K.488, as detailed in his subsequent letter to Winter of 30 September 1786.

Piano concerto in G major, K.453

i. Allegro, $\frac{4}{4}$, 349 bars; ii. Andante, $\frac{3}{4}$, 135 bars; iii. Allegretto, $\frac{2}{2}$, 346 bars.

Scoring: solo fortepiano; violins 1 & 2; violas; bass [= cello, bass]; flute; 2 oboes; 2 bassoons; 2 horns.

Composed in Vienna; dated 12 April 1784 (autograph and *Verzeichnis*).

The autograph of K.453 (on 12-stave 'Querformat' paper) was removed from the Berlin Staatsbibliothek, Preussischer Kulturbesitz at the end of World War Two; it is currently in the Jagiellonian University Library, Kraków.[1] Manuscript copies were advertised in the *Wiener Zeitung* by Lorenz Lausch on 31 August 1785; two weeks later, Johann Traeg also announced the availability of copies of this 'brand new' concerto, although the work was some eighteen months old by this date. Mozart had remarked to his father on 26 May 1784 that, in the case of K.450, 451 and 453, 'Only today I could have got 24 ducats for one of them, but I think that it will be more profitable for me to hold on to them for a few years more and then have them engraved and published.' None of these works was subsequently published during his lifetime, however, and whether the 1785 advertisements of Lausch and Traeg were part of a business arrangement with Mozart or independent ventures made possible by the circulation of pirate copies is unknown.[2] Three apparently contemporary manuscript copies survive, in Berlin, Melk and Kroměříž.[3] They seem to derive from the first edition, issued as 'op.IX' by Bossler in Speyer during 1787 (Mozart, 1787), and share with it a relatively large number of obvious textual errors and inconsistencies, suggesting that Mozart was not at all closely involved in the preparation of Bossler's print.[4] An edition by Artaria appeared the following year. Four cadenzas to K.453 survive: Mozart's autograph cadenza to the first movement;[5] two cadenzas, respectively for the first and second movements that appeared in the Artaria edition of 1788;[6] and a cadenza to the second movement, reproduced in André's 1852 edition.[7]

K.453 was one of four concerto autographs Mozart sent to his father in Salzburg on 15 May 1784,[8] later noting on 26 May 'I am quite willing to wait patiently until I get them back, so long as no one else is allowed to get hold of them.' Precisely when the autograph of K.453 was returned is unknown; however, it was among the package of Mozart's concerto autographs that were purchased by André from Constanze Mozart in 1799. The manuscript remained in the André family's possession until 1854 (when it passed to the Berlin Staatsbibilothek). On the first music-page is the legend, 'Di Wolfgango Amadeo Mozart Vienna li 12 d'Aprile 1784 per la Sigra Barbara Ployer', a date that also appears in Mozart's Thematic Catalogue, although the completion of this concerto is mentioned in a letter to Mozart's father of 10 April. It is mentioned again in letters of 26 May (in conjunction with the remarks on

Leopold's and Nannerl's preferences among Mozart's recent concertos, K.449, 450 and 451, and the extreme virtuosic demands of the latter two pieces),[9] and again on 12 June, in which Mozart advertises a performance arranged for the following day by Gottfried Ignaz von Ployer at Döbling at which 'Fräulein Babette is playing her new concerto in G'.[10] It was subsequently among the works offered *via* Sebastian Winter in a letter of 8 August 1786 to Prince von Fürstenberg, for the use of his court orchestra at Donaueschingen.[11] The theme of its variation finale is notated in a slightly altered form in Mozart's household account book on 27 May 1784, against an entry of 34 kreuzer paid for a starling which could apparently sing this theme.

A ten-bar $\frac{3}{4}$ autograph sketch in C major, possibly for the slow movement of K.453, survives.[12] It contains a number of melodic and rhythmic features similar to the eventual version (principally bars 3 and 9–10). While its harmonic and phrase disposition is considerably different – to judge from the completed parts of the sketch, which consists of only a treble and a bass line – the second of the two phrases is extended to five bars, as is the case in the opening phrase of K.453's finished Andante. Alan Tyson is of the opinion that the 39-bar sketch for a slow movement in C major, K.Anh.59 (459a),[13] may be associated with this concerto rather than, as more commonly held, K.459 in F (Tyson, 1987, p.141).[14] Its paper-type is otherwise confined in Mozart's usage to the three months of February, March and April 1784, including K.453 (entered in Mozart's *Verzeichnis* on 12 April 1784), whose last two movements are on this same paper type.

Notes

1. PL-Kj, Mus.ms.autogr. W. A. Mozart 449; Tyson, 1996, nos.55, 71, 73. The autograph was not available to the editors of NMA V/15/5. Their principal text was the André firm's 1852 edition (Mozart, 1852), advertised as 'Ausgabe nach der Originale Handschrift'. In André's print, K.453 appeared alongside K.482 (also based on the autograph), K.466, K.488, K.450 and K.467.

2. In the letter of 26 May 1784, Mozart specifically asked Leopold and Nannerl to prevent these three concertos from being copied and distributed outside of the family circle, so distrustful was he of Salzburg copyists. Traeg again advertised copies of K.453 in the *Wiener Zeitung* on 18 June and 2 July 1788: '1 Concerto in G for harpsichord, by W.A. Mozart'; Deutsch, 1965, pp.319–20.

3. D-B, Mus.Ms. 15480/1; A-M, IV 297, of c.1800, including ripieno string parts; CZ-KRa, II G 64/A3258 (playing parts). All three of these copies preserve faulty texts, deficient in matters of accuracy and articulation, though they appear to have arisen independently, rather than all deriving from a single faulty exemplar. Their general lack of staccato markings in the orchestral parts, compared to André's apparently authentic print of 1852, is especially noteworthy.

4. A selection from the first movement: bar 128, piano, left hand has bass D for C; bar 131, piano right hand, 7th semiquaver has A for G; bar 132, bassoon lacks staccatos.

5. K⁶626a/K.624, Teil i, 48; D-B, Mus.ms.autogr. W. A. Mozart 624(48); this is printed in the main text in NMA V/15/v; Tyson, 1996, no.71.

6. K⁶626a/K.624, Teil i, 49 and 51; printed in NMA V/15/v, Anhang I and II. Eva and Paul Badura-Skoda regard these as being of doubtful authenticity, principally on grounds of keyboard texture; possibly they are the work of one of Mozart's pupils (Barbara Ployer?).

7. K⁶626a/K.624, Teil i, 50, now in I-Mc, 1181/7879; this is printed in the main text in NMA V/15/v.

8. The others were K.449, K.450 and K.451.

9. See also the letter of 21 July 1784. K.453 was the second concerto Mozart composed for Ployer; the first was K.449 (*q.v.*). There had previously been mention of unspecified cadenzas which Leopold was having copied for Nannerl in a letter of 25–26 March 1785; Ruth Halliwell believes one of these to have been possibly for K.453 (Halliwell, 1998, p.479, n.25). On 14 September, Leopold Mozart wrote to Nannerl, enclosing the keyboard parts of three 'new' concertos to go with one she already had. These works were K.449, K.450, K.451 and K.453, though precisely which one Nannerl already had by this date is difficult to establish with certainty; Halliwell makes a persuasive case for it to have been K.451 (Halliwell, 1998, p.465, n.19).

10. Also performed were the Piano Quintet, K.452 (with Mozart at the keyboard), and the Sonata in D for 2 Pianos, K.448 (Mozart and Ployer).

11. The other concertos mentioned are K.451, 456, 459 and 488 (see Mozart's letter of 8 August 1786). Eventually, he sent three concertos to Fürstenberg, including that in A major, K.488, as detailed in his subsequent letter to Winter of 30 September 1786.

12. K.Anh.65 (452c); printed in NMA V/15/viii, Anhang II/1. The scoring is for an ensemble identical to that of K.453.

13. Printed in NMA V/15/8, Anhang II/2.

14. The autograph is in A-Sm, fragment 18.

Piano concerto in B flat major, K.456

i. Allegro vivace, $\frac{4}{4}$, 364 bars; ii. Andante, un poco sostenuto, $\frac{2}{4}$, 209 bars; iii. Allego vivace, $\frac{6}{8}$, 324 bars.

Scoring: solo fortepiano; violins 1 & 2; violas; bass [= cello, bass]; flute; 2 oboes; 2 bassoons; 2 horns.

Composed in Vienna; dated 30 September 1784 (*Verzeichnis*).

The autograph of K.456 (on 12-stave 'Querformat' paper) is currently in the Staatsbibliothek zu Berlin (Musikabteilung).[1] The first edition was produced by André (Mozart, 1792d), that is, some years before he acquired the Mozart *Nachlaß* from Constanze in 1799. His source for the text of K.456 is unknown. The Viennese music dealer, Johann Traeg, advertised copies of this work at 7 kr. per sheet in the *Wiener Zeitung* on 1 December 1785.[2]

An authentic copy of K.456 – on 12-stave 'Klein-Querformat' paper – survives in the M. J. Glinka Museum, Moscow;[3] Mozart signed this at the end ('Vienna. di Wolfgango Amadeo Mozart mpa. 1784'). In addition to some autograph annotations of dynamics to the solo part, its text incorporates an important alteration in the piano part at bar 127 of the first movement (namely, the addition of flats to notes 8 and 11 in the right hand, transforming the cadence from the major to the minor mode). As this same alteration is found in the autograph,[4] it seems plausible that the composer supervised the 'Moscow' copy carefully, although against this interpretation is the fact that at two points in the slow movement variations, the 'Moscow' copy departs slightly from the autograph text.[5] Perhaps this copy was one of those available from Traeg at the end of 1785.[6]

The 'Moscow' copy contains cadenzas to the first and third movements, and an *Eingang* to the third. While the cadenzas may represent examples composed by Mozart especially for the use of a pupil (or its intended executant, Mlle Paradies – see below),[7] the authenticity of the *Eingang* at bar 144 of the finale is debatable.[8] While neither its figuration nor its harmonic language are outside the boundaries of Mozart's practice, the migration to a $\frac{4}{4}$ time-signature within a $\frac{6}{8}$ movement is suspect. Two alternative cadenzas for the first movement survive among those printed by André and Artaria.[9]

This concerto was written for the blind pianist, Maria Theresia von Paradies (1759–1824). A pupil of Salieri, Kozeluch and Richter, Paradies had been blinded at the age of three, but pursued a remarkable career as a pianist and singer (see Clive, 1993). During the summer of 1783, she made a highly successful concert tour that took her to Salzburg, where she encountered the Mozarts. Possibly, K.456 was written at her request, expressly for a proposed concert tour planned for the following year. Paradies is known to have played in Paris in October 1784 and in London the following month, as part of a tour that also took in Brussels and Berlin. The date of 30 September (the date Mozart entered the concerto in his *Verzeichnis*) would coincide with that tour, but would not have given Paradies much time to learn it (assuming that this date actually records the finishing of the composition, rather than simply the date on which Mozart happened to record an already completed work in his catalogue).

Two of Mozart's own performances of this work are known. On 13 February 1785, he played K.456 at an academy given by the singer, Louisa Laschi, as reported in a letter from Leopold to Nannerl (14 February). Leopold described the piece as

> a glorious concerto, which he composed for Mlle Paradis for Paris. I was sitting only two boxes away from the very beautiful Princess of Wurttem-berg and had the great pleasure of hearing so clearly all the interplay of the instruments that for sheer delight tears came into my eyes. When your brother left the platform the Emperor waved his hat and called out 'Bravo Mozart!' And when he came on to play there was a great deal of clapping.[10]

Mozart subsequently played K.456 (and also K.503 and a fantasia – K.475? – two sets of variations and two scenas, sung by Josepha Dusek) at a benefit concert in Leipzig on 12 May 1789 (Deutsch, 1965, pp.341–2). It was one of the five piano concertos Mozart offered *via* Sebastian Winter in a letter of 8 August 1786 to Prince von Fürstenberg, for the use of his court orchestra at Donaueschingen.[11]

Notes

1. D-B, Mus.ms.autogr. W. A. Mozart 456 (bound together with the autograph of K.459); Tyson, 1996, nos.53, 56, 74, 75.
2. Deutsch, 1965, p.258 (21 December 1785). Traeg advertised the piece again on 13 May 1786 (Eisen, 1991a, no.71).
3. RUS-Mcm fond 282, 82; formerly in the collection of the Moscow Conservatoire Library (1923) and previously in the private collection of the composer, Mikhail Ippolitov-Ivanov.
4. Just visible in the facsimile on p.xviii of NMA V/15/5.
5. At bars 36 and 205–7, printed in the main text as *ossias* in NMA V/15/5.
6. Other contemporary copies of K.456 are at CZ-KRa, I G 73 (parts, of which the solo part contains some figured bass notation); CZ-Pu, M II/13, no.11. (score); and A-Wn, Mus.Hs.5733 (score) and Mus.Hs.19944 (parts). The Prague and Vienna sources derive from a late-eighteenth-century score from the private collection of Carl Bär, though neither is so closely linked with Mozart as the 'Moscow' copy.
7. K⁶626a/K.624, Teil i, 52 and 56; printed in NMA V/15/v, Anhang III/1 and 3.
8. K⁶626a/K.624, Teil i, 55; printed in NMA V/15/v, Anhang III/2.
9. The first, K⁶626a/K.624, Teil i, 54, is printed in the main text in NMA V/15/v [André, 1804, no.20; Artaria, 1801, no.vii]. The other, K⁶626a/K.624, Teil i, 53, is given in NMA V/15/v, Anhang II [André, 1804, no.19; Artaria, 1801, no.xi].

10.   Nannerl may have been sent a copy of this concerto by Leopold; see Leopold's letter dated 20–22 October 1785 (though this may have been K.459 – see Halliwell, 1998, pp.499–500, n.42).

11.   The others were K.451, 453, 459 and 488 (see Mozart's letter of 8 August 1786). Eventually, Mozart sent three concertos, including that in A major, K.488, as detailed in his subsequent letter to Winter of 30 September 1786.

Piano concerto in F major, K.459

i. Allegro vivace, $\frac{2}{2}$, 410 bars; ii. Allegretto, $\frac{6}{8}$, 159 bars; iii. Allegro assai, $\frac{2}{4}$, 506 bars.

Scoring: solo fortepiano; violins 1 & 2; violas; bass [= cello, bass]; flute; 2 oboes; 2 bassoons; 2 horns; [additionally 2 trumpets; timpani, according to the *Verzeichnis* entry]

Composed in Vienna; dated 11 December 1784 (*Verzeichnis*).

The autograph of K.459 (on 12-stave 'Querformat' paper), is today in the Staatsbibliothek zu Berlin (Musikabteilung).[1] It contains evidence of an interesting rethinking of the *tactus* of the slow movement, from $\frac{3}{8}$ to $\frac{6}{8}$.[2] Contemporary manuscript copies also exist[3] though none has any annotations by Mozart.[4] Autograph cadenzas to the outer movements, and an *Eingang* to the finale (bar 255), survive.[5] The first edition was issued by André (Mozart, 1794a).[6] The title-page of André's edition heralds K.459 as 'Krönungskonzert' (like K.537, also published in 1794): 'Ce concerto a été executé par l'auteur à Francfort sur le Mein à l'occasion du Couronnement de l'Empereur Léopold II (Bollert, 1958, pp.66–8).'

The coronation of Leopold II actually took place on 9 October 1790 in Frankfurt cathedral, whereas Mozart's concert was held in the Municipal Playhouse there on the morning of 15 October. In addition to the two piano concertos, K.459 and K.537, one in each half of the concert, according to the surviving programme (Deutsch, 1965, p.374), the event included two symphonies (or possibly component movements of the same symphony, as occurred in the case of the 'Haffner' symphony, K.385, performed in Vienna on 23 March 1783), performed at the beginning and end,[7] along with an improvised fantasy and three arias or duets. Given its performance on this occasion, K.459 deserves the epithet 'Coronation' concerto just as much as the more famous K.537 in D. Mozart, writing to his wife on 15 October 1790, described the concert as 'a splendid success from the point of view of honour and glory, but a failure as far as money was concerned',[8] We are fortunate that an independent report of this concert survives in the travel diary of Count Ludwig von Bentheim-Steinfurt, who had attended the coronation celebrations in Frankfurt:

> Mozart played a *Concerto* composed by him which was of an *extraordinary pretiness and charm*, he had a forte Piano by Stein of Augsburg which must be supreme of its kind ... Mozart's playing is a little like that of the late *Klöfler* [the Count's former director of music] but infinitely more perfect ... *In the second Act*, No.5, another concerto by Mozart, which however did not please me like the first (Deutsch, 1965, p.375).

His opinion ('extraordinary pretiness and charm') contains insufficient detail to allow a certain identification of which concerto was so pleasing to the

Count. He further notes that 'The orchestra was no more than rather weak with 5 or six violins but apart from that very accurate.' By 'weak', the Count evidently meant lacking in volume. He mentions only the small number of strings – not, regrettably, the wind and brass complement. In the *Verzeichnis*, Mozart includes a pair of trumpets and timpani among the instrumental forces for K.459[9] although no parts for these instruments are included in the autograph score, nor are any transmitted in the early sets of manuscript playing parts or in the first edition. Possibly, the instrumentation given in the *Verzeichnis* is a mistake. Alternatively, the extra parts may have been written on a separate *partitura*, for inclusion only on special ceremonial occasions (including, perhaps, 15 October 1790), as was apparently the intention in the case of K.365 and K.482. While F major is not a key associated with trumpets in Mozart's orchestral music, there is no technical reason why they could not have been employed in this key.[10]

A 39-bar sketch for a slow movement in C major, K.Anh.59 (459a),[11] may be associated with this concerto. Alan Tyson, however, believes that it may more probably be connected with the G major concerto, K.453, since its paper-type is otherwise confined in Mozart's usage to the three months of February, March and April 1784, including K.453 (entered in Mozart's Thematic Catalogue on 12 April 1784), whose last two movements are on this same paper-type (Tyson, 1987, p.141).[12]

K.459 was one of the five piano concertos Mozart offered *via* Sebastian Winter to Prince von Fürstenberg, for the exclusive use of his court orchestra at Donaueschingen in August 1786.[13]

Notes

1. D-B, Mus.ms.autogr. W. A. Mozart 459 (bound together with the autograph of K.456); Tyson, 1996, nos53, 55, 72, 76.
2. This may be seen in the facsimile reproduced in NMA V/15/5, p.xxii; Mozart here had to cancel alternate barlines.
3. A-Wn, Mus.Hs.20221; CZ-Pu, M II/13 no.3 (scores); CZ-KRa, II G 74; CZ-Bm, A.14442 (playing parts). The Kroměříž copy agrees with André's edition very closely in its musical text and replicates part of the title-page ('Ce concerto a été executé par l'auteur à Francfort sur le Mein à l'occasion du Couronnement de l'Empereur Léopold II'). The Vienna and Prague scores may have been copied directly from the autograph; the Brno parts, in turn, appear to have been copied from the Prague score.
4. A copy may have been sent to Nannerl Mozart by her father; see Leopold's letter dated 20–22 October 1785 (though this may have been K.456 – see Halliwell, 1998, pp.499–500, n.42).
5. Collection of Prof. Dr. H. Federhofer (Graz). For facsimiles, see Federhofer, 1958, esp. p.114 (Table). The cadenzas and the *Eingang* are, respectively, K[6]626a/K.624, Teil i, 58, 60 and 59; Tyson, 1996, no.58. Cadenzas by Hummel survive in manuscript at CZ-K, Sig. Schwarzenburg K.27, no.776 ('Cadenze per

sette Concerti di Mozart pe[r i]l Piano Forte ... Composte del Sigre. Giov: Nep: Hummel ... Opera 4ta ...'), copied presumably from Hummel, 1828–42.

6.   For confirmation that this work was played on this occasion, see *Rellstabs Berliner Lagerverzeichnis*, suppl. 8 (1795), reported in Deutsch and Oldman, 1932, p.345; see also Deutsch, 1931.

7.   The second symphony was not, in fact, given, owing to lack of time, according to the report of Count Ludwig von Bentheim-Steinfurt (see below).

8.   By this time, Mozart was falling seriously into debt, and he must have counted on making a significant amount from this event, given its position within the immediate aftermath of the coronation festivities. By ill luck, there was a rival event on the same morning that attracted many of Mozart's would-be patrons.

9.   The same scoring ('2 clarini et Timpany ad libitum') is given in the *Verzeichnis* for K.537 (24 February 1788).

10. The editors of NMA V/15/5 note, somewhat ambiguously, that F major is not otherwise found in any of Mozart's symphonic or concerto output. It is found within the D minor concerto, K.466, however – a work bearing the same one-flat key-signature, and potentially sharing much of the same compass and utilising many of the same available natural trumpet pitches as a work in F.

11. Printed in NMA V/15/8, Anhang II/2.

12. The autograph is in A-Sm, fragment 18.

13. The other concertos mentioned are K.451, 453, 456 and 488 (see Mozart's letter of 8 August 1786). Eventually, he sent three concertos to Fürstenberg, including that in A major, K.488, as detailed in his subsequent letter to Winter of 30 September 1786.

Piano concerto in D minor, K.466

i. Allegro, $\frac{4}{4}$, 397 bars; ii. Romanze, $\frac{2}{2}$, 162 bars; iii. Rondo. [Allegro assai], $\frac{2}{2}$, 428 bars.

Scoring: solo fortepiano; violins 1 & 2; violas; bass [= cello, bass]; flute; 2 oboes; 2 bassoons; 2 horns; 2 trumpets; timpani.

Composed in Vienna; dated 10 February 1785 (*Verzeichnis*).

The autograph of K.466 (on 12-stave 'Querformat' paper) is in the collection of the Gesellschaft der Musikfreunde, Vienna.[1] It bears, on the first music-page, the legend 'Concerto Di Amadeo Wolfgango Mozart'. Previously, it was owned by Mozart's colleague, the Abbé Maximilian von Stadler (1748–1833). After Mozart's death, Stadler, at Constanze's request, began to put the remaining autograph manuscripts in order, completing a few fragmentary compositions, and cataloguing others.[2] The first edition was published by André (Mozart, 1796), that is, three years before he purchased from Constanze a large quantity of autographs upon which his early editions of Mozart's works were based; the exemplar for this print is not known.[3] The autograph of K.466 was not among those autographs purchased by André in November 1799. Possibly it had already been given to Stadler by this time. A set of playing parts survives at St Peter's, Salzburg, in which detailed instructions for 'ripieno' performance appear in the violin parts.[4] Although no cadenzas to this work by Mozart are known, Beethoven composed examples for the first movement and finale (Beethoven, 1967); he performed the work at a benefit concert for Mozart's widow (also attended by Count Zinzendorf) in the Kärntnertortheater, Vienna, on 31 March 1795.[5]

K.466 was first performed by Mozart at the Mehlgrube Casino on 11 February 1785 (the day after it was entered in the *Verzeichnis*).[6] This was the first of six weekly 'Friday concerts' given by Mozart during spring 1785. It coincided with an extended visit to the capital by his father, and Leopold's letters to his daughter from this time provide some interesting details on the piece and the circumstances of its early performances. In a long letter written in stages between 14 and 16 February, he described Wolfgang's latest concerto in the following context:

> [On 11 February] we drove to his first subscription concert, at which a great many members of the aristocracy were present. Each person pays a souverain d'or or three ducats for these Lenten concerts. Your brother is giving them at the Mehlgrube ... The concert was magnificent and the orchestra played splendidly ... we had a new and very fine concerto [K.466] by Wolfgang, which the copyist was still copying as we arrived, and the rondo of which your brother did not even have time to play through, as he had to supervise the copying.[7]

Mozart played K.466 again – this time in rather less haste – at a concert on 15 February in the Burgtheater organised by the singer Elisabeth Distler. Leopold reported that on this occasion, Mozart 'played his new grand concerto in D minor magnificently'.[8]

There is evidence in the autograph that Mozart may have intended this concerto for performance by a fortepiano with an extra pedalboard. At bars 88–90 of the first movement, the autograph contains, in addition to the notated left-hand crotchet chords on beats 1 and 3, supplementary low crotchets D and A – unplayable by the left-hand alone without ugly spreading that would ruin the effect of punctuation beneath the running semiquaver patterns. Alternatively, if played by the feet, these notes could have quite the opposite effect of reinforcing the chordal tonic–dominant punctuation at this point (the pitches are otherwise supplied only by the trumpets and timpani). It is known that Mozart had a specially adapted fortepiano with pedal attachment available for the 1785 series. He used it for performances of the contemporary K.467, and it was described by his father in a letter of 12 March.[9]

Mozart sent Leopold his autograph score of the work (along with that of K.467 and engraved copies of the six string quartets dedicated to Haydn, K.387, 421, 428, 458, 464 and 465) at the end of November 1785.[10] Leopold noted that the copying of the parts would be a lengthy task and that the solo parts (of K.466 and 467) were being copied first 'for the concertos will require a great deal of practice'. Evidently, the solo part of K.466 was sent to Nannerl in St Gilgen early in 1786, since, in a letter of 4–5 January, Leopold, referring to one of these recently copied concertos, specifically identified its slow movement as a 'Romance'. Describing a subsequent performance in Salzburg by Heinrich Wilhelm Marchand (1769–c.1812) on 22 March 1786[11] Leopold remarked that:

> As you have the clavier part, he [Marchand] played it from the score and [Michael] Haydn turned over the pages for him and at the same time had the pleasure of seeing with what art it is composed, how delightfully the parts are interwoven and what a difficult concerto it is ... We rehearsed it in the morning and had to practise the rondo three times before the orchestra could manage it, for Marchand took it rather quickly.[12]

A rather later performance of K.466 is recorded by Thomas Attwood in a letter to an unnamed correspondent probably dating from 1828–30 (Eisen, 1991a, no.64). According to Attwood's recollection of events occurring some forty years previously, Mozart 'was very kind to all of Talent who came to Vienna & generally played at their Benefit Concerts with the Pianofortes ... The last time I heard him, He play'd his concerto in D minor & "Non temere" [that is, "Ch'io mi scordi di te ... Non temer, amato bene", K.505] at [Nancy] Storace's Benefit [concert]'. This was probably Nancy Storace's farewell concert at the Kärntnerthortheater on 23 February 1787 (Deutsch, 1965, p.285).

Notes

1.   A-Wgm, Signatur A 160 (formerly VII 3405); Tyson, 1996, nos.61, 71, 76.
2.   Stadler's catalogue appeared as an appendix to Nissen, 1828. Further on Stadler, see Clive, 1993.
3.   An edition by Artaria also appeared in 1796, as 'Op.39' (Verlagsno.650).
4.   A-Ssp, Moz.275.1, a copy prepared between 1 December 1785 and 5 January 1786 (see correspondence discussed below). For details of the ripieno parts, see Chapter Seven (at p.136). Also Schmid, 1980–83. Other contemporary copies: I-Mc, 12269; CZ-KRa, II G 76; CZ-Pu, M II/13, no.8.
5.   Manuscript cadenzas to the first and last movements dating probably from c.1790 by Emmanuel Aloys Förster are in A-Wn, S.m.1241; reproduced in facsimile in Edge, 1996c, fig.4. A generation later, this concerto was in the repertoire of Mendelssohn who frequently performed it during the 1830s and early 1840s. His own cadenzas are lost, though some indication of the structure of the first-movement cadenza – unusually, for the 1830s, drawing on Mozart's principal themes rather than lapsing into gratuitous virtuoso display – is given in a letter to Mendelssohn's sister, Fanny. See Todd, 1991.
6.   For details on this location, see Morrow, 1988, pp.100–101.
7.   Later in the same letter, Leopold mentions that Mozart was to play a concerto, possibly K.466, that night (16 February) at a concert given by Gottfried Ignaz von Ployer at his residence in Döbling.
8.   Letter to Nannerl Mozart, 16 February 1785.
9.   Further on the use of this instrument, see the entry for K.467 below. Mozart's pupil, Thomas Attwood, claimed that Mozart had the pedal attachment fitted because 'He was so fond of Sebastian Bach's Preludes & Fugues' (Eisen, 1991a, no.64); the pedalboard presumably allowed Mozart to realise these pieces in a more 'polyphonic' manner than was possible on the fortepiano keyboard alone. For a detailed account of the instrument, see Maunder and Rowland, 1995.
10. See Leopold's letter to Nannerl of 2 December 1785.
11. Letter to Nannerl of 23 March 1786.
12. By 'the score' Leopold may have been referring to the autograph rather than a copy of it. When this was subsequently returned to Wolfgang in Vienna is unknown. It is possible that it was only returned *via* Nannerl upon Leopold's death in May 1787. On 1 August that year, Wolfgang asks his sister, 'Please do not forget my *scores*' (original emphasis); 'scores' may refer to those important autographs (for instance, of piano concertos that Mozart hoped one day to publish) that had been sent to Leopold and not returned. Leopold's remarks seem to suggest that Marchand's performance of a piano concerto *from a score* was an unusual circumstance. For a detailed account of Marchand's performances of this work (among others) see Halliwell, 1998, pp.507–23 *passim*.

Piano concerto in C major, K.467

i. [Allegro maestoso], $\frac{4}{4}$, 417 bars; ii. Andante, $\frac{4}{4}$, 104 bars; iii. Allegro vivace assai, $\frac{2}{4}$, 447 bars.

Scoring: solo fortepiano; violins 1 & 2; violas; bass [= cello, bass]; flute; 2 oboes; 2 bassoons; 2 horns; 2 trumpets; timpani.

Composed in Vienna; dated 9 March 1785 (*Verzeichnis*).

The autograph of K.467 (on 12-stave 'Querformat' paper) is in the Pierpoint Morgan Library, New York.[1] On the first music-page is the legend 'Di Wolfgango Amadeo Mozart nel Febraio 1785'. K.467 was evidently not among the autographs purchased from Constanze by André in November 1799, and on which he was to base most of his own editions, 'faite d'après le manuscrit original de l'auteur' that appeared from 1800 onwards.[2] Although André did produce editions of this concerto (Mozart, 1800d; Mozart, 1800e), his efforts were preceded by a volume of Breitkopf & Härtel's *Oeuvres complettes de Mozart* which appeared in (probably) April 1800 (Mozart, 1800c). In the *Allgemeine Musikalische Zeitung, Intelligenz-blatt ix* (March 1800), Breitkopf announced that this work engraved 'nach dem uns vor dem Witwe Mozart überlassenen Originalmanuscript' would appear 'by the end of next month'. Apparent confirmation that Constanze had passed over the autograph score of this work to Breitkopf is provided by her statement of 13 March 1800 that:

> After I had passed on to Messrs. Breitkopf and Härtel in Leipzic against an honorarium some few original manuscripts of my late husband, consisting solely of songs, canons, fugues, a harmonica quintet [K.617], a march for the pianoforte, a pair of sonatas and one piano forte concerto ... and after I had sold them the plates of the pianoforte concerto published by me [K.503, *q.v.*], I voluntarily offered them [Breitkopf and Härtel] my entire large collection for sale in one lot ... they did not avail themselves of my offer. Herr André ... has since purchased it from me and has thus become the sole legal possessor (Deutsch, 1965, pp.495–6).

Possibly, though, Constanze was mistaken (or guarded with the truth) about the manuscript score sent to Breitkopf. André's edition is described on the title-page as 'faite d'après le manuscript original de l'auteur'. She cannot have sold the same autograph to both publishers; probably the Breitkopf edition was based on a manuscript copy made from the autograph, rather than the autograph itself.

Along with the autograph score of K.466, the autograph of K.467 was sent to Leopold in Salzburg at the end of 1785, and was immediately copied, for the use of Nannerl Mozart.[3] Regrettably, none of these playing parts survive. On 14 January 1786, he remarked of the piece:

> Indeed it is astonishingly difficult. But I very much doubt whether there are any mistakes [in the copy owned by Nannerl], as the copyist has checked it. Several passages may not harmonise unless one hears all the instruments playing together. But of course it is quite possible that the copyist may have misread a sharp for a flat in the score, or something of the kind, for if so it cannot be right. I shall get to the bottom of it all when I see the original score.

This final comment may indicate that by 14 January 1786, Leopold had returned the autograph to Wolfgang in Vienna; had the 'original score' still been in Leopold's possession at this stage, he could have answered Nannerl's queries.[4] No cadenzas to K.467 by Mozart are known to survive.

K.467 was first performed by Mozart on 10 March 1785 at the Burgtheater, Vienna.[5] As was almost certainly the case with K.466 in D minor, Mozart's own early performances of K.467 were on a fortepiano for which he had procured a specially made pedal attachment. This contraption was described by Leopold in a letter to his daughter of 12 March 1785, in which he attempts to paint a picture of the hectic concert schedule in which her brother was then engaged:

> We never get to bed before one o'clock and I never get up before nine. We lunch at two or half past ... Every day there are concerts [either Mozart's own, or performances that he gave in concerts arranged by others]; and the whole time is given up to teaching, music, composing and so forth ... If only all the concerts were over! It is impossible for me to describe the rush and bustle. Since my arrival [on 11 February] your brother's fortepiano has been taken at least a dozen times to the theatre or to some other house. He has had a large fortepiano pedal made, which stands under the instrument and is about two feet longer and extremely heavy. It is taken to the Mehl-grube every Friday, and has also been taken to Count Zichy's and Prince Kaunitz's.

The special pedal instrument is highlighted in an advertisement for Mozart's concert on 10 March:

> On Thursday 10 March 1785 Herr Kapellmeister *Mozart* will have the honour of giving at the Imperial and Royal National Court Theatre a Grand Musical Concert for his benefit, at which not only a *new*, just *finished* [K.467, entered in Mozart's *Verzeichnis* only the previous day] *Forte piano concerto* will be played by him, but also an especially *large Forte piano pedale* will be used by him in *improvising* ... (Deutsch, 1965, p.239).[6]

Mozart's use of the pedal was, according to this advertisement, 'in *impro-vising*'. Nevertheless, it is unthinkable that, given the inconvenience of trans-porting the pedalboard noted by Leopold, Mozart would have restricted its usage to solo items when he could also present it in a new piano concerto scored for a large orchestra, including trumpets and timpani, and in which it would have plenty of opportunities to augment the depth of tone within the solo part (at bars 158–63 of the first movement, for example), to reinforce the bass line in tutti passages during which the piano is marked 'Col Basso' and to enhance the effect at important moments of tonal articulation. Almost certainly, the advertisement was drawing attention to the fact that this concert would provide listeners with an occasion to hear an unusual fortepiano.

Notes

1. US-NYpm, Heinemann Ms.266; Tyson, 1996, nos.62, 73, 76. For a useful facsimile see Mozart, 1985. Jan LaRue's penetrating examination, in this facsimile edition, of some of the tiny amendments made to scoring during the writing of the autograph is much to be recommended. One particularly telling example is the alteration of the register of bar 325 of the solo part in the first movement (which Mozart first wrote an octave higher); the final version subtly enhances the decoration in bar 326 by means of register contrast, made possible here by the particular coincidence of the returning tessitura of the tonic, C major, and the range of Mozart's keyboard (a similar upward transposition would have been impossible at bars 140–44 of the solo exposition, where this figure occurs initially at a slightly higher register in the dominant, G). A sketchleaf, containing material possibly pertaining to this concerto, survives in A-Sm; see Plath, 1959 (including also a facsimile).

2. Following a list of manuscripts to be handed over to André as part of the deal is a note that '211 engraved copies of Mozart's Clavier Concerto in C. major which are to be obtained from *Breitkopf and Härtel*' would also be forthcoming. The work in question was probably K.503 (*q.v.*, which Constanze had previously published at her own expense) rather than K.467. K.467 was eventually issued as one of the 'Op.82' concertos that André published later in 1800 (Mozart 1800d, comprising K.467, 482, 488, 491, 503 and 595), of which K.467 was Op.82, no.6. André subsequently published a volume of cadenzas to 'Op.82' (Hoffmann, 1801–03), composed by the Mainz virtuoso Philipp Karl Hoffmann (1769–1842). Surviving contemporary manuscript copies of this concerto include those in CZ-KRa, II G 77 and CZ-Pu, M II/13, no.1. The former has extensive orchestral cues for tutti sections in the right hand of the solo part.

3. In a letter of 23 March 1786, Leopold remarks that Nannerl has the solo parts of all Mozart's concertos, including K.467.

4. Alternatively, Leopold may simply not have had the score immediately to hand. He had explained to Nannerl on 2 December 1785 that 'the copyist at the moment has enough to copy and it will be slow work. I am letting him do the clavier parts first of all'; in this case, by 14 January 1786 the copyist might have been at work on the orchestral parts of K.467, explaining why Leopold could not answer Nannerl's questions directly.

5. For details on this theatre, see Morrow, 1988, pp.66–81.

6. A facsimile of this handbill is reproduced in Mozart, 1985, p.vii.

Piano concerto in E flat major, K.482

i. Allegro, $\frac{4}{4}$, 383 bars; ii. Andante, $\frac{3}{8}$, 213 bars; iii. Allegro, $\frac{6}{8}$, 435 bars.

Scoring: solo fortepiano; violins 1 & 2; violas; bass [= cello, bass]; flute; 2 clarinets; 2 bassoons; 2 horns; 2 trumpets; timpani.

Composed in Vienna; dated 16 December 1785 (Autograph and *Verzeichnis*).

The autograph of K.482 (on 12-stave 'Querformat' paper) is today in the Staatsbibliothek zu Berlin (Musikabteilung).[1] On the first music page is the legend, 'Concerto per il Cembalo. Di Wolfgango Amadeo Mozart mp.[ia] Vienna li 16 di Dec. 1785.' Johann Traeg advertised manuscript copies of playing parts for K.482 for sale in the *Wiener Zeitung* on 1 August 1789.[2] The first edition, 'faite d'après le manuscrit original de l'auteur', was produced by André (Mozart, 1800d).[3] The trumpet and timpani parts are not notated in the main body of the autograph score; instead they are set out on a separate sheet (fol.57) at the end of the autograph.[4] The provision of such a partitura for the trumpets and timpani is by no means unusual in, for example, operatic works of this period;[5] indeed, the use of 12-stave paper may have offered Mozart no comfortable opportunity to notate these instrumental lines throughout the score. Alternatively, Mozart may only have decided to include these particular parts at a relatively late stage in the composition, as in the D major concerto, K.537,[6] by which time the layout of his score could not be interfered with, necessitating the separate partitura. Possibly, Mozart may have envisaged performance of K.482 either with or without these instruments: trumpet and timpani parts were frequently regarded in the late eighteenth century as 'ad libitum', and were so described by Mozart in the list of instrumentation entered into his *Verzeichnis* for K.537.

Like its better-known neighbours, K.488 and K.491, K.482 was possibly performed in the series of subscription concerts that Mozart arranged for Lent 1786, though there is no documentary evidence of performances besides that of 23 December 1785 in the Burgtheater where it was probably played by Mozart as an Entr'act ('a pianoforte Concerto newly composed by W. A. Mozart') during a production of Dittersdorf's oratorio, *Esther* (Deutsch, 1965, pp.258–9).[7] Leopold reported to his daughter in a letter of 13 January 1786 that, according to Wolfgang, K.482 was among the works he had performed at three hastily arranged subscription concerts towards the end of December, and that the Andante was so popular that he had to repeat it.[8] Possibly it was the sheer expressiveness of the Andante that so pleased this audience. The theme's minor mode is subtly coloured by chromatic harmonies (especially neapolitan and augmented-6th chords), and this feature is exploited throughout the course of the movement, for example, the solo statement at bars 93–124. Another remarkable aspect of the Andante is its scoring. Prolonged soloistic use is made of the wind – the clarinets especially – creating many enchanting sonorous effects, including the use of clarinets and horns in octaves (bars 69–70 and 88–92), flute and bassoon in dialogue in the central C major section and *obbligato* bassoon reinforcing the bass progressions at bars 193–200. The sensitivity with which the various instrumental forces are disposed in this movement, exploiting the potential for blend and contrast in equal measure, is reinforced by Mozart's unusual provision of separate cello and bass lines.[9] Occasionally, cellos play without bass support; elsewhere there are passages for the cellos and basses in unison, octaves and double-octaves. *Divisi* viola polyphony is also found (bars 177–92). Like K.488 and K.491, completed on 2 and 22 March 1786 respectively, K.482 includes parts for clarinets, and was possibly conceived as the first item in a set of three piano concertos prominently exploiting the sonority of that instrument.

Notes

1. D-B, Mus.ms.autogr. W. A. Mozart 482; Tyson, 1996, nos.66, 78, 80, 81. Facsimiles in NMA V/15/6, pp.xx–xxii; Federhofer, 1958 (including a facsimile of sketches to the first movement, bars 19–20 and 27–8 in Federhofer's own collection).
2. An apparently contemporary copy of performance materials is in CZ-Pu, M II/13, no.6.
3. K.482 is 'Op.82, no.4'. The six concertos included in this publication are K.467, 482, 488, 491, 503 and 595. André also published a volume of cadenzas to 'Op.82' (Hoffmann, 1801–03), composed by the Mainz virtuoso, Philipp Karl Hoffmann (1769–1842). The autograph was one of those purchased by André from Constanze in 1799.
4. In the first movement, these parts bear a handwritten alteration of the number of bars' rest in the passage starting at bar 274 from 23 to 25. This is to take account of an apparent oversight in the writing out of the autograph: bars 282 and 283 were omitted (see NMA V/15/6, pp.xx for a facsimile of this page, and cf. bars 27–8 of the same movement); once restored, the silent trumpets and timpani needed to count an additional two bars' rest before their next entry (at bar 296). Although an autograph leaf (in a private Austrian collection) relates to these missing two bars in the recapitulation, it is worthy of note that the only complete eighteenth-century texts of this movement (that is, containing bars 281 and 282) are copies and prints.
5. See also the remarks on K.365 above.
6. In which, to judge from the autograph, participation of trumpets and timpani was only envisaged during the composition of the finale; see the entry for K.537 below.
7. This performance is also referred to in the minutes of the Wiener Tonkünstler-Sozietät (noted in Deutsch, 1965, pp.259 and Pohl, 1867, p.61); see also Eisen, 1991a, no.66, where it is further noted that the orchestral personnel of the Tonkünstler-Sozietät on this occasion did not include clarinetists; the clarinet parts in K.482 were probably played by the oboists. Dexter Edge is of the opinion that K.482 was not the work performed on this occasion (because of the apparent lack of clarinetists). He has expressed the view that K.482 was perhaps premièred 'at a musical academy of the Masonic lodge, "Zur gekrönten Hoffnung" on 15 December 1782

[*recte* 1785], the day before he entered the work in his *Verzeichnüß*'; see Edge, 1996a, at p.448, n.9, and Edge, 1992, at p.149. In no other case is the first known performance of a piano concerto earlier than the date on which it was entered into the *Verzeichnis*, however.

8. Wolfgang's letter, to which Leopold refers, was apparently dated 28 December 1785, so this performance of K.482 was perhaps during the last week of December, following Dittersdorf's oratorio. Wolfgang must have been referring to a performance other than that of 23 December (Dittersdorf's concert) since he also noted that 120 people had subscribed to his 'three concerts'. Exactly where and when these performances took place is unknown as Wolfgang's letter to Leopold is lost.

9. See the facsimile of the first page of the Andante as it appears in the autograph in NMAV/15/6, pp.xxi, xxii.

Piano concerto in A major, K.488

i. Allegro, $\frac{4}{4}$, 313 bars; ii. Adagio, $\frac{6}{8}$, 99 bars; iii. Allegro assai, $\frac{2}{2}$, 524 bars.

Scoring: solo fortepiano; violins 1 & 2; violas; bass [= cello, bass]; flute; 2 clarinets; 2 bassoons; 2 horns.

Composed in Vienna; dated 2 March 1786 (*Verzeichnis*).

The autograph of K.488 (on 12-stave 'Querformat' paper) is in the Bibliothèque Nationale (Département de la Musique), Paris.[1] The first edition was produced by André (Mozart, 1800d), prepared 'd'après la partition en manuscrit [de l'auteur].'[2] Unusually, Mozart wrote out the first movement cadenza straight into the main autograph score.[3] Among contemporary copies of K.488 is a manuscript in the Berlin Staatsbibliothek[4] containing fulsome ornamentation to the right hand of the solo part of the slow movement. According to Köchel, 1905 the ornamentation is, by implication, Mozart's autograph, but although the ornamentation may indirectly emanate from the composer, the handwriting is not his. Possibly the scribe was Mozart's pupil, Barbara Ployer; the notated embellishments may represent her recollection of suggestions made by Mozart.[5]

Despite the precise date in Mozart's *Verzeichnis* (2 March 1786), there is good evidence that K.488 was composed in at least two separate bursts of activity. According to Alan Tyson's investigation of the watermarks found in the autograph, its first eight leaves are written on a paper-type associated with other works dating from the period March 1784 to February 1785 (Tyson, 1996, no.73), that is, a period of intense activity in piano concerto composition (K.450, 451, 453 and 467 all date from this time and all share the same paper-type found at the beginning of K.488). Evidently K.488 was originally destined for either the 1783–84 or 1784–85 concert season in Vienna, but was put aside unfinished. The stimulus to complete it was probably the series of subscription concerts organised by Mozart in Vienna during the spring of 1786. Significantly, on revisiting the 'particella' of K.488, he decided to revise its scoring, replacing the original oboes with clarinets. Close examination of the first page of the autograph score of K.488 shows that staves 5 and 6, on which the clarinet lines occur, had originally (1784–85) been allocated to oboes. The part-designation ('2 oboi') to the left of these staves is erased and replaced by '2 clarinetti', and the clarinets' opening phrase (beginning at bar 9 with a restatement of the main theme) occurs at *untransposed* pitch (that is, the pitch at which the oboes would have played it), preceded by a *siglum* (X) evidently referring to fol.26r of the autograph, on which Mozart wrote out this opening phrase for the clarinets in A at their proper transposing pitch.[6] That Mozart went to the trouble of revising the instrumentation of K.488 must surely indicate the availability of clarinets for his projected Viennese performances, and it is an interesting coincidence that two other concertos completed and entered in his *Verzeichnis* at about this time, K.482 (16 December 1785) and K.491 (24 March 1786), also include parts for clarinets. Perhaps, given the opportunity to write for clarinets in the 1786 season, Mozart envisaged K.482, K.488 and K.491 as a group of three new piano concertos to be premièred at his subscription concerts, each prominently featuring this particular woodwind sonority.[7]

Various sketches for the slow movement and finale survive on separate leaves datable between December 1785 and December 1786 and therefore unquestionably from the second phase of composition of K.488 (spring 1786).[8] All except one is scored for clarinets rather than oboes.[9] K.Anh.58 (488a) is a ten-bar $\frac{3}{4}$ movement in D major – a far more conventional key for a slow movement to a work in A than the F sharp minor eventually preferred. To judge from the fragment, the clarinets would have played an important role in advancing the melodic material; in bars [5–6] the clarinet 1 offers an echo of the violin's cadential gesture.[10] Of the three sketches for a finale, possibly K.deest[11] is the simplest: at just 11 bars, it is not very far developed; its instrumentation is not fixed; it consists for the most part of a single melodic line (piano only); and even the barring is fragmentary. Nevertheless, its semiquaver passagework (in $\frac{2}{4}$ time) hints at some features of K.488's eventual finale. It begins with the solo unaccompanied; its general melodic profile foreshadows that of K.488 (note especially the prominently placed e″ and a″ in the right hand on the first beats of bars [1] and [2] and the f sharp″–e″ motion at the beginning of bar [3]); and the harmonic division, ending after four bars with a half-cadence on the dominant, E. K.Anh.63 (488b) is a 23-bar finale sketch in stately $\frac{2}{2}$ time, beginning, like K.deest and the eventual finale, with piano alone (bars 1–8), answered by the tutti (only the violin 1 and bass are notated in Mozart's sketch of the continuation).[12] Whereas in the final version the tutti entry repeats the material of the opening, in K.Anh.63 bars 8–23 introduce a succession of new ideas. Like K.deest, K.Anh.63 begins with a prominent, gavotte-like upbeat, discarded in the eventual finale which is characterised by a firm 'downbeat' scansion. The place of the finale sketch, K.Anh.64 (488c), in the sequence of sketches is difficult to determine. At 20 bars, it is more fully developed than K.deest, and at least equal in status to K.Anh.63.[13] Details of instrumentation are quite fully worked out. Following an opening four-bar statement by the solo (this time, cadencing on the tonic, A), the material is immediately repeated by the clarinet 1 (bars 1–8); the pattern of solo–clarinet 1 is continued in bars 9–16, after which the strings introduce new material, in what was probably intended to be an extended tutti passage within the opening ritornello. However, Mozart chose not to continue with this possibility. What may have prompted him to abandon this sketch is its relationship to the preceding movement. Had he persisted with the $\frac{2}{4}$ time D major slow movement begun in K.Anh.58, a $\frac{6}{8}$ finale would have posed no problems. But he decided instead on the memorably limpid siciliana in F sharp minor, after which another $\frac{6}{8}$ movement would have given insufficient contrast, despite a quicker tempo. In fact, the melodic and rhythmic patterns of K.Anh.64 are not dissimilar to those of K.488's Adagio, and it may even be the case that Mozart's sketching of a putative finale in $\frac{6}{8}$ suggested to him the character of a siciliana that was eventually to serve as the slow movement, superseding his original $\frac{3}{4}$ sketch in D. At any event, it is likely that his $\frac{6}{8}$ sketch for the finale preceded rather than followed the eventual Adagio. The two remaining duple-time sketches for the finale relate more closely to his eventual choice and may have been written after the Adagio was complete.

K.488 was among the five concertos offered *via* Sebastian Winter in a letter of 8 August 1786 to Prince von Fürstenberg, for the use of his court orchestra at Donaueschingen.[14] Eventually, Mozart sent three concertos, as detailed in his subsequent letter of 30 September that same year, noting that

> the compositions which I keep for myself or for a small circle of music–lovers and connoisseurs (who promise not to let them out of their hands) cannot possibly be known elsewhere as they are not even known in Vienna. And this is the case with the three concertos which I have the honour of sending to His Highness ... I must ask His Highness not to let them out of his hands. There are two clarinets in the A major concerto. Should His Highness not have any clarinets at his court, a competent clarinettist might transpose the parts into the suitable keys, in which case the first part should be played by a violin and the second by a viola.

The remark that K.488 was a work 'not even known in Vienna' is rather puzzling. There are indeed no documented performances of the A major concerto by Mozart in Vienna, although there can be little doubt that he did include it in his 1786 subscription concerts, especially given the trouble he took over the scoring and the design of the finale. Possibly Mozart was being a little economical with the truth here: by 'not known in Vienna' he perhaps meant to indicate not that the works (including K.488) had never been produced there, but that they had not been published. An authorised copy of such a work, supplied by the composer himself, would doubtless have carried more weight with Fürstenberg than a piece that could be routinely purchased through a publisher's agent.

Notes

1. F-Pn, Sig. Malherbe 226; Tyson, 1996, nos.73, 74, 78, 80.
2. K.488 is 'Op.82, no.5' in this collection. The six concertos issued by André as 'Op.82' (Mozart, 1800d), comprise K.467, 482, 488, 491, 503 and 595. André also published a volume of cadenzas to 'Op.82' (Hoffmann, 1801–03), composed by the Mainz virtuoso, Philipp Karl Hoffmann (1769–1842). The autograph was one of those purchased by André from Constanze in 1799. A facsimile of the first leaf is reproduced in NMA V/15/7, p.xii; the opening of the slow movement is

reproduced in Wyzewa and Saint-Foix, 1912–46, vol.iv, p.138. A contemporary manuscript set of parts is in CZ-Pu, M II/13, no.2.

3. $K^6$626a/K.624, Teil i, 61; on this cadenza, see Whitmore, 1991, p.142, and Chapter Seven above.

4.   D-B, Mus.ms.15486/5: 'Adagio dell concerto Ex A Ex fis Minor'.

5.   See NMA V/15/7, *Kritische Berichte*, pp.10–14 (with facsimile on pp.106–9). These embellishments have been vilified by, among others, Joseph Kerman (see Kerman, 1989, p.52).

6.   This first page of the autograph score is reproduced in NMA V/15/7, p.xii.

7.   Mozart's emendations to the autograph extend also to the solo part, and include two excised passages: the first (originally standing between bars 113 and 114) is given in NMA V/15/7, Anhang Ia; the second (from bar 126) in NMA V/15/7, Anhang Ib. Another sketchleaf containing melodic ideas for the first movement of K.488 is D-B, Mus.ms.autogr. W. A. Mozart 624(2), also including cadenzas to K.414 ($K^6$626a/K.624, Teil i, 27, 32, 33 and 34).

8.   K.Anh.58 (488a), A-Sm, fragment 16 (one leaf); K.deest, private collection of Dr Jan Racek, Brno (one leaf); K.Anh.63 (488b), A-Sm, fragment 17 (two leaves); K.Anh.64 (488c), A-Sm, fragment 14 (one leaf). They are transcribed in NMA V/15/8, Anhang II (see below). In the case of the single leaf, K.Anh.64 (488c), Alan Tyson has identified the opposite half of the bifolium to which it originally belonged; it is a 12-stave leaf in the former Karl Marx Universität, Leipzig (now Universität Leipzig), Sammlung Kestner, I, CII, 277, containing an additional seven bars for violin 1 (stave 1) and bass (stave 12) not reproduced in NMA V/15/8, Anhang II.

9.   They are discussed in Küster, 1996, pp.205–14; see also Kidger, 1992. The exception, K.deest (NMA V/15/8, Anhang II/6), has no woodwind instrumentation specified.

10. For this fragment, see NMA V/15/8, Anhang II/3.

11. NMA V/15/8, Anhang II/6.

12. NMA V/15/8, Anhang II/4.

13. NMA V/15/8, Anhang II/5.

14. The other concertos mentioned are K.451, 453, 456 and 459.

Piano concerto in C minor, K.491

i. Allegro, $\frac{3}{4}$, 523 bars; ii. Larghetto, $\frac{2}{2}$, 89 bars; iii. [Allegretto], $\frac{2}{2}$, 287 bars.

Scoring: solo fortepiano; violins 1 & 2; violas; bass [= cello, bass]; flute; 2 oboes; 2 clarinets; 2 bassoons; 2 horns; 2 trumpets; timpani.

Composed in Vienna; dated 24 March 1786 (*Verzeichnis*).

The autograph of K.491 is in the library of the Royal College of Music, London.[1] Uniquely among the later piano concertos, it was written throughout on paper of a single type, a factor determined by the unusually large woodwind section, which includes pairs of oboes and clarinets. For this task, Mozart had to use a 16-stave 'Querformat' paper.[2] K.491 was among the autographs purchased from Constanze by André in 1799; he produced the first edition of the work (Mozart, 1800d).[3] An autograph sketchleaf, on the same 16-stave paper, contains ideas for a piano concerto slow movement in E flat. Although only the piano part is notated (lasting just three bars and a beat), it is written into score, and the blank staves are specifically designated for an ensemble identical to that of K.491, leaving little doubt that this fragment was originally intended for the C minor concerto.[4]

The autograph of K.491 is remarkably untidy in its appearance, containing a large number of erasures, cancellations and alterations scattered liberally throughout all three movements. It betrays frequent signs of hasty preparation, suggesting that the composer was working in the face of an imminent deadline (that is, a performance).[5] Leopold's comment, in relation to the finale of K.466, that Mozart did not have time to play the piece through before the first performance because he was still busy supervising the copying, rings true also in respect of the C minor concerto, in which Mozart often applies 'shorthand' notation to save time in writing out the score. This is particularly evident in the outer movements. Towards the end of the first movement, for instance, following the cadenza, sections of the tutti that are straightforward repetitions of earlier music are not written out again but are indicated by idiosyncratic 'Dal Segno' symbols referring to the particular bars from earlier in the move- ment that required insertion. Specifically, bars 492–508 are not notated on fol.17r: they are equivalent to bars 82–98, notated on fols.2v–3v.[6] After bar 98 on fol.3v is a direction to proceed to the 'Coda' (bar 509 to the end of the movement) notated on fols.17r–17v.

This is one kind of 'shorthand'. Another relates to the notating of the solo part. Mozart's normal practice in writing his concerto scores was, first, to draft the main melodic ingredients (namely, the string parts, the right hand of the solo piano, some leading wind entries and the orchestral bass line), and after- wards to fill in the left-hand solo accompaniments and the remaining wind and brass.[7] In K.491, however, he followed a different and quite unusual course.

Judging from the appearance of his score, Mozart concentrated first of all on completing the orchestral staves, devoting little attention to the solo part. Even a cursory glance at the autograph displays a marked difference in appearance between tutti and solo staves: the tutti parts are written out quite neatly, with many precise indications of articulation and dynamics; by contrast, the solo part is in the main only very sketchily written – scrawled, even – and is at times virtually illegible. Evidently Mozart, pressed for time, ruthlessly prioritised his work. He saw to it that at least the orchestral parts, containing a great deal of quite unfamiliar notational detail – melodic and harmonic chromaticism, for instance – and which would require the most careful copying before the first performance, were sufficiently neat and accurate for reproduction. The solo part, which he would play himself, required less attention at the preliminary stage, and substantial portions of it (principally involving extended passage-work in the first movement and in the variation finale) were at first written into the piano staves only in sketch form, giving just enough information about its harmonic content, direction of movement, note-values, register and span to enable him to realise it accurately and completely once time permitted. Thus the solo part was advanced in separate chronological stages, recoverable from the autograph as 'layers' of notation. In the simplest cases, Mozart's detailed realisations of these sketches were added to the score by writing over the sketch itself in a much blacker ink and a thicker nib, as on fol.6 (bars 165–77 of the first movement). Frequently, though, his sketches left no more than vague hints, and required significant recomposition on the (normally blank) timpani stave that stood just above the right-hand piano stave in Mozart's score. Such a passage occurs on fol.8, containing bars 223–8 of the first move-ment, for which only the barest outline of the semiquaver arpeggios was orig-inally drafted. Elsewhere, Mozart worked out the implications of his initial sketch more than once, and the succeeding layers of realisation, cancelled and redrafted, are stacked gradually up the page beyond the timpani staves on to those for the trumpet and even bassoon parts.[8] Occasionally, and perhaps deliberately, Mozart neglected to cancel one or other alternative layers of real-isation, resulting in passages for which no 'definitive' text ever emerged, as, for instance, at bars 45–8, 60–62 and 69–71 of the finale.[9]

Significant revision of the score was undertaken at some point (possibly before the work was entered in the *Verzeichnis* on 24 March 1786, and certainly before the parts were copied for the first known performance on 3 April). Among many instances, two will be considered here. The first concerns bar 34 of the Larghetto, in which Mozart decided to adapt the harmony of beats 3–4 from a first-inversion C minor chord to the more piquant dimin-ished-seventh that stands in the 'final' text. Underpinning this change, the orig-inal bass line for bar 34 (F–E flat) had to be altered to F–F sharp, and the proof that this revision came at a relatively late stage, simultaneously with Mozart's notation of the left-hand accompaniment in the solo part, is that the left-hand stave contains *only* the pitches f′ and f sharp′ – that is, there were no pre-existing notes requiring cancellation and adaptation to the revised harmonies. By contrast, the right-hand part needed minor alteration, and was rewritten on the (blank) timpani stave immediately above. Finally, the string parts were adapted to the new harmonic scheme, the violin 1 and bass being rewritten on the blank staves at the top and bottom of the leaf (fol.20v), respectively.

More serious revisions were undertaken within the first movement. The autograph betrays substantial rethinking of the detailed succession of ideas within the tutti exposition, as follows (bar numbers refer to the NMA text):

- the woodwind phrase ending at bar 43 was originally followed by the tutti, *forte*, from bars 63–90
- this in turn was followed by bars 44–62
- the tutti then concluded with bars 91–9

By means of a system of *sigla* (⊖; ✕) placed above and below the staves on fols.2–3v (presumably for the benefit of a copyist), Mozart indicated the shuffling of these segments into the continuous sequence with which we are familiar today. One possible reason for the re-ordering of these segments is that Mozart felt that the rhythm pattern ♪|♩♩♩|♩♩ (with its prominent upward leap at the close) was overdone in the original succession (bars 35–43, followed immediately by bars 63–72). Their eventual separation by the contrasting episode, bars 44–62, featuring mainly stepwise motion instead, allows the subsequent return of the strong rhythmic profile to play a more convincing role as a structural 'marker', clarifying, rather than saturating the continuity of ideas. Alternatively, these revisions may have stemmed from a measure of dissatisfaction with the part-writing in the original succession. The resolution of the flute, oboes and bassoons from bar 43 into bar 63 is certainly ungainly, but is easily surpassed in ineptitude by the continuation of bar 90 into bar 44, in which the second oboe, along with clarinets, horns and second violins, is left hanging in the air, while the first violins' leading-note semi-quaver B natural at the end of bar 90 resolves clumsily *via* a drop to G and an intervening quaver rest. Mozart would probably not have tolerated such grammatical faults in the work of a pupil. Given the appalling succession of bars 90 and 44, it is at least conceivable that Mozart's substantive revisions occurred exactly at this point in the process of composition (that is, the middle of fol.3), as a convenient escape from the temporary muddle into which he had fallen.[10]

For a concerto that was to become one of the most popular in the developing concert life of the early nineteenth century and which has since remained one of Mozart's most popular works in any genre, remarkably little is known of its early performance history. Mozart probably composed K.491 for one of a series of three subscription concerts that he arranged in spring 1786. He performed it at the third of these on 3 April;[11] on 7 April he held a concert at the Burgtheater at which he probably repeated it along with some others of his recent compositions.[12] Like K.482 and K.488, completed on 16 December 1785 and 2 March 1786 respectively, K.491 includes parts for clarinets, and was possibly conceived as the final item in a set of three piano concertos prominently exploiting the sonority of that instrument.

Notes

1.   GB-Lcm, Ms.402.
2.   Tyson, 1996, no. 84. This 16-stave paper is found only in K.491 and in the terzetto, 'Das Bandel', K.441. Two facsimile editions of K.491 are available: Mozart, 1964 and Mozart, 1979. Surviving contemporary manuscript copies of this concerto include those in CZ-Pu, M II/13 and CZ-KRa, II G 78 (playing parts), the latter very probably copied directly from the autograph (incorporating, for instance, the final stage of Mozart's revisions to the solo piano part), and differing from it in only a very few details of articulation. No cadenzas to K.491 by Mozart survive.
3.   K.491 is Op.82, no.3. in this publication, which comprises K.467, 482, 488, 491, 503 and 595. André also published a volume of cadenzas to 'Op.82' (Hoffmann, 1801–03), composed by the Mainz virtuoso, Philipp Karl Hoffmann (1769–1842).
4.   K.Anh.62 (491a). The sketchleaf is in A-Sm, fragment 13; for a transcription, see NMA V/15/8, Anhang II/7.
5.   An interesting point of detail, illustrating something of the haste with which the solo part was designed, concerns bar 40 of the Larghetto. This bar occurs in the course of the second reprise of the opening melody. Mozart evidently copied the solo part directly from the opening not noticing that, in this different location, there was a conflict between the piano harmonisation and that of the wind. Had he had the luxury of time to check the text carefully, Mozart would surely have spotted the mistake. See also Levin, 1996, at p.41. The faulty text is reproduced in almost all modern editions, including NMA.
6.   Not all of the section written on to fols.2v–3v is to be transplanted to the coda, however; at some point in the composition of the movement, Mozart changed his mind about the precise ordering of sections, and included on fols.3r–3v is a phrase that he subsequently transplanted (it eventually became bars 44–62). This is dealt with below.
7.   This sequence of events is suggested by the prominent variations in ink colour observable in the autographs, according to which separate stages of writing may be inferred. To some extent, this is observable in the facsimile reproductions of K.467 and K.537 referred to in the entries for those pieces.
8.   Among the most extreme illustrations of this are fols.26–26v (bars 37–61 of the finale), partially shown in facsimile in NMA V/15/7, p.xiv.
9.   Another kind of 'shorthand' notation involved passages such as bars 145, 157 and 163 of the finale, in which Mozart probably intended the left hand to be more florid than indicated by the simple bass line; the NMA text gives editorial realisations of such passages (shown in small notes).
10. It may be objected that the eventual succession of bars 62–3 and 90–91 are not ideal, at least in the upper woodwind.

11.   According to a report in the *Wiener Zeitung* (no.28, Anhang).
12.   Described as 'a grand musical concert' in the *Wiener Zeitung* the following day, although no specific details of the programme are given. K.491 was in Mendelssohn's repertoire, and he performed it quite often during the 1820s and 1830s; see Todd, 1991.

Piano concerto in C major, K.503

i. Allegro maestoso, $\frac{4}{4}$, 432 bars; ii. Andante, $\frac{3}{4}$, 109 bars; iii. [Allegretto], $\frac{2}{4}$, 382 bars.

Scoring: solo fortepiano; violins 1 & 2; violas; bass [= cello, bass]; flute; 2 oboes; 2 bassoons; 2 horns; 2 trumpets; timpani.

Composed in Vienna; dated 4 December 1786 (*Verzeichnis*).

The autograph of K.503 (on 12-stave 'Querformat' paper) is in the Berlin Staatsbibliothek.[1] The first edition was produced by Mozart's widow, at her own expense (Mozart, 1798b).[2] K.503 was among the autographs purchased from Constanze by André in 1799, and on which he was to base his own editions, 'faite d'après le manuscrit original de l'auteur'.[3] Mozart may have completed K.503 for performance in one of a series of four concerts arranged in the Trattner Casino during Advent 1786 which are mentioned in Leopold Mozart's letter to Nannerl of 8 December 1786.[4] It may have been the concerto performed by Mozart's pupil, Walburga Willmann, at the Kärntnertortheater on 7 March 1787 (Deutsch, 1965, p.286; Eisen, 1991a, no.77).[5] Mozart performed the work himself (along with K.456 in B flat) at a benefit concert in the Gewandhaus, Leipzig, on 12 May 1789 (Deutsch, 1965, p.342). No original cadenzas or *Eingänge* for K.503 survive.

As with several other piano concertos entered in Mozart's *Verzeichnis*, the precise date of K.503 (4 December 1786) apparently refers only to the date of completion, and is not to be taken as indicating a single burst of compositional activity in the immediately preceding days or weeks. The first three bifolia of the first movement are on paper of a different type from that found on the remainder of the autograph. Alan Tyson has shown that this particular paper is quite rare in Mozart's usage, and can be found only in a few compositions whose dates are quite firmly circumscribed (Tyson, 1987, pp.151–2). Among these other works are the F major concerto, K.459 (entered in Mozart's *Verzeichnis* on 11 December 1784), the D minor concerto, K.466 (10 February 1785), and the C major concerto, K.467 (whose autograph is dated February 1785, and which was entered in the *Verzeichnis* on 9 March). Thus it would seem that the earliest phase of composition of K.503 also dates from this time and that it was only completed much later. Probably, the first six leaves of K.503 on the '1784–85' paper represent Mozart's original draft of a grand piano concerto in C (including a pair of trumpets and timpani) intended for his concerts in spring 1785 (some of which were attended by his father). For some reason, though, composition of this work proceeded only as far as bar 127 of the first movement.[6] It may be that ideas for a different C major movement (?K.467) captured his attention instead and he abandoned his work on K.503 until the opportunity of an Advent concert presented itself in December 1786.

A leaf of sketches pertaining to K.503 survives. It is the so-called 'Berliner Skizzenblatt', containing on the other side sketches for the first movement of the 'Prague' Symphony, K.504.[7] The sketches for K.503 all relate to the first movement and occupy staves 1–8 (the rest of the leaf continues with sketches for an unidentified work, possibly for K.503, although no trace of similar patterns may be found in the finished work).[8] They are of two distinct types. On staves 1–2, Mozart jots down an idea for a chromatic approach to a dominant cadence that had perhaps occurred to him during the process of composing the first movement, but for which he had, as yet, found no suitable opportunity (in fact, these bars appear, slightly modified, at bars 208–14, the cadential close of the solo exposition in G). On staves 3–8, by contrast, we have a 'continuity draft' relating to the first piano entry from bar 96. Three versions of this passage survive, two within the main body of the autograph and one on this sketchleaf. Mozart initially wrote into the autograph a version of bars 96 foll. that is rather shorter and less melodically developed than the eventual text.[9] His evident dissatisfaction with this justifies the sketch on staves 3–8 of the 'Berliner Skizzenblatt', which comes very close to the eventual text which Mozart then wrote into the main body of the autograph, initially on two blank staves immediately above the cancelled solo part, and the remainder on a newly inserted leaf, continuing up to bar 112, at which point the postponed main theme returns. The differences between the continuity draft on the sketchleaf and the version ultimately written into the autograph concern matters of ornamentation. Bars 97–8 of the eventual text decorate the original pattern of bar 96 (first in semiquavers, then in chromatic triplet quavers), creating a sense of evolutionary growth throughout the phrase; in the continuity draft, the right hand of bar [96] is simply repeated twice. Similarly, the melodic termination in bar 100 of K.503 represents an advance on the continuity draft, in which this phrase ends more simply with a falling step from crotchet g″ to quaver f″ in beats 3–4.[10] In the remainder of the continuity draft there are only minor departures from the eventual text of K.503 (concerning the application of accidentals, and octave registers of accompanying left-hand chords), the only significant discrepancy being in bar [110], the first four semiquavers of which are given as c″–g′–f sharp′– g′ and continuing to the end of the bar in an unbroken chromatic scale one semitone higher in pitch (from a flat′ at the beginning of beat 2) than the final version.[11]

Notes

1. D-B, Mus.ms.autogr. W. A. Mozart 503; Tyson, 1996, nos.76, 78, 80, 81.
2. Constanze sold the plates to Breitkopf & Härtel, who marketed K.503 as no.16 of their *Oeuvres complettes de W. A. Mozart*. By February 1800 the 211 unsold copies were returned to Constanze, who sold them on to André. The dedication to Prince Louis of Prussia parallels that of the 'Op.82' concertos published shortly

afterwards by André (Mozart, 1800d), comprising K.467, 482, 488, 491, 503 and 595), of which K.503 was Op.82, no.1. André also published a volume of cadenzas to 'Op.82' (Hoffmann, 1801), composed by the Mainz virtuoso, Philipp Karl Hoffmann (1769–1842). Surviving contemporary manuscript copies include those in A-M, IV 296, c.1800(?), including ripieno string parts; and CZ-Pu, M II/13, no.7. An ornamented version of the slow movement from the collection of Mozart's son, Wolfgang Amadeus (but not in his handwriting), is in I-Mc (no shelfmark available).

3. An edition issued in Bonn by Simrock is a score prepared from Constanze's 1798 print and not, as suggested by Deutsch and Oldman, 1932, p.351, the first edition.

4. That is, according to Abert, 1919, p.1015. There is, however, no documentary evidence that these concerts took place, nor that K.503 was actually performed then.

5. For information on this theatre, see Morrow, 1988, pp.66–81.

6. On this topic, see Gerstenberg, 1953, which notes differences in the handwriting between the earlier and later phases of composition traceable in Mozart's autograph.

7. D-B, Mus.ms.autogr. W. A. Mozart 503, Skizzen 2. Published in facsimile in Schünemann 1936, pp.50–1. Other facsimiles of the sketchleaf for K.503 are in NMA V/15/7, p.xvi (with a transcription in Anhang IIb), and Robbins Landon, 1991, pl.26. See also Somfai, 1996.

8. The sketches are transcribed in NMA V/15/8, Anhang III. See also NMA X/30/3, 74 (Skb 1786b).

9. This is transcribed in NMA V/15/7, Anhang IIa; a partial facsimile (showing the first bars of the emendation to the autograph score) is given in NMA V/15/7, p.xv.

10. Interestingly, while Mozart's final thoughts add extra layers of sophistication in terms of articulation, the sketches do include prominent slurs, suggesting that this dimension was, for him, not supplementary to the pitch-content of his music, but an integral part of it.

11. Beats 2–4 are notated in shorthand in the sketch, by a flat sign, indicating the a flat' on beat 2, and an ascending stroke leading to the pitch g'' notated just before the barline. For the precise transcription, see NMA V/15/7, Anhang IIb.

Piano concerto in D major, K.537

i. Allegro, $\frac{4}{4}$, 422 bars; ii. [Larghetto], $\frac{2}{2}$, 110 bars; iii. [Allegretto], $\frac{2}{4}$, 374 bars.

Scoring: solo fortepiano; violins 1 & 2; violas; bass [= cello, bass]; flute; 2 oboes; 2 bassoons; 2 horns; 2 trumpets; timpani.

Composed in Vienna; dated 24 February 1788 (*Verzeichnis*).

The autograph of K.537 (on 12-stave 'Querformat' paper) is today in the Pierpoint Morgan Library, New York.[1] Manuscript copies of playing parts ('Op.20') were advertised for sale by Johann Traeg in the *Wiener Zeitung* on 25 July 1792.[2] No authentic cadenzas or *Eingänge* to K.537 are known.[3] The first edition was issued by André (Mozart, 1794b), the source for which is unknown. Comparison with the autograph reveals that this text cannot have served as André's *Stichvorlage* since the edition incorporates a number of passages omitted in the autograph. For example, the left-hand staves for the whole of the slow movement are left blank in Mozart's manuscript, which notates only the treble part; the left-hand accompaniment in the first edition is probably the work of André himself. Similar omissions are scattered throughout the autograph: the first piano entry, for instance, begins at bar 81 of the first movement, but there is nothing for the left hand until bar 108; some quite extended stretches of the finale (for instance, bars 48–77 and bars 188–224) also lack left-hand support.[4] In performances by Mozart himself, these omissions would have been unproblematic, of course, since he would have made up a suitable accompaniment. He might also have varied the identically notated reprises of the main melody in the slow movement. The fact that the left-hand part could be left un-notated is nevertheless silent evidence of the sort of texture Mozart envisaged for this work: that is, predominantly melodic in character, supported by straightforwardly chordal accompaniments (sometimes lightly embellished) rather than integrated counterpoint.

Probably, Mozart had originally envisaged performance opportunities for K.537 during the 1788 season,[5] but although completed, according to the *Verzeichnis*, on 24 February 1788, the earliest documented performance of this concerto took place on 14 April 1789, when Mozart played it at the Dresden Court.[6] André's edition notes on its title-page that 'Ce concerto a été executé par l'auteur à Francfort sur le Mein à l'occasion du Couronnement de l'Empereur Léopold II', hence the work's nickname, 'Coronation'. The Frankfurt concert took place in the Municipal Playhouse on 15 October 1790, almost a week after the actual coronation.[7] In a letter to his wife written that same day, Mozart noted that the concert was a great triumph in terms of prestige, but a dismal financial failure.[8]

The physical state of the autograph of K.537 offers some interesting clues about the work's genesis. Mozart wrote K.537 on no fewer than six different types of paper. The first two types are datable to spring 1787, and are found also in the autograph of the G minor String Quintet (finished on 16 May 1787).[9] The former[10] was used throughout the first sixteen folios of the first movement (bars 1–264) and all of the slow movement; the latter[11] was used only in fols.17–20 of the first movement (bars 265–313). The remainder of the autograph was written on papers otherwise found in works dating from 1788.[12] It would therefore seem that much of the first movement and all of the slow movement of K.537 were written in 1787. The concerto was then put aside, possibly because of impending work on *Don Giovanni,* premièred at the National Theatre in Prague on 29 October that year. Mozart returned to the concerto early in 1788, completing it on 24 February.

Exactly how much of the first movement had been completed in 1787? This question is difficult to answer with certainty, but close analysis of the final bifolium of 1787 paper (fols.19–20v) provides some clues. The contents of these leaves are as follows:

fol.19   bars 292–301
fol.19v   bars 302–5; four cancelled bars [equivalent to bars 95–8]
fol.20   ten cancelled bars [equivalent to bars 99–108]
fol.20v   bars 306–13

It is clear that Mozart began the '1788' phase on the last bifolium of 1787 paper, since the string staves on fols.19v and 20v (either side of the cancelled portion) were written using a nib that continues throughout the remainder of the movement (fols.21–8). Having used up the remainder of the last bifolium of 1787 paper Mozart proceeded with new, 1788 paper from fol.21r. There are several musically sensible points from which composition might have restarted early in 1788: bar 292 (fol.19r); bar 300 (fol.19r); the first bar of fol.20 (a cadence corresponding to bar 99); the fifth bar of fol.20 (a cadence corresponding to bar 103); and the cadence on A at bar 311 on fol.20v. The first three of these may be ruled-out. Analysis of the ink colour and nib thickness seems to suggest that all of the material from fol.1 up to the fifth cancelled bar on fol.20r was written in a single, uninterrupted phase of activity. By contrast, the piano entry in that bar, reprising the material of bar 103 and occupying the last six bars of fol.20r, continues in a markedly lighter ink and thicker nib (moreover, there are subtle differences in the script, particularly the formation of semiquaver beams). Possibly, then, these six bars were not written immediately after the first five on fol.20r, and may have been Mozart's starting-point in 1788. In this case, one of his first tasks would have been to revise the recapitulation transition, omitting the fourteen bars on fols.19v–20 (corresponding to bars 95–108 earlier in the movement). Having decided against reprising this passage, Mozart cancelled it heavily, and returned to bar 305 (fol.19v), adjusting the semiquaver groups at the end of that bar so that they would now lead into an arpeggiated continuation on a chord of A major (bar 306). That continuation appears at the start of fol.20v (the final leaf of '1787' paper) extending to the low A in the left hand at bar 311. Intriguingly, the following phrase, beginning with the piano's right-hand triplets, is in yet another combination of ink-colour and nib-thickness, used, in the solo part, from this point until the end of the movement. Possibly, then, bar 311 marks the point at which Mozart recommenced work on K.537 in 1788, the decision to omit part of the recapitulation transition having been made previously, in 1787, occasioning a temporary interruption in the 'flow' that accounts for the odd succession of scripts on fols.19v, 20 and 20v.

Throughout most of the autograph score, clear and consistent 'patterns' of ink-colour and nib-thickness may be seen, extending horizontally across the page. Wolfgang Rehm has attempted to show that these patterns represent distinct and systematic stages in the writing of the score.[13] According to his interpretation, within the first movement, the string and piano parts (staves 2–4; 9–11) were written first, using a fairly broad nib and in a relatively light brown ink;[14] the woodwind and horn parts (staves 5–8) were written subsequently with a thinner nib and darker brown ink. The script in which the wind parts are written is consistent in both ink-colour and nib-thickness throughout the entire movement (that is, both its '1787' and '1788' portions), suggesting that Mozart added those parts only after the solo piano and string parts had been completed, and possibly simultaneously with the trumpet and timpani parts on staves 1 and 12, which share the same nib and ink-shade.[15] For the other movements, Mozart adopted different scribal procedures. Judging by the ink and nib patterns observable in the Larghetto, the violin 1, string bass and solo piano (staves 2, 9, 11) conform to one pattern, violin 2, viola and wind to another (staves 3–8). In the first four leaves of the finale, the same patterning applies as in the first movement, but from fol.5 to the end the inking and nib thickness are uniform across the whole vertical span of the score, suggesting completion in a single, relatively short burst of activity, rather than chronologically distinguishable phases.

Rehm is certainly correct to focus attention on Mozart's 'layered' approach to writing out this score. His supposition that the wind parts were added only once the piano and strings parts of the '1787' phase were complete is supported by the musical characteristics of the flute and first oboe parts, which show every sign of having been designed to complement an already-existing first violin line (for example, from bars 13 to 32). At only one point in the first movement does the woodwind pursue an independent course from the strings (bars 216–23). Here, Mozart grafts a hint of canon at the octave between first bassoon, flute and first oboe onto the pre-existing string texture (founded on a simple 'ostinato', alternating tonic and dominant-7th harmonies), the wind's four-square 'downbeat' scansion nicely complementing the syncopations in the first violin. However, Rehm's template considerably over-simplifies

Mozart's procedures in K.537, especially in relation to the first movement. The distinction that he draws between two 'profiles', one for strings and piano, the other for wind, is too undiscriminating and is at times quite difficult to reconcile with the appearance of the autograph. His claim that, in the first movement, the piano and string parts exhibit a single ink-and-nib profile (that is, a fairly broad nib and a relatively light brown ink) is certainly not borne out by fols.6v–10v, for which the nib used to notate the piano staves is much thinner than that used for the strings, suggesting two quite separate phases of writing. The consistency that Rehm's interpretation implies would only be apparent if Mozart's practice had been to advance the piano and strings *together*, a bar (or a few bars) at a time, spreading vertically down the score. Actually, Mozart tended to concentrate on extending just the leading melodic part, sometimes across several successive folios, before returning to the previous starting-point and filling-in the supporting harmonies. Close inspection of the solo piano staves in the first movement of K.537 reveals a consistent pattern running through the notation of that part, according to which his nib becomes steadily blunter; was sharpened; became blunter once again; was re-sharpened, and so on, unfolding horizontally folio after folio.

In fact, the autograph of the first movement of K.537 displays many discrete variations in both shade and thickness of Mozart's script, the most obvious distinction being that between fols.1–20v, written in 1787, and fols.21–8, added the following year. The materials that Mozart used for writing the '1788' portion of the movement (fols.21–8) produce a script manifestly different in appearance from that of the earlier portion (fols.1–20v). Generally speaking, in fols.1–20v, Mozart seems to have advanced both piano and strings together, as Rehm's template suggests, staves 2–4 and 9–11 being relatively homogenous in appearance. However, this is not true of that portion of the movement completed in 1788 (fols.21–8). Here, the solo part appears to have been written separately from the strings using a slightly thicker nib, producing a significantly more 'definite' profile than that of the accompanying string parts. Probably, in this later portion of the movement, Mozart wrote the extended, and uninterrupted, sections of the solo part first of all (that is, bars 311–83; 388–409), and completed the accompanying string parts in a separate, subsequent phase of activity. All in all, the subtleties of Mozart's script throughout the first movement of K.537 are only partially decipherable through analysis of the ink and nib configurations. It is certainly dangerous to infer too much from the present-day appearance of a score susceptible to chemical changes over two centuries. While Rehm's template provides a useful basic foundation for understanding the genesis of K.537, it would be a mistake to infer too systematic a set of procedures from it.

Finally, a note on the scoring of K.537. Mozart's trumpet and timpani parts are described in his *Verzeichnis* as *ad libitum*. They appear in the autograph, though, oddly notated. Only from fol.10r in the finale (bar 173) are these parts integrated into the main brace of the score (between the staves for the horns and the solo piano). Earlier in the finale and in the first movement, they appear respectively on the top and bottom staves of the 12-stave paper, above and below the central ten staves utilised for the rest of the ensemble. Fol.10r of the finale is datable to 1788,[16] and Tyson suggests that it was at this stage, and not in 1790, as claimed by Einstein (Köchel, 1937; K[6]), that Mozart decided to augment the orchestral group. Wolfgang Rehm intriguingly proposes that the 'ad libitum' designation refers not simply to the trumpets and timpani, but to the entire wind complement, placing K.537 in a parallel case to, say, K.413–15, performable either with or without wind ('à quattro').[17] This possibility is borne out to some degree by the diverse ink shadings in the first 20 folios of the first movement (that is, the portion apparently begun in 1787), which suggest that the piano solo and string parts were written at one time and the wind subsequently. Rehm's thesis derives from the precise wording of Mozart's *Verzeichnis* entry, in which, unusually, the instrumentation reads '... *à 2 Violini, Viola e Baßo...* ', that is, with the 'Baßo' inscribed *before* the enumeration of wind instruments, rather than at the end of the entire list, as was his usual practice elsewhere in his catalogue.[18]

Notes

1. US-NYpm, Heinemann Ms.156; Tyson, 1996, nos.55, 56, 61, 82, 86, 95. (Note that paper 61 is not identical with that found in the autographs of K.414 and K.449 (*q.v.*), which, though bearing the same watermark, is ruled with staves of a broader span.) A facsimile of K.537 is available (Mozart, 1991).

2. Surviving early copies of K.537 include a set of parts at A-M, IV 295, of c.1800, including ripieno string parts and another set copied from the André edition of 1794 at CZ-CH, Sig.717.

3. Examples by Hummel survive in manuscript at CZ-K, Sig. Schwarzenburg K.27, no.776 ('Cadenze per sette Concerti di Mozart pe[r i]l Piano Forte ... Composte del Sigre. Giov: Nep: Hummel ... Opera 4ta ...').

4. In NMA 15/V/8 the 'editorial' left-hand parts deriving from André's edition are helpfully supplied in small type.

5. In a letter to Michael Puchberg written at the beginning of June that year, in which Mozart requests a loan of 100 gulden, he refers to concerts beginning at the Trattner Casino that month from which he expected to make money, although no reports of the projected concerts survive, and the fact that he wrote a further letter to Puchberg before the end of the month asking for yet more money may indicate that none of the projected concerts took place.

6. See Mozart's letter to Constanze of 16 April, in which he describes K.537 as 'the new concerto in D'.

7. Mozart also performed the F major concerto, K.459 (*q.v.*, likewise published as a 'Kronungskonzert' by André in 1794).

8. For this and other comments on this concert, see the entry for K.459 above.

9. Tyson, 1996, nos.61 and 86. Interestingly, an autograph sketchleaf, now in the possession of the Mayeda Ikutoku Foundation, Tokyo, Japan, contains sketches

for both K.537's Romanze and the finale of the quintet: Tyson, 1996, no.67. This leaf is reproduced in the facsimile referred to above, p.x. See also NMA X/30/3, 81 (Skb 1787c). Interestingly, on this sketchleaf the Larghetto is entitled 'Romance'.

10.   Tyson, 1996, no.61.
11.   Tyson, 1996, no.86.
12.   Tyson, 1996, nos.55, 56, 82 and 95. For fuller details on the sequence of paper-types in the manuscript of K.537, see Tyson's introduction to the facsimile edition, pp.vii–xi.
13.   NMA V/15/8, *Kritische Berichte*, pp.h9/10.
14.   The precise colour shades visible in the autograph manuscript itself are more difficult to determine in the facsimile cited previously (a black and white repro-duction), although the sequence of events described here is evident enough.
15.   For further discussion of these parts, see below.
16.   Tyson, 1996, no.95.
17.   See his comments in NMA 15/V/8, p. xxii.
18.   Only in the entry for K.595 is this pattern broken ('*Begleitung*. 2 Violini, 1 flauto, 2 oboe, 2 fagotti, 2 corni, Viole e Baßi'). Rehm's point is arguably strengthened by the *Verzeichnis* entry for K.449 (the first work in Mozart's catalogue), which reads 'Begleitung. 2 Violini, Viola e Basso. (2 oboe, 2 corni ad libitum).' Mozart describes this concerto in a letter of 15 May 1784 as performable without wind.

Piano concerto in B flat major, K.595

i. Allegro, $\frac{4}{4}$, 369 bars; ii. Larghetto, $\frac{4}{4}$, 130 bars; iii. Allegro, $\frac{6}{8}$, 355 bars.

Scoring: solo fortepiano; violins 1 & 2; violas; bass [= cello, bass]; flute; 2 oboes; 2 bassoons; 2 horns.

Composed in Vienna; dated 5 January 1791 (*Verzeichnis*).

The autograph of K.595 (on 12-stave 'Querformat' paper), removed from the Berlin Staatsbibliothek, Preussischer Kulturbesitz at the end of World War Two, is today in the Jagiellonian University Library, Kraków.[1] A set of playing parts survives at St Peter's, Salzburg.[2] The first edition was produced in Vienna by Artaria (Mozart, 1791).[3] Subsequently, K.595 was published by Hummel in 1794;[4] André also produced an edition (Mozart, 1800d),[5] bearing the legend, 'Edition faite d'après la manuscrit partition en manuscrit' (K.595 was among the concerto autographs that André purchased from Constanze Mozart in 1799). Cadenzas for the first and third movements[6] were not included in the autograph of K.595, but were notated subsequently by Mozart on separate sheets of paper;[7] in all probability, they postdate his own perform-ance of the work at a concert arranged by the clarinettist, Joseph Beer (1770–1819), in Ignaz Jahn's Restauranthalle in the Himmelpfortgasse[8] on 4 March 1791. The concert was reviewed in the *Wiener Zeitung* on 12 March: 'Herr Kapellmeister Mozart played a Concerto on the *forte piano*, and every one admired his art, in composition as well as performance' (Deutsch, 1965, p.387). This concert, at which Beer played the clarinet and Aloisia Lange (Weber) sang some arias, was to be Mozart's last public appearance as a soloist.[9]

Despite Mozart's *Verzeichnis* date of 5 January 1791, close study of the watermarks in the autograph of K.595 reveals that it was written in two different phases. The first and second movements, as well as the beginning of the finale (fols. 1–7), are written on a paper that is found only in Mozart's scores from between December 1787 and February 1789; the remainder is on a much later paper dating from 1791 (Tyson, 1987, pp. 156, 134–5; Tyson, 1991, at p.225). Alan Tyson's initial examination of the autograph after it had become accessible to modern scholarship once again in the early 1980s suggested that there was evidence within it of a 'particella' comprising bars 1–300 of the first movement and bars 1–39 of the finale, consisting of the leading melodic parts (typically strings, woodwind solos and the solo piano part) written with a relatively broad nib and in dark brown ink. The remaining parts throughout these sections were subsequently written using a thinner nib and paler ink. By contrast, bars 40 foll. of the finale (written on the 1791 paper) were apparently written in a single sweep, all the parts exhibiting the same nib thickness and ink-shade.[10] The implication of Tyson's findings is that bars 1–

300 of the first movement and bars 1–39 of the finale (and possibly all of the slow movement too) were drafted no later than February 1789 and that the concerto existed as an uncompleted fragment from that stage until its completion early in 1791 (for which the immediate stimulus was perhaps the opportunity of a performance at Beer's concert on 4 March). An objection to this interpretation was advanced by the late Wolfgang Plath.[11] Plath's study of the handwriting revealed no appreciable change in Mozart's script between fols.1–19v of the first movement (bars 1–300) and fols.20–23 (the remainder). By contrast, Plath observed quite a significant change in the script between fols.32–33v (bars 1–39 of the finale) and fols.34–50 (the remainder, including the portion written on the '1791' paper from fol.39). If Tyson's reasoning is correct, and parts of at least the outer movements of K.595 remained fragments for some two years, then one would expect a notable and consistent change in the handwriting both at fols.19v/20 and 33v/34 (marking in each case the breach between chronologically separated phases of compositional activity). That there is none between fols. 19v and 20 leads Plath to conclude that a gap of two intervening years in the writing of bars 1–300 and the remainder of the first movement is untenable, and that this movement was in fact completed in a fairly continuous stream of activity.

The remarkable chromatic passage from bars 47–53 of the first movement in the NMA text is omitted from almost all modern editions.[12] These bars (identical to bars 358–64 following the cadenza), appear in all early editions and are present in Mozart's autograph, but not obviously so. What appears to have happened is that Mozart omitted to notate these bars in the tutti exposition and, on checking the manuscript prior to publication, noticed his mistake and inserted a *signum* ('NB: 7 Takt') after bar 46 directing the typesetter to the seven-bar passage after the cadenza on fol.23 of his manuscript.[13] Alternatively, Mozart may originally have intended to follow bar 46 with bar 54, and only at a later compositional stage – that is, at the tutti following the cadenza – decided to introduce what we know as bars 47–53. Whatever the true explanation, these bars are certainly authentic.

Notes

1.   PL-Kj, Mus.ms.autogr. W. A. Mozart 595; Tyson, 1996, nos.95, 99. The autograph was not available to the editor of NMA V/15/28.
2.   A-Ssp, Moz.280.1. According to Schmid, 1970 the copyist (his 'Schreiber 15') was the same person responsible for the surviving orchestral parts in this collection of K.413–15, although some doubt has been cast on this recently by Dexter Edge (Edge, 1996c, p.61 (n.8)).
3.   It was advertised in the *Wiener Zeitung* on 10 August. Surviving early copies (all scores) include those in CZ-Pu, M II/13, no.15; A-M, Sig.IV 295; and in the private collection of Hans Kindler (Washington, US), the latter evidently copied

from the individual parts of the Artaria first edition.

4. In which K.595 is 'Op.V no.1'; Verlagsno.763.

5. K.595 is 'Op.82 no.2' in this set, which comprises K.467, 482, 488, 491, 503 and 595. André also published a volume of cadenzas to 'Op.82' (Hoffmann, 1801–3), composed by the Mainz virtuoso, Philipp Karl Hoffmann (1769–1842).

6. K^{6}626a/K.624, Teil i, 62, 63 ('nach der ersten Fermate', bar 130 – a ten-bar *Eingang*) and 64 ('nach der letzten Fermate', bar 272). The earliest printed text of these is Artaria, 1801. An *Eingang* is clearly also required at bar 181, though none survives in the autograph or early prints.

7. K^{6}626a/K.624, Teil i, 62, 63 and 64. The authenticity of 63 was questioned in NMA V/15/8, p.xxvi, but an autograph bifolium containing it (and also the cadenzas to the outer movements of K.595) has subsequently been found in a collection of composers' autographs ('Autographen berühmter Componisten und Sängerinnen', of which the Mozart item is no.121) in the Estnisches Historisches Museum, Tallinn, Estonia (no shelfmark). See Rehm, 1986. It is reproduced in the *Kritische Berichte* to NMA V/15/8, p.h/102 (see also pp.h/43–4).

8. For a description of this hall, see Morrow, 1988, pp.101–2.

9. The following month (26 April), K.595 was performed again (by Jan Vitásek) in a concert at the Royal National Theatre, Prague, given by Josepha Dusek (Deutsch, 1965, p.393). Dexter Edge has suggested that Beer's concert may not have been the one in which K.595 was performed, offering as an alternative a concert of 9 January 1791 in which Mozart's pupil, Barbara Ployer, performed; see Edge, 1996b, at pp.89–91. Edge's speculation is in keeping with the typically brief time lapse between the entry of a completed concerto in the *Verzeichnis* and its first performance (in this case, the gap is four days); whether Ployer could have learnt this concerto in such a short space of time (shorter still, if we allow for the copying of a piano part) is debatable, however. In the case of the two other concertos that Mozart wrote for Ployer (K.449 and K.453) there was a much more substantial time delay between completion and Ployer's performance, six weeks and two months, respectively.

10. But according to Tyson, 1987, p.156, n.45, there is no evidence of a 'particella' in the slow movement.

11. Plath's letter, expressing his view, is quoted in the *Kritische Berichte* to NMA V/15/8, pp.h/42–3.

12. Including, for instance, the 'old' Breitkopf & Härtel *Mozart Ausgabe* and the Eulenburg score, no.775. On this passage, see Rosen, 1987.

13. See the facsimile on p.xxxiv of NMA V/15/8.

Bibliography

A Editions of music

Wolfgang Amadeus Mozart: Neue Ausgabe Sämtliche Werke [*Neue Mozart-Ausgabe* (NMA)], Kassel: Bärenreiter/Salzburg: Internationale Stiftung Mozarteum (1955–98).
Wolfgang Amadeus Mozarts Werke, Serie XVI/i–iv, Leipzig: Breitkopf & Härtel (1877–79).

i) *Works by Mozart: eighteenth- and nineteenth-century printed sources and facsimile editions*

Mozart, 1784: Trois sonates pour le pianoforte composées par W.A. Mozart Oeuvre VI. Vienna: Artaria. [K.330, 331, 332]

Mozart, 1785a: *Premier/Concerto/Pour le Clavecin avec Accompagnement/de deux Violons, Alto, Basse,/Hautbois, Flûte et Cors ad Libitum/Composé/par Amedée Mozart ...* Paris: Boyer. [K.175]

Mozart, 1785b: [Trois] *Grand Concert[s]/pour/Le Clavecin ou Forte-Piano/ avec l'Accompagnement des deux Violons, Alto,/et Basse, deux Hautbois, et Deux Cors/composé par/W.A. Mozart/Oeuvre IV. Livre 1 [2; 3]*. Vienna: Artaria. [K.413, 414, 415]

Mozart, 1787: *Grand Concert/pour le/Clavecin ou Piano-Forté/avec Accompagnement/de Plusieurs Instruments,par/MR W.A. Mozart./Oeuvre IX.* Speyer: Bossler. Verlags no.346. [K.453]

Mozart, 1791: *Concerto/Per Il./Clavicembalo o Forte-Piano/Con l'Accompagnemento/Piano.Violini, Viola e Basso, 2 Oboe, 2 Corni, 2 Fagotti, Flauto/ Composto/Dal Sig^r W.A. Mozart/Opera 17*. Vienna: Artaria. Verlags no.346. [K.595]

Mozart, 1792a: *Concerto/pour le/Clavecin ou Piano Forté/avec Accompagnement/de plusieurs instruments,/Composé/par/Mr Mozart./Oeuvre 26me*. Offenbach-am-Main: André. Verlags no.529. [K.271]

Mozart, 1792b: *Concerto/pour le/Clavecin ou Piano-Forté/avec Accompagnement/de plusieurs instruments,/composé/par/Mr Mozart/Oeuvre 23me*. Offenbach-am-Main: André. Verlags no.526. [K.449]

Mozart, 1792c: *Concert/pour le/Forté-Piano/avec l'Accompagnement de deux Violons, [Alto,] 1 Flutte, 2 Obois, 2 Cors, 2 Fagottes,/2 Clarin:, Timp: et Basse,/composé par/W.A. Mozart/Op.18*. Speyer: Bossler. Verlags no.228. [K.451]

Mozart, 1792d: *Concerto/pour le/Clavecin ou Forté-Piano/avec accompagnement/de plusieurs Instruments,/composé par/Mr Mozart./Oeuvre 21me*. Offenbach-am-Main: André. Verlags no.479. [K.456]

Mozart, 1793: *Concerto/pour le/Clavecin ou Piano Forté/avec Accompagnement/de plusieurs instruments,/Composé/par/Mr Mozart./Oeuvre 35me*. Offenbach-am-Main: André. [K.238]

Mozart, 1794a: *Concerto/Pour le/Clavecin ou Piano-Forté/avec Accompagnement/de grand Orchestre,/composé par/W.A. Mozart/Oeuvre 44me*. Offenbach-am-Main: André. Verlags no.684. [K.459]

Mozart, 1794b: *Concerto/Pour le/Clavecin ou Piano-Forté/avec Accompagnement/de grand Orchestre,/composé par/W.A. Mozart/Oeuvre 44me*. Offenbach-am-Main: André. Verlags no.715. [K.537]

Mozart, 1796: *Concerto/Pour le/Clavecin ou Piano-Forté/avec Accompagnement de grand Orchestre,/composé par/W.A. Mozart/Oeuvre 54me*. Offenbach-am-Main: André. Verlags no.923. [K.466]

Mozart, 1798a: *Concerto/Pour le/Clavecin ou Piano-Forté/avec Accompagnement de grand Orchestre,/Composé et dédié/aux amateurs/par/W.A. Mozart/ Oeuvre 33*. Vienna: Artaria. Verlags no.768. [K.450]

Mozart, 1798b: *No.1 del retaggio del defunto publicato alle spese della vedove ... all'Altezza Reale di Principe Luigi di Prussia*. Vienna. [K.503]

Mozart, 1800a: *Concerto facile/pour le Piano-Forté/Composé/par/W.A. Mozart./Oeuvre 84*. Offenbach-am-Main: André. Verlags no.1422. [K.246]

Mozart, 1800b: *Concerto/pour/deux Clavecins/Composé/par/W.A. Mozart./ Oeuvre 83me*. Offenbach-am-Main: André. Verlags no.1421. [K.365]

Mozart, 1800c: *Concert pour le Pianoforte/avec Accompagnement/de 2 Violons, Alto et Basse, Flûte, 2 Hautbois, 2 Bassons, 2 Cors,/2 Trompetes et Timballes,/par/W.A. Mozart/No.I*. Leipzig: Breitkopf & Härtel. Verlags no.227. [K.467]

Mozart, 1800d: *Six grands concertos/pour le/Piano-Forté,/composés par/W.A. Mozart,/et respectuesement dédiés à/S.A.R./Le Prince Louis Ferdinand de Prusse/par l'éditeur/Oeuvre 82./Edition faite d'après la partition en manuscrit*. Offenbach-am-Main: André. [K.467, 482, 488, 491, 503, 595]

Mozart, 1800e: *Six grands Concertos/dédiés au Prince Louis Ferdinand de Prusse*. Offenbach-am-Main: André. [K.467, 482, 488, 491, 503, 595]

Mozart, 1800f: *Concerto pour le Pianoforte/avec Accompagnement/de 2 Violons, Alto et Basse, Flûte, 2 Clarinettes, 2 Bassons, 2 Cors/par/W.A. Mozart/Nr.2 ...* Leipzig: Breitkopf & Härtel. [K.488]

Mozart, 1802a: *Concerto/pour/Piano-Forte,/avec Accompagnement d'orchestre/ composé par/W. A. Mozart./Oeuvre 7*. Offenbach-am-Main: André. Verlags no.1558. [K.175]

Mozart, 1802b: *Deuxième Concerto/pour 2 Claviers,/par W. A. Mozart,/ Oeuvre 102*. Offenbach-am-Main: André. [K.242, in version for 2 pianos]

Mozart, 1802c: *Grand Concerto[s]/pour le/Piano-Forte/avec accompagne-*

ment de/plusieurs instrumens/composé par/W.A. Mozart/Oeuvre 4eme L[ivre] 1 [2. 3.]/Edition faite d'après le manuscrit original/de l'auteur. Offenbach-am-Main: André. [K.413, 414, 415]

Mozart, 1804: *Concert/pour/deux Pianofortes/avec Accompagnement de/2 Violons,/Alto et Basse,/2 Hautbois, 2 Bassons, 2 Cors,/par/W. A. Mozart./ No. 17.* Leipzig: Breitkopf. [K.365]

Mozart, 1852: *W.A. Mozarts/Klavierkonzerte/in Partitur./Herausgegeben von einem Verein von Tonkünstlern und Musikgelehrten in Frankfurt ª/M./mit Bearbeitung/der Orchesterbegleitung für das/Klavier/von/F.X. Gleichauf...* Offenbach-am-Main: André. [K.453, K.482]

Mozart, 1964: *Wolfgang Amadeus Mozart: Piano Concerto K.491.* Washington: The Robert Owen Lehman Foundation.

Mozart, 1979: *Mozart: Piano Concerto K.491*, Foreword by Watkins Shaw and Critical Introduction by Denis Matthews. Kilkenny: Boethius Press.

Mozart, 1985: *Wolfgang Amadeus Mozart: Piano Concerto no.21 in C major, K.467.* Facsimile edition, Introduction by Jan LaRue and J. Rigbie Turner. New York: New York Public Library/Dover.

Mozart, 1991: *Wolfgang Amadeus Mozart: Piano Concerto no.26 in D major ('Coronation'), K.537.* Facsimile edition, Introduction by Alan Tyson and J. Rigbie Turner. New York: New York Public Library/Dover.

ii)   Published cadenzas by Mozart (eighteenth- and nineteenth-century sources)

André, 1804: [W.A. Mozart] *Trente-cinq Cadences ou points d'orgue pour pianoforte.* Offenbach-am-Main: André.

Artaria, 1801: [W.A. Mozart] *Cadances originales se rapportant à ses Concerto[s] pour le Clavecin ou Pianoforte, dédiées à Mr. l'Abbeé Gelinek.* Vienna: Artaria.

iii)   Other eighteenth- and nineteenth-century editions and arrangements

Bach, 1760: Carl Phillip Emmanuel Bach, *Sechs Sonaten fürs Clavier mit veränderten Reprisen* (Berlin, 1760). Facsimile reprint ed. E. Darbellay (Courlay: Editions Fuzeau, 1985).

Bach, 1770a: Johann Christian Bach, *Six Favourite Overtures in VIII Parts ...* (London, c.1770).

Bach, 1770b: Johann Christian Bach, *A second Sett of Six Concertos for the Harpsichord or Piano Forte With Accompaniment for two Violins & a Violoncello ... Opera VII* (London: Welcker; 1770).

Bach, 1777a: Johann Christian Bach, *A Third Sett of Six Concertos for the Harpsichord, or Piano Forte With Accompaniments for two Violins and a Bass, two Hautboys and two French Horns ad Libitum ... Opera XIII* (London, 1777).

Bach, 1777b: Johann Christian Bach, *Six concertos pour le claveçin ou forte piano, op.15 ...* (Paris, 1777) [actually op.13; corrected in later impressions].

Beethoven, 1967: Ludwig van Beethoven, *Beethovens Werke: Kadenzen zu Klavierkonzerten,* ed. Joseph Schmidt-Görg, Serie vii, Bd.vii, Munich and Duisburg: Henle.

Cramer, 1825–37: Johann Baptist Cramer, *Mozart's Celebrated Concertos, Newly Arranged for the Piano Forte, with Additional Keys, and Accompaniments of Violin, Flute and Violoncello* (London, 1825–37). [= K.450, 459 (with a slow movement actually imported from K.449), 466, 467, 482, 491.]

Eckard, 1763: Johann Gottfried Eckard, *Six Sonates Pour le Claveçin 1er Oeuvre ...* (Paris, [1763]).

Hoffmann, 1801–3: Philipp Karl Hoffmann: *Cadences se rapportant aux six grands concertos pour le piano-Forte, Op.82 de Mozart, composées et dédiées à Mre M. Clementi.* (Offenbach-am-Main, 1801; 1803). [K.467, 482, 488, 491, 503 and 595.] [Transcribed in King, 1959].

Honauer, 1765a: Leontzi Honauer, *Six sonates pour le claveçin, livre premier* (Paris, c.1765).

Honauer, 1765b: Leontzi Honauer, *Six sonates pour le claveçin, livre second* (Paris, c.1765).

Hummel, 1828–42: Johann Nepomuk Hummel, *Douze Grands Concertos de W. A. Mozart arrangés pour Piano seul ou avec Accompagnement de Flûte, Violin et Violoncelle avec Cadences et Ornaments* (Mainz, 1828–42). [Actually, only seven works were ultimately published: K.365, 456, 466, 482, 491, 503, 537.]

Raupach, 1765: Hermann Friedrich Raupach, *Six Sonates pour le Claveçin. Avec Accompagnement de Violon ... oeuvre Ier* (Paris, c.1765).

Schobert, 1765: Johann Schobert, *IV sonates pour le claveçin avec accompagnement de violon* (Paris, c.1765).

Schröter, 1774: Johann Samuel Schröter, *Six/Concertos/for the Harpsichord, or Piano Forte:/With an Accompanyment/for two Violins and a Bass ...* (London, 1774).

Schröter, 1777: Johann Samuel Schröter, *Six concertos pour le claveçin ou le forte piano avec accompagnement de deux violons et basse* (Paris, c.1777).

B   Literature – primary sources (eighteenth and nineteenth centuries)

Bach, 1753: Carl Phillip Emmanuel Bach, *Versuch über die wahre Art des Clavier zu spielen* (Berlin and Hamburg, 1753; 1762), William J. Mitchell trans. *Essay on the True Art of Playing Keyboard Instruments* (New York: Norton, 1949).

Batteux, 1746: Charles Batteux, *Les Beaux-Arts réduits à un même principe* (Paris, 1746). Facsimile edn of the 1773 edition (Geneva: Minkoff, 1979).

Burney, 1775: Charles Burney, *The Present State of Music in Germany, the Netherlands and United Provinces; or, The journal of a tour through those countries, undertaken to collect materials for a general history of music* London: Becket, Robson, Robinson, 1775).

Czerny, 1797–98: Carl Czerny, *Anleitung zur Erfindung der Melodie* (Vienna, 1797–98).

Czerny, 1834: Carl Czerny, *Vollständiges Lehrbuch der musikalischen Composition* (Vienna, 1834) [translation of Reicha, 1826].

Czerny, 1839: Carl Czerny, *Complete Theoretical-Practical Pianoforte School* (London, 1839).

Czerny, 1848: Carl Czerny, *School of Practical Composition*, trans. J. Bishop (London, 1848).

Czerny, 1850: Carl Czerny, *Die Schule der practischen Tonsetzkunst* (Bonn, 1850).

Daube, 1771: Johann Friedrich Daube, *Der Musikalische Dilettant; eine Abhandlung der Komposition* (Vienna, 1771).

Daube, 1797–98: Johann Friedrich Daube, *Anleitung zur Erfindung der Melodie* (Vienna, 1797–98).

Forkel, 1784: Johann Nikolaus Forkel, *Musikalischer Almanach für Deutschland auf das Jahr 1784*.

Forkel, 1788: Johann Nikolaus Forkel, *Allgemeine Geschichte der Musik* (Leipzig, 1788).

Fux, 1725: Johann Joseph Fux, *Gradus ad Parnassum* (Vienna, 1725).

Galeazzi, 1796: Francesco Galeazzi, *Elementi teorico-pratici di musica*, 2 vols. (Rome, 1796).

Gerber, 1812–14: Ernst Ludwig Gerber, *Neues historisch-biographisches Lexicon der Tonkünstler* (Leipzig, 1812–14).

Gottsched, 1736: Johann Christoph Gottsched, *Ausführliche Redekunst* (Augsburg, 1736).

Gottsched, 1748: Johann Christoph Gottsched, *Grundlegung einer Deutschen Sprachkunst* (Augsburg, 1748).

Gottsched, 1754: *Auszug aus des Herrn Batteux schönen Künsten aus dem einzigen Grundsätze der Nachahmung hergeleitet* (Leipzig, 1754).

Heinichen, 1728: Johann David Heinichen, *Der General-Bass in der Composition* (Dresden, 1728).

Jahn, 1882: Otto Jahn, *Life of Mozart*, trans. Pauline D. Townsend (London: Novello, Ewer, 1882).

Kirnberger, 1771–79: Johann Philipp Kirnberger, *Die Kunst des reinen Satzes in der Musik*, 3 vols. (Berlin and Königsberg, 1771–79). (See also Thym and Beach, 1982.)

Koch, 1782–93: Heinrich Christoph Koch, *Versuch einer Anleitung zur Composition*, 3 vols. (vol.i, Leipzig, 1782; vol.ii, Leipzig, 1787; vol.iii, Rudolstadt, 1793). Facsimile reprint (Hildesheim: G. Olms Verlag, 2000). (See also Baker, 1983; Baker and Christensen, 1996.)

Koch, 1802: Heinrich Christoph Koch, *Musikalisches Lexicon* (Frankfurt, 1802). Facsimile reprint Hildesheim: G . Olms Verlag (1970).

Kollmann, 1799: August Frederic Christopher Kollmann, *An Essay on Practical Musical Composition According to the Nature of that Science and the Principles of the Greatest Musical Authors* (London, 1799).

Marpurg, 1755–57: Friedrich Wilhelm Marpurg, *Historische-Kritische Beyträge zur Aufnahme der Musik*, vols. i–iii (1755–57).

Marx, 1845: Adolph Bernhard Marx, *Die Lehre von der Musikalischen Komposition*, vol.iii (Leipzig, 1845).

Marx, 1847: Adolph Bernhard Marx, *Die Lehre von der Musikalischen Komposition*, vol.iv (Leipzig, 1847).

Mattheson, 1737: Johann Mattheson, *Kern melodischer Wissenschaft* (Hamburg, 1737).

Mattheson, 1739: Johann Mattheson, *Das vollkommene Kapellmeister* (Hamburg, 1739).

Momigny, 1806: Jérome-Joseph Momigny, *Cours Complet d'Harmonie et de Composition*, 3 vols. (Paris, 1806).

Mozart, 1756: Leopold Mozart, *Versuch einer gründliche Violinschule* (Augsburg, 1756), trans. Editha Knocker, *A Treatise on the Fundamental Principles of Violin Playing* (London, 1951).

Nichelmann, 1755: Christoph Nichelmann, *Die Melodie nach ihrem Wesen ...* (Danzig, 1755).

Niemetschek, 1798: F. X. Niemetschek, *Leben der k.k. Kapellmeisters Wolfgang Gottlieb Mozart nach Originalquellen beschrieben* (Prague, 1798; 2nd. edn 1808).

Nissen, 1828: Georg Nicolaus von Nissen, *Biographie W.A. Mozarts* (Leipzig, 1828).

Pezzl, 1809: Johann Pezzl, *Beschreibung und Grundriss der Haupt- und Residenzstadt Wien* (Vienna, 1809).

Pichler, 1844: Karoline Pichler, *Denkwürdigkeiten aus meinem Leben* [Vienna, 1844] E. K. Blümml, 2 vols. (Munich: G. Müller, 1914).

Portmann, 1789: Johann Georg Portmann, *Leichtes Lehrbuch der Harmonie, Composition, und des General-basses ...* (Darmstadt, 1789).

Quantz, 1752: Johann Joachim Quantz, *Versuch einer Anweisung die Flöte traversière zu spielen* (Berlin, 1752).

Reicha, 1814: Antoine Reicha, *Traité de Mélodie* (Paris, 1814).

Reicha, 1826: Antoine Reicha, *Traité de Haute Composition Musicale*, 2 vols. (Paris, 1826).

Riemann, 1882: Hugo Riemann, *Musik-Lexicon* (Leipzig, 1882).

Riemann, 1900: Hugo Riemann, *Musik-Lexicon* (5th edn, Leipzig, 1900).

Riepel, 1752: Josef Riepel, *Anfangsgründe zur musikalischen Setzkunst ...* 2 vols.: I: *Von der Taktordnung* (Regensburg and Vienna, 1752).

Riepel, 1755: Josef Riepel, *Anfangsgründe zur musikalischen Setzkunst ...* 2

vols.: II: *Grundregln der Tonordnung insgemein* (Frankfurt and Leipzig, 1755).

Scheibe, 1737: Johann Adolphe Scheibe, *Der critische Musicus* (Leipzig, 1737).

Schilling, 1835: Gerhard Schilling (ed.), *Encyclopädie der gesammten musikalischen Wissenschaften* (Stuttgart, 1835–38; 1842).

Sulzer, 1771: Johann Georg Sulzer, *Allgemeine Theorie der schönen Künste* (Leipzig, 1771–74).

Türk, 1789: Daniel Gottlob Türk, *Clavierschule* (Leipzig, 1789).

Türk, 1800: Daniel Gottlob Türk, *Anweisung zum Generalbaßspielen* (Halle and Leipzig, 1800).

Vogler, 1778–79: Georg Joseph Vogler, *Betrachtungen der Mannheimer Tonschule* (vol.i, 1778; vol.ii, 1779, pp.36–9). Facsimile reprint: (Hildesheim: G. Olms Verlag, 1974).

Wolf, 1787: Friedrich Wolf, *Allgemeines musikalisches Lexicon* (Halle, 1787; Vienna, 1801).

C   Literature – secondary sources

Abert, Hermann (1919), *W. A. Mozart – Neu bearbeitete und erweiterte Ausgabe von O. Jahns 'Mozart'*, Leipzig: Breitkopf.

Agawu, V. Kofi (1991), *Playing with Signs: a Semiotic Interpretation of Classic Music*, Princeton: Princeton University Press.

————, (1996a), 'Mozart's Art of Variation: Remarks on the First Movement of K.503', in Zaslaw, 1996b, pp.303–13.

————, (1996b), 'Prospects for a Theory-based Analysis of the Instrumental Music', in Sadie, 1996, pp.121–31.

Allanbrook, Wye J. (1983), *Rhythmic Gesture in Mozart: Le Nozze di Figaro and Don Giovanni*, Chicago: Chicago University Press.

————, (1996a), 'Comic Issues in Mozart's Piano Concertos', in Zaslaw, 1996b, pp.75–106.

————, (1996b), ' "To Serve the Private Pleasure": Expression and Form in the String quartets', in Sadie, 1996, pp.132–60.

————, (ed.) (1998), *Strunk's Source Readings in Music History. Revised Edition*, vol.5: *The Late Eighteenth Century*, New York and London: Norton.

Anderson, Emily (1983), *The Letters of Mozart and his Family*, 3rd edn., ed. Stanley Sadie and Fiona Smart, London: Macmillan.

Aristotle, see Freese, 1991; Heath, 1996; Tredennick and Forster, 1989.

Arthur, John (1996), 'Some Chronological Problems in Mozart: the Contribution of Ink-Studies', in Sadie, 1996, pp.35–52.

Badura-Skoda, Eva and Paul (1962), *Interpreting Mozart on the Piano*, New York and London: Barrie & Rockliffe.

Badura-Skoda, Eva (1996), 'On Improvised Embellishments and Cadenzas in Mozart's Piano Concertos', in Zaslaw, 1996, pp. 365–71.

Badura-Skoda, Paul (1967), *Kadenzen, Eingänge und Auszierungen zu Klavierkonzerten von Wolfgang Amadeus Mozart*, Kassel: Bärenreiter.

Baker, Nancy K. (1976), 'Heinrich Koch and the Theory of Melody', in *Journal of Music Theory*, **20**, 1–48.

———, (ed. and trans.) (1983), *Heinrich Christoph Koch: Introductory Essay on Composition – The Mechanical Rules of Melody, Sections 3 and 4*, New Haven & London: Yale University Press.

———, (1988), '"Der Urstoff der Musik": Implications for Harmony and Melody in the Theory of Heinrich Koch', in *Music Analysis*, **7**, 3–30.

Baker, Nancy K. and Christensen, Thomas (1996) (eds.), *Aesthetics and the Art of Composition in the German Enlightenment: Selected Writings of Johann Georg Sulzer and Heinrich Christoph Koch,* Cambridge: Cambridge University Press.

Barthes, Roland (1977), 'The Death of the Author', in *Image – Music – Text*, ed. Stephen Heath, London: Fontana/Collins, pp.142–8.

Bauer, Wilhelm A., Deutsch, Otto E. and Eibl, Joseph H. (1962–75) (eds.), *Mozart: Briefe und Aufzeichnungen. Gesamtausgabe*, Kassel: Bärenreiter.

Beghin, Tom (1997), 'Haydn as Orator: A Rhetorical Analysis of his Keyboard Sonata in D Major, Hob.XVI:42', in Sisman, Elaine (ed.), *Haydn and his World*, Princeton: Princeton University Press, pp.201–54.

Berger, Karol (1992), 'Toward a History of Hearing: the Classic Concerto, a Simple Case', in Allanbrook, W. J., Levy, J. M. and Mahrt, W. P. (eds.), *Convention in Eighteenth- and Nineteenth-Century Music: Essays in Honor of Leonard G. Ratner*, Stuyvesant, NY: Pendragon, pp.405–29.

———, (1996), 'The First-Movement Punctuation Form in Mozart's Piano Concertos', in Zaslaw, 1996b, pp.239–59.

Bilson, Malcolm (1976), 'Some General Thoughts on Ornamentation in Mozart's Keyboard Works', in *Piano Quarterly*, **95**, 26.

Blume, Friedrich (1956), 'The Concertos (1): Their Sources', in Robbins Landon and Mitchell 1956, pp.200–33.

Bollert, Walter (1958), 'Bemerkungen zu Mozarts Klavierkonzert F-Dur (KV 459)', in *Bericht über den Internationalen Musikwissenschaftlichen Kongreß, Wien, Mozart-jahr 1956*, Graz and Cologne: Böhlhaus, pp.66–8.

Bonds, Mark Evan (1991), *Wordless Rhetoric: Musical Form and the Metaphor of the Oration*, Cambridge, Mass.: Harvard University Press.

Bossuyt, Ignace (1989), *W. A. Mozart (1756–1791) en het Pianoconcerto*, Leuven: Leuven University Press.

Bowie, Andrew (2002), 'Music and the Rise of Aesthetics', in Samson, Jim (ed.), *The Cambridge History of Nineteenth-Century Music*, Cambridge: Cambridge University Press, pp.29–54.

Braunbehrens, Volkmar (1986), *Mozart in Vienna*, trans. Timothy Bell, Oxford: Oxford University Press.

Brown, Howard Mayer and Sadie, Stanley (eds.) (1990), *Performance Practice: Music after 1600*, London: Macmillan.

Butler, H. E. (trans.) (1989), *Quintilian, Institutio Oratoria*, Loeb Classical Library, nos.124–7, Cambridge, Mass., and London: Heinemann.

Caplan, H. (trans.) (1989), *Ad Herennium*, Loeb Classical Library, no. 403, Cambridge, Mass., and London: Heinemann.

Churgin, Bathia (1968), 'Francesco Galeazzi's Description (1796) of Sonata Form', in *Journal of the American Musicological Society*, **21**, 181–99.

Cicero; [pseudo-Cicero], see Hubbell, 1976; Sutton and Rackham, 1988; Caplan, 1989.

Clark, Stephen L. (ed.), 1988, *C. P. E. Bach Studies*, Oxford and New York: Oxford University Press.

Clive, Peter (1993), *Mozart and his Circle*, London: Dent.

Cole, Malcolm S. (1969), 'Sonata-Rondo, the Formulation of a Theoretical Concept in the 18th and 19th Centuries', in *The Musical Quarterly*, **55**, 180–92.

Croll, Gerhard (1966), 'Eine neuentdeckte Bach-Fuge für Streichquartett von Mozart', in *Österreichische Musikzeitschrift, Sonderschrift* (October), 12–18.

Davis, Shelley (1983), 'H. C. Koch, the Classic Concertos and the Sonata-Form Retransition', in *Journal of the American Musicological Society*, **36**, 45–61.

———, (1988), 'C. P. E. Bach and the Early History of the Recapitulatory Tutti in North Germany', in Clark, 1988, pp.65–82.

Derr, Ellwood (1996a), '*Basso Continuo* in Mozart's Piano Concertos: Dimensions of Compositional Completion and Performance Practice', in Zaslaw, 1996b, pp.393–410.

———, (1996b), 'Some Thoughts on the Design of Mozart's Opus 4, the "Subscription Concertos" (K.414, 413 and 415)', in Zaslaw, 1996b, pp.187–210.

Deutsch, Otto E. (1931), 'Mozarts Krönungs-Akademie in Frankfurt', in *Stadt-blatt der Frankfurter Zeitung*, 29 January.

———, (1961), *Mozart. Die Dokumente seines Lebens,* Kassel: Bärenreiter.

———, (1965), *Mozart: a Documentary Biography*, trans. Eric Blom, Peter Branscombe, and Jeremy Noble, London: Barrie & Rockliffe.

Deutsch, Otto E. and Oldman, Cecil B. (1932), 'Mozart-Drücke: Eine bibliographisches Ergänzung zu Köchels Werkverzeichnis', in *Zeitschrift für Musikwissenschaft*, **14**, 337–55.

DeVal, Dorothy (1996), Review of Komlós, 1995, in *Music and Letters*, **77**, 122–4.

Devriès, Annik and Lesure, François (eds.) (1979), *Dictionnaire des Editeurs de Musique français*, vol.i: *Des Origines à environ 1820*, Geneva: Minkoff.

Dover, Kenneth (ed.) (1993), *Aristophanes: Frogs*, Oxford: Oxford University Press.

Drummond, Pippa (1980), *The German Concerto: Five Eighteenth-Century Studies*, Oxford and New York: Oxford University Press.

Edge, Dexter (1992), review-article of Morrow, 1988, in *The Haydn Yearbook*, **17**, 108–66.

———, (1996a), 'Manuscript Parts as Evidence of Orchestral Size', in Zaslaw, 1996b, pp.427–60.

———, (1996b), 'Mozart's Reception in Vienna, 1787–91', in Sadie, 1996, pp.66–117.

———, (1996c), 'Recent Discoveries in Viennese Copies of Mozart's Concertos' in Zaslaw, 1996b, pp.51–65.

Eibl, Joseph (1965), *Wolfgang Amadeus Mozart. Chronik seines Lebens*, Kassel: Bärenreiter.

Einstein, Alfred (1946), *Mozart: his Character, his Work*, London: Cassell.

Eisen, Cliff (1991a), *New Mozart Documents: a Supplement to O. E. Deutsch's Documentary Biography*, Stanford: Stanford University Press.

———, (1991b), 'The Mozarts' Salzburg Copyists: Aspects of Attribution, Chronology, Text, Style and Performance Practice', in Eisen 1991d, pp.253–[307].

———, (1991c), 'The Old and New Mozart Editions', in *Early Music,* **19**, 513–32.

———, (ed.) (1991d), *Mozart Studies*, Oxford: Oxford University Press.

———, (1996), 'The Scoring of the Orchestral Bass Part in Mozart's Salzburg Keyboard Concertos: the Evidence of the Authentic Copies', in Zaslaw, 1996b, pp.411–25.

Federhofer, Helmut (1958), 'Mozartiana in Steirmark (Ergänzung)', in *Mozart Jahrbuch*, 109–[18].

Feldman, Martha (1996), 'Staging the Virtuoso: Ritornello Procedure in Mozart, from Aria to Concerto', in Zaslaw, 1966b, pp.149–86.

Ferguson, Faye (1983), ' "Col Basso" and "General Bass" in Mozart's Keyboard Concertos: Notation, Performance Theory, and Practice', unpublished PhD thesis, University of Princeton.

———, (1984), 'The Classical Keyboard Concerto: Some Thoughts on Authentic Performance', in *Early Music*, **12**, 437–45.

Fish, Stanley (1980), *Is there a Text in this Class? The Authority of Interpretative Communities,* Cambridge, Mass.: Harvard University Press.

Flothuis, Marius (1998), *Mozarts Klavierkonzerte: ein musikalischer Werkführer*, Munich: Beck.

Forman, Denis (1971), *Mozart's Concerto Form: The First Movements of the Piano Concertos,* London and New York: Hart-Davis.

Freeman, Daniel L. (1985–86), 'The Earliest Italian Keyboard Concertos', in *The Journal of Musicology*, **4**, 121–45.

Freeman, Robert N. (1971), 'The Practice of Music at Melk Monastery in the Eighteenth Century', unpublished PhD thesis, University of California, Los Angeles.

Galand, Joel (1990), 'Rondo-Form Problems in Eighteenth- and Nineteenth-Century Instrumental Music, with Reference to the Application of Schenker's Form Theory to Historical Criticism', unpublished PhD thesis, Yale University.

Gerstenberg, Walter (1953), 'Zum Autograph des Klavierkonzertes KV.503 (C-Dur): Anmerkung zu Mozarts Schaffenweise' in *Mozart-Jahrbuch*, 38–46.

Girdlestone, Cuthbert (1958), *Mozart's Piano Concertos*, 2nd edn, London: Cassell.

Gjerdingen, Robert O. (1996), 'Courtly Behaviours', in *Music Perception*, **13**, 365–82.

Grayson, David (1996), 'Whose Authenticity? Ornaments by Hummel and Cramer for Mozart's Piano Concertos', in Zaslaw, 1996b, pp.373–91.

———, (1999), *Mozart: Piano Concertos nos.20 and 21*, Cambridge: Cambridge University Press.

Grove (1980), *The New Grove Dictionary of Music and Musicians*, 6th edn, London: Macmillan.

———, (2001), *The Revised New Grove Dictionary of Music and Musicians*, London: Macmillan.

Haberkamp, Gertraut (1986), *Die Erstdrücke der Werke von W. A. Mozart*, Tutzing: Schneider.

Haggh, Raymond (trans. and ed.) (1982), *Daniel Gottlob Türk, School of Clavier Playing or Instructions in Playing the Clavier for Teachers & Students*, Lincoln, Nebr. and London: University of Nebraska Press.

Halliwell, Ruth (1998), *The Mozart Family: Four Lives in a Social Context*, Oxford: Oxford University Press.

Hamilton, W. (trans.) (1973), *Plato, Phaedrus and Letters VII and VIII*, Harmondsworth and London: Penguin.

Heath, Malcolm (trans.) (1996), *Aristotle, Poetics*, Harmondsworth: Penguin.

Herbert, Trevor and Wallace, John (eds.) (1997), *The Cambridge Companion to Brass Instruments,* Cambridge: Cambridge University Press.

Hintermaier, Ernst (1972), 'Die Salzburger Hofkapelle von 1700 bis 1806. Organisation und Personal', unpublished PhD thesis, University of Salzburg.

Hortschansky, Klaus (1989–90), 'Autographe Stimmen zu Mozarts Klavierkonzert KV 175 im Archiv André zu Offenbach', in *Mozart-Jahrbuch*, 37–54.

Hosler, Bellamy (1981), *Changing Aesthetic Views of Instrumental Music in Eighteenth-Century Germany*, Ann Arbor: University of Michigan Press.

Hoyt, Peter A. (1997), 'The Concept of *développement* in the Early Nineteenth Century', in Bent, Ian (ed.), *Music Theory in the Age of Romanticism*, Cambridge: Cambridge University Press, pp.141–62.

Hubbell, H. M. (trans.) (1976), *Cicero, De Inventione*, Loeb Classical Library no. 386, Cambridge, Mass., and London: Heinemann.

Hughes, Rosemary (ed.) (1955), *A Mozart Pilgrimage. Being the Travel Diaries of Vincent and Mary Novello in the Year 1829*, London: Novello.

Hutchings, Arthur (1948; 1998), *A Companion to Mozart's Piano Concertos*, rev. Cliff Eisen, Oxford: Oxford University Press [page refs. are to edn of 1998].

Irving, John (1996), 'Johann Schobert and Mozart's Early Sonatas', in White, Harry and Devine, Patrick (eds.), *Irish Musical Studies*, vol.v: *The Maynooth International Conference, 1995: Selected Proceedings, Part 2*, Dublin: Four Courts Press, pp.82–95.

———, (1997), *Mozart's Piano Sonatas: Contexts, Sources, Style*, Cambridge: Cambridge University Press.

———, (1998), '"Das Conzert hat viel Änlichkeiten mit der Tragedie der Alten": Mozart's Piano Concertos and Heinrich Koch's 1787 Description', in *Mozart-Jahrbuch*, 101–16.

———, (2002), 'Variation Procedures in the Adagio of Mozart's String Quintet in D, K.593,' in van Deurzen, P. (ed.), *Proceedings of the 4th European Conference on Analysis, Rotterdam, 1999*, Rotterdam, Rotterdams Konservatorium (forthcoming).

Jauss, Hans-Robert (1974), 'Literary History as a Challenge to Literary Theory', in R. Cohen (ed.), *New Directions in Literary History*, London: Routledge & Kegan Paul, pp.11–41 [a translation by E. Benzinger of chapters 5–12 of *Literaturgeschichte als Provokation der Literaturwissenschaft* (Konstanz: Konstanz Universitäts-Presse, 1967)].

Kant, Immanuel (1987), *Kritik der Urteilskraft*, trans. Werner Pluhar, Indianapolis: Hackett.

Keefe, Simon P. (1998), 'Koch's Commentary on the Late Eighteenth-Century Concerto: Dialogue, Drama and Solo/Orchestra Relations', in *Music and Letters*, **79**, 368–87.

———, (2001), *Mozart's Piano Concertos: Dramatic Dialogue in the Age of the Enlightenment*, Woodbridge: Boydell.

Keller, Hans (1956a), 'K.503: the Unity of Contrasting Themes', in *The Music Review*, **17**, 48–58 and 120–9.

———, (1956b), 'The Chamber Music', in Robbins Landon and Mitchell 1956, pp.90–137

Kennedy, George (ed.) (1989), *The Cambridge History of Literary Criticism*, vol.i: *Classical Criticism,* Cambridge: Cambridge University Press.

Kerman, Joseph (1989), 'Mozart à la Mode', in *New York Review of Books*, **38** (18 May), 50–52.

———, (1994), 'Mozart's Piano Concertos and their Audiences', in James M. Morris (ed.), *On Mozart*, Washington, D.C., and Cambridge: Woodrow Wilson Center Press and Cambridge University Press, pp.151–68.

Kidger, David M. (1992), 'Aspects of Compositional Process and Innovation in Mozart's A-Major Piano Concerto, K.488: A Primary Source Study', in *Bericht über den Internationalen Mozart-Kongreß, Salzburg, 1991*, Kassel: Bärenreiter, pp.173–81.

King, Alec Hyatt (ed.) (1959), *Cadenzas to Mozart's Piano Concertos and Elaborations of their Slow Movements,* London: Peters.

Knocker, Editha (ed. and trans.) (1951), *A Treatise on the Fundamental Principles of Violin Playing,* London and Oxford: Oxford University Press.

Köchel, Ludwig von (1862), *Chronologisch-thematisches Verzeichnis sämmtliche Tonwerke Wolfgang Amadé Mozart's. Nebst Angabe der verloren gegangenen, unvollendeten, übertragenen, zweifelhaften und unterschobenen Compositionen desselben,* 1st edn, Leipzig: Breitkopf & Härtel.

———, (1905), *Chronologisch-thematisches Verzeichnis sämmtliche Tonwerke Wolfgang Amadé Mozarts. Nebst Angabe der verloren gegangenen, angefangenen, übertragenen, zweifelhaften und unterschobenen Kompositionen desselben,* 2nd edn, ed. Paul von Waldersee, Leipzig: Breitkopf & Härtel.

———, (1937), *Chronologisch-thematisches Verzeichnis sämmtliche Tonwerke Wolfgang Amadé Mozarts, Nebst Angabe der verlorengegangenen, angefangenen, übertragenen, zweifelhaften und unterschobenen Kompositionen,* 3rd edn, ed. Alfred Einstein, Leipzig: Breitkopf & Härtel.

———, (1964), *Chronologisch-Thematisches Verzeichnis sämtliche Tonwerke Wolfgang Amadé Mozarts, nebst Angabe der verlorengegangenen, angefangenen, von fremder Hand bearbeiteten, zweifelhaften und unterschobenen Kompositionen,* 6th edn, ed. Franz Giegling, Alexander Weinmann and Gerd Sievers, Wiesbaden: Breitkopf & Härtel.

Komlós, Katalin (1991), '"Ich praeludierte und spielte Variazionen": Mozart the fortepianist', in Todd and Williams 1991, pp.27–53.

———, (1995), *Fortepianos and their Music: Germany, Austria and England, 1760–1800,* Oxford: Oxford University Press.

Konrad, Ulrich (ed.) (1998), *Wolfgang Amadeus Mozarts Werke: Skizze* [NMA supplementary volumes X/30/3], Kassel: Bärenreiter.

Küster, Konrad (1991), *Formale Aspekten der ersten Sätze des Konzerten Mozarts,* Kassel: Bärenreiter.

———, (1996), *Mozart: a Musical Biography,* trans. Mary Whittall, Oxford: Oxford University Press.

Lawson, Colin (ed.) (1995), *The Cambridge Companion to the Clarinet,* Cambridge: Cambridge University Press.

———, (1996), *Mozart: Clarinet Concerto,* Cambridge: Cambridge University Press.

Layer, Adolf (1975), *Eine Jugend in Augsburg – Leopold Mozart, 1719–1737,* Augsburg: Die Brigg.

Leeson, Daniel and Levin, Robert (1976–7), 'On the Authenticity of

K.Ahn.C14.01 (297b), a Symphonia Concertante for Four Winds and Orchestra', *Mozart-Jahrbuch*, 70–96.

Lester, Joel (1992), *Compositional Theory in the Eighteenth Century*, Cambridge, Mass.: Harvard University Press.

Levin, Robert J. (1990), 'Instrumental Ornamentation, Improvisation and Cadenzas', in Brown and Sadie (1990), pp.267–91.

———, (1992), 'Improvised Embellishments in Mozart's Keyboard Music', in *Early Music*, **20**, 221–33.

———, (1994), 'Mozart's Keyboard Concertos' in Marshall, Robert L. (ed.), *Eighteenth-Century Keyboard Music*, New York: Schirmer, pp.350–93.

———, (1996), 'The Devil's in the Details: Neglected Aspects of Mozart's Piano Concertos', in Zaslaw, 1996b, pp.29–50.

McClary, Susan (1986), 'A Musical Dialectic from the Enlightenment: Mozart's Piano Concerto in G major, K.453, Movement 2', in *Cultural Critique*, **4**, 129–69.

Maunder, Richard (1992), 'Mozart's Keyboard Instruments', in *Early Music*, **20**, 207–19.

———, (1995), *Keyboard Instruments in Eighteenth-Century Vienna*, Oxford: Oxford University Press.

Maunder, Richard and Rowland, David (1995), 'Mozart's Pedal Piano', in *Early Music*, **23**, 287–96.

Mitchell, William J. (ed.) (1949), *Essay on the True Art of Playing Keyboard Instruments*, New York: Eulenburg.

Morrow, Mary Sue (1988), *Concert Life in Haydn's Vienna: Aspects of a Developing Musical and Social Institution,* Stuyvesant, N.Y.: Pendragon.

———, (1997), *German Music Criticism in the Late Eighteenth Century: Aesthetic Issues in Instrumental Music*, Cambridge: Cambridge University Press.

Moser, Hans-Joachim (1951), 'Die Erstfassung des Mozartschen Klavierkonzerts KV 450', in *Die Musikforschung*, **4**, 202–4; 301–4.

Nattiez, Jean-Jacques (1990), 'Can we speak of "Narrativity" in Music?', in *Journal of the Royal Musical Association*, **115**, 240–57.

Neumann, Frederick (1986), *Ornamentation and Improvisation in Mozart*, Princeton: Princeton University Press.

Newcomb, Anthony (1984), 'Once More "Between Absolute and Programme Music": Schumann's Second Symphony', in *19th-Century Music*, **7**, 233–50.

Olleson, Edward (1962–3), 'Gottfried van Swieten: Patron of Haydn and Mozart', *Proceedings of the Royal Musical Association*, **89**, 63–74.

Orel, Alfred (1954), 'Gräfin Wilhelmine Thun (Mäzenatentum in Wiens klassischer Zeit)', *Mozart Jahrbuch*, 89–101.

Perrin, B. (trans.) (1916), *Plutarch's Lives*, vol.iv, Loeb Classical Library, London and New York: Heinemann.

Plath, Wolfgang (1959), 'Das Skizzenblatt KV 467a', in *Mozart-Jahrbuch*, 114–26.

———, (1960–61), 'Beiträge zur Mozart-Autographie I: Die Handschrift Leopold Mozarts', in *Mozart-Jahrbuch*, 82–117.

———, (1976–77), 'Beiträge zur Mozart-Autographie II: Schriftchronologie 1770–1780', in *Mozart-Jahrbuch*, 1976–77, 131–73.

Plato, see Hamilton, 1973; Waterfield, 1993.

Pohl, C. F. (1867), *Mozart in London*, Vienna: Gerold.

Prout, Ebenezer (1895), *Applied Forms*, London: Novello & Ewer.

Quintilian, see Butler, 1989.

Radcliffe, Philip (1978), *Mozart Piano Concertos*, London: British Broadcasting Corporation.

Ratner, Leonard (1980), *Classic Music: Expression, Form, and Style*, New York: Schirmer.

———, (1991), 'Topical Content in Mozart's Keyboard Sonatas', in *Early Music*, **19**, 615–19.

Rehm, Wolfgang (1986), 'Der Eingang zum 3.Satz des B-Dur Klavierkonzerts KV 595 ist authentisch! Mozarts Kadenzen-Autograph bringt Klarheit', in *Mitteilungen der Internationalen Stiftung Mozarteum*, **34**, 35–40.

Rink, John (1998), 'Translating Musical Meaning', in Nicholas Cook and Mark Everist (eds.), *Rethinking Music*, Oxford: Oxford University Press, pp.217–38.

Ritzel, Fred (1968), *Die Entwicklung der 'Sonatenform' im musiktheoretischen Schrifttum des 18. und 19. Jahrhunderts*, Wiesbaden: Breitkopf & Härtel.

Robbins, Mary (1992), 'Reinterpreted Elements in Mozart's Cadenzas for his Piano Concertos', in *Bericht über den Internationalen Mozart-Kongreß, Salzburg, 1991*, Kassel: Bärenreiter, pp.182–7.

Robbins Landon, H. C. (1956), 'The Concertos (2): Their Musical Origin and Development', in Robbins Landon and Mitchell 1956, pp.234–82.

———, (1989), *Mozart: The Golden Years*, London: Thames & Hudson.

———, (1991) (ed.), *The Mozart Compendium*, London: Thames & Hudson.

Robbins Landon, H. C. and Mitchell, Donald (eds.) (1956), *The Mozart Companion*, London: Faber.

Rogers, B. B. (1902–14), *The Comedies of Aristophanes*, vol.v, London: n.p.

Rosen, Charles (1971), *The Classical Style*, London: Faber.

———, (1980), *Sonata Forms*, New York: Norton.

Rosen, David (1987), 'The Composer's "Standard Operating Procedure" as Evidence of Intention: The Case of a Formal Quirk in Mozart's K.595', in *The Journal of Musicology*, **5**, 779–90.

Rosselli, John (1998), *The Life of Mozart*, Cambridge: Cambridge University Press.

Rowland, David (ed.) (1998), *The Cambridge Companion to the Piano*, Cambridge: Cambridge University Press.

Ruile-Dronke, Jutta (1978), *Ritornell und Solo in Mozarts Klavierkonzerten*, Tutzing: Schneider.

———, (1995), 'Der Ort der Solokadenz in Konzert KV537: Überlegungen zur Satzanlage bei Mozart', in Schmid, M. H. (ed.), *Mozart Studien*, **5**, Tutzing: Schneider, pp.173–82.

Russell, D. A. and Winterbottom, M. (eds.) (1989), *Classical Literary Criticism*, Oxford: Oxford University Press.

Samson, Jim (2001), 'Romanticism', in *Grove* (2001).

Schiedermair, L. (1919), *W. A. Mozarts Handschrift in zeitlich geordneten Nachbildungen*, Bückeburg and Leipzig: Beck.

Schmid, Ernst Fritz (1956), 'Neue Quellen zu Werken Mozarts', in *Mozart-Jahrbuch*, 35–45.

Schmid, Manfred Hermann (1970), *Die Musikaliensammlung der Erzabtei St. Peter in Salzburg. Katalog. Erster Teil: Leopold und Wolfgang Amadeus Mozart*, Salzburg: Internationale Stiftung Mozarteum.

———, (1980–83), 'Nannerl Mozart und ihr musikalischer Nachlaß: zu den Klavierkonzerten im Archiv St. Peter in Salzburg', in *Mozart-Jahrbuch*, 140–7.

———, (1993), 'Zur Mitwirkung des Solisten am Orchester-Tutti bei Mozarts Konzerten', in *Basler Jahrbuch für Historische Musikpraxis*, **17**, 89–112.

———, (1999), *Orchester und Solist in den Konzerten von W. A. Mozart. Mozart Studien*, **9**, Tutzing: Schneider.

Scholz-Michelitsch, H. (1962), *Das Orchester- und Kammermusikwerk von Georg Christoph Wagenseil: thematischer Katalog*, Vienna: Böhlau.

———, (1966), *Das Klavierwerk von Georg Christoph Wagenseil* Vienna: Böhlau.

Schulenberg, David (1984), *The Instrumental Music of Carl Phillipp Emmanuel Bach*, Ann Arbor: University of Michigan Research Press.

Schünemann, G. (1936), *Musiker-Handschriften von Bach bis Schumann*, Berlin and Zurich: Atlantis.

Senhal, Jirí (1971), 'Die Musikkapelle des Olmützer Bischofs Maximillian, Hamilton (1761–1776)', in *Die Musikforschung*, **24**, 411–17.

———, (1978), 'Die Musikkapelle des Olmützer Erzbischofs Anton Theodore Colloredo-Waldsee 1777–1811', in *Haydn Yearbook*, **10**, 132–50.

Senn, Walter (1962), 'Die Mozart Überlieferung im Stift Heilig Kreuz zu Augsburg', in *Zeitschrift des historischen Vereins für Schwaben*, **62–3**, 333–68.

Simon, Edwin J. (1957), 'The Double-Exposition in the Classic Concerto', in *Journal of the American Musicological Society*, **10**, 111–18.

———, (1959), 'Sonata into Concerto; a Study of Mozart's first seven concertos', in *Acta Musicologica*, **31**, 170–87.

Sisman, Elaine (1982), 'Small and Expanded Forms: Koch's Model and Haydn's Minuet', in *The Musical Quarterly*, **68**, 444–75.

————, (1993), *Haydn and the Classical Variation*, Cambridge, Mass.: Harvard University Press.

————, (1996), 'Form, Character and Genre in Mozart's Piano Concerto Variations', in Zaslaw 1996b, pp.335–61.

Snook-Luther, Susan P. (trans. and ed.) (1992), *The Musical Dilettante – A Treatise on Composition by J. F. Daube*, Cambridge: Cambridge University Press.

Somfai, László (1996), 'Sketches during the Process of Composition', in Sadie 1996, pp.53–65.

Sommerstein, Alan H. (1989), *Aeschylus, Eumenides*, Cambridge: Cambridge University Press.

Steinbeck, Wolfram (1990), 'Zur Entstehung der Konzertsatzform in den Pasticcio-Konzerten Mozarts', in *Beiträge zur Geschichte des Konzerts: Festschrift Siegfried Kross zum 60. Geburtstag*, Bonn: Schröder, pp.125–39.

Stevens, Jane R. (1971), 'An 18th-Century Description of Concerto First-Movement Form', in *Journal of the American Musicological Society*, **24**, 85–95.

————, (1974), 'Theme, Harmony, and Texture in Classic-Romantic Descriptions of Concerto First-Movement Form', in *Journal of the American Musicological Society*, **27**, 25–60.

————, (1988), 'The "Piano Climax" in the Eighteenth-Century Concerto: An Operatic Gesture?', in Clark 1988, pp.245–76.

————, (1996),'The Importance of C. P. E. Bach for Mozart's Piano Concertos', in Zaslaw, 1966b, pp.211–36.

Stock, Jonathan (1997), 'Orchestration as Structural Determinant: Mozart's Deployment of Woodwind in the Slow Movement of the C Minor Piano Concerto, K.491', in *Music and Letters*, **78**, 210–19.

Stowell, Robin (ed.) (1992), *The Cambridge Companion to the Violin*, Cambridge: Cambridge University Press.

Sutton, E. W. and Rackham, H. (trans.) (1988), *Cicero, De Oratore*, Loeb Classical Library, no.348, Cambridge, Mass.; and London: Heinemann.

Taruskin, Richard (1982), 'On Letting the Music Speak for Itself: Some Reflections on Musicology and Performance', in *The Journal of Musicology*, **1**, 338–49.

————, (1988), 'The Pastness of the Present and the Presence of the Past', in Kenyon, N. ed., *Authenticity and Early Music*, Oxford: Oxford University Press, pp. 137–210.

————, (1992), 'Tradition and Authority', in *Early Music* , **20**, 311–25.

Thym, Jürgen and Beach, David (trans.) (1982), *Johann Philipp Kirnberger, The Art of Strict Musical Composition*, New Haven and London: Yale University Press.

Tischler, Hans (1966), *A Structural Analysis of Mozart's Piano Concertos*, New York: Institute of Medieval Music.

Todd, R. Larry (1991), 'Mozart according to Mendelssohn; a Contribution to *Rezeptionsgeschichte*', in Todd and Williams 1991, pp.158–203.

Todd, R. Larry and Williams, Peter (eds.) (1991), *Perspectives on Mozart Performance*, Cambridge: Cambridge University Press.

Tovey, Donald F. (1936; 1978), 'The Classical Concerto', in *Essays in Musical Analysis*. vol.iii: *Concertos*, Oxford: Oxford University Press, pp.3–27 [page references are to edn of 1978].

Tredennick, H. and Forster, E. S. (trans.) (1989), *Aristotle, Posterior Analytics and Topica*, Loeb Classical Library, no.391, Cambridge, Mass., and London: Heinemann.

Tyson, Alan (1987), *Mozart: Studies of the Autograph Scores*, Cambridge, Mass., and London: Harvard University Press.

——, (1991), 'Proposed New Dates for Many Works and Fragments Written by Mozart from March 1781 to December 1897', in Eisen 1991d, pp.213–26.

——, (ed.) (1996), *Wolfgang Amadeus Mozarts Werke: Wasserzeichen Katalog*, 2 vols. [NMA supplementary volumes X/33/2], Salzburg: Internationale Stiftung Mozarteum.

Wagner, H. (trans. and ed.) (1972), *Wien von Maria Theresia bis zum Franzosenszeit: Aus den Tagebüchern des Grafen Karl von Zinzendorf*, Vienna: Wiener Bibliophilen Gesellschaft.

Waterfield, Robin (trans.) (1993), *Plato, Republic*, Oxford: Oxford University Press.

Webster, James (1996), 'Are Mozart's Concertos "Dramatic"? Concerto Ritornellos versus Aria Introductions in the 1780s', in Zaslaw 1996b, pp.107–38.

Webster, T. B. L. (1967), *The Tragedies of Euripides*, London: Methuen.

Whitmore, Philip (1991), *Unpremeditated Art: the Cadenza in the Classical Keyboard Concerto*, Oxford: Clarendon Press.

Wolff, Christoph (1978–79), 'Zur Chronologie der Klavierkonzert-Kadenzen Mozarts', in *Mozart-Jahrbuch*, 235–46.

——, (1984), Christoph Wolff, 'Zur Edition der Klavierkonzerte KV 246, KV 271, KV365, KV 413–15' in Hanemann, D. (ed.), *Neue Mozart-Ausgabe. Bericht über die Mitarbeitertagung in Kassel 29.–30. Mai 1981*, Kassel: Bärenreiter.

——, (1986), 'Über kompositionsgeschichtlichen Ort und Aufführungspraxis der Klavierkonzerts Mozarts', in *Mozart-Jahrbuch*, 91–2.

——, (1991), 'Cadenzas and styles of improvisation in Mozart's piano concertos', in Todd and Williams 1991, pp.228–38

Worbs, Hans Christoph (1958), 'Komponist, Publikum und Auftraggeber: eine Untersuchung an Mozarts Klavierkonzerten', in *Bericht über den Internationalen Musikwissenschaftlichen Kongreß, Wien, Mozart-jahr 1956*, Graz and Cologne: Böhlhaus, pp.754–7

Wyzewa, Théodore de and Saint-Foix, George de (1908–09a), 'Un maître inconnu de Mozart', in *Zeitschrift der Internationale Musikgesellschaft*, **10**, 139–40.

———, (1908–09b), 'Les Premiers Concerts de Mozart', in *Zeitschrift der Internationale Musikgesellschaft*, **10**, 35–41.

———, (1912–46), *W. A. Mozart. Sa vie musicale et son oeuvre*, 5 vols., Paris: Desclée de Brouwer.

Zaslaw, Neal (1989), *Mozart's Symphonies*, Oxford: Oxford University Press.

———, (1996a), 'Contexts for Mozart's Piano Concertos', in Zaslaw 1996b, pp.7–16.

———, (ed.) (1996b), *Mozart's Piano Concertos: Text, Context, Interpretation*, Ann Arbor: University of Michigan Press.

Index